WHAT LIES ACROSS THE WATER

WHAT LIES ACROSS THE WATER

THE REAL STORY OF THE CUBAN FIVE

STEPHEN KIMBER

FERNWOOD PUBLISHING • HALIFAX & WINNIPEG

Editing: Brenda Conroy
Cover design: John van der Woude
Printed and bound in Canada by Hignell Book Printing

Published in Canada by Fernwood Publishing
32 Oceanvista Lane, Black Point, Nova Scotia, B0J 1B0
and 748 Broadway Avenue, Winnipeg, Manitoba, R3G 0X3
www.fernwoodpublishing.ca

Fernwood Publishing Company Limited gratefully acknowledges the financial support
of the Government of Canada through the Canada Book Fund and the Canada Council
for the Arts, the Nova Scotia Department of Communities, Culture and Heritage,
the Manitoba Department of Culture, Heritage and Tourism under the
Manitoba Book Publishers Marketing Assistance Program and the Province of Manitoba,
through the Book Publishing Tax Credit, for our publishing program.

Library and Archives Canada Cataloguing in Publication

Kimber, Stephen
What lies across the water : the real story of the Cuban
Five / Stephen Kimber.

Includes bibliographical references and index.
ISBN 978-1-55266-542-8

1. Political prisoners--United States. 2. Prisoners, Foreign--
United States. 3. Cubans--United States. 4. Terrorism--Cuba--
Prevention. 5. Espionage, Cuban--United States. I. Title.

HV9467.8.K54 2013   365'.4509227291   C2012-908106-X

Contents

Cast of Characters

Percy Alvarado Godoy: Born 1949. Guatemalan-Cuban. Intelligence agent who infiltrated the Cuban American National Foundation. State Security code name: Monk; CANF code name: Agent 44.

José Basulto: Born 1940. Cuban-American. Contractor. Bay of Pigs, CIA veteran. Founder, Brothers to the Rescue.

Orlando Bosch Avíla: Born 1926. Pediatrician. CIA veteran. Co-founder of terrorist umbrella organization CORU. Acquitted alleged mastermind of 1976 bombing of Cubana Airlines Flight 455.

Francisco Antonio "Gordito" Chávez Abarca: Salvadoran gangster with links to Luis Posada. Hired mercenaries to plant bombs in Cuban hotels.

Raúl Ernesto Cruz León: Salvadoran mercenary hired to plant bombs in Cuban hotels.

Rodolfo Frómeta: Cuban exile, claims Castro killed members of his family. Key player in Alpha 66, founder of Comandos F-4.

Fernando González: Born 1963. Cuban illegal intelligence officer assigned to Fayetteville, North Carolina. Filled in as a vacation replacement in Miami for both Gerardo Hernández and Ramón Labañino. Operated in the United States as Ruben Campa. Code names Oscar and Vicky.

René González: Born 1956. Pilot, "defector." Cuban intelligence agent who infiltrated Brothers to the Rescue, PUND and the Democracy Movement. Code names Iselin and Castor. Married to *Olga Salanueva*.

Antonio Guerrero: Born 1958. Cuban intelligence agent assigned to penetrate the Boca Chica Naval Station. Code names Lorient, Tony. American girlfriend, *Maggie Becker.*

Francisco "Pepe" Hernandez: Cuban-American. Bay of Pigs veteran. Co-founder of the Cuban American National Foundation.

Gerardo Hernández: Born 1965. Illegal intelligence officer, head of La Red Avispa. Supervised, among others, René González, Tony Guerrero, Nilo and Linda Hernández and Alejandro Alonso. Operating in the United States as Manuel Viramóntez. Code names Giro, Giraldo. Married to *Adriana Perez.*

Ramón Labañino. Born 1963. Cuban illegal intelligence officer originally stationed in Tampa, Florida, but reassigned to Miami in 1997 to focus on the new U.S. Southern Headquarters and supervise, among others, agents Guerrero, Joseph Santos and Amarylis Silverio. Operating in the United States as Luis Medina. Code names Allan and Oso.

Jorge Mas Canosa: Born 1931. Cuban-American. Bay of Pigs, CIA veteran. Founder of the Cuban American National Foundation, the most powerful anti-Castro lobbying organization in the United States.

Luis Posada Carriles: Born 1928. Chemist. Bay of Pigs, CIA veteran, explosives expert. Co-founder of terrorist umbrella organization CORU. Alleged escaped co-mastermind of 1976 bombing of Cubana Airlines Flight 455; confessed mastermind of 1997 Havana hotel bombing campaign.

Juan Pablo Roque: Born 1955. Cuban Air Force pilot, "defector." Cuban intelligence agent who penetrated Brothers to the Rescue. Code names German and Vedette. American wife, *Ana Margarita*.

Ramón Saúl Sánchez: Born 1955. Cuban-born exile. Member of Alpha 66. Founder of the Democracy Movement.

Prologue

This is not the book I intended to write. That book was to be a novel, a love story set partly in Cuba. In the spring of 2009, I travelled to Havana to do some preliminary research for it, and got sideswiped by the truth-is-stranger-but-way-more-interesting story of the Cuban Five.

I'd vaguely heard of them. Back in 2004, my wife and I spent a week at Breezes Jibacoa, a beach resort halfway between Havana and Varadero. It was there, in fact, that I conceived the idea for the novel, perhaps for no better reason than to ensure I would have to return. Like most Cuban resorts at the time, communication with the outside world from Jibacoa was primitive: two painfully slow Internet-connected computers tucked away in a second-floor lounge. Since you invariably had to line up to use them, I filled up my waiting time one day literally reading the writing on the wall — a collection of Soviet-style government posters about the plight of a group of men known as the "Cuban Five." They were, the posters declared, "political prisoners" in the United States. The English translation was awful — "Prisoners of the Impire" was the heading on one — and the information about their case was confusing and frustratingly incomplete. As if I should already know the details. I hadn't a clue.

When I returned to Canada, I did a Google News search for "Cuban Five" but found only one mainstream American news story from the previous month — in spite of the fact lawyers for the Five were in the midst of appealing their controversial convictions up the ladder of the U.S. court system. Most of the rest of what I discovered about them on the Internet consisted of polemics, which painted the Five either as heroic young patriots worthy of veneration or as murderous villains for whom even the death penalty wasn't punishment enough.

Reading between the bombast and broadsides, the short version seemed to be that the Five were members of a Cuban intelligence network who'd surreptitiously entered the United States, infiltrated several militant anti-Castro groups, got caught by the FBI, were tried and sentenced to lengthy prison terms. I wrote a brief newspaper column about what I'd learned — and the fact no one except the Cuban government seemed to care — filed it and forgot it.

Until five years later, that is, when I met Alejandro Trelles Shaw. Alex was an energetic 70-year-old Cuban who could still vividly remember what it had been like to be an idealistic 20-year-old banker caught up in the headiest days of the life-altering Cuban revolution. Unlike the rest of his well-to-do family, who all fled to Miami or ended up in jail after Castro took power, Alex stayed. "I was the red sheep of the family," he jokes. "I looked around, saw what the revolution was trying to do. I thought, 'if this is communism, then I'm a communist.'"

He eventually became a counter-intelligence officer in Cuba's Ministry of the Interior (MININT), the all-powerful ministry responsible for foreign and domestic intelligence, among many other duties. Alex can — and will if you ask — regale you with fascinating tales of how he infiltrated CIA-backed student groups at the University of Havana, and later served as a government "minder" for Cuban delegations and sports teams when they visited other countries. Without seeming to brag, he would explain he'd also occasionally translated for the "Commander" when Castro travelled abroad. Not that he ever totally swallowed the Kool-Aid. "Part of the problem in Cuba," he told me, "is that Fidel was involved in everything. I call it the Law of the Jeep. Fidel would arrive in his Jeep, he would talk and then he would leave, and suddenly we had a new law."

When he was in his late fifties — for reasons I'm not sure I understood or that mattered all that much — Alex had a falling out with his bosses, and retired. In the mid-1990s, he got kicked out of the Communist Party but somehow managed to hold onto his prized party ID card. Like plenty of others in that distressed, depressed, post-Soviet, "Special-Period-in-Time-of-Peace" Cuba, Alex re-invented himself. He became an off-the-books entrepreneur, employing his language skills, guile and charm to survive in impossibly difficult circumstances. One of the many services he offered was as a guide and raconteur for tourists who wanted a "no-guff introduction to the real Havana."

I did. I'd read about him in a newspaper travel story before I left home, and I gave him a call soon after I arrived in Havana in May 2009. He picked me up at my hotel the next morning in his battered, Russian-made Lada. He'd been allowed to buy the car back in 1979, he told me, as a reward for being a good communist. The price: 2,200 pesos, paid off at 35 pesos a month for five years, interest-free. The engine now had over 400,000 km on it but was running "just fine."

We spent the day tooling around parts of the city I'd never have experienced on my own. But far more interesting than what I got to see — as interesting as that was — was getting the chance to listen to Alex's stories: in the car, over cigars after lunch at an outdoor restaurant where everyone knew his name, over drinks back on the terrace at the Hotel Nacional, where the security guards kept an especially watchful, wary eye on a smooth-talking Cuban in relaxed English conversation with a foreigner.

He'd been married three times, he told me, had four children and four grandchildren. These days, he lived in a one-bedroom apartment with his 18-year-old daughter, a university student. She slept in a second bedroom he'd carved out of the balcony. To save money, he never turned on the air conditioning. But he had an antenna on the roof of his building so he could watch television. And he had an Internet connection, in the name of a friend.

Alex was interested in, and thoughtful about, the world beyond Cuba. Because many of his customers came from Canada, he told me, he read the Toronto *Globe and Mail* online every day. He mentioned a recent report in that paper about a speech Nicaraguan President Daniel Ortega had given at the Summit of the Americas. "When you only get one side of the story," he noted, referring more to me than himself, "how can you be informed?" He even followed Canadian politics. "What do you think of Stephen Harper?" he asked at one point.

I was curious too. Barack Obama had just won the American presidency, and there was much wishful hoping among my liberal friends in the United States that his ascendancy might finally signal not only an overdue end to the counter-productive U.S. trade embargo but also fresh water in the poisoned well of personal relations between the two old enemies. What did Alex think Obama's victory might mean, I asked, assuming the best?

He paused, took a contemplative puff on his cigar, exhaled. "Nothing," he said simply. "It doesn't matter who is the president of the United States or who is in charge in Cuba. Nothing will change between Cuba and the United States until they resolve the issue of the Five."

The Five?

Suddenly, I was back to the Cuban Five. In Cuba — as I was about to discover — all conversations about the future of Cuba-U.S. relations invariably wind their way back to *Los Cinco*. In Cuba, their real-life story has long since transcended mere fact to become myth. Hundreds of thousands of Cubans have marched past the United States Interest Section in Havana shouting demands for their release. Their images are ubiquitous. They stare back at you from highway billboards beneath a starkly confident: "Volverán." *They Will Return.* Much younger versions of their faces are painted on fences, the sides of apartment buildings, office waiting-room walls, postage stamps, even on stickers glued to the dashboards in Old Havana Coco cabs.

Though they still rank below Fidel and Ché in the revolutionary pantheon, they have become certified, certifiable, first-name Heroes of the Revolution. Ask any Cuban school child and they can rhyme off those first names: Gerardo, René, Antonio, Ramón and Fernando. The children will inform you that *los muchachos* — though all are now well into middle age, they are usually still described in Cuban propaganda as "the young men" — are Cuban heroes unjustly imprisoned in the United States for trying to protect their homeland from terrorist attack.

The Cuban version of their story is straightforward: During the nineties, Miami-based counter-revolutionary terrorist groups were plotting — and sometimes succeeding in carrying out — violent attacks against Cuba. Since the American government seemed unable or unwilling (or both) to stop them, Cuba dispatched intelligence agents to Miami to infiltrate these violent anti-Castro organizations, find out what they were planning and, if possible, stop them before they could wreak their havoc.

Sometimes they succeeded, sometimes they didn't. An Italian-Canadian businessman was killed in one 1997 explosion at a Havana hotel. To prevent an even worse tragedy, Cuba reluctantly agreed to share the fruits of their agents' work at an unprecedented meeting between Cuban State Security and the FBI in Havana in June of 1998. But the FBI, instead of charging the terrorists the Cubans had fingered, arrested Cuba's agents instead. The Five were thrown into solitary confinement for close to a year and a half to break their will, then tried in a rabidly anti-Castro Miami, convicted and sentenced to unconscionable prison terms ranging from 15 years to something obscenely described as double life plus 15 years.

For what? For trying to prevent terrorists from attacking their homeland. Surely, in the wake of 9/11, Americans could understand the necessity of the kind of heroic work the Five had been doing. If only the American media would tell the truth… That's the Cuban version.

The American version? Actually, there are two. In most of the United States beyond South Florida, the Cuban Five are still more likely to be the Cuban Who? Or the Cuban What? As stories about their arrest, trial, conviction and sentencing played out daily on the front pages in Miami newspapers, the Five registered barely a blip on the national media radar screen. During much of that period, of course, the media's Florida antennae were jammed by another, very different, and more emotionally appealing tug of war between Miami and Havana: the crisis/circus over Elián González, and whether his Cuban father or Miami relatives should get custody of the six-year-old miracle survivor of a 1999 rafting disaster that killed his mother. That story had barely faded from public consciousness when the national media became obsessed by the might-have-been-laughable-if-it-hadn't-been-so-consequential tale of the "hanging chads" and Florida's (particularly Cuban-American Floridians) even more than usually decisive voice in determining the outcome of the 2000 U.S. presidential election. After that came 9/11 and the stunning revelation that several of the hijackers who attacked New York and Washington had learned how to fly jets on simulators at training schools in — where else? — Florida. If the Cubans hoped terrorism-terrified Americans might finally understand their rationale for sending agents to Florida, they were thinking wishfully. The media's fixed lens moved quickly from Florida, to Afghanistan, then Iraq. Three months after 9/11, while American forces were gearing up to chase the evil Taliban out of Afghanistan, the Cuban Five were being sentenced and disappeared into the abyss of the U.S. prison system.

In Miami, on the other hand, everyone knew about the Five. Most believed they got what they deserved. Or, more likely, that they got off lightly, considering... Considering that the Five were responsible for the deaths of four civilian fliers from Brothers to the Rescue. The Floridians are quick to point out that *that* story — the one about how the Brothers fliers, who were only trying to save the lives of innocent Cubans, were blown out of the sky by Cuban MiGs, and how the Five had helped murder them — is somehow left out of the Cuban narrative. (That's not quite true, I was to discover. It's just that the Cubans see the shootdown as a separate, different issue, one more example in which the exact same facts can unfurl polar opposite narratives.)

Castro's version, the Floridians added, made it seem as if his agents had somehow been sent to Florida because a few bombs — probably planted by his own agents for his own purposes — had exploded in Havana. Castro has been sending his army of infiltrators, double agents, dupes and *agent provocateurs* to Florida since the day he seized power in 1959. Don't believe it? Look at the Five. One of them "defected" to the United States in 1990, seven years before any bombs exploded in the hotels. And, despite what the Cubans claim, their agents were not just spying on legitimate, peaceful exile organizations like Brothers to the Rescue and the Cuban American National Foundation. These Cuban spies were also trying to burrow inside the United States military in order to steal secrets Cuba could use to launch a military attack on America, or peddle to fellow-traveling, terrorist rogue states like Iran or Libya.

I will confess that — on the hot spring afternoon when Alex Trelles and I were sitting on the terrace at the Hotel Nacional contemplating the view of the sparkling waters of la Bahia de la Habana, sipping mojitos, puffing cigars and discussing the future of Cuban-American relations in the Obama era — I understood almost nothing about the unfathomable pit of this abyss between the American and Cuban versions of reality. But I was intrigued. Was any of this documented, I asked?

"Fidel gave a speech," he said. "It's all there. Names, dates, places. They put it on the Internet. In English. Look it up."

Eventually, I did. The speech, which was delivered on May 20, 2005, at the José Marti Anti-imperialist Square in Havana, opens with a kind of breathless urgency. "My fellow countrymen," Fidel Castro begins, "what I will immediately read to you has been elaborated on the basis of numerous documents from our archives. I have had very little time, but many comrades have cooperated..." It was hardly a speech in the way I understood speeches, even speeches by a legendary speechmaker like Fidel Castro. It was, essentially, a remarkable 10,286-word *j'accuse* in which the Cuban leader read into the public record details of every one of the significant events of the 1997 Havana hotel bombing campaign: from April 12, 1997 ("a bomb explodes in the 'Ache' discotheque at the Melia Cohiba hotel") to September 12, 1998 ("the five comrades, now heroes of the Republic of Cuba, are arrested").

"It's all there," Alex repeated, "even the part about García Márquez."

Gabriel García Márquez? The Nobel prize-winning Colombian novelist? In the middle of the bombing campaign, it turned out, Castro had asked his good friend García Márquez to carry a top secret message about the Miami exiles' latest, even-worse-than-bombing-hotels terrorist plot to Washington. As Castro explained in his speech: "Knowing that writer Gabriel García Márquez would be traveling to the United States soon where he would be meeting with William Clinton, a reader and admirer of his books (as so many other people in the world)... I decided to send a message to the U.S. president, which I personally drafted."

After returning from his secret mission in May 1998, García Márquez wrote a chatty, finely detailed, 4,000-word report on his adventures, which Castro also proceeded to read into the record — "an exact copy without removing a word." He even included the text of a message he'd sent García Márquez the day before his speech, asking permission to publish the novelist's report: "It is indispensable that I discuss the subject of the message I sent with you about terrorist activities against our country," Castro wrote. "It is basically the message that I sent and the wonderful report you sent back to me, which is written in your unmistakable style... This will in no way," he added, perhaps unnecessarily, "damage the addressee and much less will it affect your literary glory."

According to Castro's speech, Gabriel García Márquez's visit to the White House opened a back channel that eventually led to an unprecedented meeting between Cuban State Security and the FBI in Havana in June 1998. At the conclusion of three days of face-to-face gatherings, Castro claimed, "the U.S. side acknowledged the value of the information they had been given and made a commitment to give a reply with an analysis of these materials as soon as possible. It is strange that almost three months went by without the serious response promised... On September 12 — mark my words, hardly three months had passed — the Five comrades, now heroes of the Republic of Cuba, are arrested."

"After you read that speech," Alex told me that afternoon, "you'll begin to understand why the Five matter so much here and why nothing can really be resolved between Havana and Washington until they are returned to Cuba." He paused, smiled. "But you'll only *begin* to understand... It's complicated."

It is. After I returned from Havana, I began to burrow deeper into that labyrinthian netherworld. I started with the Castro speech, then moved on — novel? what novel? — to the Miami *Herald* archive, where I read hundreds of news stories about the arrest, trial, conviction and appeals of the Cuban Five. Eventually, I tracked down an electronic copy of the 20,000-plus-page transcript[1] of *United States of America versus Gerardo Hernández, et al., Case*

---

1. It was the first time I'd ever opened a Microsoft Word document that was so long the

Number 98-721, and read it from opening gavel to final sentencing. And then began an ongoing correspondence with the Five in prison. The more I read, the more I realized I didn't know.

I began to read books about Cuba, about Cuban-American relations, about Fidel, about the exile experience, about Havana, about Miami, about migration accords and foreign policy, even novels about Cuba's Special Period and its effect on Cubans. I tried to make sense of the Alpha-66 to Omega-7 Greek alphabet soup of militant Miami exile groups who've been doing their best to topple Fidel Castro since the day he took power. I tried — and gave up trying — to add up the dozens, probably hundreds, maybe even thousands of Cuban government agents who've infiltrated, disrupted, undermined, exposed and even led those same groups. (So many prominent anti-Castro exiles have ultimately unmasked themselves, or been unmasked, or at least been accused of being Cuban intelligence agents, that even exile groups can never be certain who among them is working for Cuban State Security. Which, of course, is the goal.[2])

Nothing, it seems, is ever as it seems. Consider the Cuban American National Foundation, ostensibly the single most powerful American lobby group working for peaceful, democratic regime change in Cuba. CANF has helped elect — and influenced the Cuba policy of — every American president since Ronald Reagan. CANF's leaders hang out at the White House and in the best offices on Capitol Hill, posing for photos and peddling their stridently anti-Castro, tighten-the-embargo-screws-and-we'll-win message. Privately, however, some among them were also organizing and financing their own secret paramilitary wing whose purpose was to overthrow the Cuban government by force and, if possible, murder Fidel Castro. The fingerprints of upstanding CANF board members are smudged over more than a few of the 638 — and counting — failed plots to assassinate Castro.

All of which led me back — and forward — to Luis Posada Carriles and Orlando Bosch Ávila, the founding fathers of anti-Castro terrorism. And, of course, to those many and various turning-point moments in the history of Cuba-American relations, such as the 1961 Bay of Pigs invasion, and the 1976

Pages count read: ****of****.

2. Exile groups aren't the only ones who've found themselves fooled and/or confused by Cuban double agents. Consider the case of Florentino Azpillaga, the head of Cuban intelligence in Czechoslovakia, who sought asylum in the United States in 1987. Azpillaga told his CIA interrogators that many of the Cubans the Americans believed they were "running" in various intelligence operations were actually double agents working for Cuban State Security and feeding the CIA "misleading or useless" information. "We certainly underestimated the Cubans," one official told the *Los Angeles Times* in an August 12, 1987, story. "We never realized that the operations we thought were so good were theirs all along." Assuming, of course, that Azpillaga wasn't himself a plant... Which many believed he was.

terrorist bombing of Cubana Airlines Flight 455, which killed 73 people. But every single incident, event, deception, plot, individual, group or policy has its own 180-degree different reality, depending on which side of the Florida Straits you happen to be.

The more I investigated, the more I realized I couldn't take anything for granted.

Consider the Five themselves. Although the group that would become known as the Cuban Five consists of the five men — Gerardo Hernández, René González, Fernando González, Ramón Labañino and Antonio Guerrero — who stood in the prisoners' dock in Miami when their trial finally began in 2000, there were, initially, many more than five of them.

According to U.S. prosecutors, the Five were members of a Cuban intelligence network called La Red Avispa, or the Wasp Network, a name they discovered buried in decoded computer disks.[3] When FBI agents initially swooped in on September 12, 1998, they arrested 10 people. Five of them quickly struck deals, pleading guilty in exchange for lesser sentences and a promise to testify against their compatriots. At the same time, the FBI publicly identified four other Avispa agents it claimed had left the country before they could be arrested.

So that adds up to 14.

But reading between the lines of the thousands of pages of decoded documents and testimony presented during the Five's trial, it's clear there were other officers and agents associated with La Red Avispa, people with code names like Sol, Ariel, Laura, José, Tania, Horacio and Manny. Some of them probably returned to Cuba before the arrests. A few were likely among a scattering of Cubans arrested on other charges over the next few years and linked, at least tangentially, to the Wasp Network. And then, of course, one or two might have been FBI double agents all along.[4]

---

3. Hernández, the intelligence officer identified in court as Avispa's senior agent, told me he doesn't know how or why Avispa got its name, or what, if anything, the name was supposed to signify. He didn't even appear to think of it as a network, perhaps because most of the people in the so-called network didn't connect at all. René González and Antonio Guerrero, for example, who were both described as Avispa field agents, didn't meet — or even know of each other's existence — until after their arrest. Fernando González told me he'd known Hernández when they were students together at Havana's elite International Relations Institute but hadn't known he'd also become an intelligence officer until he was dispatched to Miami to fill in for Hernández when he returned home on vacation.

4. During the trial of the Five, prosecutors — for national security reasons — were never required to say when or why they began surveillance of La Red Avispa. In 2010, however, an exile named Edgerton Ivor Levy told an anti-Castro Miami television station he and his wife were agents Ariel and Laura, and that they'd told American authorities "what the intentions of the Castrista intelligence were… as soon as we got here." The two arrived in the Florida Keys, ostensibly as rafters, in 1993. Although

Adding up all those names and code names, I arrived at a total of 22 members of La Red Avispa. But I've seen estimates as high as 27. Not that those numbers really tell you much, other than to affirm that nothing is as it seems. During the time it operated, La Red Avispa was only one aspect of a much larger Cuban intelligence-gathering picture. Percy Alvarado, for example, wasn't a member of La Red Avispa, but his penetration of the Cuban American National Foundation as a Cuban counter-intelligence agent during the same period provided Cuba with a critical link from Luis Posada to CANF to the 1997 hotel bombing campaign. And, on a broader canvas, La Red Avispa represents just a few brush strokes in the picture of Havana-Miami spying — and terrorism — that's been painted since 1959 and is still being tinkered with today.

So, the story of the Cuban Five isn't really the story of the Five at all. Or, at least, it's not just their story. And it isn't a simple linear narrative. It's a cascading accumulation of incident and irritant, of connivance and consequence, a parallel, converging, diverging narrative featuring an ensemble cast of eclectic characters on both sides of the Straits of Florida — spies, terrorists, revolutionaries, counter-revolutionaries, cops, mercenaries, politicians, heroes, villains, journalists, innocents — whose personal ambitions, actions, loyalties, vanities, secrets, strengths and foibles collectively weave larger narratives: about Cuban-American relations, about the war on terror, about hypocrisy, about truth and fiction, about right and wrong.

Perhaps it was the quicksand complexity of it all that ultimately convinced me this story needed to be told, and needed to be told by someone who didn't already know which versions of which stories were true.

Levy claimed he'd come forward because "it bothers me to see so much propaganda based on a basic lie that [the Five] were fighting against terrorism," it is worth noting the Miami Hispanic television station paid Ivor Levy for exclusive rights to his story, so other reporters didn't have chance to question his account.

Building the Nest

December 12, 1990 — February 1994

Miami, July 17, 1990

Only in Miami! Watching his triumphal, hero-home-from-the-wars televised press conference, a casual viewer might have puzzled over how to square the image of this smiling, rubbery-faced old man in the charcoal-grey suit and open-collared shirt — blinking through thick, over-sized spectacles into the glare of the TV lights while his adoring wife and four children, along with a gaggle of cheering supporters, looked on — with the sobering reality of who this man had once been. And who he might still be.

Dr. Orlando Bosch Ávila was a convicted felon, a parole jumper, an accused mass murderer, a man who had spent all but six months of the previous 14 years behind bars, a man who had most recently entered the United States illegally, a man the FBI agent who'd rummaged through the recesses of his life had labelled "Miami's number one terrorist," a man the United States associate attorney general had described as "resolute and unwavering in his advocacy of terrorist violence," a man 31 other countries had already refused to allow to set foot inside their borders and a legend and hero in much of Miami's *el exilio* community.

To the rest of the world, Orlando Bosch was a terrorist. But in Miami, the world's worst terrorist could be a beloved freedom fighter, provided he waged his terror on behalf of *la causa* — overthrowing Fidel Castro, killing him if possible, wiping his hated communist dictatorship off the face of the earth by any and all means necessary, and restoring Cuba to its once and future glory. This had been Orlando Bosch's guiding, sole mission in life for 30 years.

One of the more intriguing twists on their mutual loathing was that Orlando Bosch and Fidel Castro had once been allies. They were Cuban contemporaries, born within a week of each other in 1926. During the 1940s, they'd both studied at the University of Havana. Castro was president of the law students' association, Bosch headed up the medical students' group. Both took part in the struggle to topple Cuba's hated dictator Fulgencio Batista. After the triumph of the rebels, Castro, the revolution's leader, had rewarded fellow traveller Bosch, who'd returned from a pediatric internship in Ohio, to join the fight, with an appointment as governor of his native Las Villas province.

But relations soon soured. Bosch quit and returned to the hills to lead an armed rebellion against Castro's revolution. By the middle of 1960, he'd fled to Miami with his wife, also a doctor, and their four small children. Like many of his fellow exiles, who assumed they would return home soon, Bosch arrived on a 60-day tourist visa. He eventually found a job as an assistant director at a small Coral Gables hospital, bought a fixer-upper house in Little Havana and a "beat-up blue Cadillac," and even watched enough TV to claim that a quirky spy drama called *Mission: Impossible* was his favourite television show. But *la causa* remained his primary — some might say only — obsession. How obsessed? Bosch was eventually fired from his job at the hospital for storing explosives on hospital property. He signed on for the ill-starred Bay of Pigs invasion, then joined the CIA and became a case officer for Operation 40, a White House–sanctioned, CIA-run covert operation to mount a Cuban exile invasion force to depose Castro.[1]

On the side, Bosch also ran an organization called the Insurrectional Movement of Revolutionary Recovery (MIRR), one of a plethora of violent, transplanted-from-Cuba exile groups that made their bones by launching attacks against their former homeland. MIRR's tactics included dropping incendiary devices from small planes on Cuba's sugar cane fields as a way to destroy the country's agricultural lifeline. According to a CIA document, one 1963 MIRR air strike killed a father and his three children. Bosch denied he had anything to do with the attacks, but also claimed they were carried out at the direction of the CIA.

In 1964, he was arrested in Miami for "towing a homemade, radio-operated torpedo through downtown in rush-hour traffic"; in 1965, he was arrested for trying to smuggle bombs out of the country; in 1966, he was arrested twice more, first for ferrying "six dynamite-stuffed, 100-pound surplus aerial bombs" up the Tamiami Trail "to a secret base where there was a boat we could use to bomb Castro," and then for trying to extort $21,000 from a fellow exile to finance his various anti-Castro operations. None of the allegations stuck. Welcome to Miami.

---

1. His fellow members included a Who's Who of figures from future American political scandals. Beginning with the man who presided over its meetings, then Vice President Richard Nixon. Watergate burglars Frank Sturgis and Bernard Barker were members of the group, as was Nixon-era White House "plumber," E. Howard Hunt. Two others, Félix Rodríguez and Luis Posada, wound up in the middle of the Iran-Contra affair. Bosch himself would be fingered as "the dark-skinned man" in the famous Zapruder film of the Kennedy assassination, as well as a participant — with other Cuban exiles — in a Dallas hotel-room meeting with Lee Harvey Oswald prior to Kennedy's assassination. Bosch, who was questioned by the U.S. House Select Committee on Assassinations about his involvement, insisted he was at home in Miami at the time.

In 1970, Bosch was finally convicted for firing (misfiring, actually) a bazooka at a Polish (which is to say communist) freighter docked at the Port of Miami. He was sentenced to 10 years in prison. He was paroled four years later, soon after re-election-seeking Governor Claude Kirk boasted to a Latin American Chamber of Commerce dinner he had been "quietly and effectively" working to get their hero released. "When I think of free men seeking a free homeland," Kirk declared, appropriately misty-eyed, "I must necessarily think of Dr. Bosch."

Back in Miami, Bosch came under police scrutiny again, this time in connection with the mysterious 1974 assassination of an exile leader named José Elias de la Torriente. By the time police showed up to question him, Bosch had skipped the country, thus violating the terms of his parole. By then, Miami didn't matter. His first wife had divorced him, he'd lost his job, and he'd abandoned any pretence of practising medicine. *La causa* had become his city — and his life.

Before he left Miami, however, Bosch had had $10 million worth of bonds printed to finance a new scheme to overthrow Castro. He peddled them — in denominations of $10 to $1,000 — throughout Little Havana. Three million dollars of the money raised, Bosch claimed, was to be set aside to assassinate the Cuban leader. The bonds, in fact, were only redeemable upon the death of Fidel Castro. Though Bosch disappeared from public view for the next two years, the American government and CIA kept remarkably careful track of their sometime asset's whereabouts — and his activities — as he wandered Latin America, changing identities as often as he changed countries. Not that the Americans wanted him back on U.S. soil. Between 1974 and 1976, U.S. authorities turned down offers from both Venezuela and Costa Rica to return the parole-violator to the United States.

Bosch was arrested in Venezuela after someone tossed dynamite into a meeting of Cuban and Venezuelan diplomats, but he was released — with a new fake passport — after he turned over the key to his apartment, a weapons-filled arsenal, to local authorities. He then moved to Chile, where he lived in a military safe house under the protection of military dictator Augusto Pinochet. U.S. government documents say he filled his days painting naïve Cuban landscapes and his nights mailing bombs to Cuban embassies in Peru, Spain, Canada and Argentina.[2]

---

2. Bosch claimed in a 2006 interview with *La Vanguardia*, a Spanish magazine, that he'd come closest to killing Castro in Chile in 1971. "Two members of our group went there posing as reporters from Venezuelan TV channel *Venevisión*," Bosch explained. The plan was supported by the head of Chilean intelligence, "whose agents told our men to throw themselves to the ground after shooting the gun, and they would pretend to arrest them. They were standing two metres away from Castro," Bosch explained. "So what happened?" the interviewer asked. "The one who had to pull the trigger

In January 1976, Bosch showed up in Costa Rica, where U.S. Secret Service agents questioned him in connection with a plot to assassinate Henry Kissinger during a visit to the Central American country. Bosch told Costa Rican authorities his target wasn't Kissinger at all, but the nephew of Chile's deposed Marxist president, Salvador Allende. Costa Rica packed him off to the Dominican Republic anyway. There, in June 1976, at a secret gathering in the town of Bonao, Bosch helped found Coordination of United Revolutionary Organizations (CORU), an umbrella organization for the most violent of the violent anti-Castro groups.[3] "I told them that we couldn't just keep bombing an embassy here and a police station there," Bosch would explain later. "We had to start taking more serious actions."

According to U.S. government documents, CORU was responsible for more than 50 terrorist operations during the next few years, including the September 1976 car-bomb assassination of Chilean diplomat Orlando Letelier in Washington.[4] CORU's most deadly action came on October 6, 1976, when two bombs blew a Cubana Airlines plane out of the sky just west of Bridgetown, Barbados, killing all 73 people aboard. The victims included two dozen Cuban fencers, most of them teenagers returning home with pockets full of medals they'd won at the Central American and Caribbean Fencing Championships. For the next 25 years — until 9/11, in fact — that attack on Cubana Airlines Flight 455 would carry the dubious distinction of being the worst incident of air terrorism in the Americas.

The CIA quickly identified Bosch and his CORU co-founder Luis Posada as the bombing's masterminds. According to a CIA cable, an informant had overheard Posada boasting a week before the bombing: "We are going to hit a Cuban airliner… Orlando has the details." Within a day, Barbadian authorities had arrested two Venezuelan men — Hernán Ricardo and Freddy Lugo — as the actual bomb planters. They'd bought tickets on the Guyana-Havana milk-run but had gotten off the plane during its Barbados stop. Ricardo, who was travelling on a false passport, had done work for Posada's Caracas-based private investigation company and served as Bosch's driver. Ricardo fingered Posada and Bosch as the men who'd directed the plot. Ricardo and Lugo were eventually returned to Venezuela, where — after several trials — they were found guilty and sentenced to 20 years in prison.

The Posada and Bosch cases dragged on much longer. In 1980, a

---

chickened out and didn't shoot," Bosch replied.

3. Bosch's co-founders included Luis Posada Carriles, Gaspar Jiménez Escobedo and Guillermo Novo Sampol, all of whom would be implicated in a multitude of terrorist actions over the years.

4. One of CORU's founders, Guillermo Novo, was among those eventually found guilty of involvement in Letelier's death. When police raided Posada's Caracas office following the Cubana Airlines bombing, they also found a map of Washington with Letelier's daily route to his office marked on it.

Venezuelan military judge acquitted both men, but the prosecutors successfully appealed, arguing the trial should have been held in a civilian court. While awaiting retrial, Posada — with help from rich exile friends in Miami — escaped, disguised as a priest, and disappeared.

Bosch wisely waited for the legal process to run its course, which only solidified his martyr status in Miami exile circles. While he was still in prison, Miami's mayor led a highly publicized (it was an election year) pilgrimage to visit him in his cell. When Bosch went on a hunger strike to protest his incarceration, a dozen sympathizers set up a tent city in Little Havana and joined his fast. City fathers in Miami, Hialeah and Sweetwater even designated March 25, 1983, as "Orlando Bosch Day" to celebrate his lifetime of unstinting devotion to *la causa*.

In 1986, Bosch was finally acquitted, largely on a technicality: the Venezuelan court refused to allow Barbadian evidence to be used in his trial because it had been submitted too late and only in English. The judge also made the fascinatingly beside-the-point argument that Bosch must be innocent because he wasn't with Hernán and Lugo "at the moment in which the Cubana plane was destroyed." The next year, Bosch, proclaiming, "I have a loving wife who resides in the United States and five American children with whom I want to share the last years of my life," resurfaced in Miami, a city that must have seemed dramatically different — and not — from the place he'd abandoned 13 years earlier. By then, Miami, as noted American writer Joan Didion put it in her 1987 nonfiction book, had become "our most graphic lesson in consequences."[5] Most of those consequences were a direct result of the presence in the city of close to half a million Cubans, many of whom had arrived in the years since Bosch left.

The first Cubans to flee to Miami following the triumph of Fidel Castro's revolution, not surprisingly, had been the most wealthy and most powerful members of the old Batista regime, along with the American mobsters who'd made Havana their own. They were soon followed by the country's business elite, many of whom already did business with the United States, or whose companies were owned by Americans. Cuba's professional classes were next to seek their exit. Many had opposed Castro from the beginning, but others — like Bosch — were early supporters who changed their minds, either because of what they saw as the excesses of the revolution or because of Castro's quick embrace of Soviet-style communism.

By the end of 1962, nearly 250,000 Cubans had landed in the United

---

5. Miami, Didion wrote in *Miami*, was "not exactly an American city as American cities have until recently been understood but a tropical capital: long on rumor, short on memory, over-built on chimera of runaway money and referring not to New York or Boston or Los Angeles or Atlanta but to Caracas and Mexico, to Havana and to Bogota and to Paris and Madrid."

States, most settling in south Florida. They saw themselves not as refugees or would-be immigrants but as exiles who had relocated temporarily to wait out the madness that had gripped their homeland. Miami — with its shared sub-tropical climate and an already established Cuban community of close to 30,000 — made a natural haven. Havana's upper classes were hardly strangers to Florida's charms, of course; before the revolution, many had vacationed in Miami Beach. And Miami was conveniently close to Havana — just a 55-minute flight across the Florida Straits — meaning they could return quickly once the political situation improved. They were so confident they would return soon many left their valuables behind in Cuba.

Why wouldn't they have been optimistic? The American government seemed committed to helping them get their country back. Under cover of an organization code-named JM Wave, the cia set up shop on the south campus of the University of Miami, doling out $50 million to hire a permanent staff of 300 to oversee the insurrectionist work of more than 6,000 Cuban exile agents.

Their dismal failure at the Bay of Pigs in the spring of 1961 initially only seemed to make the American devotion to *la causa* stronger. The cia shipped off cadres of bright young Cuban exiles — including Bosch's eventual coru compatriot Luis Posada; Felix Rodríguez, who would gain fame as the cia operative responsible for killing Ché Guevara and for running Oliver North's Iran-Contra network; and Jorge Mas Canosa, who would one day become chair of the politically influential Cuban American National Foundation — to American military bases where cia instructors helped them master the fine arts of bomb-making and sabotage.

But the exiles' dream turned into a nightmare after the 1962 Cuban missile crisis, when the Kennedy administration — as part of the price for getting the Soviet Union to remove its missile bases — agreed not to invade Cuba. Bosch himself wrote "a long bitter letter to Kennedy, charging betrayal." By then, however, the exile genie was out of the bottle. Even if it wanted to, the American government couldn't magically take back all the support and training its cia had provided to the anti-Castro militants.[6]

Not that it wanted to. The Americans were still just as eager for their exile proxies to topple Castro; they just couldn't be seen to be directing the process any longer. The result was that militant exile groups flowered in Miami's hothouse, becoming a law unto themselves as they launched raid after raid against Cuba from the safety of their bases in Florida. Despite the undeniable reality that their actions violated the U.S. Neutrality Act — which says paramilitaries can't organize or carry out attacks against other countries

---

6. In 1976, during another wave of bombings in Miami, the local police became so desperate they sent a letter to the cia asking for a list of all exiles the agency had trained to make bombs as well as the whereabouts of all plastic explosives left behind when the cia closed its exile training facilities. The cia never replied.

from U.S. soil — the FBI rarely investigated. When police did file charges, prosecutors rarely prosecuted. If they did, juries in exile Miami even more rarely convicted.

It was probably no accident, for example, that Orlando Bosch had been stopped five times in five years before finally being convicted for terrorist activities, mostly because firing a makeshift bazooka at a Polish ship from Miami's busy downtown MacArthur Causeway made him impossible to ignore.

By the 1970s, this growing culture of lawlessness had also turned inward as various exile groups tried to prove they were purer, more committed to *la causa* than the others. In 1978, for example, a respected Cuban-American banker named Bernard Benes brokered a secret, White House–encouraged deal with Fidel Castro that led to the release of 3,600 Cuban political prisoners and opened the door for Cubans to finally, if briefly, reunite with their relatives in the United States. For his efforts, Benes became, in the words of the *New York Times*, "the most prominent — and in anti-Castro circles the most hated — member of Miami's community of 430,000 Cuban exiles."

Benes, Robert M. Levine reported in his book *Secret Missions to Cuba*, "remained under FBI protection, surviving at least one and possibly two assassination attempts, and wearing a bulletproof vest... His bank was picketed and firebombed and... he lost almost all of his assets. For years, he could not even visit Little Havana without people refusing to shake his hand or look him in the eye." Why? For trying to free Cuban prisoners? For allowing exiles to see their families again? Why did Benes become such a pariah? Andrés Nazario Sargen, one of the founders of the militant Alpha 66 group, put it succinctly in an interview at the time with the Miami *Herald*: "When an American citizen talks to Castro, or helps a person in Cuba in any way," he explained, "it gives the Cubans hope, which postpones their need to risk their lives to overthrow him, which hurts the cause."

One result of that dictum was a frightening outbreak of internecine warfare. During one 18-month period in the mid-70s, there were more than a hundred bombings and an average of an assassination a week in Miami. In a report, the FBI described Miami as the "terrorist capital" of the United States.

Whoever killed José Elias de la Torriente — the 1974 murder investigators had wanted to question Bosch about before he disappeared — issued a statement calling the exile leader a "traitor to the fatherland" and promising to kill any other leader who got in the way of the "process of liberating their homeland by working only to advance their own bastard ambitions."[7] Whoever his killers were, they'd been as good as their word, murdering four

---

7. Bosch himself sounded an eerily similar note in a 1974 interview with the *Miami News*. "Nobody will dare raise a false flag here anymore, for fear for his own life," he said of Torriente's murder. "His slaying was a good lesson to the exile community, so that no one else will now come forth with phony theories to fool and rob the people."

more exile leaders and blowing the legs off a fifth. The FBI eventually arrested three individuals, who, according to the *Miami New Times*, "had one thing in common. At one time or another, they were all connected with a man named Orlando Bosch."

Soon after Bosch's return to Miami in 1987, authorities clapped him into jail for his long-ago parole violation. Before he could finish paying that debt to society, the Justice Department also challenged his petition to be allowed to stay in the country. It turned out that when Bosch lived in Miami during the sixties and early seventies, he'd never actually applied for permanent residency. And now, based on more than 700 pages of classified U.S. government evidence cataloguing Bosch's involvement in terrorist activities, the Department of Justice wanted him deported. The problem was that no other country wanted him, except Cuba, and American authorities refused to send him there.

Thanks to that impasse, Bosch had spent the last two years in limbo at the Miami Correctional Center as prisoner No. 92690-131 while friends in high places lobbied for his release. Despite — or, more likely, because of — his terrorist track record, Bosch had many friends in high places, friends like Jorge Mas Canosa, chair of the Cuban American National Foundation, the most powerful exile lobby group in the United States. Florida congressional representatives Ileana Ros-Lehtinen and Connie Mack wrote letters on his behalf. Ros-Lehtinen's campaign manager and wannabe Florida governor Jeb Bush spoke to his father — who was, conveniently, the president — on Bosch's behalf. Even the chair of the Dade County Democratic Party — Bosch was a bipartisan cause, after all, for vote-hungry politicians — spoke out in his favour. Why? "The Cuban community believes the struggle against Castro is a war," Alfredo Duran explained simply, "and in a war that kind of activity is not frowned upon." *That kind of activity?* Blowing an airplane out of the sky, killing 73 people? Organizing an umbrella group for militant anti-Castro exiles implicated in "more than 50 bombings and, possibly, political assassinations?"

Regardless, the lobbying worked. In early July 1990, the Justice Department — under pressure from an exile-friendly White House and pushed by a federal judge to either deport him or release him — offered a surprise deal for Bosch's "temporary immigration parole." The three-page agreement called for Bosch to wear an electronic monitoring device, have no contact with "convicted felons or members of groups that advocate the use of violence for achieving political goals,"[8] remain in his wife's[9] modest

---

8. Two of the organizations advocating violence that Bosch was not supposed to have contact with were Brigade 2506, the Bay of Pigs veterans' association, and Alpha 66 —both of which openly maintained offices in Miami.
9. He married his second wife Adriana during his mid-seventies sojourn in Chile.

bungalow on Seventh Street in northwest Miami for 21 hours a day, have his phone calls monitored and maintain a log of every visitor to his house.

At first, Bosch balked at the requirement he keep a log of visitors; he didn't want to be seen as a *chivato,* a hated government informant, his lawyer told reporters. After 10 days of negotiation, Bosch finally relented but in his own unrelenting way. Bosch, the Miami *Herald* reported, "said he would hang a banner on the front of his tiny pink home warning any visitors away: 'Do not knock. Please go away. No *chivato* lives here.'"

It wasn't much of a concession, but it was enough for beleaguered Justice officials. Bosch finally signed the agreement and the Department signed off on it. At 1:45 p.m. on July 17, 1990, Bosch walked out of prison and into his lawyer's red convertible Mercedes, a sort-of free man. His release had become a subject of such intense public fascination that Miami television stations broke into afternoon soaps to announce it. Several even broadcast live his 23-minute press conference from the lobby of his lawyer's office in Coconut Grove.

Although his lawyer had issued a required boilerplate statement — "Dr. Bosch reaffirms his previous statement that he has renounced terrorism in any form whatsoever as a means of political action and as a means to free Cuba from communism" — Bosch himself sounded remarkably unrepentant. During the three hours a day — 11 a.m. to 2 p.m. — he was permitted to leave his house, Bosch told reporters he would wander Little Havana's Calle Ocho and Flagler Streets. "I will speak to anyone I want, I will embrace anyone I want and I will answer any questions they might have."

He also wasn't supposed to have any contact with members of the Bay of Pigs' veterans' group, Brigade 2506, because of its support for Castro's violent overthrow, but Bosch couldn't help but praise them while slagging the American government for betraying them so many years before. "On April 17, 1961, the United States took and abandoned the Brigade 2506 at the Bay of Pigs... Those that died there are heroes of Cuba and heroes of mine."

Although Bosch told the assembled throng and those watching on TV that he was extremely grateful to his friends and supporters in Miami — "I said I couldn't find the words to reciprocate, but in the end I chose one, which is what we all say when God grants our wishes: *Gracias, muchas gracias*" — he remained scornful of the American government for failing to appreciate, or support, the exile cause. "In my long history fighting for the freedom of Cuba," Bosch declared, "the government of the United States has built an enormous file giving me the face of a terrorist. But the United States never wanted to go into the depths of that file to understand that my insistence, my persistence, even my intransigence are products of a shameful pact where the destiny and sovereignty of my country was compromised."

Was he really ready to live up to the terms of his deal with the Justice Department, agreeing not to "own a firearm nor participate in criminal activity"? Could he really give up *la causa?* Bosch was coy: "They have bought the chain," he said enigmatically, "but they don't have the monkey."

The Cuban government, of course, wasn't amused. "We cannot calmly take the news of the release of Orlando Bosch, who is a terrorist," explained a spokesperson for the Cuban Interest Section in Washington. Havana had no intention of waiting quietly for the monkey's next trick.

Boca Chica U.S. Naval Air Station, December 8, 1990

U.S. Navy air controllers picked up the small, low-flying yellow AN-2 Colt biplane on their radar screens at 2 p.m. that Saturday afternoon. They thought at first it might be a private plane from the nearby Key West International Airport that had gotten itself into distress. It wasn't. René González had stolen the plane earlier that afternoon from a public airfield at San Nicolás de Bari on the outskirts of Havana. He had only 10 minutes of fuel left in his tanks. By the time he landed a few minutes later, officials from Customs, Immigration and Naturalization Service and the FBI were all scrambling to process this latest escapee from Castro's Cuba.

It was hardly an unfamiliar exercise. The flow of Cuban migrants had ebbed and flowed over the years, driven by events and economics, policy and politics. There'd been a significant increase in the last several years, thanks largely to the collapse of the Soviet Union, which had wreaked havoc on the Cuban economy. González had been one of its victims. "He said conditions were getting bad over there," a navy spokesperson explained to reporters soon after he landed. "He said he knew the government wouldn't let him leave as a trained pilot. So he took the opportunity and split."

González, a 34-year-old pilot and veteran of Cuba's Angola war, told immigration authorities he had recently lost his job as head of the aerial sports section of an organization called the Patriotic Military Education Society, a youth training organization run by the armed forces and communist youth.

Luckily, he was an affable, easygoing guy who'd managed to maintain friendships with former co-workers. Which was why no one had been surprised to see him at the airport that morning. They couldn't have guessed he'd been planning his escape for three months, or that he had been "dreaming about it for years." He'd said goodbye to his wife Olga and daughter Irma and took the long bus ride to the flying school's practice field. It was a quiet day with few volunteers, so González offered to park a small crop duster that had been left sitting on a runway. He was in the cockpit and just about to make good on his escape plan, he explained, when two people unexpectedly walked in front of the plane. "I didn't want to run them over," he said, so he'd parked the plane incorrectly in hopes the mechanic would ask him to do it again. He did, and this time González didn't hesitate. "I gave it power, let go of the brakes at full throttle until I left Cuba behind," he told INS officials.

"I'll never forget the last I saw of Cuba," he would later tell a Miami *Herald* reporter. "The thermo-electric plant of Santa Cruz del Sur and the beach at Jibacoa... I will never forget, but I think on that day what influenced me most was the fact I had already said goodbye in my mind so many other times... When I saw the Keys, I felt like Christopher Columbus!" René González wasn't the first would-be Cuban defector to arrive in the United States by air; he wasn't even the first to arrive at this naval base in a stolen airplane. Three years earlier, a former Cuban air force brigadier general had also commandeered a small civilian plane in Cuba and flown it here.

Despite the spectacular and daring nature of his own escape, González's official reception was routine, largely because he was carrying a photocopy of his American birth certificate and other documents in his flight coveralls. René González Sehweret was, in fact, an American citizen — born in Chicago in 1956, three years before the revolution, to working-class Cuban parents. Cándido René González had come to the U.S. from Cuba in the 1950s to play professional baseball. That didn't work out, so he became a sheet metal worker in Chicago. He married Irma, an exile activist who'd organized her first union — at a greeting-card factory — when she was only 16. They were both fervent opponents of Cuban dictator Fulgencio Batista. In 1957, when the 26th of July Movement was founded, they signed up in Chicago. Three years later, the family — which now included another son, Roberto — returned home to the new Cuba.

Like many of his generation who'd lived through Cuba's troubled pre-Castro years, Cándido and his wife counted themselves among the new regime's true believers. He made sure his sons were "educated in a revolutionary environment... undertook voluntary work, kept guard in the neighborhood and in their workplaces." Now Cándido González would have to face the reality of a very different son. As would González's staunchly revolutionary mother, his wife Olga and their six-year-old daughter Irma. René González was now officially a defector from communist Cuba. González knew he would have to deal with the fallout from all of that soon enough. For now, it was enough that he had accomplished the first stage of his mission; he had made it to America.

By the end of the day, the INS had confirmed his citizenship and put him on the telephone with his grandmother in Sarasota. González arranged to travel to see her the next day. Meanwhile, the commander of the Boca Chica air base introduced him to Arturo Spinola, a Cuban-American who was the president of Key West's Latin American Chamber of Commerce. Spinola took him to dinner and found him for hotel for the night. Alone in the hotel room, René González showered, turned on the TV, lay down on the bed and took out the two photographs he'd brought with him from Cuba. One was of his wife Olga, the other of him with his daughter Irma—his lovely Irmita. He began to cry.

BUILDING THE NEST

Havana, February 1991

She'd known it as soon as she rounded the corner that night two months before. There were no lights shining from the two small front windows of their house. They weren't going to the movies. "Every time you go to San Nicolás," she'd told René that morning, "the bus breaks down." He'd gone anyway. Olga understood. René missed flying, missed the camaraderie of the airfield. Still…

On that Saturday — December 8, 1990 — Olga had spent her day volunteering at a factory. Six-year-old Irma was staying overnight at her grandmother's so René had suggested — perhaps to placate Olga — that they should see a movie after he got back from the airfield. Ever the optimist, he'd brushed past Olga's skepticism. Of course he'd be back in time. He wasn't. The house was dark when she arrived home shortly after six. She went inside, turned on a light.

Dandy! The little dog René had found on the street and brought home a few weeks before had spent the day getting into mischief. He'd dragged all the papers from the bathroom and strewn them around the house. Olga went looking for a broom to clean up the mess.

"She's there," she heard a voice outside say. "The light's on." Olga went to the door. A man was standing there.

"I've come to speak about René González," he began awkwardly. "Are you his wife?"

Olga was frightened. Had René been in an accident? She didn't say a word. Waited for the man to make the first move.

"Did you know that René had gone to San Nicolás to drop some parachute jumpers?" he asked.

"Yes," she answered warily. "I'm waiting for him. We were going to the movies."

"I'm sorry," he said, "but I have to tell you that René did not land. We don't know where he is."

Did not land? What did that mean? Olga wanted to scream but it wasn't in her nature. She kept her emotions inside. Instead, she waited, waited for the worse news he must be preparing her for. Memories flashed. Of the moment they met. April 10, 1982, shortly after 1 p.m. on the beach at Santa Maria in La Playa del Este. René almost hadn't bothered to show up. He'd grown up in Miramar, just a block from the beach, he told her later. Why should he travel all the way across the city and beyond just to go swimming? But one of his teachers at the flight school had suggested there was this girl he should meet, and he was curious.

So was Olga Salanueva. Marisol, one of her friends at work, had told her about this friend of her husband's, a student pilot. "You two would have things in common," Marisol told her.

"How old is he?" she'd asked.

"Twenty-five."

Twenty-five? Olga was 22, and 25 seemed old for a Cuban man to be still single. "Is he married?" she wanted to know. Her mother had warned her: Never marry a man who's divorced and has children already. It's always a problem, her mother said, "when the biscuit comes with a box." At Olga's urging, Marisol instructed her husband to find out more about his friend. After looking up René's file at school, he reported back that René wasn't married. And there were no kids.

Even after that, getting the two of them together hadn't been easy. At one point, René was supposed to attend a party at the home of one of Marisol's relatives, but he'd committed a minor violation of the flying school's rules and been denied a weekend pass.

But when they finally did meet that day on the beach at Santa Maria, there was… something. The next Saturday — April 17 — they went on their first official date. A year later, to the day, they got married. Marisol was the maid of honour, her husband best man. René landed a job as a flight instructor at San Nicolás. A year later, lovely little Irmita had been born. And now…

Now, the man standing in front of her looked puzzled. "You are the wife of a pilot," he said, sounding almost suspicious. "You aren't reacting the way I would have expected."

"I think you are not telling me the whole truth," Olga responded evenly. "Cuba isn't so big you can't know where the plane fell. What happened? Please tell me."

"We don't know," he said.

Just then Francisco, a pilot friend of René's, arrived at the house. A few months before, he'd offered to bring René a pig for their traditional end-of-year barbecue. He could get them one for cheaper than they'd have had to pay in Havana.

"It's lucky you're here," Olga told Francisco now. "This comrade here — " she pointed to the man — "is saying that René has disappeared."

The two men exchanged perfunctory greetings. Then the first man left after offering Olga the phone number of his office. "You can call later."

After he was gone, Francisco said to her: "Do you believe him? I don't. If the plane had crashed, they would have told you. No, René has left the country…" Left the country? Defected? It couldn't be. It wasn't possible. Not her René!

"Turn on the radio," Francisco suggested. "They will say if a pilot has gone."

Instead, Olga went looking for the telephone she and René used only for emergencies. This was an emergency. She called René's brother, Roberto, and told him what the official had told her, what Francisco had suggested. "No," he agreed with her. "René would never have defected."

She called the airfield. No one would tell her anything. She called again. And again. Begging. Insisting. Finally, one of the men told her there had been no accident. René had indeed defected. The rumour was he'd flown to Key West.

Olga couldn't believe it. Finally, the next day she did listen to Radio Marti, the American propaganda network that beamed into Cuba. A Cuban pilot named René González, it reported, had stolen an Antonov 2 aircraft from a Havana airfield and flown it to the U.S. to claim asylum. So it was true. But it still didn't make any sense.

When René's first letter arrived from Florida a month later, Olga discovered "a René I didn't know." He'd left Cuba, he explained to her, because he couldn't agree to give up being a pilot. Olga understood his frustration, of course. She knew how important being a pilot was to him. Still, she wrote back, there were other things in life besides his pilot "fantasy." He also told her he had come to "a wonderful country" where there would be lots of opportunity for all of them. He'd already investigated schools Irmita could attend. "He was talking foolish things," Olga would say later.

Now, she read again the painful words of the letter she had written in response. If this was really how he felt, she'd written, she would have nothing more to do with him. "I wish you luck in your new future but it will not be with me."

Miami, May 25, 1991

José Basulto was — he would insist to anyone who asked — a changed man. He'd had an epiphany. After studying the writings of Mahatma Gandhi and Martin Luther King, he had decided to make active non-violence his "guiding principle for the rest of his life." That was why, he explained, he'd created Brothers to the Rescue, a new humanitarian organization of small-plane pilots whose sole mission would be to save the lives of thousands of Cubans fleeing their oppressive communist homeland in rickety fishing boats and jerry-built rafts to seek their freedom in the United States. It was a stretch.

José Basulto's history, as he would be the first to admit — occasionally the first to brag about — was violent. "I was trained as a terrorist by the United States, in the use of violence to attain goals," he told a reporter for the Miami Herald. "When I was young, my Hollywood hero was John Wayne," he noted with a smile. "Now I like Luke Skywalker. I believe the Force is with us."

In 1960, as a fresh-faced 19-year-old student at the University of Havana, he was recruited by a different force — the CIA — and shipped off to a Florida island for training. Basulto took to lessons in espionage, cryptography, infiltration, weapons and explosives "like a zealot," then served his apprenticeship in what would become the *de rigueur exilio experience*: the botched Bay of Pigs finishing school. For Basulto, it had been a defining experience: he still wore a Rolex wristwatch his CIA trainers had given him before the invasion, and the Cessna he flew carried the licence number 2-5-0-6 as a tribute to the exile brigade that tried and failed to overthrow Castro in April 1961.

A few months after the Bay of Pigs, the CIA infiltrated him back into Cuba in an unsuccessful scheme to bomb a missile base. In August 1962, Basulto was "the man behind the gun," firing 15 rounds from a speed-boat-mounted-20-millimetre cannon into the dining room of a hotel on the northern coast of Cuba, where he believed some Russians were meeting with Cuban military officers.

The next year, he joined the U.S. Army in the optimistic expectation he was training for another, this time more successful invasion of Cuba. When the invasion failed to materialize, Basulto quit in disgust and began piecing together his own new life in Miami. He earned a degree in architectural engineering, became a successful builder of luxury homes, married, had kids, divorced, remarried, helped raise his blended family of five children and, oh yes — as he would put it delicately many years later — "joined many of the efforts to free his homeland."

During the 1980s, he branched out — sort of. He provided what he called "humanitarian support" to Contra rebels fighting the Sandinista government in Nicaragua. But watching events unfold in the Iran-Contra affair — which he saw as yet another American failure to follow through on its promises to support anti-communist freedom fighters — Basulto couldn't help but reflect "on the years of trying to invade Cuba, the many failed assassination plots, the stockpiles of weapons hidden throughout the community awaiting the right time to gather arms and fight again, and the incessant cries of exiles demanding the death of Fidel. *It had all been fruitless.* Violence," he concluded, "did not elicit change in anyone or anything... Change on the island had to come from within, not from Miami."

This was, as his biographer would acknowledge, "a radical departure from the anti-Castro, pro-violence extremism of the majority of Cuban exiles." But was it sincere?

Although Basulto would insist his active role in violent attacks against Cuba ended with the 1962 shelling of the hotel, Cuban State Security's file offers a very different narrative. In August 1982 — 20 years after that attack — the Cubans claimed Basulto had "prepared an explosive device for an attempt against the Cuban President." In 1983, the file notes, he helped recruit new members for anti-Castro paramilitaries through an anti-Castro organization known as the Junta Patriotica Cubana while serving as a "subordinate" to a CIA officer named Carl Jenkins, the same man who'd trained him back in 1961.

Perhaps not surprisingly, Cuban officials had little faith in Basulto's Saul-like conversion on the glide-path to the founding of Brothers to the Rescue. Just as they doubted that the true intentions of the organization — co-founded by Basulto and another Bay of Pigs veteran, Billy Schuss — were as benign as Basulto had described them at a televised press conference the week before. Which may explain why, when Brothers to the Rescue's first official mission lifted off from Tamiami Airport on May 25, 1991, José Basulto's co-pilot was a recent Cuban defector named René González, who — as it happened — was also a Cuban intelligence agent.

Two days before, González had been meeting with Captain Eduardo Ferrer, the president of the Cuban Pilots' Association, a group made up of former Cuban military and civilian pilots. Ferrer was keen to hear González's opinion on the viability of a scheme some in the group had cooked up. They wanted to build a platform on a boat they could use to launch a small, unmanned plane loaded with explosives and direct it at a target in Cuba. In the middle of that edifying conversation, José Basulto had called Ferrer to invite him to the press conference where he was announcing the founding of Brothers to the Rescue. Ferrer had invited González along, which led to Basulto's invitation to join him in the cockpit. René González would have plenty of interesting information to report back to the CP, the Centro Principal, headquarters for Cuba's Directorate of Intelligence.

Miami, Fall 1991

Christopher Marquis pressed the telephone receiver closer against his ear, tried to block out the cacophonous clatter and chatter of a newsroom on deadline. He struggled to make sense of the strange, strained voice at the other end of the line. The man was calling from somewhere in Latin America, but the connection was iffy and the man mumbled in a garbled, guttural Spanish. "Tell my story…" Marquis could decipher that much, but then he heard what sounded like slurping followed by a question: "Will you come?" Bambi was back — almost literally from the dead — and he was eager to talk.

Christopher Marquis, who had yet to celebrate his 30th birthday, was the Miami *Herald*'s chief Cuban and Central America correspondent. Although a California native who'd earned his master's in journalism from New York's Columbia University, his perceptive reporting on Latin America — particularly on Cuba — had made his stories must-read material in Washington, not to mention at major competitor newspapers, like the *New York Times*. The previous year, Marquis had investigated the mysterious attempted assassination of the man who was now at the other end of his telephone line — Luis Posada Carriles. In that story, Marquis had decorously described Posada as "one of Cuban Miami's more fascinating warriors," a characterization that barely scratched the shiny surface of Posada's spy-novel worthy résumé.

Like Orlando Bosch, Luis Posada was a contemporary of Fidel Castro who fled his homeland after the 1959 revolution. Posada also signed up for the CIA's ill-starred 1961 Bay of Pigs invasion of Cuba, though he never actually took part in the fighting. Afterward — embittered and driven — he joined the U.S. military before graduating as a paid CIA operative, a role he performed for at least a decade. He and Bosch had been first among equals at the founding of CORU in June 1976, and then, three months later, first among unequals as the alleged "intellectual authors" of the Cubana Airlines bombing.[10]

In 1985, while in Venezuela awaiting the outcome of yet another appeal on criminal charges connected to the airplane bombing, Posada escaped from prison disguised as a priest.[11] Within months, he resurfaced in the messy middle of the Iran-Contra affair. Using the pseudonym Ramón Medina, Posada served as the El Salvador-based deputy in a CIA-run operation to clandestinely ferry U.S.-supplied weapons to anti-government rebels in Nicaragua partially financed by return air shipments of drugs to the United States. When that complicated web of shady dealings finally came to light,[12] it triggered a scandal, Congressional investigations, a special presidential review board, White House resignations and firings, an International Court of Justice ruling that the United States was liable for violating Nicaraguan sovereignty and criminal charges against key Reagan aides. But not, it should be said, against Luis Posada. He quickly disappeared again from public view.

As Christopher Marquis would later piece together the sequence of events, Posada had undergone an operation "to alter his facial features, shaved off a familiar beard, gained weight and has curlier hair than before."

Posada's first post-Contra job was as a secret adviser to El Salvador's president, José Napoleón Duarte. After Duarte lost the presidency, Posada — operating under a new alias, Juan José Rivas Lopez — relocated next door to Guatemala, where the state-owned telephone company officially employed him as a security consultant. In fact, Guatemala's president, Vincio Cerezo, had hired him to set up a sophisticated, well-financed secret security force independent of both the national police and the minister of the interior, and answerable only to him. As part of Posada's compensation package, Cerezo provided him with a luxury, high-rise apartment in the capital.

At 9 a.m. on February 26, 1990, Posada was driving to work in his black Suzuki Jeep in the middle of Guatemala City's morning rush hour when two cars pulled up on either side of his vehicle. Gunmen suddenly began spraying Posada's car with automatic weapons fire. In just a few seconds, the gunmen had fired more than 40 nine-millimetre rounds into Posada's vehicle. Most

---

10. According to declassified CIA documents, Posada was no longer on its payroll by this point.

11. In his memoir *Los Caminos del Guerrero* (The Paths of the Warrior), Posada claimed that Mas Canosa, head of the influential Cuban American National Foundation, had planned and financed his escape.

12. When one of the planes running guns to the Contras was shot down and its pilot captured, the pilot claimed his boss — a man he knew as Ramón Medina — was working for the CIA. It didn't take long to connect the dots from Medina to Posada.

missed their intended target. Three did not. One bullet slammed into his chest, "rubbing" his heart, a second grazed his arm, and a third caught him full in the face, shattering his jawbone and nearly severing his tongue. Somehow, Posada managed to grab the nine-millimetre handgun he kept on his lap for just such emergencies and returned fire, chasing off the attackers.[13] Bleeding profusely from his various wounds, Posada drove for another half mile before finally swerving to a stop in front of an Esso gas station.

The station's owner later told Marquis he found Posada slumped over the car's steering wheel in a "bloody heap." Looking up at him, Posada made the sign of the cross and gestured urgently for a pencil and some paper. "Allergic to penicillin," he wrote in Spanish, then added: "I'm an advisor to Cerezo," and gave the gas station owner a phone number to call. Within 15 minutes, two of Cerezo's senior aides arrived to take charge. Posada was whisked to the nearby El Pinar Sanatorium, an exclusive medical clinic, where doctors struggled to save his life. National police officers and members of the presidential guard took up positions outside his hospital room to provide 24-hour protection.

Although Cerezo would publicly deny even knowing Posada and never visited him at the hospital, Posada would later tell Marquis that the president had "sent word for Posada not to worry." The president would take care of all his expenses. It didn't work out that way. A month later, while Posada was still awaiting corrective surgery on his badly damaged jaw, Cerezo's aides showed up at his hospital room, helped him pack, handed him a bill for $20,000 — Cerezo's promised largesse had apparently only covered the hospital bed, not the surgeon's fee — drove him to the airport and unceremoniously put him on a plane out of the country. Destination unknown.

Now, a year later, out of the blue, Luis Posada was calling the young reporter who'd chronicled his assassination attempt, inviting him to visit him to hear his version of the story — and more. "I bought a plane ticket and called him back with the flight information," Marquis would write later. "'How will I know you?' [Posada] demanded. 'I'm young,' I say, 'with a gringo face and a portable computer.' But I was plainly an amateur. 'Carry a newspaper,' he advised."

Marquis was met at a "cluttered, subtropical airport in a Latin American city" by a garrulous "Cuban-American arms dealer... I'll call Emilio" and a silent, tall, grey-haired man "who must be Posada." Emilio drove Marquis to an iron-gated safe house 15 minutes from the centre of the nameless town.

Marquis noted Posada's "craggy face, green eyes, a thick crop of dark grey hair. He is trim but his cheeks slide into flappy jowls, almost as though his jaw were unhinged. He can't chew. Spittle collects on his lower lip... Posada

---

13. One of Posada's bullets actually killed a bystander, but Posada told Marquis that Guatemalan officials "covered up the incident. He shrugs: 'These things happen in war.'"

nibbles at a cigar, smiles and apologizes for his sloppy speech. It's his tongue, you see; it was almost shot clean out of his mouth. 'Hanging out like a piece of liver,'" as he described it to Marquis. Later, Posada pressed Marquis's palm against his chin so the reporter could feel where the jaw failed to fuse properly, then stripped off his shirt to show him "the puckered skin where two other bullets penetrated."

Who was responsible for trying to kill him? At the time the shooting occurred, Posada offered Guatemalan investigators a number of possibilities, including the right-wing extremists in El Salvador he'd infiltrated on behalf of Duarte, or Nicaraguan Sandinistas, or perhaps agents from Castro's Cuba. If Posada had been attacked in the aftermath of his escape from prison in Venezuela, one diplomat told Marquis, "I'd have said it was the Cubans. But… in 1989 or '90, I'd say there's a lot of people who might want to take him out."

Posada seemed in a reflective, almost ambivalent mood. "We have maintained the belligerence," he told Marquis. "When [other exiles] were immersed [in Miami] trying to live well, trying to forget Cuba, we did what we could to continue the fight. We didn't give up. Right or wrong… When you think about it," he added almost wistfully, "we've grown old with our enemies. [Orlando] Bosch is really old. Fidel Castro is old. And I'm old."

Right or wrong? Had Posada's own views moderated, Marquis wanted to know? Posada nodded. "There was a time when I thought this was the way to liberate Cuba: Attack everything that served Fidel. Make him lose an embassy here, a consulate there. Whatever. Obviously, the world has changed. Many Cubans don't dare to say that… I fought Venezuelan terrorists, and I was a terrorist myself, if that is the word. Things have changed."

"Who is this man whose history reads like a personal challenge to Castro's expansionist dreams?" Marquis couldn't help but wonder. In the magazine piece he completed after he returned to Miami, he asked: "Is he a vessel of exiles' hopes? Or a cartoon of their despair? Or is he, simply, a thug?" Marquis's own conclusion: "Posada is a marooned Japanese soldier still fighting World War II. He is trapped in *la causa*. He is 61. In the smoky, unstirred heat of his urban hideaway, I sense something: Luis Posada, lost warrior, wants to come in from the cold."

Posada didn't deny it. Still, he seemed more resigned to his fate than resigned from it. "I'm bigger than whatever can happen to me," he explained. "Now I'm in a very difficult predicament in my life: I'm injured, decrepit, unable to eat. But I keep on, and I will to the end of my life."

In the offices of Cuban State Security in Havana, where the Miami *Herald* was required reading, analysts would sift the tea leaves of Posada's latest communiqué, read between the lines of Marquis's 8,500-word profile, try to make sense of what he was planning next. He was, they were certain, still planning something.

BUILDING THE NEST

Miami, May 21, 1992

It ended with faux smiles and a handshake at a Dade County Easter Seals fundraiser. "For the good of the community," as Jorge Mas Canosa would so decorously frame it. As he made his way into the Radisson Mart Plaza Hotel to share the platform with his fellow guest speaker and hearts-and-minds rival David Lawrence — publisher of the Miami *Herald* — Mas told reporters he was unilaterally ending his high-profile, four-month campaign to bludgeon the English-language *Herald* and its Spanish-speaking sister *El Nuevo Herald* into portraying Cuba and Fidel Castro in the same absolutist way he and his powerful Cuban American National Foundation did.

Ostensibly, the dispute — which featured billboards and bumper stickers, dueling op-ed commentaries, vandalism, even death threats — began innocently enough with a January 18, 1992, editorial in the *Herald* under the headline "Bad Strategy for Cuba." The editorial was critical of a draft Congressional bill called the Cuban Democracy Act, which was being promoted by Robert Torricelli, a Democrat from New Jersey. The legislation was designed to tighten the 29-year-old embargo on Cuba by prohibiting offshore subsidiaries of U.S. companies from trading with Cuba, or claiming tax deductions for expenses related to such trade, and even blocking foreign vessels that traded with Cuba from docking at American ports. Describing the proposed legislation as "a jumble of embargo-tightening measures that would punish countries that do business with Fidel Castro's government," the newspaper argued its intentions were "at odds with its likely results" and called for the bill's defeat. Mas was not amused. He not only supported the Torricelli bill — CANF's Political Action Committee had given Torricelli $35,000 — but he was also its mastermind.

Jorge Mas Canosa was the heroic, larger-than-life 53-year-old chair of the board of CANF, the most powerful, important and effective anti-Castro lobbying machine in the United States. Which made Jorge Mas Canosa the most powerful, important and effective Cuban-American exile in the United States. Mas was the living embodiment of the rags-to-riches, poor-but-ambitious refugee who had made very, very good in his adopted homeland. Not that Mas Canosa ever considered himself anything other than a visitor in that new land.

Born in Santiago de Cuba in 1939, the son of a local veterinarian who'd served as a major in Batista's army, Jorge had been shipped off to junior college in North Carolina at age 18, thus missing all the fun of the revolution. He returned home to go to law school one week after Castro came to power. His official biography explains it this way: "Following months of intense struggle as a student leader in Cuba, first, against the Batista dictatorship and then against Castro's communism, he was arrested and persecuted for his democratic ideals until he was given no other choice but to seek exile. In Miami, he joined the ranks of Brigade 2506 and following the failed invasion" — no need, in *exilio*-speak, to describe it further — "graduated as a Second Army Lieutenant at Fort Benning, Georgia."

Which was true, as far as it went. Officially, the 22-year-old Mas Canosa served as a squad leader, 1st Rifle Company, 3rd Squad in the invasion's El Grupo Nino Díaz. But Díaz's troops never made it closer to Cuba than somewhere off the coast of Oriente province. They beat a hasty retreat back to Miami as soon as they learned that the main force had been decimated. "Mas," explained Miami writer Gaeton Fonzi in a 1993 *Esquire* profile, "never got his feet wet."

But because he was classified as a Bay of Pigs veteran, Mas Canosa did qualify for officer training in the U.S. Army and went to Fort Benning, where he did graduate as a second lieutenant. Conveniently missing from the official biography is the fact that Fort Benning at that time served as a base "where men in civilian suits came and gave special courses in such specialties as clandestine communications, intelligence and propaganda," and where Mas Canosa's fellow exiles-in-training included Felix Rodríguez and Luis Posada, another El Grupo Nino alumni.

Though the details had been carefully airbrushed from his life story, Mas Canosa then became one of the leaders of Representación Cubana en El Exilio — RECE — a CIA-backed exile terror group operating out of Miami in the sixties. At one point, he personally delivered $5,000 in expenses to Luis Posada, who was in Mexico to blow up a Cuban ship.

Later, according to an FBI report, Mas Canosa encouraged Posada to "travel to Spain, Mexico, and other Latin American countries at RECE's expense and place bombs in communist installations such as embassies and information service libraries." Mas Canosa's official biography skips quickly back to Miami where "he married Irma Santos, his high school sweetheart." Which is where the narrative of the patriotic young Cuban democrat, forced to flee his homeland with nothing but the clothes on his back and dreams of a free Cuba in his pocket, really takes shape. From lowly hotel dishwasher, to shoe salesman, to milkman, to stevedore, to… well, hugely successful self-made man, Jorge Mas Canosa shinnied up the slippery pole of the American Dream with dizzying speed.

In 1968 — he wasn't 30 yet — Mas convinced a Cuban exile banker to loan him $50,000 to buy the failing company he worked for. The small firm — called Iglesias and Torres after the surnames of its founders — had been unsuccessfully attempting to win contract work with telephone companies. Mas anglicized its name to Church and Tower and, within the year, landed a multimillion contract with Bell Southern. It was the first of many his emerging "engineering contracting firm specializing in telecommunications infrastructure" would win.

The official history again: "That company went on to become MasTec, a multinational corporation, still headquartered in Miami, once named the largest U.S.-Hispanic owned business in the country and the first Hispanic owned corporation to be featured on the New York Stock Exchange. The company today employs over 8,000 individuals around the globe."

As for Mas Canosa himself? "He bought a sprawling, Spanish-style mansion south of Miami with high walls, towering Royal palms, a tear-drop swimming pool," Fonzi wrote in *Esquire*. "He drove a Mercedes, had a box seat at the Dolphins games, took his family skiing at Vail. He had become a very successful capitalist and began to itch with the power that came with that success. In Miami," Fonzi added, "that power had its own special twist."

In 1981, the stars of Mas Canosa's emergence as the most prominent Cuban-American business leader aligned neatly with a scheme by Richard Allen, newly elected President Ronald Reagan's National Security Advisor, to promote the president's "pro-active foreign policy." If the exiles could form a high-profile lobbying organization to support Reagan's hard-line anti-communist agenda, Allen suggested there would be — as one exile leader would later put it — "a chance of doing something" to promote their own dream of getting rid of Castro. And so the Cuban American National Foundation — modelled on the spectacularly successful Israeli lobby, the American Israeli Public Affairs Committee, was born. CANF, with separate non-profit, political action and lobbying wings, quickly became so success-ful in its own right that one former Senate foreign affairs staff member told Fonzi: "The Israeli lobby could take lessons from CANF."

In 1983, Mas Canosa convinced the Reagan administration — and Congress — to fund Radio Martí, a propaganda broadcasting operation he wanted beamed into Cuba to counter the official Castro media and "fight communism." To make it happen, CANF successfully bulldozed over objections from the government's own Voice of America, which argued that another publicly funded broadcaster wasn't needed; conventional American broad-casters, who feared it would provoke the Cuban government into blocking their broadcast signals; the International Telecommunications Union, which said the station was illegal; the U.S. State Department and the usually powerful Senate Foreign Relations Committee, both of which objected on all manner of political, legal and tactical grounds. Radio Martí began broadcasting in 1985. Five years later, Mas Canosa convinced Washington to underwrite a TV Martí too.

Part of CANF's success can be attributed to good old fashioned politi-cal schmoozing. In 1983, Mas Canosa invited Reagan to speak at a Cuban Independence Day rally in Miami. Reagan, dressed in a traditional *guayabera* wowed the huge crowd with shouts of "Viva Cuba Libre!" and "Cuba si, Castro no!" Soon after, Miami named a street in Little Havana after the president.

Mas Canosa, like many of the early Cuban exiles, was instinctively, viscerally anti-Democrat. He blamed President John F. Kennedy for abandoning their cause after the Bay of Pigs debacle and would still claim, decades later, that the man he hated most — after Fidel Castro, of course — was Kennedy. But Mas Canosa was smart enough not to allow even such deeply ingrained partisan loyalties get in the way of the greater cause. In 1988, for example, he helped engineer the defeat of a moderate Connecticut Republican, Lowell Weicker, who'd made the mistake of publicly promoting dialogue with Cuban leader Fidel Castro. CANF's Political Action Committee put its money and its muscle behind Weicker's right-wing Democratic opponent, Joe Lieberman. Weicker lost.

Mas Canosa was just as flexible when it came to the issue of violence. In 1978 — just three years before CANF's founding — he'd batted away a Miami *Herald* reporter's question about whether he supported violence. "Am I non-violent?" he asked rhetorically, then answered: "No, I am pro-violence." After he became the public face of the most powerful and influential exile lobby group in the United States, however, Mas sang from a new songbook. "We can defeat a communist tyranny in our sphere of influence without shooting one bullet," he now said. At least officially.

In 1985, he'd helped finance and organize the prison break of his old friend and compatriot, the self-confessed terrorist Luis Posada. Five years later, Mas underwrote Posada's hospital costs after his original benefactor cut him loose. And just last year, he'd lobbied hard to get Bosch, who'd also been labelled a terrorist, a pardon. And there was more — and more about to unfold.

Like Orlando Bosch, like José Basulto, like Luis Posada, Jorge Mas Canosa had publicly renounced terrorism. But, like them too, he hadn't really abandoned it as the best — perhaps only — means to achieve *la causa*. Not that Mas had any intention of explaining that. Not now. It was easier — and politically more useful — to emasculate the Miami *Herald*. Following the newspaper's initial editorial attack on the Torricelli bill, Mas took to the airwaves. In written statements read on Spanish-language radio stations, he denounced both the *Herald* and *El Nuevo Herald* as "tools of the Castro regime." Lauding Torricelli as "a friend of the Cubans," Mas upped the ante, thundering that the *Herald* was guilty of "a continuous and systematic campaign against Cuban Americans, their institutions, values, ethics and ideals," while *El Nuevo Herald* "manipulates information just like [Cuban state newspaper] *Granma*." He even called on the paper's two highest-ranking Cuban-American executives — one of whom was the president of the papers' parent publishing company — to resign in protest. They didn't.

Mas's vitriol must have seemed surprising to casual readers, especially considering that the newspapers' coverage of Mas had generally been so reverential that the local alternative weekly, the *Miami New Times*, referred to *Herald* publisher Lawrence as "Doormat Dave." Indeed the newspaper's initial response to Mas's full frontal assault seemed more puzzled and hurt than righteously aggrieved. "We have worked hard to be fair, and feel badly when anyone thinks otherwise," Lawrence said in a statement. "We will always remain willing to try and do even better."

But Mas didn't play nice. He quickly helped orchestrate the creation of a group called the Cuban Anti-Defamation League — fronted by Miami mayor Xavier Suarez and Republic National Bank chair Luis Botifoll — "to defend the character, the good name and the influence of this community… against those who would distort, defame and attack our community." Mas, of course, was one of the new organization's "senior advisers," and its first formal complaints — just as unsurprisingly — were filed by the Cuban American National Foundation against the *Herald* and *El Nuevo Herald*.

To press its case against the newspapers, CANF rented a billboard in Little Havana and brought space on 60 of Dade County's 536 buses, boldly declaring — in English or Spanish, depending on the route — YO NO CREO EN EL HERALD… I DON'T BELIEVE THE MIAMI HERALD. And it sent ominous letters to the newspapers' advertisers to "raise awareness [of the] bias and half-truths" the *Herald* was feeding its readers. The campaign had an impact. Dozens of newspaper vending machines were vandalized, some covered in excrement. Lawrence and two other senior executives received anonymous death threat letters. There was a bomb scare at the newspaper.

For the first time in its 50-year history, an organization called the Inter American Press Association — which fights for press freedom in the Western Hemisphere — felt compelled to launch an investigation into press freedom threats against an American newspaper. "We are concerned that when passions in the community are already running high," the IAPA report concluded, "campaigns of denunciation and criticism based on emotions run the risk of inflaming some members of the community to the point of violence."

Although Mas was quick to distance CANF from the threats and property damage, it seemed clear to many readers that the *Herald* was being intimidated. "The clearest indication of who was winning the battle," Gaeton Fonzi later noted, "came when Lawrence, after filling a half-page column with what he thought was a tough, firm stance, topped it with a banner headline: 'PLEASE MR. MAS, BE FAIR.' It had the sad sound of a big newspaper whining." Which explained why Mas was ready to end his feud with the newspaper at the Easter Seals fundraiser. But not, of course, before getting in a few last shots. During his speech, the *Herald* reported, Mas "made fun" of the newspaper publisher's efforts to speak Spanish on television while "'looking like a scared deer' in the headlights of a truck. But he ended his remarks on a conciliatory note," the paper added. "'I take my hat off in respect to Dave

Lawrence,' Mas Canosa said. 'He really stood up and put up a hell of a fight on behalf of his people, no matter how wrong they are.'"

The noisy war of words had another, perhaps intended consequence. CANF was gearing up for its annual meeting in Naples, Florida. And some in the group were making plans they would not want reported.

Naples, Florida, June 1992

By 1992, the Miami exiles' ever hopeful next-year-in-Havana greeting had turned into a doubtful dirge. Cuba should have been ripe for the counter-revolutionary plucking. Its primary benefactor, the Soviet Union, had imploded, turning off its cash taps. One after another, countries of the former Soviet empire — Poland, Hungary, Czechoslovakia, East Germany — had abandoned communism for the free market. But not Cuba. Not Castro.

Jorge Mas Canosa had assumed it would happen. The year before, the Cuban American National Foundation had even hired a public relations firm to answer the question: "How can the Cuban American National Foundation assure itself of the position as the only logical choice as leader in the establishment of the government and economy of the new Cuba?" CANF drafted a new constitution and legal codes so it would be ready when Castro fell. It established a blue-ribbon commission to come up with an economic reconstruction blueprint for a post-Castro Cuba, and sprinkled it with political friends like Ileana Ros-Lehtinen and Connie Mack, as well as luminaries from Republican economist Arthur Laffer and *Forbes* publisher Malcolm Forbes Jr., to former U.N. ambassador Jeane Kirkpatrick. CANF encouraged corporate members — Hyatt Hotels, Royal Caribbean Cruise Lines, BellSouth — to pony up $25,000 or more to get in on the ground floor. And Mas Canosa travelled to Wall Street to pitch his plan for a $500 million bond issue to underwrite "a post-Castro boom to rival the California gold rush."

Before the final collapse of the Soviet Union, he'd flown to Moscow to lobby Mikhail Gorbachev to cut off all aid to Cuba, then embarked on a whirlwind tour of former communist capitals — convincing Hungary's parliament to endorse a "statement of solidarity" with CANF's campaign to overthrow Castro — and invited the increasingly powerful Boris Yeltsin to Miami to speak at a university seminar. CANF followed that up by announcing it was opening its own Moscow office!

The Cubans themselves were not forgotten either. Mas Canosa recorded a videotape he had smuggled into the island, touting the economic successes of the exiles in Florida and promising to transform them from *proletarios* into *propietarios* too. "What we want through our example is to show you, the Cubans on the island, that if we were to change the system on the island… those who may wish to sacrifice themselves, to work hard, to endeavor, will be able to achieve the same as we have in exile." In case that sounded too smug and self-serving — and it did — Mas Canosa was quick to reassure his unseen audience they had nothing to fear from the wealthy, powerful and well-connected members of the Cuban American National Foundation. "We have more than enough resources to live comfortably here in exile," he explained. Not that Jorge Mas Canosa intended to live in exile much longer. "I have never assimilated," he told the Los Angeles *Times*. "I never intended to. I am a Cuban first. I live here only as an extension of Cuba." Next year in Havana.

But none of it changed anything. Fidel Castro was still in power in Havana. And Mas Canosa was still in Miami. Those simmering frustrations among the exile leadership over the failure of history to unfold as they believed it should had finally boiled over during the Foundation's annual general meeting in Naples. One director suggested it was past time they did "more than lobbying in Washington" to overthrow Castro. Others agreed. Before they left the meeting, "about 20" of CANF's "most trusted leaders" had quietly agreed among themselves to set up El Grupo Belico, the War Group, a secret paramilitary group whose goal would be "destabilizing the communist government of Castro." They agreed that Mas Canosa and CANF's president, Pepe Hernández, would be delegated to choose the members of the new secret armed group. Hernández, who was Luis Posada's cousin, would lead the paramilitary operations because, as one participant put it, of "his known record as a fighter in the 2506 Brigade and the Marines."

The man charged with providing the financial and logistical support for CANF's new paramilitary wing was José Antonio "Toñin" Llama, a successful self-made exile who ran a business exporting automobile air conditioning systems. Llama would put up $1.4 million to finance the purchase of 10 small radio-controlled ultra-light airplanes, a cargo helicopter that could serve as an "operation base for the planes, explosives (purchased through a company owned by another exile who was authorized to acquire them "to open up sewage canals for South Florida's sugar industry") and seven satellite-radio-and-phone equipped vessels for staging attacks on Cuba by sea. Plans also called for the Foundation's paramilitary wing to acquire a high-speed yacht that could quickly ferry Mas Canosa himself back to Cuba at the appropriate post-revolutionary moment to assume his rightful place as the president of a new "democratic" Cuba.

Perhaps not surprisingly, given its recent bruising encounter with Mas and the Foundation, the Miami *Herald* wouldn't delve into the details of what happened at the meeting for close to 15 years.[14]

---

14. That's not quite true. When the Cuban government claimed in 1998 that CANF had set up a secret paramilitary, the *Herald* reported the story but essentially dismissed the suggestion as more Castro propaganda. It wasn't until 2006, when CANF board member Toñin Llama confessed his involvement with the group, that the *Herald* finally began to take it seriously.

WHAT LIES ACROSS THE WATER

Tampa, October 27, 1992

Though most of the participants were quick to characterize the private meeting with Bill Clinton — which lasted only 15 minutes — as "more social than political," there was no downplaying its historic significance. A week before Americans were scheduled to go to the polls to elect their next president, Jorge Mas Canosa and key members of CANF — rock-ribbed Republicans all — travelled to Tampa for a cordial face-to-face with the Democratic presidential candidate to express their appreciation for Clinton's "crucial" help in getting Robert Torricelli's Cuban Democracy Act through Congress. The Foundation stopped short of endorsing Clinton's bid to be president, but peek-a-boo short. "We think it is safe to say that if one year ago someone suggested we would be meeting here today with the Democratic nominee for president of the United States, no one would have believed it," Mas Canosa acknowledged in a statement. Cuban Americans had traditionally supported the Republican Party, he said, because it was "the party that expressed concern and solidarity with the tragedy of the Cuban nation, introducing policies designed to bring that nightmare to an end." But then he added: "Any fears that the Cuban-American community may have had about a Clinton administration... have dissipated today. We are pleased and satisfied with Governor Clinton's deep-seated commitment to continue exerting pressure on the Castro regime until a free and democratic Cuba becomes a reality. Thank you for taking this time to visit with us... Bienvenido a Tampa, Governor Clinton."

Mas Canosa had had to swallow hard. He'd never voted Democrat, and he was a personal friend as well as a political supporter of current U.S. President George Bush. "He didn't want to make the statement," admitted Jerry Berlin, a Miami-based Democratic Party fundraiser who informally advised the Foundation, and had not only orchestrated the Clinton-Mas meeting but also helped draft Mas's everything-but-an-endorsement statement. "He finally agreed, but it was very, very reluctant."

But earlier that year, after erstwhile ally Republican President Bush had expressed tepid reservations about the Torricelli bill, Mas Canosa pointedly invited Clinton to speak at CANF's Independence Day celebrations. Clinton dutifully declared his support for CANF-supported legislation, and four local Cuban-American businessmen then dutifully contributed $100,000 to his campaign coffers.

Suddenly reminded of the importance of Florida to his own re-election hopes, Bush quickly announced — over the objections of his own State Department — an embargo-tightening executive order, which seemed in remarkable lockstep with CANF's wishes. "State Department officials admit," wrote syndicated columnist Georgie Anne Geyer, "that Mr. Mas's Foundation... has been responsible for the fact that the United States has basically formulated no policy of its own toward Cuba because of fear of the

Foundation's tactics." Paraphrasing her frustrated sources, Geyer added that suggestions that U.S. foreign policy toward Cuba was "being run by a bunch of nuts and ambitious egomaniacs is not too far from the truth."

They might have been nuts and egomaniacs, but they were also politically canny. By late October, Mas realized Bush's re-election campaign was in deep trouble, including in what had been the Republican bastion of Florida. The latest opinion polls showed that the state, which hadn't supported a Democratic presidential candidate since Jimmy Carter in 1976, was tilting Democratic and that Clinton's support among Cuban Americans had almost doubled in a month. Mas may have still planned to vote for Bush personally, but the cause was bigger than any individual, any party. If Bill Clinton was about to take the White House, Jorge Mas Canosa wanted to make sure the new president — like the current president and the president before him — would continue to do his bidding on Cuba.

Miami, November 11, 1992

Even in a city where everyone was suspect and no one knew for certain who was spying for whom — even after the fact — this latest confession was beyond stunning. Francisco Avila Azcuy, the chief of operations for Alpha 66, one of the oldest and most militant of the anti-Castro groups, went on a Spanish-language Miami television program to declare that he had been a spy for Cuba for the past 13 years. And not just a spy for Cuba. During almost that entire time, he said, he had been informing on Alpha 66's activities to the FBI too.

According to Avila, Cuban authorities had arrested him during an Alpha 66 raid on the island in 1967. He'd been tried, convicted and sentenced to 25 years in prison. During his time in prison, however, Cuban intelligence officers approached him with an offer of early release if he agreed to become a spy for them. He did but then, soon after he arrived back in the U.S., he says he contacted an "American counter-intelligence agency" — the FBI — and offered to work for them too. He had come forward now, he told the interviewer, because he was worried the Castro government would soon fall and his role as a secret agent might be exposed.

In Miami, callers to Hispanic phone-in shows debated whether it was worse to be a spy for Castro or a snitch for the FBI. And who else might be a spy. And, of course, whether Avila was even telling the truth, or if he was now a Castro disinformation agent trying to confuse the confusion. If so, it worked.

Key West, March 1993

Maggie Becker wasn't sure what to call it. Not love… not yet anyway. She liked to dance. He taught salsa dancing. He was Cuban, some kind of engineer, he'd said, but he spoke virtually no English so it was difficult to know for sure. She was from Pennsylvania, an artsy type; her rudimentary Spanish — *¡Hola¡ Me llamo Maggie* — dredged up from the memory recesses of a mostly forgotten semester back in college. For now there was dancing. And that seemed to be more than enough.

They'd met by chance a few weeks earlier. Maggie's landlady and her roommate, who'd spent the evening drinking and dancing at a local waterfront bar called the Pier House, had met a couple of guys and brought them home. Maggie was already asleep when they arrived around midnight. "I woke to the sound of a crash," she would remember later. "I thought the cat had knocked over the keyboard of my computer." When she went to the apartment's living room to investigate, she discovered a salsa dance party in preparation. "They were moving all the furniture and rolling up the rug." They invited Maggie to join them but — even though she definitely liked to dance salsa — "I was tired and it was late. Besides, there were already four of them." So she made her excuses, breezed through the perfunctory introductions — "Maggie, this is…" some guy who played in a band and another guy who didn't speak English — and went back to sleep.

But the guy who didn't speak English — Antonio Guerrero, a bus boy at the Pier House — was clearly intrigued by Maggie. Later, he'd asked her landlady about her and if he could ask her out to dance. "This isn't Cuba," she told him. And, well, one thing had led to another. And now Maggie wasn't sure what this thing had become.

With a mix of rudimentary words and gestures, they'd told each other their life stories. She told him about growing up in Pennsylvania, about how she'd gone to college but dropped out two credits shy of her degree, about how she'd started coming to Florida for winter vacations in the early eighties, about how those escape vacations got longer and longer until she eventually decided she would stay. She'd settled in artsy, progressive Key West and, at the suggestion of an ex-boyfriend, taken up massage therapy.

He told her he was Cuban, but that he'd actually been born in Miami. His dad had been a professional ballplayer. He showed Maggie his baseball card. In 1959, after his father was injured playing ball, the family resettled in Havana. Tony was only a toddler at the time. In 1978 when he was 19, he won a scholarship to study aeronautical and construction engineering in the old Soviet Union. There, he acknowledged without apology, he'd married a Cuban woman. In 1983 after he graduated, they'd returned to Cuba where he got a job working on an expansion to the airport at Santiago de Cuba. They had a child — Antonio, Jr. — in 1985, but the marriage hadn't worked out, and they'd divorced in 1989. Antonio had then moved to Panama, where he'd had another relationship — at least he was honest — with another woman whom he'd married. She was pregnant when he decided to move to the United States last year in search of better opportunities. She'd been supposed to join him, he said, but, well, that hadn't worked out either.

That was the bad news — along with the fact Tony liked the syrupy popular Spanish singer Julio Iglesias. The good news was that he had been honest about his romantic history. Plus, he was, Maggie had already discovered, a "brilliant" chess player, a painter and a musician, not to forget an excellent salsa dancer. Whatever this was, whatever it would become, it seemed worth exploring — without worrying too much too soon about what to call it.

Maggie wasn't the only one wondering what to call their relationship — and how to explain it to others. While Tony had been honest about his various romantic entanglements, there were pieces of his life history he'd left out. For starters, he was a Cuban intelligence agent. When he'd moved to Panama in 1991, it was on orders of Cuban State Security. He'd arrived with a shopping list of assignments: "search for political-military information via radio intelligence and visual intelligence, create a network of support agents, access and penetrat[e] prioritized main objectives — military bases, political and diplomatic installations — and... look for information about special Panamanian groups." But his primary objective had been to establish a history for himself there that would make an eventual move to Miami seem more natural.

But his Panamanian wife — who didn't have a clue about his other life either — had balked when Tony's bosses back in Havana told him he was moving to Florida in May 1992. As one Cuban State Security report noted, the woman "would not accept any of the explanations given about the advantages they would enjoy in the U.S. After this, she asked for a divorce and [Tony] accepted." What would his bosses back in Havana think of Tony getting involved with another woman? What did *he* think of it?

Havana, May 3, 1993

The Cuban diplomatic note began with the fusty fussiness common to official communications between governments, even those, like the United States and Cuba, whose relations with one another were so strained they didn't maintain embassies in each other's countries and communicated mostly through the good offices of neutral third parties, like Switzerland. "The Ministry of Foreign Relations extends its cordial greetings to the Honorable Swiss Embassy and the United States Foreign Interest Section" — this particular note began, then quickly got down to the business at hand — "It is known that the self-named terrorist group, Alpha 66... whose leader is the well-known terrorist Andres Nazario Sargen..."

Cuban intelligence had apparently been busy. The note documented what the Cubans claimed was an Alpha 66 training camp known as "Rumbo Sur" at 40th Street sw and 172nd Avenue in Miami. According to the note, the camp's instructors included four former U.S. Marines. Some of the group's impressive array of weaponry — "60 rifles, M-16; 20 rifles AR-15; 10 fifty-calibre machine guns; 10 machine guns, M-60; 400 rifles, AK-47, some of them semiautomatic; 30 grenade launchers for rifle M-16; over 500 carbines M-1, Garand and other types; over a hundred shotguns; as well as an unknown amount of high-power plastic explosives, hand grenades and hand guns" — had been hidden around the camp while the rest was stored in "residences and country farms owned by the terrorist leader Nazario Sargen and several of his followers." The group, the Cuban note said, also had a number of vessels "in order to carry out its subversive acts against Cuba." The note went on to identify each vessel and where American authorities could find them.

Which was the point. "The Cuban Government expects that this information about the subversive activities, which are carried out by the terrorist group Alpha 66 in North American territory, is useful to the United States authorities to take the necessary steps in order to put an end to the criminal actions of this terrorist group. The Cuban Government requests from the North American authorities information regarding the results of the pertinent investigations, as well as the legal actions that arise from such investigations."

Having made its request, the note reverted to etiquette: "The Ministry of Foreign Relations avails itself of this opportunity to renew to the Honorable Swiss Embassy and the United States Foreign Interest Section its assurances of their highest consideration and respect."

Key West, May 18, 1993

Dalila Borrego had another job Tony could apply for — also at the Boca Chica Naval Air Station. It was temporary, she said, like the last job. But at least it didn't involve digging ditches or repairing sewers. Borrego — an employment counsellor for Job Services, a state agency that matched job seekers with employers — had first met Antonio Guerrero a few months before when he showed up at her office one day looking for work. A personable young man who spoke very little English, Guerrero explained that he'd just moved from Miami and planned to settle in Key West. Borrego not only helped him land his first job — in the kitchen at the Pier House — but she'd also combed through the newspaper's real estate section that day to help him find a place to live.

The job at the Pier House hadn't worked out — someone stole his wallet and he quit — so she'd helped him find a short-term job at the Days Inn, then the ditch-digging job through AIA Employment, a temp agency that had a contract at the naval air station. "I knew I could get him in," she would explain later, "because I had been the only one in Job Services who would fill those positions with my clients." Tony wasn't picky about where he worked; he just wanted a job.

But Borrego knew that job was temporary and "dirty," so she had been on the lookout for something better. And now she thought she'd found it. The janitorial position at the base, a civilian position but a federal government job, was temporary too. The job was a long way from matching Tony's qualifications as an engineer. But, given his language skills, it seemed like a job he could land. She gave him the application to fill out. It was dated May 18, 1993. When could he begin work, the form asked? May 19, 1993, he wrote.

Miami, October 16, 1993

At first glance, it might have seemed like an appropriate place for a man who was, after all, a pediatrician by training to end up. Dr. Orlando Bosch had just set up shop in a modest, low-rise Coral Way office building filled with other doctors, medical supply companies and health care organizations. But Bosch, as he explained cheerfully to a reporter from the Miami *Herald,* had no intention of returning to ministering to the medical needs of Miami's infants and children. His new offices were to be world headquarters for the People's Protagonist Party, a political party he had launched to raise money to buy weapons and other military supplies to send to Cuban dissidents. Its slogan was "Mix for the Masses."

What did that mean, the reporter asked?

Bosch smiled. "We're not talking about flowers, or hot meat pies."

Weapons, the reporter asked?

Bosch didn't say a word. Instead, Antonio Dominguez, a man the reporter would describe as his "collaborator," answered.

"Yes," he said.

Wouldn't that, well, violate the terms of Bosch's parole? Though Immigration had relaxed some of the conditions of his 1990 release from jail — he was now allowed to spend eight hours outside his home each day instead of the original three — he was still prohibited from hanging around with "members of groups that advocate the use of violence for achieving political goals."

Wouldn't he? Didn't they?…

Bosch told the reporter he understood he might indeed be violating his parole terms, but he didn't care. "That's the problem of the authorities," he explained. "I consider those restrictions to have expired."

Later, the reporter called the U.S. Attorney's office seeking an official reaction. "A spokesman… declined comment," the newspaper reported.

Miami, November 5, 1993

Abel Viera was excited for his old friend. "You will meet them tonight," he'd announced grandly when he telephoned Percy Alvarado earlier in the day to give him the news. Now, as Viera drove the few short blocks from the duplex where Alvarado was staying to the rendezvous site, Percy Alvarado tried to keep his focus on the season's first storefront Christmas displays, the reality of so many poor people rummaging in their pockets to buy what they could not afford, willed himself not to think about the risks he faced… or the potential importance of the connection he was about to make. Viera pulled into the big Sunoco gas station at the corner of Calle Ocho and 27th Avenue in Miami's Little Havana and proceeded directly to a secluded parking area at the rear of the property. He stopped, turned off the lights. Through the windshield, Alvarado could see a silver Toyota parked beside them, a dark figure inside.

Alvarado and Viera had been neighbours back in the real Havana. Viera, who long ago moved to Florida, employed his old friend Alvarado — a Guatemalan-Cuban whose passport allowed him to travel easily between the U.S. and Cuba — to ferry money to Viera's relatives in Cuba. Alvarado was more than happy to oblige, for a 20 percent commission, of course.

Alvarado was a Marxism professor at the University of Havana, but with a taste for the good life a Cuban professor's salary couldn't support. During the past five years, he had developed a lucrative business as a "mule." In exchange for his cut, Alvarado smuggled thousands of American dollars that well-to-do — and guilty-feeling — Miami exiles wanted to send back to needy relatives on the island.

On the first Thursday of each month, Alvarado would travel to Miami for four days. He'd stay in a room in Ricardo Deliano's house in the 800-block of Northwest 32nd Avenue, which Deliano let him live in for free in exchange for carrying money and gifts back to Deliano's family in Cuba. When Alvarado wasn't cadging meals from Deliano or hitching rides to the Opa-locka flea market so he could buy cheap vcrs and watches to peddle back in Havana, he held court in his room, meeting as many as 10 Cuban exile-supplicants a day — most by appointment — who would show up at the house bearing cash, medicines, clothing, radios for him to take to Havana.

For his percentage — and for the bits and pieces of useful gossip and information he could gather for his real bosses back in Havana — Alvarado willingly put up with "interminable" stories from customers like Viera who liked to boast about their long-past "feats" fighting Castro, not to forget their next grand schemes to overthrow the dictator and free Cuba from its communist shackles. And, oh yes, Alvarado thought to himself, make a lot of money for themselves in the new capitalist Cuba.

Perhaps Alvarado could help their cause, Viera had suggested. Because he had the freedom to travel back and forth to Cuba, Viera explained, there were things he could do for them. "Them," it turned out, was the Cuban American National Foundation, the powerful anti-Castro lobby. Viera, as he was fond of boasting to his former neighbour, was not only an important member of the group but he knew people who knew people. Alvarado had allowed that he'd consider the idea, but only if there was something in it for him. That's how Viera had come to set up this clandestine meeting between Alvarado and a mysterious unnamed "leader" from the Foundation.

Viera and Alvarado got out of Viera's car and slipped into the Toyota. Alvarado sat on the passenger side, Viera got into the back seat. As he sat down, Alvarado stole a glance at the driver. He was in his mid-40s, balding with close-set eyes and thin lips. He wore a white shirt, open at the collar to show off the gold chain on his chest and a silver watch on his wrist. Alvarado noted the time. Midnight. He looked again at the man beside him. He had recognized him immediately. His was a familiar face to anyone who watched Hispanic television in Miami. The man was Luis Zuñiga Rey. Officially, he was a vice president of the Foundation's Spain-based front group, the Continental Peace Association. On TV and in the newspapers, he played the role of a defender of human rights in his homeland.[15]

Thanks to his bosses in Havana, however, Alvarado already knew something of Zuñiga's other history as a counter-revolutionary. Zuñiga had left Cuba in 1962 but kept re-appearing in the country enmeshed in one terrorist plot or another. In 1974, he'd been arrested trying to sneak weapons into Cuba and sentenced to 30 years in jail. He'd been released in 1988 after 14 years and shipped off to the United States. Since then, he had become a key player in the Foundation — and, more ominously, its recently established paramilitary offshoot. According to Cuban State Security, in fact, Zuñiga had begun recruiting agents inside Cuba to sabotage its thermoelectric plants, port terminals and oil refineries. And now...

"Nice to meet you," Zuñiga said simply.

"Nice to meet you too," Alvarado responded as respectfully as he could manage.

Zuñiga quickly got down to business. "Abel tells me he's known you for a long time," he said. "He says you are very capable and that you're willing to join us. Is that true?"

"Well, Luis," Alvarado answered cautiously, "that depends on what you want from me."

What Zuñiga wanted, he explained, was for Alvarado to set up a clandestine cell in Cuba to carry out bombings and acts of sabotage. The fake Frente Nacional Cubano, or the Cuban National Front, which would be portrayed as an organization made up of disgruntled officers from inside the Cuban military, would claim credit for their actions. Zuñiga would provide weapons and explosives as well as, of course, money.

Alvarado remained coy. He had become "disappointed" with Castro, he explained, "but I will not run those risks for the sake of it... Do you understand? I want to be well off and live comfortably. This is the most important

---

15. In 2004, U.S. President George W. Bush appointed Zuñiga as an official delegate to the United Nations 60th anniversary Human Rights Commission conference in Geneva.

thing for me at present… I want to be well recompensed. That is the only way to obtain my cooperation. The rest has no interest for me."

Zuñiga smiled. He already knew from Viera that his old friend was motivated by greed rather than patriotism. That was fine. Zuñiga and his friends would be more than happy to supply the patriotism — and the cash. "You should not worry about money," Zuñiga said. "You will have in the future many dollars — and much power." They had a deal.

Opa-locka Airport, November 1993

Perhaps it was because they'd both fled Fidel Castro's Cuba by swimming to freedom across Guantanamo Bay: José Basulto in 1961 in the wake of the Bay of Pigs debacle; Juan Pablo Roque more than 30 years later after he'd become so disillusioned with his life under communism he "pulled on some scuba gear and flippered his way to the U.S. naval base in Guantanamo," where he demanded asylum. Or perhaps, Basulto thought, he liked the young defector so much simply because his story seemed so compelling, and he told it so well.

Juan Pablo Roque had never quite belonged in Castro's Cuba, he explained. He didn't consider himself a communist or revolutionary and, as a young man, preferred reading "contraband" muscle magazines to political tracts. Despite his ambivalence, Roque was bright enough to have been plucked, while still a teenager, from the masses and shipped overseas to study in the Soviet Union. Seven years later, he returned to his homeland, a Cuban Air Force MiG pilot. Though Roque loved flying — something else that endeared him to Basulto — he was too much the individualist to fit comfortably within the boxes of Castro's military. Partly because he didn't drink rum or coffee and wasn't crazy about baseball — he was a bodybuilder and obsessive about his diet — his fellow pilots had dismissed him as "not Cuban enough."

Roque was more than Cuban enough to fly with Brothers to the Rescue, Basulto told him when they first met a few months before. Brothers' lawyer Sofia Powell-Cosio had introduced the two men. She and Roque were both members of Puente de Jóvenes Profesionales Cubanos, another fledgling anti-Castro organization in Miami that was trying to rally the next generation to *la causa*. Though Basulto himself had quickly taken a shine to the 33-year-old defector, not everyone in the organization felt the same way. Some of the other pilots dismissed him as a publicity-loving narcissist and grumbled among themselves about the newcomer's chumminess with Basulto, who'd not only tried to find him work but also hired him as his own personal trainer.

Basulto's interest in Roque was partly personal and partly practical. Brothers needed publicity in order to raise money for its missions. Roque was chiselled, dimpled, movie-star handsome — one reporter would write that he looked more like Richard Gere than Richard Gere — and he was eager to tell and re-tell his life story whenever a camera appeared. When he did tell his story, Basulto couldn't help but notice, he inevitably also told reporters all about the important work Basulto and Brothers to the Rescue were doing "saving from death those [Cubans] who plunge into the sea in their quest for the land of hope," he offered eloquently. "They are brothers — not brothers-in-arms, as Raúl Castro described his Russian masters — but Latin and Anglo brothers, symbols of a new way of thinking, of a new dawn."

Today, Roque was taking part in a special Brothers mission flown by members of Officers and Professionals for Democracy, a group of 16 former Cuban military and civilian pilots that included not only the Bay of Pigs old-timers like Basulto and co-founder Billy Schuss but also recent arrivals: a former parachute instructor at Cuba's Naval Academy, a former officer at its Civil Aeronautics Institute, a newly defected MiG pilot Roque had met during his training days in the Soviet Union, and, of course, René González, the genial civilian pilot who'd escaped Cuba three years before.

On this day, they'd flown over the Straits of Florida "sending a message of love and unity to the members of the Armed Forces of Cuba" — and looked for rafters. During the flight, Roque had spotted three of them in a leaky vessel near the Anguilla Cays, 40 miles off the Cuban coast. He'd notified the Coast Guard of their coordinates, then made a number of low-level passes, dropping fresh water and dried fruit to the "poor people" below and letting them know help was on the way.

As he flew over the water, Roque would explain later, he couldn't help thinking about a fellow Cuban pilot who'd crashed in Angola while making a similar low-level reconnaissance pass during the 1980s. "I got to thinking on the difference between two palpably different philosophies," he would write in *Desertor*, his 1995 autobiography, "the rescue mission in which I risked my life… [and] the political fanaticism for which my comrades risked their lives in the land of King Kong, where we had no reason to be, defending people with whom we had no link or relationship… I reached a logical and eloquent conclusion: I was now defending my roots, my customs; risking my life for what was mine. As (José Marti) said: 'Our wine is bitter, but it's ours.'" Back in Florida, the pilots celebrated their spotting success and their freedom with lunch. "What a great table had been set," Roque would write. "What a great group of men these were."

Basulto couldn't have agreed more. He just didn't know two of that great group, including Roque, were Cuban intelligence agents, whose job was to report back on everything the Brothers did or said.

Miami, November 13, 1993

The 55-word story was so seemingly routine it only appeared in the Miami *Herald's* "Names in the News" briefs section. "U.S. Rep. Ileana Ros-Lehtinen, R-Fla.," the article began, "was given a certificate of appreciation Friday

by Alpha 66 in appreciation of her efforts toward the liberation of Cuba."
Alpha 66's Comandante Rodolfo Frómeta had been fulsome in his praise of
the Cuban-America Republican from Florida's 18th Congressional District:
"She has always been willing to help us when we've needed her help on our
mission to liberate Cuba," he said.

It was what wasn't said that made the article so interesting. Less than
two months before — on September 25 — Frómeta and five other heavily
armed members of Alpha 66 had been stopped in the Florida Keys in a truck
that had been reported stolen. Police uncovered a terrorist's treasure trove:
"tripod-mounted rifles that fire 50-calibre bullets, Soviet-made AK-47 semi-
automatic assault rifles… a grenade launcher and missiles to launch… 5,000
rounds of ammunition," along with maps of Cuba "with markings indicating
plans for raiding the island." Alpha 66's "Military Chief" matter-of-factly
acknowledged his men had gone to the Keys to do some training "before
carrying out a mission against Cuba."

It certainly wasn't the first time Alpha 66 members had run afoul of the
law, not even the first time that year. In May, U.S. Customs Service agents
boarded a twin-engine, 28-foot boat moored near the KOA Campground in
Sunshine Key, Florida. They found nine, camouflage-clad Alpha 66 members
on board and seized a bag filled with two illegal pipe bombs, four hand grenades, a grenade launcher, several semi-automatic weapons and an illegally
modified, fully automatic weapon. What were they planning? A spokesperson for the group told reporters they had been about to set off on a mission
dubbed "Operation Independence." Were they planning to attack Cuba?
"People have to act as circumstances present themselves," the spokesperson
said not so mysteriously. Though the men were eventually charged in that
case, a judge acquitted them in late August (just a month before their next
arrest) because prosecutors couldn't — or at least didn't — prove any of them
knew anything about all those illegal weapons that just happened to have
been stashed on their vessel.

That next incident — the one that occurred just two months before the
Ros-Lehtinen certificate-of-appreciation event — didn't even lead to court. It
turned out the truck hadn't actually been stolen and the weapons themselves
were legal, so they were returned. No one apparently thought to consider
charging the men under the Neutrality Act, a venerable American law that
explicitly bans paramilitary actions launched against other countries from
American soil. And no one thought to mention to Ileana Ros-Lehtinen — or
maybe she just didn't care — that she was being honoured by a group that
was intimately linked to terrorist plots. And, perhaps most importantly, no
one told Rodolfo Frómeta it was time to stop launching attacks on a foreign
country.[16]

---

16. Frómeta remained unapologetic about his various schemes to attack Cuba and his

BUILDING THE NEST

Miami, February 1994

He took the unfamiliar coins from his pockets, inserted them into the slot in the motel's unfamiliar vending machine, considered the too many soft-drink choices staring back at him. Grape soda? Grape soda. Why not? He had never tried it. He pressed the selection button. Was his hand shaking?

It was his first time. The guys back in Havana joked that your first time was always the hardest, that it was like losing your virginity. He took a sip of the liquid, barely noted its sickly, sweet taste, looked around in the darkness of the motel parking lot. He wasn't a virgin anymore.

It had been a long, strange few days of changing clothes, cities, countries, hotels, flights, passports and personas. In the process, he had shed the person he'd been born — Gerardo Hernández Nordelo, thin, beginning-to-be-balding, mustachioed, a Cuban citizen, communist, son, brother, husband, veteran of the Angola war, sometime cartoonist, freshly minted diplomat on his way to serve his country in Argentina — and become the person on the birth certificate he now carried, the man he must be in order to do the job he'd been assigned to do in Miami.

His new name was Manuel Viramóntez. Like Gerardo Hernández, Manuel Viramóntez was 27 years old. Other than that — and the photos and physical characteristics noted on their identity documents — Gerardo Hernández and Manuel Viramóntez appeared to be two very different people. Manuel Viramóntez was Puerto Rican, the son of an accountant father and a secretary mother. His parents met in the mid-sixties while both were students at the University of Edinburgh in Texas. After graduation, they married and had two children in Texas — a daughter and a son, Manuel, born January 26, 1967 — before returning to Puerto Rico in 1970. The family lived in Hato Rey, Puerto Rico, a neighbourhood "with many stolen cars." If you asked him, Manuel could tell you the names of the various schools he attended, the teachers who taught him. After studying sales and marketing at college, he took a job in San Juan as a sales agent for a liquor company. He moved in with his mother after his father died of bone marrow cancer on October 23, 1991. He inherited his father's car, a two-door Oldsmobile Delta 88, because his mother — whose own parents had died in a car crash in 1956 caused by a drunk driver — was still too traumatized to drive a car herself. At the time, he had a girlfriend, a law student at the University of Puerto Rico, but that relationship hadn't lasted. So he'd moved to Mexico to start his life over. There, he met and married another woman but... well, that hadn't worked out either. They'd recently separated, and he had decided he needed another fresh start. Which was why he'd come to Miami. That, at least, was the legend.

---

desire to kill Fidel Castro, which he justified as "an attempt to do justice about a person who has killed thousands and thousands of persons." He blamed Castro, in fact, for the deaths of his son, father and brother.

Gerardo had memorized Manuel Viramóntez so well he had become — he believed/hoped — his alter ego. He had to be convincing if he was to do his job without being questioned, or discovered, or... Hernández had learned to speak Spanish with a Puerto Rican accent. He read Puerto Rican newspapers and followed the island's — Puerto Rico's, not Cuba's — popular culture. Understanding local pop culture, he knew, was just as critical to passing as Manuel Viramóntez as knowing the intimate details of the fictional Manuel's life story. "If someone asks me today as a Cuban how high the Pico Turquino [mountain] is, I swear on my mother that I do not remember," Gerardo — as Gerardo — would explain to his bosses back in Havana. "But if I am Cuban, I would have to know who the Doctor of Salsa is, even if I do not like music, because everyone talks about him. It is the same with Puerto Ricans."

But Gerardo Hernández was not just Manuel Viramóntez. There were other identities he'd had to learn too, names and life stories he had to be ready to assume at a moment's notice. If he thought his Viramóntez identity was about to be compromised or he might be arrested, for example, he was supposed to morph into Daniel Cabrera Olivera. Cabrera was his escape identity, for which he carried, hidden from view, yet another passport, Social Security card and driver's licence. If he was forced to become Cabrera, things were clearly becoming dangerous, and he had instructions to leave the United States as quickly as possible: "Avoid airports in New York, Washington, Miami and Los Angeles," he had been told. "These are among airports with the tightest security in the U.S. They are not to be used upon initiating escape plan travel." Instead, if possible, he should fly to San Antonio, Texas, cross the border at El Paso, then catch a bus or plane to Mexico City. If that wasn't possible, he should travel from Florida to some other state and book a flight to Nicaragua, or head farther north, crossing the U.S.-Canadian border at Niagara Falls.

Hernández had yet another identity for an even worse-case, please-don't-let-this-happen scenario. If he was arrested and the authorities discovered who he wasn't, he was to claim to be someone named Roberto García Fernandez, an unemployed dropout who'd arrived illegally in Florida from Cuba during the 1980 Mariel boat lift. And, oh yes, there was a final instruction: "Under no circumstances will Giraldo ever admit to being part of, or linked to Cuban intelligence or any other Cuban government organization."

Giraldo? Gerardo Hernández — a.k.a. Manuel Viramóntez, a.k.a. Daniel Cabrera, a.k.a. Roberto García — was also "Giraldo," or "Giro," or "Manny." They were the code names he was supposed to use when communicating, always in the third person, with his bosses back at the CP — the Centro Principal — the headquarters of the Cuban Directorate of Intelligence in Havana. In the parlance of the trade, Hernández was an "illegal officer" for Cuban intelligence.

To understand what that means, it helps to know there were legal officers too. Legal intelligence officers operated under their real names, carried diplomatic passports and had diplomatic immunity. They were based in so-called "legal centres" within diplomatic posts like the Cuban Interest Section in Washington and the United Nations Mission in New York. Their job — like their counterparts in virtually every other diplomatic mission in virtually every other country in the world — was intelligence gathering, processing and reporting. But the primary benefit of being classified as a legal officer — diplomatic immunity — came with a price. Cuban diplomats were not permitted to travel beyond a 25-mile radius of the American city in which they were based without special permission from the United States State Department. And they were often under surveillance. Which made it more than a little difficult for legal officers to meet with field agents — men like René González, Tony Guerrero and Juan Pablo Roque — who were based, for obvious reasons, in Florida.

That's where illegal officers like Hernández fit in. Like their legal counterparts, they were highly trained, including in the spy arts — cryptography, counter-surveillance, high frequency radio transmitting, microdot and water-soluble paper messaging, etc. — and worked full time for Cuban intelligence. But, unlike their legal counterparts, they slipped surreptitiously into and out of the countries where they worked, operated off the official radar, used fake identities and didn't have the comforting safety net of diplomatic immunity if they got caught. Each illegal officer supervised a small group of field agents. These agents — the third and perhaps most critical layer in Cuba's intelligence-gathering network — were not merely Cuba's eyes and ears in America, they were also the heart and soul of what was regarded, even by its enemies, as the best organized and most effective intelligence network in the world.[17]

Though agents were carefully recruited and vetted, rigorously trained and strategically deployed, they were, for the most part, poorly paid.[18] They did it because they believed in the revolution, and that was what made them so successful. They lived in America, usually under their own identities,[19] held

---

17. Through its Directorate of Intelligence (DI), Cuba's Ministry of the Interior (MININT) is responsible for most of Cuba's foreign intelligence gathering, primarily in the United States. The DI itself includes a labyrinth of interconnected departments, each one designated by the letter M followed by numbers. M-1, not surprisingly, deals with intelligence related to American "targets." M-5 is the department responsible for the work of illegal officers. And M-9 comes up with what are known as "active measures" to influence or disrupt plans from anti-Cuba forces. M-19 deals with counter-revolutionary groups. And M-10 is the office of the chief of intelligence, the person responsible for making the entire octopus-like apparatus work as one being.

18. Most of the Avispa agents received $400 per month for "operational expenditures and economic aid." Agents like Percy Alvarado, the money mule, were also permitted to keep what they earned illicitly from their agent roles.

19. Many, like González and Guerrero, had been born in the U.S. but raised in Cuba. Their American citizenship made it easier for them to enter, live and work in the U.S.

down regular jobs, sometimes two, juggled rent and car payments, worried about their love lives, rented movies at Blockbuster and, oh yes, in between, they infiltrated militant anti-Castro exile groups to find out what new and nefarious schemes its members might be hatching, kept watchful eyes on nearby military bases looking for unusual activities that might indicate the United States was planning to attack Cuba and took on whatever other tasks their superiors back in Havana decided needed doing for the good of the revolution.

Havana communicated with these boots-on-the-ground agents mostly indirectly through illegal officers like Hernández. Havana would send the illegal officer coded messages and instructions, which he would decode and pass on the appropriate details to his field agents during clandestine meetings. The illegal officer would also collect the agents' activity reports and send them — often with his own editorial comments — back to Havana. Though illegal officers didn't infiltrate exile groups directly, they were responsible for gathering and interpreting other information, much of it from newspapers and public sources, that would all become part of the intelligence stew[20] their supervisors in Havana would use to stay one step ahead of the enemy.

Hernández had been dispatched to Miami to supervise a small group of agents, including González, Roque, Guerrero, a husband-and-wife team[21] — Nilo and Linda Hernández, collectively known as "The Juniors," who'd moved to Miami from New Jersey in 1992 and had infiltrated Alpha 66 and the Latin American Chamber of Commerce — and Alejandro Alonso, a boat pilot who was known by the code name Franklyn.

Though Roque and González obviously knew each other through their work with Brothers to the Rescue, most field agents operated independently and unknown to one another. It wasn't unusual, in fact, for more than one agent to infiltrate the same organization and report back on the activities of another agent they didn't realize was doing the same about them. Very few people — including the illegal officers — ever got to see, or comprehend the full intelligence picture. Hernández, for example, didn't know what Percy Alvarado was doing inside the Cuban American National Foundation, though he might eventually receive assignments based on the fruits of Alvarado's reports to their superiors. Alvarado, for his part, had no idea Hernández even existed. It was all about compartmentalization. The fewer people who understood everything the less likelihood that one agent or officer could

---

without arousing suspicion.

20. Within the Directorate of Intelligence, there is a separate department — M-3 — which does nothing but analyze intelligence and information gathered from all sources.

21. Another husband-and-wife team — Joseph Santos and his wife, Amarylis Silverio — were added to the network in 1996 to provide information on Southcom, the U.S. Southern Command military headquarters, which was relocating from Panama to Miami.

compromise an entire operation.

Hernández's assignment in Miami — his first as an illegal officer — was to oversee what was to become a broader network of agents whose primary focus would be to infiltrate newly energized anti-Castro exile groups, of which there were many. His network's official code name was La Red Avispa — the Wasp Network — but the name itself wasn't significant or even especially noteworthy except, of course, when it came to dealing with budgets and the bureaucracy back in Havana.

Managing all of that would be part of Gerardo Hernández's job too. He'd been well schooled for it. Like many of his fellow intelligence officers, Hernández had been recruited specifically for secret work while still a student at the Instituto Superior de Relaciones Internacionales, the elite Havana post-graduate institute that also trained many of the island's best and brightest for the diplomatic corps. Being selected from among that elite to become part of an even more elite cadre of intelligence agents was an honour, of course, but it was also a burden, in part because you weren't allowed to tell anyone about it. Not even — or perhaps especially — your own family.

For Gerardo, that was the hardest part. He willed himself now not to go there. He took another swallow of the grape soda. Adriana... He couldn't help himself. He remembered the day they met. October 20, 1986. He was 21; she was 16. He still lived with his parents in Arroyo Naranjo, a suburban neighbourhood 11 miles from the old city. To get to university, he had to get up at four in the morning and take three different buses. Luckily, his father had a car and would usually drop him off within walking distance of the school on his own way to work. In exchange, Gerardo washed his father's car. But one day when his father asked him to wash it, Gerardo begged off, claiming he was too busy.

"You're never too busy when you need a ride," his father retorted.

Gerardo took offence — "it kind of hurt my teenager feelings, even though I was already in my twenties," he would joke later — so the next morning he got up before dawn to make the long journey to school on his own. He'd made it as far as the third and final bus stop on his journey when he noticed her. She was standing in line with some friends. For reasons he would never be able to explain, it was "love at first sight." For him at least.

"He put his eye on me," Adriana Pérez O'Connor would recall with a laugh many years later. "But I didn't notice him. Not then."

By the next day, she didn't have a choice. Gerardo, who had once again skipped the convenience of a drive to school with his father in order to make the arduous bus journey in order to see her again, handed her a poem he'd written during his international law class the day before. Entitled "Poem to the Girl at the Bus Stop" — he didn't know her name! — it began: I can hardly make out the figure before me/bent over, making didactic gestures/

legal concepts and international conflicts/the details almost make it to my ears/but my mind is filled with that girl/at the bus stop.

Adriana wasn't immediately won over. "I wasn't interested in a relationship at that time." To discourage him, she even got up before her own usual time the next morning and took an earlier bus. The day after that, Gerardo showed up even earlier and was already waiting — with another poem and roses, stolen from a neighbour's garden. Adriana's friends were quick to realize "something" was beginning. They held seats for Gerardo and Adriana on the bus and then "talked among themselves so I had to talk to him." Not that that turned out to be so difficult. He was a gentleman with a sense of humour, and he wasn't hard on the eyes either.

A month later, they went on an outing to Morro Castle, the historic Havana landmark that doubled as a convenient spot for young lovers. "Look over there," Gerardo said as they sat together on a hillside overlooking the harbour. "There's a very beautiful boat on your left." As she turned to look, he said. "There's another one, over there, to your right."

"As I turned this way and that to look for the boat," Adriana would recall, "he kissed me... and from that moment — November 7, 1986 — we were together."

Not for long. They married July 15, 1988, but the day before they could celebrate their first anniversary, Gerardo left for a year's military service in Angola. And now, less than four years after he returned, he'd left again, this time for his new post in the Cuban embassy in Argentina. That, at least, is what he'd told Adriana. It was hard. They'd confided their innermost thoughts, hopes and dreams to one another, but now he'd had to lie. For his sake. For hers.

The fact he'd had to leave Cuba without his wife was easily understood. Cuba was not a rich country, even at the best of times, and this was not the best of times. The country was in the deepest depths of what Fidel Castro had delicately described as the "Special Period in Time of Peace." There were shortages of everything, including fuel and food. The government simply couldn't afford to pay for Adriana to accompany her husband to his new job. In fact, he probably wouldn't even be able to return home for vacation each year. He couldn't be sure when he'd see her next.

To complicate Gerardo's own emotional roller coaster ride, he knew that Adriana — who was living in Arroyo Naranjo with Gerardo's widowed mother — was in the last intense, exhausting and stressful months of her own studies at the university in chemistry and engineering. In a few months, she would have to submit her thesis, and he could not be there to support her.

Instead... Gerardo Hernández looked down, realized suddenly that he'd drunk the entire can of grape soda without even being aware of it. A wave of nausea swept over him. He threw up, purging himself finally of all the traces of these last few emotionally wrenching, nerve-wracking, tension-filled days, of the grape soda he would never drink again. He was Manuel Viramóntez now. And he was ready.

Rescuing the Brothers
March 8, 1994 – December 1995

Miami, March 8, 1994

Pepe Hernández was apologetic. He was pleased to have learned from his friend Zuñiga and from Alfredo Domingo Otero, his chief of operations, that Percy Alvarado was now working with their organization. "But you'll understand that we are obliged to distrust everyone. Experience has shown that Castro's agents are everywhere." As Hernández spoke, Alvarado eyed the man whose own eyes continued to scrutinize him, to take his measure, to look for... something. "That's why, without wanting to make you angry," Hernández continued smoothly, "we want to propose to you that — in order for us to continue with our work together — you first pass a lie detector." Percy Alvarado hadn't been expecting that. He tried to keep his face a mask, not let his panic show. He could not allow himself to think about what might happen if he said no to the polygraph or what could happen if he said yes. He had come too far too fast for everything to fall apart.

It had been just four months since his former neighbour, Abel Viera, introduced him to Zuñiga. Zuñiga had since provided Alvarado with an identity — Agent 44 — a compass to find locations for secret meetings on the high seas, two lanterns with infrared light accessories for signalling between vessels, two portable Realistic brand radios through which he would get instructions from Miami and $200 for expenses.

Alvarado had — at Zuñiga's instruction — assembled a clandestine cell back in Cuba. He'd lined up Bichicho, a friend who had a fishing boat they could use to rendezvous at sea; Rodolfo, a disgruntled retired colonel and explosives expert from the Armed Forces, who would serve as their sapper; and a young man Alvarado referred to only as the Kamikaze because he was "willing to risk everything" in order to make good his own escape to the United States. Bichicho, Rodolfo and the Kamikaze were, in truth, all Cuban State Security agents. Alvarado's Havana bosses had assigned them to help him with his real mission: to discover and disrupt the Foundation's plans.

Alvarado wasn't State Security's only source inside the Foundation. Somehow — no one told Alvarado how, of course — State Security had uncovered the identities of two "real" counter-revolutionary agents the Foundation had recruited. They'd already "neutralized" one of them — Agent 22 — whose assignment had been to set off bombs in Matanzas, an industrial city 60 miles from Havana. The second agent, a Havana man named Orfíris Pérez Cabrera — known as Agent 18 and also recruited by Zuñiga — had been assigned to conduct reconnaissance for possible attacks, including sabotaging tourism vehicles, burning sugar cane fields, poisoning livestock, planting bombs at the famous Tropicana night club.

State Security instructed Alvarado to befriend Agent 18, loosen his tongue, get him to confide the details of his role and then leverage that confession to undermine him back in Miami with the Foundation. Though he'd been skeptical the plan would work, Alvarado had done as he was told. On his next visit to Miami in early December — during which Zuñiga introduced him to Otero, who would "attend to you concerning everything related to the plans we talked about" — Alvarado played his Agent 18 card.

"When I was in Havana," Alvarado began calmly, looking at Zuñiga, "I had the chance to talk with an old man who said he knew you. He told me that you, Luis, had given him the number 18 as a code name." He stopped, let this revelation sink in.

Zuñiga, Alvarado noted with satisfaction, had turned pale. Otero appeared shocked. Alvarado feigning anger, continued. "I'm worried you are connected with people who easily spill the beans to anyone," he said. "What happens if he learns about me? I don't want something to happen to me just because of negligence on the part of some stupid idiot like that old man in Havana." He paused, began again. "Listen to me carefully, you two. You put me at risk and I swear I'll tell you, 'go to hell' and never speak to you again." His voice rose: "If that is the way it's to be, you tell me now and it's all over."

Alvarado enjoyed their obvious discomfort, their eagerness to make amends. "That guy saying he knows me is a liar, Percy," Zuñiga responded quickly. "And you can be sure that, except for us, no one else knows of your involvement. You can stay calm. The most important thing for us is your security."

"I hope so," Alvarado answered evenly. "My security is certainly the most important thing for me too. I would not want you to forget that and put your foot in it."

Agent 18 had been neutralized. Percy Alvarado's stock had gone up.

Alvarado had also returned from the December meeting in Miami with new information for Cuban State Security about yet another scheme he said Otero *et al.* had concocted. Within weeks, the Foundation was to deliver four bombs and a dozen phosphorus capsules to Alvarado's cell. The handover was to occur during a high seas rendezvous 10 to 12 miles off the Cuban coast between Santa Fe and Jaimanitas. "Don't worry about getting caught coming back to port," Otero had said. "We'll bring you a lot of fresh fish too to justify your 'fishing' trip."

Alvarado was to set off the bombs at four Havana hotels on Christmas Eve and Christmas Day, and to place the phosphorus devices in cinemas and theatres around the city in order to start fires and create panic. "The most important thing," Otero explained, "is to fuck Castro's year-end."

Back in Havana — while his bosses tried to come up with a scheme that could derail the Foundation's plans without exposing Alvarado — Alvarado and his "cell members" placed stickers promoting the Cuban National Front on walls at various tourist sites in Havana, photographed them for Miami and left, after which State Security officials moved in and removed them. Alvarado also prepared reports on a number of economic targets the Foundation had identified, including Cuba's vital sugar industry. Alvarado had, in fact, once worked for the National Centre for Sugar Cane Workers, so the Foundation knew he could access information about the harvest. The trick was "to combine untrue data with real information," so the Foundation would be convinced by his carefully constructed disinformation.

Meanwhile, Alvarado's bosses in Havana mounted an offensive of their own, increasing the actual numbers and frequency of high-speed boat patrols on its northwestern coast and used its other agents in Cuba and Florida to make sure the Foundation knew about the increased security and the impossibility of sneaking weapons into Cuba by sea.

Whatever the reasons — it turned out, as Alvarado learned when he returned to Miami in January, the Foundation had had problems acquiring bomb components — the Christmas bombing plan had fizzled. But in February, Otero had given Alvarado more assignments, including preparing reports on the movement of oil tankers in Havana harbour and the potential for industrial sabotage in Matanzas.

When Alvarado returned to Miami this week and turned in his report, Otero caught him off guard by announcing grandly: "I have a surprise for you Percy. Tomorrow, you'll meet an important member of the Foundation." The meeting had been held at Otero's house, a sprawling white bungalow with a swimming pool and elegant, art-filled interior that reminded Alvarado of a showroom. He and Otero sat at the poolside bar drinking Chivas Regal while they waited for their mystery guest to appear. They'd just begun their second Scotch when the doorbell rang. Otero left to answer it and returned a few moments later with a dark-skinned man dressed in a white shirt and blue trousers. Alvarado took note of the penetrating eyes and aquiline nose.

"Percy," Otero declared, with what Alvarado would later describe as "a pompous air and without concealing a genuflection... 'I introduce you to my boss.'" Which was how Percy Alvarado came face to face with Francisco José "Pepe" Hernández, the president of the Cuban American National

Foundation, yet another Bay of Pigs veteran — though one who'd actually landed in Cuba and been captured, spending two years in prison — and a former CIA operative. Hernández had been one of the founding members of the Cuban American National Foundation in 1981 and now, along with Mas Canosa, he was the head of CANF's secret paramilitary.

Alvarado's excitement at having so quickly negotiated his way up the Foundation's power ladder, however, instantly turned to panic when Hernández asked him to take the polygraph test. But he couldn't show it. Hernández was watching him "the same way an eagle does with its prey."

Alvarado took a slow sip of his drink, fought to calm his nerves. "Look, Pepe," he said finally, "I understand you have to take all necessary precautions. I'd be worried if you didn't. If you want me to, let's go right now and take the test — "

"It's not so complicated," Otero jumped in, trying to defuse the moment while Hernández kept his eyes fixed on Alvarado.

"Excuse me, Otero," Alvarado cut him off. "Since your boss has been sincere with me, I will be with you. I know the risk. I don't like what is going on in Cuba. But I'm tired of coming back and forth to Miami just to earn a few cents. If you pay well, I guarantee my work. So, if I pass that lie detector... let's get on with it."

Pepe Hernández laughed. "Don't worry, Percy," he said, "the polygraph test isn't today. Your reaction... that's enough for now."

Percy Alvarado had passed the test. By pretending to want to take it! He could breathe again. For the moment.

The conversation moved on. Their ultimate goal, Hernández told him, was to "eliminate Fidel Castro. If we can put them — both Fidel and his brother — out of the game, Cuba's problems will be solved."

"What can I do to help achieve that?" Alvarado asked.

"A lot, Percy, you can do a lot." Hernández wanted Alvarado to find out everything he could about Fidel's health and whether there were any policy disputes between Fidel and his henchman that the Foundation might be able to exploit. Most importantly, he said, he wanted Alvarado to check out the routes Castro travels "especially along 5th Avenue," so the Foundation could plan an attack on him there. "If it turns out successfully," he added, "you will live like a millionaire for the rest of your life."

"It will not be easy, Pepe," Alvarado answered.

"We know that. It is difficult, but it can be done. What we need to know is whether you are capable of fulfilling our expectations — up to and including eliminating Castro. What do you say?"

"Count me in," he said.

WHAT LIES ACROSS THE WATER

Miami, May 24, 1994

> Remember I want to be with you at the beach in September and I am not losing hope. I am sending you a very big kiss and a lot of love. From your dear husband waiting impatiently with open arms to close around you in the most tender and loving hug.

René González looked again at the words he'd just written. It had been three years, five months and 16 days since his "defection" — three years, five months and 16 days since he had last seen Olga and their daughter Irma. Despite the time that had passed, René could still feel the righteous sting from that first letter Olga had written him. It had arrived about a month after he'd landed in the United States. He'd gone to Miami for a weekend visit. His grandmother telephoned from Sarasota. "You have a letter," she said. "From Olga." René had rushed back, excited, eager, tore open the letter and… found himself "torn apart."

"I wish you luck in your new future," Olga had written, "but it will not be with me."

For the next week, he had wandered aimlessly, "like a zombie," trying to come to terms with what those words meant. On the one hand — the hand that had willingly come to the United States to perform a patriotic mission for his homeland — René was proud of her "most dignified, moving and strong response to my defection." He had expected nothing less. But on the other hand — that hand that desperately missed his wife, the hand that wanted to watch his little girl grow up in front of him — he was devastated.

But he refused to give up. It wasn't in his nature. Even as he had gone about the tasks at hand — finding a job, a car, a place to live, befriending fellow exiles, joining anti-Castro groups, working as a roofer for a year in post-Hurricane Andrew Florida to earn money for his flight instructor licence, volunteering as a pilot with José Basulto's Brothers to the Rescue group, trying to set up his own flight training school — he continued to write, to call Olga through friends, to plead for forgiveness, for the chance to reunite their family once again.

His cause had been aided — inadvertently and unfortunately — by events unfolding at home. After the collapse of the Soviet Union, Cuba's economy collapsed. There were shortages of everything from electricity to food. People — literally — starved. Olga herself reported their house had been robbed, and everything of value stolen. To make matters worse, the neighbours gossiped, sometimes loudly and pointedly, about René's "treason." Irma was old enough to ask questions, so Olga decided to move them to a smaller apartment in another Havana neighbourhood, closer to her parents. But then that building's stairs collapsed, and they'd been forced to move into a temporary shelter. Eventually, events and René's persistence — and, of course, the reality that she still loved and missed the man she had married — wore her down. Olga finally relented. René applied to U.S. Immigration for a visa to bring her and Irma to Florida.

"Speaking of that," he wrote cheerfully, "I don't know if I already told you that I received the notice of receipt from Immigration... They tell me that the process should take between 90 and 120 days. I imagine that, within that time, they will have already made an appointment with you at the [U.S.] Interest Section in Havana to see if you are the same in the photograph I turned in... It was difficult for me to let go of that photograph, but it was the only one that more or less fit the requirements they were asking for. Besides, I imagine that it is more pleasant to grant a visa to a woman as pretty as you are than to any other woman. Anyway, I decided to sacrifice such a pretty photograph as long as I could have with me the original who is prettier still. Finally when you are here, I will be able to take hundreds of photos of you.

"As for me," he continued in the same upbeat, chatty tone, "I am fine. As you must already know, I returned from Mexico... I am processing all the information I got there to start a [flying school] business I think will be successful... If it goes the way I hope, I think I can get a slice of what I have put up my sleeve to make money... With about 10 students, I could be assured of a good salary that would prepare me for when you all arrive."

He skipped from subject to subject. His grandmother had had to postpone her planned trip back to Cuba because of her husband's illness, he wrote. "Speaking of trips to Cuba, I have been thinking about what could be a new alternative for you. Those who leave legally may travel [back to Cuba] a year after their departure. That means once you are here a year, you are free to travel there to visit whenever you want to. Unfortunately," he added, "I can't go with you because they would tear me to pieces if I show up there.

"Well, Tuti, I take leave in order to write a letter to your mother-in-law and another one to your daughter... Don't fail to tell me when they call you at the Interest Section so I know the process is going smoothly."

Of course René González still couldn't tell his wife the truth about what he was really doing in the United States. If only.

Miami, June 2, 1994

"The Sergeant" unfurled the heavy poncho, revealing a collection of U.S. military containers on the warehouse floor. He pried opened one of the boxes, carefully removed a Stinger missile from its case, showed it to his two clearly impressed visitors. One of them was Rodolfo Frómeta, the former head of Alpha 66. Two months before, he and the man to his right, Fausto Marimon, another Cuban exile, had co-founded a new group called Commandos F-4.[1]

---

1. The name meant "fire from all four sides."

Frómeta had decided to start the new group, he explained at the time, because Alpha 66 wasn't "aggressive enough" in its plans to attack Cuba.[2] By the time Frómeta had been introduced to the Sergeant in May, he had a business card: "Commandante en Jefe," it read, and then below: "Comando F-4 Por La Libertad de Cuba." New splinter organization, same old objective.

A friend of a friend had put Frómeta and Marimon together with the Sergeant. The Sergeant was an Army supply sergeant from a military base in Georgia, the friend explained, but he also operated a sideline business peddling American military hardware to people who wanted it but weren't supposed to have it. Frómeta, who certainly wasn't supposed to have it, was in the market for some serious weaponry.

"I've seen his stuff," the friend told Frómeta. "This guy is really legit." Meaning, of course, illegitimate.

They met first in early May aboard a vessel in the Miami River. In the hold, the Sergeant showed Frómeta and Marimon a crate filled with M-16s. "I stole 'em," the Sergeant boasted. "Reported them broken. But they're all brand new, in perfect working order. These ones aren't for you. Some Colombians have already spoken for these. But I can get you the same… better if you have the cash." Short term, Frómeta told him, he was looking for ammunition for the M-16s he already owned. But, yes, he was interested in other stuff too. They'd met again a few days later in front of Alpha 66's office in Little Havana. Frómeta was inside with a few other men when he spotted the Sergeant waiting on the sidewalk and hurried to meet him. By now, Frómeta's shopping list had become longer and more detailed. He was interested in buying some C-4 explosives, he said, a grenade launcher, a few anti-tank rockets and a Redeye.

The Sergeant knew as soon as Frómeta mentioned Redeye that the man's enthusiasm outweighed his knowledge. A Redeye was what the manufacturer called a Stinger when it first started making the missiles several generations ago. "I can do you even better," he said.

They'd haggled over price, and it was equally clear Frómeta didn't have a lot of cash. They could start with just a few items and go from there, the Sergeant finally agreed. How about $15,000? That sounded good to Frómeta. "Not that it matters," the Sergeant said, "but where are you going to use this

---

2. Not that it hadn't been trying. In February 1994, Frómeta and seven fellow members of Alpha 66 had been arrested *again* — his third time in less than a year — aboard yet another boat loaded with still more weapons. Frómeta claimed he and his shipmates had travelled to Cuba "to set up a contact" but failed and returned to Miami. But Andres Nazario Sargen, Alpha 66's secretary, said Frómeta and his crew had actually gone to a secret base called Caribbean Point 8 to pick up the weapons and three other men for a planned raid on Cuba. Whatever version you chose to believe, the result, in a by-now-familiar story, was that the vessel developed engine trouble off Key Biscayne. The Coast Guard boarded it, seizing shotguns, assault rifles and pistols. Equally familiarly, the Coast Guard eventually returned the weapons and laid no charges.

stuff?" Cuba, Frómeta said. They had a deal. Which is how Frómeta and Marimon had ended up in this South Dade warehouse with the Sergeant and his military-issue display cases of stolen weapons.

"How's that work?" Marimon asked of the Stinger. The Sergeant gently placed the heavy weapon on Marimon's shoulder, gave him the *Reader's Digest* version. "It's a heat-seeking missile," he said, "so it looks for the hottest point — an aircraft engine or, in a helicopter, just below the rotor. You just put it on your shoulder, aim for the sky, wait for the tone that says it's locked on, and fire. You can take out an airplane at 10,000 feet with this baby. But you have to be careful. This baby doesn't have any eyes so once you shoot it goes. You lock on the wrong target, you could miss the helicopter, hit a passenger plane instead. Even if you hit the helicopter, it can come straight down, land on a building, kill a bunch of people."

Marimon laughed. "A two-for-one shot," he said. He took the Stinger off his shoulder, handed it to Frómeta, who also hefted it, took aim, pronounced himself satisfied.

The Sergeant put the Stinger back, opened another box, this one containing a LAW rocket, another shoulder-mounted weapon designed to be fired at tanks but which could be also used to obliterate a car or other vehicle. While the two examined this toy, the Sergeant sliced through the outer layer of what looked like a large white candy bar, peeled back a layer. "C-4," he said, "a pound of the malleable plastic explosive to start with."

All that was left was the money. "Uh…" Frómeta was apologetic. They hadn't been able to round up all the money, he said. *Yet.* But they did have $5,000. They could pay the rest with the next order. And there would be a next order, Frómeta insisted. They were going to become very good customers. The Sergeant calculated, relented, reluctantly. He had come too far to walk away now.

Marimon hurried outside to get their van, backed it into the warehouse. He and Frómeta began to load up the van while the Sergeant closed the garage doors so no one would see their clandestine transaction.

Actually, that wasn't the real reason. FBI and U.S. Customs agents had been watching every step of this exchange from a nearby command centre. The warehouse — like the boat where they'd first met — had been completely wired for audio and video. And the Sergeant — who was not a sergeant at all but an FBI special agent named Raymond Lopez — had closed the warehouse door because he was under orders not to allow those real weapons to leave the warehouse under any circumstances.

The Sergeant's cell phone rang. He answered, looked over at Frómeta and Marimon as they continued to load the van. "I got to take this," he shrugged and turned to leave. As he did, the warehouse filled up with men wearing bulletproof vests and carrying weapons. "FBI! FBI! On your knees!" they shouted.

For the fourth time in the past year, Rodolfo Frómeta had been caught red-handed with weapons intended to be used to launch attacks on Cuba. Would he walk again?

Miami, November 5, 1994

Pepe Hernández carefully checked the GPS coordinates Percy Alvarado had brought with him from Havana against the longitude and latitude marks on the map spread out tonight on Alfredo Domingo Otero's dining room table. As Hernández's fingers traced the lines, Alvarado noted the name of the map issuer — the U.S. Army. It figured. Hernández's fingers found what they were looking for: the location of the Antonio Guiteras Thermoelectric Plant in Matanzas. Pinpointing the plant's location had been one of Percy Alvarado's most recent reconnaissance assignments. With the help of his bosses at State Security, he had gotten the numbers just wrong enough to seem right.

"Good work, Percy," Hernández said and pointed again to the spot on the map. "When the time comes, other people — our friends — will make good use of this information." He folded the map. "Now, my friend, it's time to forget all this GPS and intelligence-gathering work. It's time to focus on the Tropicana."

Two months before, during a regular remittance-gathering trip to Miami, Alvarado had met with Otero. Pepe Hernández hadn't been able to join them, Otero explained, because he was busy making sure the Clinton administration didn't make a deal with the Cuban government to solve the rafters' crisis the wrong way. But Hernández had left specific instructions for Alvarado to proceed with plans to scope out the Tropicana. Back in Havana, Alvarado had attended a show, taken some photos, made some sketches, brought them back for Otero.

"Those mulatto girls," Otero had offered admiringly as he examined the photos the night before, "they're very beautiful."

"Don't you worry about the possibility they could die if we set off a bomb there," Alvarado asked?

"Don't you worry about that," Otero dismissed his concerns. "We only want to make a big noise. Scare people." He'd laughed. "Do you think I'd let these beautiful women die?"

Tonight, Hernández riffled more distractedly through the photos. He was only interested in — and concerned about — the sketches Alvarado had brought. They showed two locations where Alvarado thought he could plant a bomb: both were outside the club.

"We want you to place the bomb *inside*, not outside," Hernández reminded him.

"It's too dangerous, Pepe," Alvarado replied. "Someone could be hurt."

"No one is going to get hurt," Hernández insisted. "You have to trust me. Trust Otero. All it will do is make a noise."

"But I don't know how to make a bomb."

"Don't worry," Hernández said. "You just go back to Havana and wait for a telephone call. When you get the call, you'll go to Guatemala, check in at the Camino Real Hotel. Our guy will find you there. He's an explosives expert. He'll show you how to make the bombs, how to get them into Cuba, how to put them together, everything you'll need to know. He'll give you two bombs. You'll plant one at the Tropicana, the other one wherever you like. It doesn't matter so long as there's a big bang and people hear about it."

Alvarado was about to protest again when Otero cut him off. "Here's the first thousand," he said, handing him a wad of cash. "For your expenses. If you need any more, you just tell our guy in Guatemala. He'll get it for you." Otero had already explained they would pay Alvarado $10,000 for every bomb that exploded.

"When will I get paid?" Alvarado asked.

"Three days after the bombs explode," Hernández replied, "you come back here to Miami and you'll get your money. If the results are good," he added, smiling, "who knows? There might even be more money for you."

Alvarado smiled. "OK then." How would his bosses back in Havana figure a way around this latest scheme — without blowing up the Tropicana, or blowing his cover?

Guantanamo Bay, November 10, 1994

It was "there," José Basulto would explain. At 12:40 p.m., the Brothers to the Rescue founder had taken off from the airfield at the U.S. Naval base at Guantánamo Bay, Cuba. He was ferrying Miami's former mayor, Xavier Suarez, back to Florida after an unhappy, unsuccessful attempt to visit some of the 24,000 Cuban rafters being held at a makeshift encampment on the American military base at the far eastern end of the island.

At 1:13 p.m., as his Cessna aircraft rounded Punta de Maisí to begin the four-hour journey home — Cuba, of course, had refused him permission to take the shorter route across its territory — Basulto suddenly had an idea. Instead of flying north, he banked the plane to the left and headed — illegally — into Cuban airspace. Why not? It was there. It all happened quickly — just like the crisis with the rafters.

Thanks to Cuba's increasingly desperate economic plight, more and more Cubans had been hopping into leaky boats and jerry-built rafts for the perilous 90-mile journey to Florida. Four months ago, in July, one group even stole a tugboat. It collided with — some claimed was rammed by — another pursuing Cuban tug. Thirty-two people drowned. Even that didn't deter those desperate to get out. Two weeks later, someone else tried to hijack a Havana Bay ferry. There were clashes between police and those anxious to leave, no matter how.

Finally, on August 11, 1994, Fidel Castro stunned his countrymen — and the U.S. government — by announcing that any Cuban who wanted to leave was free to go. It wasn't the first time Castro had turned on the exit taps in order to turn off unrest at home. In 1980, during earlier economic troubles, he had allowed 125,000 Cubans — a few criminals, mental patients and other "undesirables," as well as legitimate refugees — to leave through the port of Mariel. By the time he turned off the tap six and a half months later, the American Coast Guard had been forced to mount its largest ever peacetime operation and the military had been called out to provide security at refugee compounds around Miami and beyond.

Part of the problem, from the Cuban point of view, was America's much-more-than-welcoming open-door policy for Cuban migrants, a policy specifically crafted to undermine and destabilize the Castro government. Under the 1966 Cuban Adjustment Act, Cubans — unlike immigrants from any other country in the world — didn't have to be sponsored by family members, or demonstrate employment prospects, or enter the U.S. through a recognized port of entry, or deal with any of the usual immigration quotas and hurdles. In fact — thanks to the influence of the Cuban-American lobby — any Cuban who managed to be in the United States for a year or longer, no matter how they got there, was entitled to apply for permanent residency.

Now, in the aftermath of Castro's pronouncement, tens of thousands more Cubans had jumped into boats that weren't fit to float. When that happened, Basulto's Brothers to the Rescue stepped up its missions, "patrolling the Straits in anything that could fly." But they, like the U.S. Coast Guard, which was intercepting 300 rafts a day, were simply overwhelmed.

Then, on September 9, 1994, the Clinton administration announced it had struck a deal with the Cubans. The United States would no longer automatically allow Cubans picked up in the Straits to come to America, a reversal of its decades-old policy. Instead, rafters intercepted at sea would be dispatched to "safe haven" camps in Panama or Guantanamo. No one seemed to know what would happen to them from there. In future, to accommodate ordinary Cubans who did want to immigrate, the U.S. agreed to legally admit no fewer than 20,000 each year, but through normal channels. In exchange, Cuba promised to use "persuasive methods" to discourage its citizens from trying to make their way by sea.

No wonder José Basulto was pissed. At Castro, of course, for creating this mess in the first place. But also at Clinton for having, with the stroke of a pen, transformed Cuban political refugees into just another group of "migrants" — as if they were somehow no different than the Haitians or economic immigrants attempting to get into the U.S. from the Dominican Republic. The Cubans were different, Basulto would insist. It was the Cubans "who were abandoned at the Bay of Pigs; it was the Cubans whom President Kennedy promised that their national flag would be returned to... in a free Cuba. It was the Cubans who fled political, not economic persecution... For better or worse, Cuba was different."

To show his displeasure at the deal, Basulto helped organize demonstrations that choked traffic in Miami for a week.

The new U.S.-Cuba agreement had an unintended consequence. Suddenly, Brothers to the Rescue had no one to rescue. Once the rafters realized they would be shipped off to Guantanamo or Panama if Brothers' pilots notified the Coast Guard of their coordinates, they began angrily waving off their would-be saviours the moment they spotted one of their aircraft overhead. And with no one to rescue — and no publicity for having done it — donations also began to dry up. Basulto tried to stir up new interest by pitching fund-raising drives, telethons and collections to support the dissident movement inside Cuba, but those pleas had fallen flat. The new mission, dismissed a Miami *Herald* columnist, seemed "less sexy" than plucking rafters from the waves.

On April 17, 1994, to mark the anniversary of the Bay of Pigs invasion, Basulto had teamed up with Militares y Profesionales por la Democracia, an exile military group headed by former Cuban General Rafael Del Pino, for what would become Basulto's first, highly publicized incursion into Cuban airspace.

Three or four of the exile aircraft slipped inside Cuban airspace and flew to within three miles of Havana, at which point the pilots set off flares and smoke grenades. As an urgently scrambled Cuban MiG circled overhead, Basulto radioed: "On behalf of the Cuban exiles... we wish to Cuba, the Cuban people, the armed forces that you could make freedom for Cuba possible and to do everything you can to bring an end to Castro's regime."

The MiG pilot didn't respond to Basulto's entreaty to defect — or fire on the aircraft that had illegally entered Cuban territory — but that wasn't really the point. Accompanying Basulto in the plane that day was Bernadette Pardo, a reporter for Miami's Univision Channel 23, who was videotaping Basulto's "daring" mission for the evening news. Now that had been great publicity. Perhaps...

Basulto was still looking for his new mission when he heard that 24 Miami lawyers had filed a lawsuit against what they called "the unlawful detention of innocent men, women and children... in cramped dusty tents surrounded by barbed wire" at Guantanamo. Basulto and his fellow pilots agreed to fly a small delegation of them to Guantanamo so they could meet face to face with their clients.

But Basulto was now convinced the U.S. military brass had done everything in its power to make the lawyers' work as difficult as possible. Officials refused to tell the lawyers the names of the designated leaders in each camp, for example, and insisted the detainees add their names to a dauntingly long list if they wanted to meet personally with the lawyers. As if to grind salt into the wound, Guantanamo base bureaucrats hadn't even allowed Basulto or any of his pilots to visit the encampments where the detainees were living. How many of these Cuban refugees — call them by their right name! — were alive today because of the work of Brothers to the Rescue? All he'd wanted to do, Basulto insisted, was to visit "my people."

Part of him was happy to be flying away from this unhappy place. But not before… As he made his way into Cuban airspace today, Basulto turned around, rummaged under the plane's rear seat, found what he was looking for: packages of Brothers to the Rescue bumper stickers. He looked down at the Cuban countryside, saw a small town. His father had been born in this part of Cuba. He opened the plane's window, scattered the stickers into the air.

Miami, November 17, 1994

The fact that nine Miami police officers had to be assigned to protective duty at Little Havana's Centro Vasco restaurant during today's official presentation of the release of Human Rights Watch's most recent report on freedom of expression in Miami spoke volumes about the state of that freedom. Two years before, the 25-year-old non-governmental organization set up to monitor human rights had published its first ever report on freedom of expression in an American city. That 30-page report — which documented more than 20 years of "bombings, vandalism, beatings, death threats and other examples of violence and harassment directed mostly against politically moderate exiles" — concluded that Miami's exile community was "dominated by fiercely anti-communist forces who are strongly opposed to contrary viewpoints."

Among many other villains, the report singled out the Cuban American National Foundation for its campaign against the Miami *Herald*, and its chair, Jorge Mas Canosa, for having used his White House connections to sic government investigators on anyone favouring improved relations with Cuba. "Ironically," the report concluded, "many anti-Castro Miami Cubans have a good deal in common with the regime they loathe." Ouch.

Now, two years later, investigators had returned to see what had changed. Not much. "Overall the atmosphere for unpopular political speech remains marked by fear and danger, while government officials maintain a conspicuous silence in the face of threats to free expression."

This time, the group's report focused in on what had happened to a group of Miami residents who attended an April gathering in Havana, the first face-to-face meeting between Cuban exiles and the Cuban government since 1978. When the participants returned to Miami after the highly publicized meetings, FBI agents and local police had to meet them at the airport and escort them away from a menacing crowd of screaming exiles.

The participants, whose only crime seemed to have been that they accepted an invitation from the Cuban government to take part in the meetings, were verbally attacked on Spanish-language radio talk shows and sometimes physically assaulted in the streets. They were shunned. One restaurant took out a newspaper advertisement to announce that "participants in the recent conference in Havana are not welcome in our establishment." Businesspeople who attended the meeting in Havana reported customers abandoning them; one entrepreneur claimed he lost 95 percent of his business in the first two weeks after the conference and a banker said exile clients were threatening to close their accounts. There were harassing phone messages, even death threats. "Communist, *vendepatria* [sellout], son of a bitch, pig, traitor and shit," read the gentle salutation on one fax. "Be very careful, as I think there are many who would like to see you dead." "We're going to take care of you," said a telephone caller. "You'll be floating in the Miami River with flies in your mouth." Another caller gleefully described what would happen at the participant's funeral.

The Human Rights Watch report concluded that local, state and national leaders had "failed" to protect the First Amendment rights of Miami's moderate exile community. "We urge them to end their silence and to begin to protect the rights of all South Florida residents."

The Miami *Herald*, of course, was one of those opinion leaders, not to mention an organization with a vested interest in free speech. But, perhaps still wary from its last encounter with Mas and his Foundation, it wasn't about to stand tall for those who'd met with the Cuban government. While offering pro forma criticism of the "hateful actions of some Cuban exiles," the paper was quick to argue that Human Rights Watch "misleadingly characterizes as 'political moderates'" those who took part in the Havana meeting. "In a video broadcast on Miami television," a *Herald* editorial noted with what sounded like shock, "some of those émigrés were shown greeting, kissing, or showering praise on Fidel Castro. Is it a sign of widespread 'intolerance,'" the editorial demanded, "for Cuban exiles, who are Castro's victims, to denounce such conduct?"

There's denouncing… and then there's denouncing.

Guatemala City, November 23, 1994

Percy Alvarado heard the knock he'd been expecting on his hotel room door. He'd arrived, as instructed, in Guatemala City the day before, checked into the Camino Real. It was strange being in Guatemala again: the country of his birth and the source of the passport that made him so valuable to the Cuban American National Foundation — and to Cuban State Security. Except for one brief visit, he hadn't been back here since he was 11, the year his family settled in Cuba. He'd actually spent most of his childhood in Argentina after his parents were forced into exile because… best not to think of that, or of his parents and what they knew or didn't know about who he had become. He had work to do.

According to the directions he'd been given over the telephone, Alvarado first called Otero in Miami to let him know he'd arrived. "Don't leave the room," Otero told him. "A friend will call. He'll identify himself as Pumarejo. Don't worry."

"I'm not worried," Alvarado had replied. "But I'm going to need more money." He looked around the room. "This hotel is expensive."

"Don't worry," Otero said again. "Pumarejo will give you whatever you need."

In fact, Pumarejo hadn't finally telephoned until 9:30 this morning. Fifteen minutes later, he knocked on the door. There were two of them. The first, an "affable, hearty, extroverted" man in his sixties stuck out his hand as he entered. "Call me Pumarejo," he said. The other man didn't introduce himself. He simply stared at Alvarado, suspicious, wary. He was tall, stooped and appeared to be older than his companion. Alvarado noted a scar on the right side of the man's face and his difficulty breathing. They sat down at a small round table near the window in the hotel room. Alvarado brought out the bottle of Havana Club rum he'd brought as a gift from Cuba. Pumarejo explained that they hadn't called earlier because they were having trouble tracking down one of the components for the bomb. Their friend "Bassas" should have it soon. "Can you stick around for a few more days?"

"No, no," Alvarado cut him off. This wasn't in the plan. He felt the fear return. Did they know something? He would have to improvise. "Pepe has already said he wants these bombs to go off before the end of the month, and I have other things I have to do back in Havana."

"Okay, don't worry," Pumarejo offered reassuringly. "We'll get what we need." As if to placate him, he took out his wallet, handed Alvarado five $100 bills. "We'll be back at 8 tonight with everything you'll need."

The other man finally spoke. Alvarado had to strain to make out the words. "Stay here in case we need to contact you," he admonished Alvarado. "And don't talk to anyone else. You never know who might be a Castro agent." Alvarado didn't allow himself even the hint of a smile.

In the end, the two men returned 40 minutes later than promised, but this time they seemed to have brought everything they needed. Pumarejo opened a plastic bag with the name of the hotel on it, emptied the contents on the table. There were two plastic Silkience bottles, one labelled shampoo, the other conditioner, six marker pens, two black, analog wrist watches and a package of AAA batteries.

At this point, the other man — clearly the explosives expert — took over. He carefully showed Alvarado how to take the contents from each bottle, which had been re-filled with C-4 plastic explosives, assemble them with a detonator-marker and watch-timer to transform the benign pieces into dangerous bombs. While Alvarado tried it himself, his instructor "positioned himself on a removed plane, watching how I projected myself … He interrupted on two or three occasions, just to adjust the technical explanations about the handling of the explosives. He was like a hawk on a hunt." Alvarado felt the man as a "cold gaze watching me, expectant, calculating, as if he were evaluating me, measuring me." Or perhaps that was just Alvarado projecting.

Once it was clear that Alvarado had learned his lessons well and quickly, the man relaxed. So too did Pumarejo. "After this is all done," Pumarejo said, "you'll come back here and we'll celebrate with a bottle of Old Gold."

After the two men left, Percy Alvarado waited in his hotel room until just before dawn. Then he slipped out with the cache of bomb-making material and briskly walked the two blocks to meet his Cuban State Security handlers. They'd been in the city the whole time, watching, waiting. Alvarado happily handed over the bombs to "friendly hands" to carry back to Cuba for analysis.

The trick now would be to figure out how to not set off the bombs without setting off suspicion.

Miami, December 20, 1994

Given the almost festive mood among the spectators in the Miami courtroom, you'd have been hard-pressed to believe their heroes had not only been convicted but also sentenced to prison. Perhaps it was because of the backhanded way in which Judge Frederico Moreno announced he was sentencing Rodolfo Frómeta and Fausto Marimon to 41 and 12 months respectively for their roles in attempting to buy a Stinger missile and assorted other weaponry from an undercover FBI agent.

"No matter how good the cause may be," Moreno told the two men, "no one may violate the laws of the United States." It was almost as if the crush of Comandos F-4 supporters in the courtroom hadn't heard the second part of the sentence. "Long live a free Cuba!" they shouted as marshalls led the two out of the courtroom. Frómeta didn't let them down. "We'll keep on struggling," he shouted back.

Miami, January 7, 1995

"Dear Mr. Basulto," the letter began. "Thanks for your inquiry about the L-29s." The L-29, more formally the Aero L-29 Delfín, was a Czech designed and built military jet aircraft popular for flight and weapons training among militaries in the former Soviet Union. Now that the Soviet Union was no more, there were many such planes available. The letter, from a Minnesota-based used airplane salesman, was upbeat. "It is easy to check out, great fun to fly," it explained. "Take a look at the accompanying fact sheet for its capabilities. It is even designed for operation on soft fields." Which could be useful if you might someday want to land your plane in Cuba.

Miami, January 9, 1995

Alfredo Otero had finally calmed down, though it was clear he had not yet forgotten — nor forgiven — Percy Alvarado for failing to detonate the bombs. Alvarado's instructions had been clear enough: on the night of November 29, he was to hide the first bomb at the Tropicana between some areca palm trees "in a spot near the orchestra and the tourists." And boom! But there was no boom. And no word at all from Alvarado. In fact, he didn't finally return to Miami to explain himself until nine days later. By then, Otero was beside himself.

"Shit, this is unbelievable," he shouted before Alvarado could say a word. "Pepe is very annoyed. He says I'm not to give you another cent until those bombs explode!"

Alvarado was frightened. He and his Cuban State Security handlers had come up with what they hoped would be an explanation that would fit Alvarado's persona, that would make sense and allow him to continue his work. But they couldn't know until he tried it. If they were wrong…?

"Otero, you know I've never failed you before," Alvarado began, sounding cockier than he felt. "But the truth is that you failed me. *You* lied to me!"

Otero was clearly taken aback. "That's not true," he stammered.

"Not true? Not true! You told me those bombs wouldn't hurt anybody. Just make some noise… Well, those explosives you guys gave me were high-powered bombs!" It was true. When Cuban State Security emptied the contents of the shampoo bottles, they discovered 900 grams of C-4, more than enough to have killed several hundred people attending the show that night at the Tropicana. Not that Alvarado could actually admit his information came from State Security. "I didn't agree to kill anyone," he said.

"That can't be true," Otero replied, but he clearly seemed nervous. Did he know the truth? Or had Posada lied to him too?

Posada! After he'd returned to Havana, Alvarado picked out Posada's photo as the man who taught him to assemble the bombs. Posada's partner in crime, the one who'd called himself "Pumarejo," was another Cuban exile, Gaspar Jiménez Escobedo. Jiménez — another of the co-founders of the terrorist group CORU — had been convicted in connection with the murder of the Cuban consul's bodyguard during a botched kidnapping attempt in Mexico in 1976. And "Bassas," the friend Pumarejo had said was helping to track down the bomb components? Cuban intelligence believed he was Enrique Bassas, a Miami businessman who, though not a direct participant in terrorist actions, helped finance them.

"What makes you think those bombs could have killed anyone?" Otero demanded.

Alvarado was more than ready for that question. "Rodolfo," he said. Rodolfo was the retired Cuban Armed Forces explosives expert Alvarado had supposedly recruited, at Hernández's request, to be part of his clandestine cell. In truth, of course, he was a State Security agent like Alvarado. "I gave everything to Rodolfo to prepare the bombs, and he told me your *little* package contained 900 grams of C-4. Do you have any idea how many people we would have killed? I'm not going to be a murderer! I told you that already."

"Calm down, Percy. I swear I didn't know. That isn't what they told me."

"Well, it's true," Alvarado replied. "So let me be very clear. I will never plant those bombs. Never. As soon as I can, I'm going to dump them in the ocean."

"No, no, don't do that, Percy," Otero jumped in frantically. "You'll get me into big trouble if you don't plant those bombs."

"I'm the one who will get into trouble if I plant them. Just me. The other members of my cell now know what you tried to get me to do, and they're scared. Can you imagine what will happen to me if one of them talks?"

They'd left it at that. Percy couldn't believe how easy it had turned out to be to turn the tables on Otero, twist his anger into fear, fear about what might happen to Otero if Alvarado didn't plant his bombs. He hoped that would be the end of it.

But Otero wasn't giving up on having Alvarado set off the Tropicana bomb. "If it's a matter of money," Otero pressed him again, "I can get you more. Plant the bombs and I'll personally make sure you get $10,000 more."

"Money isn't the issue. I told you that. I won't kill anyone."

"I think you're making a mistake," Otero said evenly. "Fidel has very little time left and your hesitation may be misinterpreted by my bosses."

This was not going well. "Look," Alvarado repeated himself as forcefully he could. "I will not plant those bombs. Never. I'm not a murderer. But, listen, if you want me to do other things for you, things in Cuba, you can rely on me." He could only hope Otero would get the last part of that message to his bosses at the Foundation.

But Otero had already moved on. He picked up the cell phone Alvarado had just returned to him — Hernández had given the phone to Alvarado back in the fall to use to contact Miami — and dialed a number. Guillermo Novo Sampol, Otero mouthed, pointing to the phone. Alvarado knew who he was. Yet another founder of CORU. Novo had been a member of one of the earliest militant anti-Castro organizations, the Cuban Nationalist Movement, which the FBI had credited with "acts of violence in the United States and Canada," including a botched attack in New York during Ché Guevara's 1964 speech at the United Nations. In 1976, he and his brother Ignacio, both Bay of Pigs veterans and CIA operatives, had been convicted, then "absolved" of planting the remote-controlled car bomb that killed former Chilean diplomat Orlando Letelier in Washington. In the late eighties, Novo had joined the Cuban American National Foundation.

Alvarado knew his bosses back in Cuba would be interested to learn who Otero was calling on Pepe Hernández's cell phone. Before Alvarado had returned the phone to Otero, Cuban State Security had noted its make — Cellstar by NEC — and serial number — 0317111543. All of which would prove useful just a few months later.

Key West, 1995

Arrested! Maggie Becker still couldn't believe what had happened after their vessel docked back in Key West today. A friend had told her about these voyages to Cuba a local good-Samaritan group organized to deliver medical supplies and other goods. "Do you want to go next time," she'd asked? Maggie did. She was keen to learn everything she could about her boyfriend's homeland. She'd asked Tony to come, but he couldn't get the time. He was still a janitor at the base in Boca Chica — still frustratingly not in a job that matched his qualifications, but he seemed okay with it. Tony, she joked, was amazingly zen-like in his approach to life.

"You should go," he'd encouraged her. "You could meet my family."

The crossing had taken longer — seven or eight hours — and been far rougher than Maggie anticipated. But Tony's older sister Maruchi and his mother Mirta[3] had been waiting in the rain to greet her when the boat landed at Marina Hemingway, at the western edge of Havana.

Though neither Maruchi nor Mirta could speak English and Maggie's Spanish was still — even after two years with Tony — rudimentary, Maggie immediately felt welcomed into the family. Maruchi took her salsa dancing. Mirta told Maggie the story of how she'd raised the children back in Havana after her husband died, and about the closeness of the bond that had developed among mother, daughter and son. Maggie had even met Tony's son. A bright boy. What kind of step-mother would she make, Maggie wondered? Or mother? Could she ever live in Havana? She noted how Tony's family's neighbours helped each other out. If someone's car needed fixing, someone else would pitch in just because that person was good at fixing automobiles. "Just seeing all that," Maggie would tell friends later, "helped me understand Tony better."

Maggie had been eager to report back to Tony on her adventures with

---

3. Both Maruchi and Mirta knew Tony was working as a secret agent for Cuban intelligence. Maruchi, described in one report as a "militant member of the Communist Party... is our collaborator and the person through which we render assistance to the family."

his family, to tell him how keen she was to go back to Cuba with him. But the first thing Tony wanted to know was what U.S. Customs agents were doing on the vessel when it landed. It turned out they'd arrested the captain for smuggling Cuban cigars into the U.S. Before the passengers had been allowed to disembark, they'd each been interviewed by agents. Did they know what the captain was doing? Did they see anything? Tony, whose English still wasn't good enough to understand all the nuances, told her he worried she'd gotten into trouble for having gone to Cuba. She reassured him it was just about cigars, nothing to do with her. Or, he hoped, with him.

Miami, March 1995

Percy Alvarado's handlers still hadn't entirely given up on the plan to bomb the Tropicana. When Otero contacted Alvarado during his most recent visit to Miami, he didn't mention the bombings at first, only suggested there was another member of CANF's inner circle who wanted to meet him. They drove to a house in North Miami Beach where they met Arnaldo Monzón, who introduced himself as a director of the Foundation.

Monzón, a Cuban-born New Jersey businessman, owned a network of more than 40 successful shops operating under the name Arnold Fashions. He'd also co-founded a bank in Union City, the Pan American National Bank, which had led him to a spot of legal bother: in 1985, he'd pled guilty to laundering $100,000 through the bank. These days, Monzón — now in his early sixties — was selling off his businesses and dividing his time between New Jersey and Florida. After having helped found the New Jersey branch of the Cuban American National Foundation and having served as one of the biggest donors for anti-Castro New Jersey politicians like Robert Menendez and Robert Torricelli, Monzón was eager to do his part for *la causa* in Florida too. Which is why he'd become involved in financing and directing the Foundation's secret paramilitary wing.

"Otero has told me you decided not to carry out our plans at the Tropicana," Monzón told Alvarado after the initial pleasantries. "I think you should reflect on that." It seemed like the beginning of what had become a familiar, tiresome back and forth. But then Monzón quickly switched subjects. "We'll talk about that later," he said. "For now I have another job for you back in Cuba. Do you have any problems with that?" Monzón wanted him to travel to Cienfuegos, a port city on Cuba's south coast that, perhaps coincidentally, happened to be the birthplace of both Monzón and his boyhood friend Luis Posada, and gather information on the city's thermoelectric plant, oil refinery and Soviet-built submarine base. "It would be good," Monzón added, "if you could make some videos." By the time he left, Monzón had given Alvarado an additional $500 for expenses.

WHAT LIES ACROSS THE WATER

Havana, March 20 1995

This time it wasn't Cuban State Security that had stymied some would-be bombers; it was an alert Mexican customs inspector in Cancun. He questioned the identification documents carried by the two Costa Rican tourists returning home from a Cuban vacation. Unsatisfied, he sent them back to Havana. It didn't take long for their cover stories to unravel and for Cuban interrogators to follow the threads back to the Cuban American National Foundation.

Santos Armando Martínez Rueda and José Enrique Ramirez Oro were two Cuban men who'd grown up to together in Puerto Padre, a sheltered inlet in Las Tunas province on the northeast coast. The year before, they'd hijacked a boat and made their way to Florida. There, they told Cuban authorities, they'd been recruited by a man who liked to be called "Mr. Bill," but whose real name was Guillermo Novo Sampol. They'd become members of a militant exile organization that called itself the Cuban American Veterans' Association, but was really another front for CANF's paramilitary wing.

At Novo Sampol's instructions — and with cash from Arnaldo Monzón — the two men had assembled their collection of mischief-making material: a plastic bucket, 12 electric detonators, 25 metres of detonating wire, wire clippers, some plastic Cosmos Quartz clocks, packages of low voltage batteries, transformers, adhesive tape and, oh yes, two Baikal-Makarov 9-millimetre pistols with ammunition. Novo Sampol also gave them a GPS to mark tourist destinations and a cell phone to communicate with him while they were in Cuba.

On February 27, 1995, Martínez Rueda and Ramirez Oro added two small landing craft — one they'd picked up at Novo Sampol's furniture store, the other from his home — to their travel kit and made their way to a Miami River dock, where they were met by a group of men they didn't know. They boarded a high-powered vessel and headed out to sea, where they were met, in international waters, by a second vessel. During the rendezvous, the men on the second vessel transferred a plastic tank filled with more than 20 kilograms of C-4 explosive material to their boat. The second vessel departed, and the boat carrying them continued on to a spot near the coast of Cuba off Puerto Padre. Under cover of darkness, the two Cubans slipped ashore in their landing craft. While Ramirez Oro stood guard, Martínez Rueda buried their cache near the lighthouse, and then the two men returned to the waiting vessel, which brought them back to Miami.

A few days later, carrying false passports and U.S. residency cards — which Novo Sampol had supplied and which made them appear to be ordinary Costa Rican tourists — the two men flew into Havana's José Marti airport. After a few days spent casing Havana hotels and the Plaza of the Revolution as possible bombing targets, they'd proceeded to Puerto Padre, where they played the more familiar role of local boys who'd gone off to America and had returned home for a visit. Under this convenient cover, they located their hiding place and collected some of the bomb-making paraphernalia. On their way back to Havana, they made a brief stop at the Sol Palmeras beachfront resort in Varadero, where they planted a bomb timed to explode after they'd left the country.

Thanks to the observant Mexican customs officer, however, Ramirez Oro and Martínez Rueda had been caught, returned to Cuba, questioned and confessed in time for investigators to defuse their bomb before it could do its damage. Once investigators began trying to corroborate the story the two men told, they discovered calls had been made from their confiscated cell phone to both Novo Sampol and Luis Zuñiga of the Cuban American National Foundation. The cell phone itself? When they checked the serial number, they discovered it was the same phone Pepe Hernández had previously given Percy Alvarado to use. The dots kept connecting.

Coral Gables, April 1, 1995

It was a marriage made in *el exilio* heaven — or at least in Bible classes at the University Baptist Church in Coral Gables. And Ana Margarita Martinez would be happy to tell you when, where and under what circumstances she'd met the man who was about to become her husband.

It was March 15, 1992. She'd attended church services with her grandmother and her two children, Sasha and Omar. Juan Pablo Roque had been in a nearby pew with his cousins. Ana Margarita already knew who he was. She'd seen him on TV a few days earlier — the courageous Cuban Air Force pilot who'd swum through "shark-infested waters" across Guantanamo Bay to American freedom. Ana Margarita liked that. She also liked the chiseled, buff way he looked, the confident way he carried himself. He reminded her of a movie star. After church, one of Juan Pablo's cousins, an FBI agent in Miami, introduced them. Juan Pablo was interested in her too. She could see it in his eyes.

Ana Margarita wasn't looking for a husband. She'd had two already, and neither had worked out all that well. She was Cuban, born in 1960, the year after the revolution. Her mother and father split up when she was one; when she was six, her mother brought her to the United States. They'd initially settled in New York, but when Ana Margarita was 19, she moved to Miami "to start my own life. I married my first love." That quickly fell apart and, three years later, she married again. The romance ended the day the marriage started. "He became very possessive, and he abused me emotionally and physically." She divorced him in 1989, but by then she was also the sole support for two children. She had to juggle two or three jobs just to pay rent and put food on the table. She lost interest in trying to find another man. She hadn't dated in years.

Her relations with Roque began innocently enough with glances across the room at nightly Bible classes. Two months later, at a Memorial Day party at the church, Ana Margarita worked up the courage to make small talk. That led to a dance — he was a good dancer — and then another, and another. After the party ended, they stopped by a nearby nightclub for more dancing. Juan Pablo wasn't a conventional romantic. But he mowed her lawn and fixed her car and painted her house. "He liked salads and steamed vegetables, french fries with nearly every main course. For a treat, a three-scoop sundae at Baskin-Robbins, chocolate syrup over chocolate ice-cream and plenty of nuts, please." Most importantly, he seemed to be a loving father to her children. He even took them on a visit to Walt Disney World.

By the fall of 1992, J.P., as Ana Margarita called him, had moved in. Not that he helped a lot with the household expenses. Although he'd been an Air Force major back in Cuba, he didn't have any marketable skills in America. He'd applied for a job as a Miami *Herald* delivery manager, claiming experience in "management, supervision and human resources." He didn't get the position, mostly because his English language skills were considered too rudimentary. He tried to peddle stories to *CubaNews*, a monthly Spanish-language newsletter the *Herald* published, but all he got were rejection letters. He skipped from temporary job to temporary job: as what he described on his résumé as a "personnel assistant" at Mercantil Services Corporation, a Venezuelan bank in Coral Gables (which the bank would later call a fill-in filing clerk's position), as a construction worker, as a stock clerk at a Fedco drug store, as an aircraft fueller at the Opa-locka airport.

His boss at the airport was a fellow member of the Brothers to the Rescue organization. Brothers, in fact, had become Juan Pablo Roque's primary social, emotional and political outlet. Though he'd flown fewer than a dozen actual missions, he hung out at the Brothers' Opa-Locka hangar, helping prepare the food, water and radios the other fliers would drop to Cuban rafters in the waters below. He'd become especially close with Brothers' founder José Basulto. After Roque found out that his older brother was trying to escape from Cuba in a makeshift raft, Basulto organized a search party to try to locate him. When Roque said he wanted to write a book — a memoir of his life in and escape from Castro's Cuba — Basulto arranged for him to meet with members of the Cuban American National Foundation, who agreed to finance its publication.

Today, there were plenty of fellow Brothers on hand at University Baptist Church to watch J.P. wed Ana Margarita. Guillermo Lares, an Argentinian-born Brothers pilot, was Roque's best man. Basulto was there too, of course. So was René González, another pilot-defector, even though Basulto had removed González from the Brothers' flying roster several years before.

The problem had started after González had begun moonlighting as a pilot with the one-plane "air wing" of another militant anti-Castro exile group, Partido Unidad Nacional Democracia (PUND), which was made up of what González himself would later describe as "the not uncommon mix of bandits, ex-CIA (including Frank Fiorini, one of the Watergate plumbers), anti-Castroites and drug dealers." One day when González and some fellow PUND members landed at Tamiami airport after a trip to Marathon Key, Drug Enforcement Agency agents detained them, forcing them all to lie face-down and spread-eagled on the ground, while the agents searched the plane. Guillermo Lares saw the takedown and reported it to Basulto, who questioned González about it. González insisted he knew nothing about any drugs; he was only interested in the group because it, like Brothers, was anti-Castro.

"Those guys aren't clean," Basulto warned him. Even though Basulto liked González — "he was *buena gente,* good people" — and believed his protesta-tions of innocence, he couldn't risk the Brothers' reputation being tarnished by drug charges against one of its pilots. "Clip his wings," he instructed Lares. Still, González had continued to volunteer around the hangar and showed up at Brothers' events. His popularity with the other pilots made his presence among today's wedding guests perfectly logical.

Oscar Montoto wasn't among the wedding guests. Which was logical too. Montoto was Roque's FBI controller, and neither of them wanted any-one else to know about their relationship. For close to two years, Roque had been serving as a secret paid informant inside Brothers, supplying Montoto with tidbits he picked about exile maneuverings, even about a drug deal he'd discovered. He'd earned more than $5,000 in secret payments already — enough for a down payment on a new Jeep Cherokee. No one thought to ask how he could afford it. José Basulto knew nothing of his protégé's other life as an FBI informant. Neither did Ana Margarita. But that was par for the Roque course. Neither of them — nor Montoto — had a clue about Roque's *other* other life: as a Cuban intelligence agent inside Brothers to the Rescue.

Perhaps because he seemed so committed to their relationship — even pressing her to have a child with him — Ana Margarita didn't question J.P.'s reluctance to talk about his own past. She knew he'd been married before, to a woman in Cuba with whom he'd had two children he never mentioned and from whom he was now divorced. She knew even less about his first marriage, to the daughter of a Soviet Air Force officer he'd met while he was pilot training in Russia in the 1980s. She knew he wasn't close with his own family but she didn't know why. She only knew that one of his brothers, who'd defected after Juan Pablo, had warned her against marrying him.

Ana Margarita wasn't thinking about any of that today, of course. She was thinking how pretty she looked in her white — yes, white — gown with its "full skirt, tulle around the décolletage, her dark hair in a becoming up-do with ringlets cascading along her cheeks, a crown of diamonds clasping her veil," and how handsome her new husband looked in his black tuxedo and white tie. After the ceremony, there would be a reception at the home of friends and then "Guille," the best man, would fly the happy couple to a honeymoon resort in the Bahamas as his wedding gift.

New York, Spring 1995

The automatic garage door opened, and the driver eased his official vehicle out of the underground parkade and into New York's early evening air. He turned left on East 38th Street, drove slowly past the assorted security cameras, the police guard and the marked and unmarked vehicles — U.S. Secret Service, FBI — keeping their usual wary eyes on the comings and goings at Cuba's Permanent Mission to the United Nations. Security was even more vigilant tonight because Cuba's National Assembly president, Ricardo Alarcón, was in the city for talks with American State Department and Immigration officials. They were trying to come up with a more permanent settlement to the rafters' crisis. The two sides had agreed last September on a deal to stanch the flood of Cubans fleeing their homeland by boat by diverting rafters plucked from the Florida Straits to temporary camps in Panama and the American base at Guantanamo. The issue, among others, was what to do with them now.

The official talks were not going well, in part because some of the American officials, including Dennis Hays, the State Department's coordinator of Cuban Affairs, were balking at any compromise to end the impasse. Though a career diplomat, many in State — and among the Cuban delegation — believed Hays was too cozy with Miami's exile leadership. Which may explain why Peter Tarnoff, the U.S. under secretary of state for political affairs, the point man for the American government in the negotiations, had quietly suggested to Alarcón they find a place to meet away from the madding crowd of officials. (The need to keep a high-ranking American official's own senior advisors out of the negotiating loop, Alarcón would allow with a smile years later, was "one of the curiosities of the American administration.")

Alarcón and Tarnoff had known — and liked — each other since the late 1970s, when Tarnoff served as a special assistant to U.S. President Jimmy Carter's two secretaries of state and Alarcón was Cuba's permanent representative at the United Nations. But getting together now for a private chat wasn't easy. Because the U.S. Secret Service was responsible for providing security for foreign dignitaries while they were on American soil, Alarcón had to travel to and from his meetings in a Secret Service limousine driven by a U.S. government driver.

Tonight — as they had the past several nights — Cuban officials released the Secret Service driver soon after he brought Alarcón back from the day's official talks. "The president will not be going out for the rest of the day," they explained. "Please return to pick him up in the morning."

Soon after the American limousine left, one of the Cuban government's own cars entered the Mission parkade, stayed inside for a few minutes and then left as it had entered, empty except for the driver at the wheel. Well, not really. Alarcón was crouched on the floor in the car's back seat, remaining in that uncomfortable position for several blocks before getting back into his seat as his driver sped up Madison to the Carlyle, a luxury hotel where he and Tarnoff could dine quietly and discuss how best to end the impasse.

The rafters wasn't the only issue they discussed. "I know you don't watch Miami TV in Washington," Alarcón said to Tarnoff at one point, "but, in Havana, we watch Miami TV all the time. I have a DVD I can give you so you'll see how some people in Miami act." The DVD included an interview from a right-wing Miami TV station featuring Andres Nazario Sargen, the leader of Alpha 66, and a second man who appeared with his face covered. They were bragging about their latest "attack on a Cuban fishing village." Alarcón's purpose, he would explain later, was to make sure Tarnoff understood that, even as the two sides were making limited progress toward a rapprochement on the rafters, extremists in Miami were "plotting to undermine any advances."

After they finished dinner, Tarnoff and Alarcón made their way through the hotel lobby toward the exit. Suddenly, they were accosted by a phalanx of photographers and flashing lights. "I thought, 'Oh my God, they found us,'" Alarcón would joke later. "I looked at Peter and he just stood there frozen."

But the moment passed, the photographers hurried past. Their quarry, in fact, was the actor Woody Allen, who sometimes played his jazz clarinet at the Café Carlyle bar. Tarnoff and Alarcón looked at one another, laughed, shook hands. Alarcón walked off to find his car. Their secret was safe for another day.

Miami, June 13, 1995

Another day, another plot. And another assignment for Gerardo Hernández and his Avispa agents. Information about this particular plot — as with many others — had come from M-19, the department within the Directorate of Intelligence responsible for monitoring American counter-revolutionary groups and, if possible, neutralizing their nefarious plots. The problem was that one never knew for certain just how reliable M-19 sources were. But every tip, rumour, tidbit of gossip had to be checked out. Often, the most unbelievable ones turned out to be true.

Consider the latest. An M-19 source reported that four Cuban military defectors had met recently in Atlanta to discuss "the Commander's trip to New York." Fidel Castro was planning to attend the celebration of the United Nations 50th anniversary in New York in October. One of those attending the Atlanta gathering was a former deputy chief of the Cuban Air Force named Rafael del Pino, who'd broken with Fidel over Cuba's role in Africa and defected to the U.S. in 1987. According to M-19's source, "Del Pino offered to pilot a fighter jet which must intercept the Commander's plane and bring it down between Cuba and the Bahamas."

M-19 believed Del Pino was now in Miami looking for a plane he could use for such an attack and "might be trying to contact Basulto to use one of two aircraft which Brothers to the Rescue bought not too long ago." Using a rogue fighter jet to blow Fidel Castro's plane out of the air? Incredible! But was it really any more incredible — or impossible — than the idea of poisoning the Cuban leader's cigars?

Over Cuban Territorial Waters, July 13, 1995

José Basulto had to do something. From the cockpit of his Cessna, he could see two armed, brown and grey Cuban government gunboats menacing a much smaller, unarmed vessel. *Not again.* The vessel, the *Democracia*, was the pointy end of a 13-boat flotilla filled with 100 Cuban exiles determined to mark the anniversary of an incident the year before during which 41 people had drowned. On July 13, 1994, a group of 72 Cubans desperate to get to Florida hijacked a tugboat, the *Trece de Marzo*, in Havana harbour. They were making their escape when they were overtaken by fellow Cubans in other tugs, who rammed the vessel, then turned their water hoses on it, sinking the runaway boat.[4]

Those aboard today's small-boat flotilla planned to sail to the spot, six miles inside Cuban territorial waters, where the tug had gone down and lay wreaths. It was a memorial but also, of course, a provocation. "Our purpose," explained organizer Ramón Saúl Sánchez, founder of the Democracy Movement, "is to have Castro be concerned, to bring a message of solidarity to the Cuban people and to show that we are willing to take risks."

Shortly after 2:30 p.m., Sánchez announced the vessel had crossed into Cuban waters. Those aboard began singing the Cuban national anthem. Before the final verse, the first gunboats arrived. "You have entered Cuban territorial waters," an officer hailed them in Spanish over his bullhorn. "You have violated Cuban territorial waters."

"We are Cubans, you are Cubans," Sánchez shouted back over the noise of the engines. "We have as much right to be here in Cuban waters as you."

While the exiles aboard threw flowers into the ocean and the small planes overhead buzzed the patrol boats, the *Democracia*'s captain ignored the Cuban warning and continued toward Havana.

"You have violated Cuban national waters," the officer repeated, louder this time. "We will not be responsible for what happens."

The *Democracia* didn't change course or even slow down. At 2:50 p.m.,

---

4. The Cuban Coast Guard arrived soon after and rescued the remaining 31 people aboard the *Trece de Marzo*.

the two gunboats approached either side of the *Democracia*, squeezing closer, closer, until finally they crunched the *Democracia's* fiberglass hull between them, knocking many of those on the deck off their feet.

Basulto and his fellow pilots[5] watched this drama unfold below them. Basulto decided he had to do something — and now. He made a split-second decision, he would explain later, and radioed fellow pilot Billy Schuss. "Follow me," he said, and the two planes peeled off south toward Havana, deliberately violating Cuban air space in hopes they could distract the Cuban military from sinking the flotilla. For 13 minutes, they flew not only inside Cuban territory but directly over the city of Havana. As Basulto flew, his co-pilot Guillermo Lares rained thousands of religious medallions and "Not Comrades, Brothers" bumper stickers on the streets below.

Back in Miami, Basulto was unrepentant. "We are proud of what we did," he said. "Ultimately, it serves as a message to the people of Cuba. The regime is not invulnerable."

In fact, Basulto's allegedly split-second decision seemed anything but spontaneous. As even he would later acknowledge, flying over Havana was always "a Plan B in case something went awry." But, he insisted he would not have flown over Havana "had the attack against the *Democracia* not occurred." Even before the planes took off that day, however, Billy Schuss had confided to René González that their plan was to fly "all the way to the Malecón." (It wouldn't have been the first time. González, the Cuban intelligence agent, had been one of the pilots participating in Basulto's April 1994 flight over Havana.)

Others, including the Criminal Intelligence Bureau of the Miami-Dade police department and the Federal Aviation Administration, weren't buying Basulto's Plan B explanation either. In a report a week before the flotilla, Miami detective Luis Rodríguez wrote: "Recent information received from various sources has revealed the intention of several organizers to create an international incident during the course of the aforementioned event." He singled out both Basulto and Sánchez, and suggested they were "presently involved in an effort to obtain a vessel which will be utilized solely to enter Cuban territorial waters and attempt to disembark in the Port of Havana." If not a vessel, a plane would do.

Before July 13, Basulto had met with the FAA's Charles Smith, who'd warned him not to fly into Cuban airspace during the flotilla. "Chuck, you know I always play by the rules," Basulto told Smith, "but you must understand I have a mission in life to perform." Not to forget an organization to resuscitate.

---

5. Basulto and five other Brothers planes had accompanied the flotilla from Key West, as did a number of other small aircraft, including one flown by the Democracy Movement's René González. González, the Cuban intelligence agent, would later describe the planes' buzzing of the Cuban patrol vessels as "a display of reckless, dangerous maneuvering."

In 1993, at the height of the rafters' crisis, Brothers to the Rescue had raised nearly a million dollars in public contributions. Last year, Brothers had taken in less than a third of that. Basulto, who'd long since given up his day job, had been forced to drop his own $60,000 annual salary down to $37,000. "Our basic mission of rescuing rafters remains," Basulto argued, even though they hadn't rescued a single one in over a year. "It is true the number of rafters has diminished dramatically," he acknowledged, "but we will continue looking for them. But I would also say that flying into Cuban airspace and showing solidarity with the Cuban people is itself a rescue action." José Basulto had found a new — and, he hoped, more lucrative — mission for Brothers to the Rescue. Agents provocateur!

Miami, September 2, 1995

José Basulto wasn't the only one to have discovered the fundraising potential in provoking the Cuban government. Ramón Saúl "Ramóncito" Sánchez had arrived in the United States with his parents as a 12-year-old in 1967, dropped out of Miami Senior High five years later, joined Alpha 66, participated in eight to ten "missions" inside Cuba and ended up in an American prison for four and a half years for "refusing to bear witness against his compatriots." In his everyday life, Sánchez, now 40, was a $300-a-week paper pusher at a small Miami export firm, a modest man "with two suits, both black, two pairs of shoes, one black, one brown and some work boots.'" But in his other larger-than-life persona, he was the founder of Movimiento Democracia, an influential umbrella group of exile organizations dedicated to peaceful change — with a little nose-tweaking civil disobedience for good measure.

According to a police intelligence report, Sánchez had spent part of August fundraising among Cuban exiles in New Jersey to underwrite his plan for another larger flotilla to Cuba on September 2, as well as a protest in New York during Fidel Castro's upcoming visit to the United Nations.

Like Basulto — and Jorge Mas Canosa and Orlando Bosch — Sánchez publicly claimed to have abandoned violence as a way to bring about regime change. During his years in prison, he said, he'd come to realize violence made no sense. "We had gone down roads that we had thought would work. We were wrong." As he explained his epiphany in an interview with Miami *Herald* publisher David Lawrence, "it struck me as strange that an idea so beautiful as freedom had to be obtained through a means so degrading as violence." Like Basulto, Sánchez now claimed to be a fan of Mahatma Gandhi and Martin Luther King Jr.

But while Sánchez, in meetings with local detectives during the summer of 1995, "reiterated his organization's passive philosophy," the police were clearly concerned about Sánchez's fellow travellers. "At present time," explained an August 10 intelligence report, "it is known that several Cuban exile organizations are planning to stage acts of sabotage against Cuban government installations. Such acts, though independent from flotilla plans, are due to occur on September 2, 1995." In fact, on the day before the July 13 flotilla, the FBI detained three members of PUND who'd been plotting to stage a raid on Cuba under the guise of participating in the *Democracia* flotilla.

As for Sánchez himself? According to the intelligence report, he'd "warned that if hampered by federal government regulations that would seek to derail plans, he would call for local acts of disobedience as a form of protest." The federal government did want to derail the protesters' plans. Officials worried about the potential fallout from another incursion into Cuban territory. In August, the State Department had even warned the protesters directly about possible "arrest or other enforcement action by Cuban authorities. [The Cuban government] warns that any boat from abroad can be sunk and any airplane downed," the State Department said, adding: "The Department takes this statement seriously."

José Basulto didn't. Though the FAA had written him that week to say it intended to suspend his pilot's licence for 120 days as a result of his July 13 over-flight, Basulto professed unconcern. "It's a bunch of pages," he said of the FAA letter. "I will talk to my lawyer, but I won't do anything with this until next week." Which, of course, just happened to be after the upcoming flotilla. Basulto had 15 days to appeal the decision. Even if the ruling was upheld, Basulto could appeal again to the National Transportation Safety Board. That could take another year. And then... The Cuban government was not amused.

Havana, October 11, 1995

"The United States of America Interest Section of the Embassy of Switzerland presents its compliments to the Ministry of Foreign Relations of the Republic of Cuba," American Department of State diplomatic note 553 began in the usual formal fashion, "and has the honor to refer to a request by the United States Federal Aviation Administration." In an earlier note — in response to a still earlier note from the Cubans protesting Basulto's incursion — the Americans promised the FAA would investigate "with a view to taking appropriate enforcement actions." Now it was ready to report. "The FAA is charging José Basulto, a leader of the Brothers to the Rescue, with violating federal aviation regulations FAR 91.703, operating a U.S. registered aircraft within a foreign country in noncompliance with the regulations of that country, and FAR 91.13, operating an aircraft in a careless or reckless manner so as to endanger the life or property of another." To assist with prosecution, the American diplomatic note continued, the FAA wanted Cuba to provide "any evidence that might be relevant to the charges against Basulto, such as statements provided by Cuban air traffic controllers who observed the flight into Cuban air space or any other data to that effect...

"The United States of America Interest Section of the Embassy of Switzerland avails itself of this opportunity to convey to the Ministry of Foreign Relations of the Republic of Cuba the assurances of its consideration."

Miami, October 21, 1995

Saúl Sánchez had a plan. His group's flagship vessel, *Democracia,* was undergoing repairs after accidentally colliding with a bridge post a few days before so wouldn't be available to participate in the next flotilla. But it was seaworthy enough to at least serve as a decoy. Sánchez had already announced that this Saturday's flotilla — the third[6] — would sail to the edge of Cuban territorial waters and beam into Cuban homes two hours of pre-recording programming, including a video reprise of his stirring July 13 high-seas confrontation with authorities.

The problem, as a spokesperson for the Coast Guard had already publicly pointed out, was that such broadcasts were illegal. "Under Article 109 of the International Law of the Sea, the authorities of any nation have the jurisdiction on the high seas to arrest any person or ship engaged in unauthorized broadcasts into that nation and seize the broadcasting equipment."

During a meeting with volunteers earlier in the week, Sánchez suggested it might soon be time for the flotilla to "defy the government more openly." In fact, he asked those present for "support in disobeying any measures designed to incarcerate any leader or group of the organization as a result of such broadcasts." To prevent the U.S. Coast Guard from grounding the flotilla before it could get close enough to Cuba to beam its signal, Sánchez had come up with a diversionary tactic. Democracy volunteers would ostentatiously install some communications equipment aboard the *Democracia,* and the vessel would then sail from Miami — apparently bound for the Keys to join the rest of the flotilla. The Coast Guard would follow the *Democracia* on what would turn out to be a pleasure voyage to nowhere. Meanwhile, another vessel — the *Reflected Gloria* — carrying the real communications equipment would slip out of Key West on what would be billed as an "excursion." Later, it would rendezvous with the rest of the flotilla and make for Cuba.

While Coast Guard officials may not have known what Sánchez was planning, the Cuban government certainly did. René González had attended the planning meetings and reported to Gerardo Hernández, who, in turn, sent high-frequency messages back to Havana. Since he'd stopped flying for Basulto's Brothers last year, González had focused his infiltration attentions

---

6. Sánchez hadn't had much luck with his flotillas. His close encounter with the gunboats had put an end to his first seagoing adventure in July and he'd had to abandon his plans to sail to Cuba again on September 2 when one of the boats sank — this time having nothing to do with Cuban gunboats — and a man died.

on PUND as well as on Democracy, where he'd become "under-secretary of air affairs."

González told Hernández he'd seen Basulto and Sánchez in private conversation after one meeting. "I fear that they may decide to act using some plane of Brothers to the Rescue on the same Saturday," González told Hernández. "They are eager to emulate the coup they managed by flying over Havana."

Luckily for the authorities, a storm expected to kick up seas of nine feet in the Straits was forecast for flotilla weekend. Two days before it was to take place, Sánchez cancelled the flotilla. Unluckily, from Cuba's point of view, that gave Sánchez more time to work on his next upcoming protest — a separate flotilla on New York's East River to coincide with Fidel Castro's 50th anniversary United Nations speech.

Miami, November 1995

Juan Pablo Roque was where he preferred to be: smack in the middle of the spotlight. A beaming Roque stood at a podium at the front of Le Festival Restaurant in Coral Gables. He was celebrating the launch of *Desertor*, his 120-page polemic-memoir. While Ana Margarita videotaped, Roque thanked "an endless list" of those who'd made it possible, including José Basulto, his mentor at Brothers to the Rescue, and Jorge Mas Canosa, his financial angel at the Cuban American National Foundation, which had put up the money to print his vanity book.

During two short years in Miami, the handsome, far from camera shy and more than quotable Roque had made himself something of a media darling. When two Cuban Air Force pilots defected within a single week in the fall of 1993, for example, the Miami *Herald* had sought out Roque — whom it described as director of "a newly formed group of military defectors that began beaming short-wave messages to the island earlier this month" — who explained why he believed fewer Cuban jets were now equipped with weapons: "They are afraid that one of these days, one pilot will turn around and bomb the Palace of the Revolution instead of flying to Miami."

Desertor was just as acerbic in its portrayal of the Castro regime. Party members, he wrote, were "fat communists, heavy beer drinkers." Cuba's foreign minister, Roberto Robaina, was Fidel's "puppet... a paranoid communist clown, intent in profiteering and living the good life, urging others to 'do as I say, not as I do." Roque not only plunked Cuba's economic woes at the feet of Fidel, who "misspent the credits and commercial incentives given... by the former Communist bloc... [and] squandered blood and money... in a campaign to export revolution to Africa," but he also claimed the Cuban government itself was involved in drug trafficking "and that Fidel got a share of the profits."

Reading the book — filled with photos of a smiling Roque with Basulto, with Mas Canosa — no one would have guessed he was actually a Cuban agent. That, of course, was the idea.

Miami, November 29, 1995

Juan Pablo Roque was losing it, Manny Ruiz warned his bosses back in Havana. Ruiz, who was substituting for the vacationing Gerardo Hernández, had arrived in Miami in late October.[7] Hernández had handed him the keys to his North Miami apartment and his car — which Ruiz would use during Hernández's absence — and gave him the only copy of the magic floppy disk needed to decode messages to and from Havana. Hernández also briefed Ruiz on his agents' assignments as well as their personal issues — of which there were many. Antonio Guerrero, code-named Lorient, was still fretting about his relationship with Maggie Becker, his non-combatant American girlfriend who was eager to marry and have children. René González, also known by his code names Iselin and Castor,[8] was eager for news about when his wife would be allowed join him in Florida. And then, of course, there was Juan Pablo Roque, alias German or Vedette, the high-strung defector who was even more anxiously waiting to learn when he would be allowed to return to Cuba.

Ruiz had met with Roque two days before at a McDonald's in Coconut Grove, where Roque had shared Basulto's latest hare-brained scheme. Basulto, Roque explained, wanted to apply for official permission to fly to Havana to deliver humanitarian aid to political prisoners. Roque "seemed to think these flights might be authorized by Cuba," Ruiz incredulously reported back to Havana. Roque had even described with enthusiasm how good it would be if such flights were allowed to take place. He would accompany Basulto, land in Cuba, and say, 'That's it for me'... [Roque spoke about] how much of an impact it would have for one of the pilots of Brothers to the Rescue to stay." Ruiz told him he was dreaming in Technicolor.

Now two days later, the two men were meeting once again, this time at another fast food joint, the Pollo Tropical near the Miami airport. Roque's mood had careened from delusional to paranoid. Despite their apparent close friendship, Roque had gotten it into his head that Basulto suspected

---

7. He'd initially introduced himself to Hernández as Miguel, though he also carried documents identifying him as a businessman in the import-export trade named either Alberto Manuel "Manny" Ruiz or Francisco Salgado Nieves. Miguel didn't tell Hernández his real name or about his other identities. Hernández didn't ask. Compartmentalization, need to know... The less one knew the less one could tell. In case...

8. González chose the name Iselin to "honor my best friend, who died in Angola." Castor? "No idea who came up with 'Castor.'"

him. Roque's concerns were likely less a reflection of reality than of Roque's own increasing desperation to get his bosses to bring him home to Cuba.

Since the end of 1993, Roque had been pressuring Havana to end his mission because of what he called "different personal and family problems." In March 1995, the CP reluctantly agreed, but for a variety of reasons it hadn't happened. During a recent telephone conversation with his wife — the one in Cuba, not Florida — Roque had apparently made it seem he'd be returning immediately. Which only added to pressure on the CP. During the meeting with Ruiz, Roque made it clear he "definitely" needed to be home before his son's birthday, which was February 26.

State Security was understandably reluctant to give up such an important covert asset. Despite his tendency to showboat — his over-the-top autobiography had not won him any friends in Havana — Roque had, in the words of one Top Secret memo, "accumulated an important, informative fund coming from diverse sources or spheres of the counter-revolution." Thanks to Roque, Cuban State Security knew all about José Basulto's "interest in acquiring long-range weapons for attempts on the Commander-in-Chief's life [and] his money-gathering for attempts on some people's lives in Cuba." Roque had also told his bosses about instructions he'd received from Brothers on ways to "interfere" with the air traffic control towers at Cuban airports. Even Roque's autobiography had produced positive, if unexpected intelligence: the Cuban American National Foundation, which had underwritten its publication, asked Roque to provide a "technical assessment of using arrow-rockets to [make an] attempt on the Commander-in-Chief's life."

The continuing conundrum was that even today, in the middle of demanding to be brought home, Roque provided Ruiz with yet another juicy insider tidbit. "He said that Basulto had told him about plans he has with a 'secret weapon' that was very effective during the Second World War," Ruiz reported back to Havana, "and has not been manufactured anymore even though it is not very costly." Ruiz pressed him for more information but Roque said he hadn't been able to find out anything more than that it was "an anti-personnel" weapon. Havana would want to know more.

Miami, December 1995

Manny Ruiz wasn't the only illegal officer sitting in for Gerardo Hernández. Fernando González — who'd been Hernández's fellow student at the Instituto Superior de Relaciones Internacionales in the 1980s and whose false documents now identified him as Ruben Campa — had also temporarily relocated to Miami from his regular base in North Carolina.

His mission: to oversee Operation Rainbow. Rainbow had grown out of an earlier assignment to follow and find out everything there was to know about a target code-named Rayo, or "bolt of lightning." "Our operation,"

Havana had explained at the time, "is to find Rayo and learn his habitual movements, the places he frequents and visits, what his relationships are, who he goes out with, where he goes with his family, etc... so that when the need arises we will know just where to go to take measures against him." Rayo's real name was Orlando Bosch.

M-19, the department in Cuba's Directorate of Intelligence that kept track of the revolution's enemies, had been following Bosch forever, of course, but its interest had intensified again after 1993 when Bosch launched his new "political party" and announced plans to raise money to buy weapons to send to Cuba. Bosch's schemes, Cuban intelligence had learned, were beginning to bear fruit.

On April 10, 1995, one of M-19's Florida operatives reported that Bosch was "preparing book bombs to mail to different individuals in Cuba." On July 18, another source reported Bosch had met with members of Commandos L, yet another militant anti-Castro group, to discuss ways to smuggle explosives, including C-4, into Cuba. State Security had managed to plant a female field agent known as Sol inside the inner circle around Bosch. She'd recently been meeting with Bosch and another exile named Ruben Dario Lopez Castro. The two men wanted her help to ship weapons into Cuba to kill Castro.

Dario Lopez was a member of both Alpha 66 and PUND — two organizations with long histories of attacks against Cuba — and had his own almost-as-lengthy terrorist rap sheet. Back in 1973, according to Cuban intelligence, he had been involved in an attack that left a Cuban fisherman dead. More recently, in 1993, he and two other men had been caught by Bahamian authorities headed for Cuba in a boat filled with grenades and other weapons. More recently still — in late September, in fact — FBI agents had visited both Lopez and Bosch to quietly warn them "not to participate in terrorist activities" when Fidel Castro was in New York for the 50th anniversary of the United Nations. That seemed a milquetoast admonition considering that these were men the FBI itself believed were plotting terrorist activities. *Do what you will, just don't do it on American soil or when the world is watching.*

So State Security had come up with a scheme of its own. Operation Rainbow. Fernando González had come to Miami to organize a team of agents, including Nilo and Linda Hernández, one of Gerardo Hernández's husband-and-wife agent teams, to secretly film Sol meeting with Bosch and Lopez. The goal was to use the video to publicly discredit Bosch and — hopefully — embarrass American authorities into putting a stop to his plans.[9] Hopefully.

---

9. Although there was testimony about Operation Rainbow during the trial of the Cuban Five, no evidence was offered to indicate González and his team actually succeeded in filming the meeting. No video has ever been released.

Shootdown
January 1996 – December 1996

Miami, Early January 1996

Even a spy needs a break. Extended vacations at home in Cuba were one of the few perks Cuban State Security offered its illegal officers as a less-than-fair exchange for spending the rest of their lives living alone as people they were not, in places that were not home, enduring the constant risk of exposure, or arrest, or worse.

In late October, Manuel Viramóntez, a Puerto Rican-born graphic designer from Miami, had driven to Tampa and boarded a flight to Cancun, Mexico, for a vacation. There, he briefly became Damian Perez Oquendo, an employee at Cine Foto, a Puerto Rican retail photo supply chain, whose boss had asked him to travel to Cuba to investigate business opportunities in the new tourist economy. The next day, he'd arrived in Havana aboard Mexicana Airlines Flight MX-321 to re-emerge as Gerardo Hernández, the man he'd been born. But he was still posing, this time as a Cuban diplomat home for a welcome respite from his posting at the embassy in Buenos Aires. He'd spend his vacation with family and friends, regaling them with unexciting tales from the life of a mid-level diplomat abroad.

Adriana didn't — but did — know what her husband really did for a living. "This subject," as Hernández would delicately explain it in a note to his superiors, "has always been treated with the 'care' which its complexity and novelty confer upon it." But he and Adriana both wanted children — and soon. They wanted to raise their family together, either in Havana or… Though they'd limited their conversations to the "concrete details if it were to happen," the issue of living together again was becoming more pressing with each prolonged absence.

In early January 1996, his vacation over, Hernández reported to a secret State Security work house in Havana to prep for his return to Florida. Work houses were otherwise nondescript houses or apartments in residential areas where agents could come and go, meet, be trained, briefed or debriefed without attracting unwanted attention. Because he was a covert agent, Hernández was "strictly prohibited from entering any establishment [publicly] connected to the clandestine services, as that could reveal my real job and jeopardize my mission. This was true, even in Cuba, where we knew the United States had counter-intelligence agents."

Hernández wasn't the only one being prepared for duty at this particular work house. Olga Salanueva, René González's wife, was here too.[1] Five years after her husband "defected," Cuban State Security finally told her what René was doing in the United States, and had recently begun training her in radio communications techniques so she could assist him when the U.S. Interest Section gave her permission to join him in Florida.

During his days at the work house, Hernández and his supervisors discussed the details of Avispa's bare-bones operating budget for the upcoming year — $35,935 for everything, including expenses for himself and his agents.[2] Hernández's handlers also briefed him on the role they wanted him to play in Operation Venecia, a newly hatched scheme to bring disgruntled agent Roque home to Cuba. The double purpose of Operation Venecia, as Hernández's bosses explained it to him, was to bring Roque back to Cuba and then use publicity about his defection to force Basulto to rethink his flyover strategy. What if, for example, Roque was to steal a Brothers to the Rescue plane and fly it to Havana? Imagine Basulto's embarrassment! Hernández's assignment was to figure out the logistics for Roque's safe return — and soon.

Miami, January 5, 1996

While the CP prepared Gerardo Hernández in the Havana work house, Manny Ruiz took care of Venecia's preliminaries in Miami. It wasn't easy. He'd tried to contact Roque but Roque didn't respond to beeper messages. When they finally did connect, Roque claimed he hadn't remembered Ruiz's number. In the meantime — and more productively — Ruiz had coached René González on his public part in the upcoming drama. Because González and Roque had been good friends within the Brothers organization, it would be essential for González to find ways to "totally discredit and disassociate himself" from Roque, even before Roque popped up in Havana. Luckily, Roque's life provided plenty of fodder. "He likes to be in the press," Ruiz suggested. "He likes to be known and he wrote a book about his defection, which didn't sell well, but he thought it was pretty good…"

Once Basulto discovered Roque's deception, Ruiz noted, it would be critical for González to appear deceived too. Ruiz also reminded González he would need to be "extremely careful" dealing with Roque's FBI contact, Oscar

---

1. That Olga was at the work house too is referenced in a Cuban State Security document. Hernández says he doesn't remember her being there.
2. Like any good bureaucracy Cuban State Security required a detailed accounting of all Hernández's expenditures: "two glasses" ($2.14); air freshener ($2.17); a Mother's Day gift for one of the agents (a $30 floral arrangement); English grammar book ($18).

Montoto. González had recently called the agent to tip him off about another exile drug smuggling operation, but since Roque had initially introduced him to Montoto, the agent was bound to be suspicious once Roque "defected" back to Cuba. The important thing, Ruiz told González, was to avoid being obvious. Not that anyone had to remind him of that. René González hadn't survived more than five years in the belly of the American beast by being obvious.

Miami, January 15, 1996

José Basulto was clearly enjoying himself. "Let's just say we take responsibility for those leaflets," he told a reporter from the Miami *Herald* two days after reports that thousands of pamphlets urging Cubans to rise up against Fidel Castro mysteriously dropped from the sky onto the streets of Havana. "But I cannot give you any of the technical details of how we did it," he added.[3] Nudge, nudge, wink, wink. Basulto wasn't about to take public credit for doing again what the FAA already wanted to suspend his pilot's licence for. But he wasn't about to deny it either.

Basulto acknowledged he had copies of the leaflets in question (with messages like "Your Neighbors Feel the Same Way You Do — Change Things Now"); that he knew half a million leaflets had been printed; that they had been dropped from the skies above Havana at about 2 p.m.; that it was raining then; that the skies over the city were dark and cloudy; and that the Cuban military hadn't fired on... whoever did the dropping.[4] So did that mean...? Basulto simply smiled.

Later that day, a Radio Marti interviewer asked him why he thought Cuba's military hadn't retaliated against this latest incursion, which was, in fact, the second in four days. Basulto's reply seemed as much as a challenge to any Cubans who might be listening as a direct answer. "That is the same question that our compatriots on the Island should ask when they fear the Cuban government," he said. "We have been willing to take personal risks for this. They should be willing to do the same. They should see that this regime isn't invulnerable, that Castro isn't impenetrable, that many things are within our reach to be done."

---

3. Basulto would later claim Brothers planes dropped the leaflets from "13 miles off the coast of Havana" and that they were "carried by the winds" into Havana.

4. During his testimony in the trial of the Five, Basulto acknowledged not only making the flight but also testified he and fellow BTTR pilots Arnaldo Iglesias and Billy Schuss had made a pre-flight videotape they left behind in case they were forced to land in Cuba. "If anything happens, being that we might be made to land in Cuba, we would like to clarify that, under pressure, any human being may say anything against his beli[efs]," Basulto declared. Iglesias, who explained he had a habit of blinking his eyes when he talked, said he was "going to make a great effort not to blink. Which means that what I'm saying, I don't really feel." Schuss declared he would do the opposite. If captured, he would "blink continually."

What about the American government, the interviewer asked? What did he think about its lack of response to his… er, *this* latest overflight? Basulto's reply was dismissive. "The United States," he said, "is on vacation." Finally. Something Basulto and the Cuban government agreed on.

Havana, January 19, 1996

The two men were both old baseball players, each better in their remembering than in reality. Bill Richardson, the United States ambassador to the United Nations, was fond of telling people he'd been drafted straight out of college baseball by the Kansas City A's. And Fidel Castro didn't do much to squelch the story that he'd once been invited to try out by a major league baseball team. While neither story could survive a reality check,[5] they did both like to watch — and talk — baseball. Which was why taking in a Cuban Baseball League game together tonight seemed a fitting way to end Richardson's three-day visit to Havana.

The idea of face-to-face meetings between Castro and Bill Clinton's closest confidante on foreign policy reflected the recent relative warming in relations between the two countries. Last spring, Ricardo Alarcón and Peter Tarnoff had secretly negotiated a new immigration accord, eliminating one of the key irritants between Washington and Havana. In early October, the White House okayed plans by 45 business owners, including flamboyant developer Donald Trump and Time-Warner chair Gerald Levin, to travel to Havana to discuss future American investment. That same day, Clinton himself announced he was relaxing restrictions on travel to Cuba, allowing U.S. news organizations to set up shop there and increasing public funding for non-governmental groups pushing "democracy and the free flow of ideas" in Cuba.

None of it had been easy. Even before the immigration accords, two right-wing Republican politicians — Congress Representative Dan Burton and Senator Jessie Helms, the chair of the Foreign Relations Committee — introduced the Cuban Liberty and Democratic Solidarity Act (the Helms-Burton bill) to tighten the screws on Cuba and make life more difficult, even for foreign companies doing business in Cuba. With the Cuban American National Foundation riding lobbying herd, the Helms-Burton bill had already sailed through the House of Representatives by a vote of 294 to 130.

---

5. According to the Albuquerque *Journal,* which investigated the Richardson story in 2005, there is no record of Richardson having been drafted by the A's or any other team. Richardson, who'd publicly claimed for years that he had, issued a statement acknowledging that, "after researching the matter… I came to the conclusion I was not drafted by the A's." And Yale professor Roberto Gonzales, who has studied Latin baseball, debunked persistent reports that Fidel was offered a tryout by either the Yankees or the Washington Senators. "It is a fabrication by an American journalist whose name is now lost," he wrote in an online posting, adding that the story "is never told in Cuba because everyone would know it to be false."

Senior administration officials were doing their best to stiffen the spine of resistance to the bill as it worked its way through the Senate, and they knew a positive gesture from the Cuban government might convince the wavering. The idea for the Havana tête-à-tête had first been broached at a private meeting between Richardson and Castro during the Cuban leader's visit to the United Nations in New York in late October. When word of the talks leaked out, Miami's exile leadership waxed predictably apoplectic. Mas Canosa took to the airwaves to denounce this "negotiating behind the backs of Americans and Cuban exiles" as "shameful." Clinton's spokesperson was forced to deny a newspaper report that the administration had told Castro Clinton would veto Helms-Burton if the Cubans agreed to release some political prisoners.

That's not to say political prisoners weren't discussed. During his first night in Havana, Richardson and Castro had stayed up until two in the morning talking about all sorts of irritants. The Americans brought up political prisoners — Richardson handed Castro a list of 10 prisoners of conscience the U.S. wanted released — as well as human rights, extradition of American fugitives in Cuba and reducing fees for Cuban emigrants to the U.S.

Castro had countered that he wanted to talk about Brothers to the Rescue. Castro was convinced the U.S. administration could clip Basulto's wings if it really wanted to. American officials responded that, given constitutional protections against "prior restraint," grounding Basulto wasn't as easy as ordering it.

Now, on Richardson's final night in Havana, the two men had decided to forget the issues that divided them and enjoy a baseball game. "We talked an hour about baseball," Richardson would recall. "I said, 'You have no pitching here. You have great hitters.'"

But Castro eventually returned to Brothers and their continuing provocations. Castro, Richardson explained, "warned me about these overflights, and he wanted us to do something about them." Though Richardson would later insist the notion of a deal to stop the Brothers was "total fiction, fantasy," the Cubans came away from the meetings convinced the Americans had agreed to stop the overflights. Havana even began making plans to release a small number of political prisoners as a sign of good faith.

But Castro wasn't prepared to take everything on faith. He quietly gave the commander of the Cuban Air Force and Air Defences the go-ahead if there were any future incursions — "if such a situation arose again, to decide personally on military interception and shooting down, if so required."

Washington, January 22, 1996

The early morning email from Cecilia Capestany, a manager in the Federal Aviation Administration's Office of International Aviation, was addressed to half a dozen FAA and other officials who were trying to prevent the Brothers to the Rescue incursions into Cuban airspace from continuing. "In light of last week's intrusion," she wrote, "this latest overflight can only be seen as further taunting of the Cuban government. [The State Department] is increasingly concerned about Cuban reactions to these flagrant violations. They are also asking from the FAA, 'What is this agency doing to prevent/deter these actions?' … Worst case scenario is that one of these days the Cubans will shoot down one of these planes and the FAA better have all its ducks in a row." It was signed "Cecilia."

Miami, Late January 1996

The FBI — like Cuban intelligence — seemed to prefer fast food joints for clandestine meets. And why not? They were inevitably busy, noisy public gathering areas where it was easy to talk without arousing suspicion. Besides, the food was inexpensive, no small matter for budget-conscious bureaucracies in both countries. Today, FBI Special Agent Alex Barbeito was at a Burger King near the Tamiami airport to meet a potential drug informant named René González. The month before, González, who was working as a flight instructor at the airport for Aero Club International, had confided to Oscar Montoto, his Roque-connected FBI contact, that he'd been approached by some people to fly to Honduras to pick up a shipment of cocaine. He was uncomfortable with the idea, he told Montoto. Montoto passed the info on to Barbeito, an agent with the drug squad.

Barbeito listened as González explained how a guy named Hector Viamonte, whom he'd known through PUND, had asked him to transport the drugs. Would González be prepared to testify if the case ever went to trial, Barbeito asked? He would. Would he wear a wire? González wasn't keen. What would happen if they caught him, he asked? Barbeito decided to leave that issue for another day. For now, he simply explained the rules of the informant game: González could not use any unlawful techniques to get information; he couldn't participate in any acts of violence; and he had to report any contact with Viamonte to Barbeito. González agreed. Barbeito said he would do up the paperwork, and René González would become a paid FBI informant — provided, of course, his information proved useful.[6]

René González wasn't concerned whether his information would help the FBI convict Viamonte for drug dealing — though he would be happy if it did — but rather in making sure Viamonte and his exile friends couldn't use their illicit drug profits to buy more weapons to attack Cuba. If he could help the FBI do its job and help Cuban State Security protect his country at the same time, it seemed a win-win.

---

6. González's information didn't lead directly to an indictment — the planned drug deal fell through — but Viamonte was convicted in December 1997 of conspiracy to import and distribute close to 3,000 pounds of cocaine and sentenced to nine years in prison.

Miami, January 27, 1996

Juan Pablo Roque wasn't keen on stealing a Brothers to the Rescue aircraft to make his escape more dramatic, but the CP — as it had made clear in its most recent messages — was "interested in this variable. Analyze again with him." Ever since he'd arrived back from Havana, Gerardo Hernández had been delicately attempting to navigate this difference of opinion between Roque and headquarters. It wasn't easy — and not just because of Roque. Manny Ruiz was still in Miami, still in Hernández's apartment, still controlling the decoding disk Hernández needed to send and receive his messages to Havana. Not that there was much he could do about that. Ruiz, a major in the State Security hierarchy, outranked Hernández, a mere lieutenant. Ruiz seemed to be busy with projects of his own for the CP — and with the decoder disk.

Despite the limitations, Hernández did his best to convey Havana's arguments to his recalcitrant agent, including suggestions that he could ask to "borrow" a plane "to pick up his children."

"Give [Roque] the argument that plane will not be stolen nor violent action be taken," the CP made clear. "It can be any BTTR plane. Look for opportune moment. Travel alone. That way we can denounce BTTR's role with spectacular proof and raise the spirit of the population facing BTTR's impunity," the message from the CP concluded, adding one final argument designed to appeal directly to Roque's ego. "It will be the culmination of the heroic activity carried out by a loyal pilot."

Hernández had trotted out that too, but Roque hadn't budged. And the window for arguing over details was closing quickly. Both Hernández and the CP would need to sort out final logistics soon if they were to get Roque back to Havana in time for his son's birthday. "Inform extremely urgent [Roque's] decision," the CP messaged finally. Hernández already knew what the decision was. He just had to get the decoding disk back from Ruiz to convey it to Havana.

Miami, January 29, 1996

Venecia wasn't the only Cuban operation targeting Basulto and Brothers to the Rescue. There was also Scorpion. On January 29, Havana sent a high frequency message to Manny Ruiz in Miami: "Superior headquarters," it said, "approved Operation Scorpion in order to perfect the confrontation of counter-revolutionary actions of Brothers to the Rescue."

What perfecting the confrontation might actually mean in practical terms wasn't clear from the rest of the message, but Havana informed Ruiz it needed to know "without a doubt" when Basulto was flying a Brothers mission, "whether or not activity of dropping of leaflets or violation of air space." The CP also wanted its agents on the ground — Roque and González

— to "report urgently on the types of aircraft BTTR would be flying, their registration numbers, pilots, passengers, flight plans, etc."

Given recent communication snafus, the CP also instructed Ruiz to "establish more than one route" to contact Roque. "Avoid arguments [Roque] used regarding confusion he had about your beeper number." The CP was clearly losing patience with Roque for all sorts of reasons, not the least of which had been his excuse for failing to respond to a message from Ruiz earlier in the month. "We were surprised," Havana noted icily, "that [Roque] would confuse your beeper number at such an important time."

Havana — apparently having forgotten that González had stopped flying with BTTR more than two years before, though he was still supplying intelligence gleaned around the hangar — instructed Ruiz to tell both González and Roque to "find excuse not to fly" if asked. "If they cannot avoid it," the CP added, González should "transmit over the airplane radio the slogan for the July 13 Viva Cuba, and [Roque] should call his neighbor Amelia and tell her he will call her on Wednesday. If he cannot call, he should say over the radio, 'Long live Brothers to the Rescue and Democracia.'"[7] Something was clearly about to happen. But what?

Miami, February 1996

While they tackled their various assignments to smooth Roque's return to Havana, Ruiz and Hernández also had to deal with more routine matters, including the hand-off of a new husband-and-wife agent team activated while Hernández was on vacation. Like René González and Tony Guerrero, Joseph Santos had been born in America but returned to Cuba as a child with his parents after the revolution. An electrical engineering professor, Santos was recruited into Cuban intelligence in 1984. After passing the usual battery of physical, medical and psychological tests, he'd begun his training in a Santa Clara work house, juggling his day duties at the university with two to three hours a day of instruction in the secret arts. He learned, for example, how to

---

7. Two weeks later, those same instructions — adopting almost precisely the same wording as the original and picking up on Havana's mistaken notion González was still flying with Brothers to the Rescue — were sent to René González. That message, which was signed using the code names for both Ruiz and Gerardo Hernández, would become a critical piece of evidence in the "conspiracy to commit murder" indictment against Hernández three years later. But Hernández insisted in a 2010 affidavit that he was never part of Operation Scorpion. "I did not write or send the message of February 12, 1996," he wrote. "I do not know why my name was added to that document as a signatory." He pointed out he would have been well aware that González was no longer a Brothers pilot and noted that the message refers to González using the code name Iselin, which he never used. Although the affidavit didn't specifically say Ruiz wrote the message, Hernández also explained that "it wasn't until early March that [Ruiz] was directed to turn over the decoding program to me."

photograph and develop documents or reports so the resulting image — no larger than a square millimetre — could be embedded, undetected, inside an ordinary object and sent back to headquarters; how to distinguish specific number sequences in high speed Morse code radio messages and translate their meaning using code books; how to encrypt and decrypt messages using special computer programs and modems. After Santos married Amarylis Silverio García, who had a degree in mathematical cybernetics, Cuban intelligence trained her too.

In 1993 — nearly a decade after he'd been recruited — Santos was given his first assignment. He and Amarylis were to relocate to Puerto Rico, settle there and "develop whatever intelligence they would request of me," particularly relating to what was going on at American military bases that would likely be used in any attack against Cuba. As part of the development of his legend, Santos was initially sent to New Jersey and instructed to wait there for further instructions. In May 1995, he was contacted by a man who gave him the correct "sign and countersign" passwords. The man introduced himself as Manolo, but his real name was Nilo Hernández, one half of another husband-and-wife team Gerardo Hernández was supervising. Manolo handed him a laptop, $2,000 and a collection of Puerto Rican employment ads. He told him he was to fly there to look for work and, once he found it, to move to Puerto Rico with his wife.

Two months later Manolo contacted him again. There'd been a change in plans. Santos, his wife and their daughter were to move to Miami instead. The reason was obvious. In March 1995, Bill Clinton had announced that the Department of Defense had chosen Miami-Dade as the new headquarters of the U.S. Southern Command. Southcom — which was responsible for military planning and action in Central and South America and the Caribbean, including Cuba — had previously been headquartered in Panama. The decision to relocate was partly a reflection of Miami's growing importance in Latin America, and partly a bit of political and economic pump-priming in the wake of the closure of Homestead Air Force Base and the devastation wrought by 1992's Hurricane Andrew.

To the Cuban government, however, the move not only meant Southcom's headquarters would suddenly be 10 times closer to its shores but also — and even more ominously — Miami's anti-Castro exile community would be in a much better position to influence senior American military officials. "If there's a coup in Haiti, a toppling of the communist government in Cuba, a need to capture Panama's leader and charge him with drug trafficking, or any other situation in Latin America and the Caribbean that requires U.S. intervention," the Miami *Herald* exulted, combining recent real history with wishful thinking, "the shots will be called from this new command center." Although the move wasn't scheduled to actually happen until late 1997,

Cuban intelligence knew it would need to plant its spy seeds early if they were to flower when needed.

Despite their unquestioned ability to penetrate exile groups, the Cubans had not been nearly so successful when it came to gathering military information. Agents like Tony Guerrero, whose assignment was the Boca Chica Naval Air Station in Key West, provided information that was mostly either publicly available, like base newspaper reports, or easily accessible, like the number of jets on the base, which could be observed from a nearby highway with the naked eye. But even mundane public information might ultimately prove to be valuable; it would certainly be bisected, dissected and desiccated by analysts back in Havana in order to discover clues to American intentions toward Cuba.

Joseph Santos and his wife's first assignment was simply to settle into their new lives in Miami. Manolo, whom the couple now knew by his real name, Nilo, hired Amarylis to do "legitimate" work at an advertising company he owned, and Joseph eventually found work at a factory. Soon after they arrived, Nilo introduced them to Manny Ruiz, whose job would be to babysit them until Gerardo Hernández returned from vacation. Initially, they mostly observed — and provided cover. For example, Santos, his wife and daughter accompanied Ruiz on what was supposed to look like a "regular tourist trip" to Key West so Ruiz could videotape an aerostatic balloon used to transmit Radio Marti signals to Cuba. While they were there, Ruiz also dispatched Santos and family to spend some time at a children's park while he met "a brother."

When Gerardo Hernández returned to Miami in late January, it was time to transfer their supervision to him. Hernández and Ruiz met with Santos at a Pollo Tropical near the airport.[8] Ruiz introduced Hernández. When he filed his reports, Santos was told, he would address him by his code name, Giro. Santos wasn't told Hernández's real name. The Santos's own code names were Mario and Julia.

This first meeting was just a getting-to-know-you session. Since the CP hadn't yet come up with specific Southcom-related assignments, Hernández asked his new agents to handle some seemingly routine but important tasks, including making a comparative analysis of using FedEx, UPS and the U.S. postal system for deliveries. Now that everyone else seemed to be using the mails to send computer disks, the CP was considering doing the same rather than continuing to personally hand them back and forth. It just needed to know which company was most efficient — and inexpensive.

---

8. While Santos testified during the trial of the Five that he believed this meeting took place in November or December of 1995, Hernández was in Havana at the time. It's much more likely it took place in late January or early February, after his return.

Havana, February 1996

Eugene Carroll understood immediately he was being asked to deliver a message — and that the message was urgent. The retired rear-admiral-turned-American-security-expert had spent the first week of February in Cuba as part of a U.S. delegation, which also included other retired American military and foreign service officers and a retired U.S. ambassador to Latin America. They'd visited the Cuban naval base at Cienfuegos, a nuclear site at Juraguá, several military training sites and the defence college, and met twice with senior Cuban military officers, including the chief of staff of the Cuban Armed Forces.

The official agenda called for the two sides to discuss the future of Cuba-U.S. relations in the post-Soviet era, but the Cubans kept bringing up the Brothers' overflights. At one point, Cuban Air Force Brigadier General Arnaldo Tamayo Méndez[9] complained that, despite Cuban protests, the flights had continued. "Even worse," Carroll would remember him saying, "the pilots had gone on television in Florida to boast they were doing this, and this proved that Cuba was defenseless, weak, impotent."

Tamayo looked at Carroll. "What," he asked pointedly, "would be the reaction of your military if we shot one of those planes down. We can, you know."

Carroll was taken aback. When he and his group returned to Washington, they arranged to meet with State Department and Defense Intelligence Agency officials to brief them on their trip, but especially the Cuban warning, which "we thought was intended for us to carry back to Washington." Carroll delivered the message. But had it been received? And, perhaps more importantly, could the recipients — even if they wanted to — prevent what appeared to be a looming confrontation?

Havana, February 16, 1996

Yet another meeting at the Swiss embassy to deliver yet another diplomatic note. The Americans had called this meeting to formally express the FAA's gratitude to the Cubans for having allowed one of their air traffic coordinators to testify before it. But now, the message explained, "the FAA has requested the following additional information… the altitude at which [Basulto's] aircraft penetrated the Havana flight information region; the dangerous zones located within the Havana flight information region; and the altitude at which the aircraft penetrated the Havana air traffic control zone."

More than seven months after Basulto's July 13 flight, the FAA was still gathering information — and only about this earlier flight! When would its investigators get around to looking into last month's incursion? Or next month's?

---

9. In 1980, Tamayo had been the first Cuban, first Hispanic and first black person to travel in space, spending nearly eight days aboard the Soyuz 38 Soviet space mission.

WHAT LIES ACROSS THE WATER

Havana, February 17, 1996

Now that the final decision had been made — Juan Pablo Roque would return to Havana by commercial aircraft — Gerardo Hernández had plenty on his plate. For starters, the CP wanted another copy — or better still, the original — of the video Roque's wife Ana had taken at his book launch. The copy he'd sent was "mutilated in several places," Havana reported. The CP was keen to show the video at Roque's press conference to embarrass both Basulto and CANF members who'd attended. Which was why Hernández had been directed to make a second videotape, showing Roque entering and leaving CANF headquarters.

Roque's final escape plan involved driving from Miami to Fort Lauderdale on either February 23 or 27, boarding a flight to Tampa, and then flying on to Cancun on Northwest Airlines. Manny Ruiz would purchase that ticket using the false name Roque was to assume. Hernández had already provided Roque with that character's legend so he could study and appear to be who he would claim to be. A senior intelligence officer from the CP would be standing by in Cancun waiting to provide Roque with a second set of false documents for the last leg of his journey home. Operation Venecia was going to be a propaganda coup.

Miami, February 20, 1996

Cuban State Security wasn't alone in wanting to "perfect the confrontation." On Valentine's Day, José Basulto had staged a showy press conference at La Ermita de la Caridad, the Cuban exile shrine on Bay Biscayne, to announce Brothers' financial support for a proposed gathering of dissident groups in Havana later in the month — and to take yet another potshot at Washington. The donation was destined for Concilio Cubano, a four-month-old coalition of 131 pro-democracy groups inside Cuba. The organization, which was demanding immediate amnesty for all of the island's political prisoners as well as a gradual transition to multi-party democracy, had recently applied to the Cuban government for permission to stage a three-day national conference in Havana beginning February 24. The date was not coincidental. It marked the beginning of island-wide insurrections in 1895, which signalled the start of Cuba's final war of independence from Spain.

Concilio's objectives — not to mention its cheekiness in citing Articles 54 and 63 of Cuba's own constitution, allowing peaceful assembly, to justify its gathering — had caught the fancy of many in Miami's exile community. "Of all the opposition organizations that have sprung up in Cuba in the last two decades," the *Herald* editorialized, "the Concilio has the greatest potential for kindling massive resistance to Castro's thuggish rule."

Basulto was eager to show his support too and, of course, to get publicity for Brothers. That had been the main reason he'd called a press conference

— to present one of the dissident group's leaders with a cheque for what the newspaper described as an "undisclosed amount" of money to underwrite the conference. The meeting with the press also gave Basulto another opportunity to attack the U.S. government. Brothers had applied to the Treasury Department for the licence required to transfer money to a Cuban non-government organization, he said, but hadn't received a response. So Basulto — who also still had his pilot's licence, thanks to Washington's slow, grinding bureaucratic gears — decided to ignore the licence and deliver the money anyway. "The process of change in Cuba cannot wait for the government of the United States," he declared.

The actual amount of the cheque — $2,000 — was relatively small, which may have been why it was undisclosed. But it created anxiety in both Havana and Washington, and not just at the Treasury. Joseph Sullivan, the head of the U.S. Interest Section in the Cuban capital, called Richard Nuccio, Clinton's special advisor on Cuba, to express concern that the Cuban government would use publicity about Basulto's donation to claim "the dissident movement inside Cuba was nothing more than a creature of the exile community and the CIA and the U.S. government… and be used… against members of Concilio."

Sullivan was right on both counts. On February 19, a senior official in Cuba's Ministry of the Interior personally visited the home of one of Concilio's leaders to inform him the government had denied the group permission to hold its meeting. According to Concilio supporters, the cancellation was followed by "a wave of repression against members of [Concilio], which has included police raids on some homes, the detention of numerous dissidents and the harassment of others."

Cuba's crackdown brought instant international condemnation — and not just from the U.S. government and the Miami exile community. The European Union, Amnesty International, Americas Watch and even American moderates like Wayne Smith, a former head of the U.S. Interest Section who'd been lobbying to end sanctions against Cuba, all weighed in against the Cuban action. For its part, the Cuban government countered — as Sullivan had anticipated it would — that the Concilio conference had been "organized, conceived, sponsored and financed by the government of the United States." So much for rapprochement. José Basulto's press conference had had its desired effect.

Miami, February 21, 1996

René González had asked for tonight's meeting. González was seeking José Basulto's advice on how to get two Cuban-American politicians — Ileana Ros-Lehtinen and Lincoln Diaz-Balart — to write letters to the State Department supporting his application to bring his wife and daughter to Miami from

Havana. It was both a real request and another way to establish his exile *bona fides*. But Basulto was distracted, angry. He'd offered to let the Miami-based Concilio organizers use his office for an upcoming meeting, he told González, but they'd "slammed the door" in his face. He was still not part of the *exilio* in-crowd.

As Basulto ranted, his phone rang. It was Carlos Costa, Brothers' chief of pilots, asking about an upcoming mission that hadn't yet been announced. Basulto was discreet but he made the point that all the Brothers aircraft would take part in the operation.

As soon as he got back to his house that night, González prepared a report for Hernández. "I have the feeling," he wrote, "Basulto is planning something expressly for the Concilio meeting."

Miami, February 23, 1996

The squeak of his shoes on the tile floor in their bedroom woke her. Ana Margarita squinted over at the alarm clock on the night table. Three o'clock in the morning. Then she remembered. The day before, J.P. had told her he was going to Key West for three days. On a business trip. Something about transporting a boat for a friend. He'd make $2,000 for his troubles, he said, money they could definitely use. Still… She could see him picking up the vinyl suitcase preparing to leave. Ana Margarita sat up in bed, caught her husband's eye, motioned for him to sit down on the bed beside her.

"J.P.," she said, "you don't love me."

He'd looked puzzled. "Why do you say that?"

"Because you're leaving me all alone." It was a joke, though she would miss him. Juan Pablo Roque didn't say a word. He kissed her on the cheek and walked out the door. Forever.

When Ana Margarita woke a few hours later, she noticed J.P. had left his cell phone charger behind. After she got to work, she tried to call him. His phone was turned off. When she got home that night, she looked in his clothes closet. It was totally empty, except for his wallet and all his credit cards. His wallet and his credit cards?

Washington, February 23, 1996

Cecilia Capestany, the FAA manager liaising with State on the Basulto file, hit the Send button on her computer. It was Friday at 2:40 p.m. This email was entitled "Cuba Alert," and marked "Urgent." "As you might be aware by now," Capestany began her latest message, "Cuba's crackdown on dissidents has resulted in a number of arrests in Havana and the cancellation of a meeting that was to have been convened by the umbrella dissident organization Concilio Cubano tomorrow." Brothers to the Rescue had announced it would make a humanitarian mission over the Straits of Florida on Saturday to mark the 101st anniversary of "the rallying cry of José Marti that began the War of Independence" — and to express solidarity with those arrested.

It "would not be unlikely," Capestany wrote, for Brothers to the Rescue to make another "unauthorized flight into Cuban air space tomorrow," and it would be even more unlikely for the Cuban government "to show restraint in an unauthorized flight scenario this time around. I have reiterated to State that the FAA cannot PREVENT flights such as this potential one," she concluded, "but that we will alert our folks in case it happens, and we will document it as best we can for compliance/enforcement purposes."

Over at the White House, Richard Nuccio, the administration's point man on Cuba, had asked the FAA to issue another specific warning to Basulto not to taunt the Cubans yet again. But a senior FAA official "rebuffed our concerns and said if they happen to run into him, they would mention it," Nuccio explained later. "But they would not make a special effort, that [Basulto] was already quite annoyed and they didn't want to bother him further." Alarmed, Nuccio left a number of phone messages for Sandy Berger, Clinton's deputy national security advisor, but Berger didn't return his calls.

Finally at quarter to seven, Nuccio, who was scheduled to attend a performance by the Cuban National Ballet Company in Washington that night,[10] emailed Berger. Nuccio warned another incursion "may finally trip the Cubans toward an attempt to shoot down or force down the planes." Nuccio didn't get a response from Berger until the next day — after the Cuban government had blown two Brothers to the Rescue aircraft out of the sky and triggered an international incident.

Over the Florida Straits, February 24, 1996

The sky was cloudless as the three Cessnas lifted off from Opa-locka Airport at 1:15 p.m.

José Basulto, as usual, was piloting Seagull One (N2506 Sierra), with veteran spotter Arnaldo Iglesias and two first-time observers, husband-and-wife anti-Castro activists Andres and Sylvia Iriondo. Mario de la Pena, 24, who'd been one of the Brothers activists involved in last July's flyover of Havana, piloted Seagull Mike (N5485 Sierra). His spotter was a 45-year-old exile militant named Armando Alejandre. The year before, Alejandre had been arrested twice: once at a demonstration outside the Cuban Interest Section in Washington and again in Key West when he smashed in the glass front door of a building being used "by a group recognized by the Cuban government." He'd recently been elected as a member of a Miami-based Concilio support

---

10. It was the first performance in Washington by the troupe in 14 years. Nuccio, who described such cultural contacts as "another important aspect of our Cuba policy," said he "wanted to be there to underscore that the administration was very pleased that this cultural exchange was taking place."

group, as had Pablo Morales, the 24-year-old spotter aboard the third plane, Seagull Charlie (N2456 Sierra). Two years before, Morales had himself been a rafter rescued by Brothers; today he was training to be a pilot. Seagull Charlie's actual pilot was Carlos Costa, Brothers 29-year-old chief pilot.

"Safe flight," the tower radioed as the planes headed south.

"We will need it," Basulto responded.

Before they left, the Brothers pilots, as required, filed their flight plan with the FAA, which in turn had passed it on to Cuban air traffic controllers. The flight plan called for the aircraft to travel south from Opa-locka to the northern edge of Cuba's 12-mile territorial limit near Varadero, turn west along the coast to a point northwest of Havana, then head north back to Florida. It was supposed to be a triangular rafters' search mission. Not that any Brothers flight had actually spotted a rafter in months.[11]

Without notifying either the FAA or air traffic control, however, the planes actually changed their flight plan in mid-air, heading straight toward Havana instead. Shortly before 3 p.m., the planes approached the 24th parallel, an area that is outside Cuba's territorial limit but where air traffic control switches from Florida to Havana.

"Good afternoon, Havana Center," Basulto radioed. "November 2-5-0-6 salutes you. Please, we are crossing parallel 24 in five minutes and we will maintain about three to four hours in your area."

"Received."

"For your information, Havana Center," Basulto continued, "our area of operations are north of Havana today. So we will be in your area and in contact with you. And a cordial greeting from Brothers to the Rescue and its president, Jose Basulto, who is speaking to you."

"OK. Received, sir," Havana Center replied evenly, then added: "I inform you that the zone north of Havana is active. You run danger by penetrating that side of north 24." The Cuban government had already announced it was planning air and navy exercises in that area between February 21 and 28 and had declared the area a "military danger zone." Though other aircraft aren't banned from an active zone, most pilots avoid putting themselves in even incidental danger.

Not Basulto. "We are conscious we are in danger each time we cross the area south of 24," he told Havana Center, "but we are ready to do it. It is our right as free Cubans."

"Then, we copy information, sir," Havana replied.

A few minutes later, Basulto radioed again, this time to report he had reached the outer edge of Cuban airspace north of Havana and was proceed-

---

11. During the trial of the Cuban Five, Basulto testified that after the change in U.S. policy regarding the rafters, Brothers flew 1,800 consecutive missions without spotting a single rafter.

ing eastward. "A beautiful day and Havana looks very good from where we are," he noted. "A cordial greeting to you, to all the people of Cuba, on behalf of Brothers to the Rescue."

"Havana received."

By this point, the Brothers' Cessnas weren't the only planes in the air. At 2:55 p.m. — acting on Fidel Castro's standing order to shoot down the next plane to violate its airspace — Cuba's military authorized two MiG-29 jets to take off from the Cuban Air Force base at San Antonio de los Baños in search of the Cessnas.

They found them. At 3:19 p.m., one of the MiGs, using the call sign zero-eight, sighted Seagull Charlie, the plane piloted by Carlos Costa. "Target lock-on, authorize us," pilot Alberto Perez Perez radioed his ground controller. When he didn't hear an immediate response, he ratcheted up his urgency. "It's a Cessna 3-37. That one, that one, that one!... That's the one! Authorize us, damn it."

Seven seconds later, the controller responded: "Fire."

Perez apparently didn't hear him. "Authorize us, damn it, we have it!"

"Zero-eight... Authorized to destroy," the controller repeated.

Meanwhile, inside Basulto's Cessna, Arnaldo Eglesias had spotted the MiGs. "They are going to shoot!" he declared urgently.

Basulto had seen too. He let out a high-pitched laugh. "They're going to shoot at us!" he shouted. Then: "They shot at us. Is that a flare?"

It wasn't.

"First shot," pilot Perez reported to his controller from the cockpit of his MiG. The heat-seeking missile had found its target. "We got him, damn it! We got him!... Cojones, we got him! Fuck! This one won't fuck around anymore."

Down below in Seagull Mike, Mario de la Pena tried unsuccessfully to contact Costa. Finally he radioed Basulto: "Hey One, have you heard from Charlie?"

"Negative.... Do you see that smoke to my left?"

"I don't see anything now. I did see smoke."

"Do you see smoke below the MiG?" Basulto persisted.

"I didn't see the MiG," de la Pena responded. "I saw smoke and a flare."

Seven minutes later, Perez locked in again, this time on de la Pena's plane. Another direct hit. Another plume of smoke. "The other is destroyed, the other is destroyed," he radioed. "Fatherland or death, coño. The other is down also."

Basulto saw the second fireball, knew now it was no flare.

"Charlie, is that you?" he asked after what sounded like a burst of static. "Seagull Mike?" A few seconds later, he tried again. "Seagull Mike?" There was no response. "Going to Opa-locka, to our base, to Opa-locka," Basulto announced finally. But by now, there was no one left to hear.

Basulto dropped his aircraft down to skim just above the waves in order to avoid Cuban radar, turned off his transponder and headed northwest to Florida, hoping to avoid any pursuing MiGs. An hour and a half later, he radioed Miami air traffic control: "We are inbound Opa-locka, some 30 miles west of Key West at this time, and we're in the process of reporting a possible emergency with two aircraft. The emergency is two overdue aircraft that we think we have lost some 30 miles north of Havana. That's Brothers to the Rescue. Two aircraft. Smoke was seen in the vicinity of the area where we were tracking north of us, and we also saw two MiGs in the air."

Near... or Inside Cuba's Territorial Airspace, February 24, 1996

After more than seven months of formal and informal complaints and threats from Havana to Washington, not to forget an equal number of months' worth of official and unofficial complaints and threats from American officials to Brothers to the Rescue, Brothers had once again flown into Cuban airspace. This time, the Cubans had blown them out of the sky.

But had Brothers' aircraft actually flown into Cuban airspace? The Cubans claimed they had. Basulto claimed they hadn't. It should have been an easy argument to resolve. After Miami air traffic control routinely informed Havana that the Brothers planes were headed their way, Cuba's military air defence command immediately swung into action, alerting its five radar sites around Havana, along with the civilian one at Havana airport, to track the planes' flight paths.

They weren't the only ones with eyes on the planes. Knowing there was a possibility Brothers might violate Cuban air space again, the FAA had asked U.S. Customs and NORAD for radar data from their sites in Florida, and for a B-94 radar balloon that usually monitors drug flights to be sent aloft to see what it could see. Other American agencies, including the CIA, the Department of Defense's National Geospatial-Intelligence Agency, the National Ocean and Atmospheric Administration, NASA and the U.S. Geological Survey all also routinely monitor and photograph Cuba from above by satellite. They would almost certainly have had data from that day.

According to hand-plotted Cuban radar data tracking, the three planes were all well inside Cuba's 12-mile territorial limit — four to five miles off the coast and headed south to Havana — when the shooting began.

While U.S. electronic radar data indicated Basulto's plane did stray briefly just inside Cuban airspace at one point — 1.7 miles — it says all of the planes were in international air space and headed either north or east when Basulto first reported seeing a MiG at 3:21 p.m.

To complicate matters, Cuba claimed its civilian radar recording system wasn't working that day and said the MiG's on-board flight data recorder had been routinely erased over after the flight.

While the American "source radar information" was the same from each of its radar facilities, "the processing and presentation... at each of the agencies was different," and one of its surveillance radar recordings was also "not retained."

Both U.S. and Cuban authorities had tape recordings of the calls between the MiG pilots and ground control; the problem was that there were unexplained gaps in the Cuban recording — about a minute's worth of chatter about ships in the area that wasn't recorded.

The International Civil Aviation Authority, which is charged with investigating such incidents, would take four months to sort through what it called "significant differences... which could not be reconciled" between U.S. and Cuban evidence. In the end, the ICAO investigative team would choose to discount both countries' versions and opt instead to trust the recorded positions and track of a cruise ship called the *Majesty of the Seas,* which happened to be sailing near where the planes were shot down. Although it admitted there was "no corroborative evidence" to back up the cruise ship's declared position,[12] the ICAO investigative team would conclude, based on it, that both planes had been shot down "outside Cuban territorial airspace."[13]

The ICAO's report would have dramatic consequences. For starters, of course, it served as a heat-seeking air-to-air missile aimed directly at Cuba's stated justification for attacking the aircraft. In the view of many in Miami — and beyond — the fact the planes were shot down over international waters made the deaths of the airmen murder. The man many believed should be held accountable for those murders was the man who had been the exiles' nemesis for 37 years, Fidel Castro, who acknowledged he'd authorized his

---

12. Surprisingly, the ship's first officer acknowledged he based his conclusion about his ship's location — and therefore the location of the shootdown, on notes he wrote down on a piece of paper at the time rather than the vessel's electronic register. Brazilian writer Fernando Morais would later point out that the cruise ship's parent company, Royal Caribbean Cruise Lines, gave at least $25,000 to bankroll the Cuban American National Foundation.

13. For more than 15 years, the Cuban government has continued to insist the planes were shot down in Cuban airspace. During the trial of the Cuban Five, defence lawyers brought in expert witnesses to try to prove that the planes were, in fact, in Cuban territory when they were attacked. One expert witness — retired American Air Force colonel George Buchner — questioned the ICAO findings and suggested the only way to definitively determine exactly where the planes went down would be to examine photographs of the area that he claimed would have been taken that day by American satellites. "It is my expert opinion," Buchner testified, "that the [U.S.] government has satellite photos that would resolve this whole issue." Despite repeated freedom of information requests, the U.S. government has refused to release those images. "Several American agencies operate satellites that are constantly monitoring and photographing Cuba and the rest of the world," Cuban National Assembly President Ricardo Alarcón told me. "We don't have satellites; they have satellites. But they refuse to provide the images. Why?"

military to shoot down the next aircraft that violated Cuba's airspace.

But bringing Castro to account in a Miami courtroom, of course, would be virtually impossible. Failing Fidel, Gerardo Hernández would have to do. But that would come later. We're getting ahead of our story.

Miami, February 24, 1996

René González was reaching into the refrigerator when he heard the announcer on the TV in the next room break into regular programming with a news bulletin. González was staying with a Miami relative at the time and had just gotten home from work. *Brothers to the Rescue... planes... shot down... men missing...* "It was one of those moments," González would explain later, "you never forget what you were doing." He'd had no idea it was coming. He was in the process of moving and his computer was in storage, so he hadn't even received the no-fly message.[14] His first thought, as a pilot, was for those in the planes. He hoped they'd survived, but he knew the odds were against them. He also knew immediately there would be political consequences.[15]

Miami, February 25, 1996

Like René González, Gerardo Hernández found out about the shootdown from a television news report. Like González, he too was shocked.[16] He'd noted nothing in any of his recent messages from Havana to indicate the CP was planning — or even involved in planning — such a drastic, dramatic response. That's not to suggest Hernández didn't know shooting down the planes was a possibility — anything was possible, and the Cuban government had been publicly threatening to do so for months — but it had seemed more likely to him that "the planes would be forced down and the Brothers arrested... if anything happened at all."

Now that the worst had happened, however, Hernández didn't have time to debate the moral rights or wrongs of what his government had done. He was too busy monitoring Miami talk radio — sifting through the deluge of threats, demands, calls to send in the troops, to take out Castro, to bomb Cuba

---

14. González says he only learned about the message during his court case. "I was so far removed from BTTR," he told me, "that it made little sense. I can only assume that some overzealous guy from Havana sent it."

15. "I wouldn't deny that sometimes we questioned the Cuban government's decision" to shoot down the planes, González says, "but in the end I didn't lose sight of the big picture. In this story, Cuba is the party under siege."

16. "It surprises even me that I don't have many memories of that day," Hernández told me in a May 7, 2011, letter. "Of course they were important events but I didn't think it would be so important in my life... I'm sorry for the loss of lives and I understand the sorrow of the relatives, but my conscience is clean. First, because I didn't have anything to do with it, and, second, because Cuba has the right and duty to protect its citizens and its sovereignty."

into the stone age. He pored over every disconnected scrap in every news report he could read, watch or listen to in order to ferret out clues about what might happen next. How would Washington respond? Was the military at Boca Chica gearing up for an invasion? What about Brothers to the Rescue? The Cuban American National Foundation? Its paramilitary? The dozens of militant exile groups he and his agents had been watching for years? Would they use the shootdown to raise money, to raise an army, to launch attacks?

Hernández had been so busy gathering and urgently transmitting all of these disparate, disconnected bits and pieces of information back to Havana so intelligence analysts there could assess the threat and calibrate the government's response to it he'd barely slept in the last 48 hours.

He hadn't had time either to take satisfaction in, or even note, the fact that — in the middle of the shootdown crisis — Juan Pablo Roque had somehow arrived safely back in Havana and held his press conference. Operation Venecia had been a success.

Even if he'd had the time to think about it at the time, Gerardo Hernández could not have imagined that, in April 1999, seven months after having been charged for the intelligence gathering he was proud to acknowledge, American prosecutors would also charge him with conspiracy to commit murder for his "role" in the shootdown of the Brothers' planes. And that, as a result, he would be sentenced to a double-life-plus-15-year prison sentence. Or that U.S. officials would refuse to allow him to even see Adriana again for 15 years... and counting.

Miami, February 28, 1996

José Basulto speculated that Cuban authorities "may have threatened to hurt his son." Ana Margarita Roque agreed. Her husband, she insisted — even after Juan Pablo Roque had dismissed her ("Why should I tell my wife my intentions?") in a CNN interview from Havana — "did not go there of his own free will. I believe he was threatened." How else to explain the fact that, just last week, Roque had asked her not to wear any short nightgowns while his brother was visiting their house. "Does that sound like a man who is preparing to leave his wife?" she asked reporters.

On Monday night — two days after the shootdown of the Brothers' fliers, three days after he'd disappeared without a trace from Miami and five days after he'd picked up his last informant's payment from the FBI — Juan Pablo Roque had appeared on Cuban television. Though Roque's re-defection announcement had been planned as a public relations coup, the international furor over Cuba's shooting down of two unarmed aircraft made it seem far more like damage control.

Roque said he'd returned to Havana to expose "the true nature" of Brothers to the Rescue, which included training its pilots in paramilitary operations and weaponry as part of a larger plan to attack Cuba and its leaders. Last year, he said, he'd arranged to buy a Czech L29 military jet to train pilots on how to land and take off in Cuba. As far back as 1993, Roque said, Basulto had asked him for information he could use to attack electric transmission towers in Cienfuegos province.[17] The goal: "to provoke incidents that create greater tensions in the relations between Cuba and the United States."

Meanwhile, the FBI was in also full damage control mode. In his CNN interview, Roque claimed he had been "responsible with providing the FBI with intelligence about all the anti-Castro organizations, not just Brothers to the Rescue." He also insisted the FBI knew in advance the Cuban government would shoot down the planes. "FBI agent Oscar Montoto tells me on February 21st, 'Don't go on that mission because they are going to knock you out of the sky.' Agent Montoto told me not to go," he repeated.

The FBI categorically denied that. "There was no mention of any Cuban plans to shoot down Brothers to the Rescue aircraft or any other aircraft," declared Paul Philip, the Bureau's special agent in charge of the Miami field office.

But the FBI couldn't avoid admitting — especially after Roque disclosed Montoto's phone and beeper numbers on TV — that Roque had served as an informant since 1993 and been paid $6,722.40 for services rendered.

What was the FBI doing paying informers for information about the internal workings of legitimate humanitarian organizations like Brothers, reporters wanted to know? "We're not investigating organizations [like Brothers to the Rescue]," FBI spokesperson Paul Miller insisted. "What we're seeking is information about individuals who are planning to commit violations of the Neutrality Act, which is a criminal, federal offense."

The idea that the FBI had informers in their ranks came as old news to Miami exile organizations, of course, many of whom had been violating the Neutrality Act for decades — and mostly getting away with it. The reality that there might be spies among their numbers seemed a given.

"Greetings, compatriots," an Alpha 66 leader declared at the start of one meeting. "Greetings, too, to the agents of the FBI, of the CIA, of the Cuban G2."[18]

---

17. René González says he remembers Basulto talking about a similar plan in the fall of 1992. Basulto had summoned him to a meeting at his house to discuss the decision to remove him from Brothers' pilot roster. "During our conversation, he shows me a map of Cuba with the country's electric grid and consults me as to introducing some plane to blow up distribution towers," González recalled.

18. A generic American term referring to an Army intelligence officer, G2 in this case simply means a Cuban intelligence agent.

Havana, March 1, 1996

The coded shortwave message was brief and — mostly — clear. The Cuban Intelligence Directorate offered its Miami operatives "our profound recognition" for their roles in Operation German.

Operation German? German was Juan Pablo Roque's code name, so someone had probably mistakenly used that name when they meant to say Operation Venecia. The rest of the message seems to support that theory. "Everything turned out well," it went on to say. "The commander in chief visited [Roque] twice, being able to exchange the details of the operation. We have dealt the Miami right a hard blow, in which your role has been decisive." When the message was introduced as evidence in a Miami courtroom five years later, prosecutors would argue that the real subject for congratulation was Operation Scorpion — the plan to shoot down the Brothers to the Rescue aircraft — and Gerardo Hernández's "decisive" role in it.

Miami, March 4, 1996

"Why the hell didn't you call?" Alex Barbeito was angry. The FBI agent had been paging his new drug informant for close to a week, but René González hadn't called back. Barbeito had seen Roque giving out fellow agent Oscar Montoto's contact numbers on TV. Montoto had called later to warn Barbeito about the connection between Roque and González, and that González could be a Cuban agent too. When they did finally get together, González was calm. He was sorry, he said — he'd been in Sarasota all week painting his grandmother's house.

Barbeito wasn't placated. "Are you planning to hold your own press conference in Havana?" he asked, carefully watching González's reaction. "Because look, if you want to, I'll give you my home telephone number, my address...."

"How can you think like that about me?" González seemed genuinely upset. "I thought Roque was a friend. I trusted him. We all feel betrayed..." Eventually, they got around to what was supposed to be the subject of their meeting: an update on Hector Viamonte's plan to smuggle drugs into Florida from Honduras. That deal, González reported, had fallen through — for the moment.

Washington, March 12, 1996

"As I sign this bill into law," Bill Clinton declared solemnly, surrounded by an equally solemn group of 100 Cuban-American politicians and activists who'd jammed into a too-small briefing room at the Old Executive Office Building, "I do so in the name of the four men who were killed. In their memory, I will continue to do everything I can to help the tide of democracy that has swept our entire hemisphere finally, finally reach the shores of Cuba."

In less than three weeks, everything had changed. The White House was no longer talking, even quietly, about a tentative rapprochement with Havana. And it certainly wasn't lobbying to kill the Helms-Burton law in the Senate. In fact, in the immediate aftermath of the Brothers to the Rescue shootdown, Clinton had again "suspended charter flights to Cuba, restricted travel by Cuban officials in the United States, expanded the reach of Radio Martí and asked Congress to authorize compensation out of Cuba's blocked assets in the United States to the families of the men who were killed."

Clinton also committed himself to signing a Helms-Burton law that not only ratcheted up America's embargo but now also made it virtually impossible for any future American president to lift it without Congressional approval.[19]

The Cuban Liberty and Democratic Solidarity Act of 1996 extended the provisions of the failed 35-year-old embargo to blanket-ban foreign companies from "trafficking" in nationalized Cuban properties and barred offending senior company executives and stockholders — even their families! — from entering the United States. Getting ahead of itself, the law also imposed conditions for American recognition of a new Cuban government; it wouldn't recognize any "transitional" government that included Fidel or Raúl Castro, the legislation declared, and it wouldn't recognize any Cuban administration that refused to first compensate American corporations for property they lost in 1959.

Needless to say, the Cuban government wasn't amused. Clinton could "run out of ink" signing "absurd, stupid and condemned-to-failure" new laws, National Assembly president Alarcón declared.

The international community wasn't amused either. The European Union and most other countries that traded with Cuba — Britain, Canada, Mexico, Brazil, Argentina, etc. — condemned Helms-Burton as a violation of international law and sovereignty; some would even pass their own laws to negate its application.

Not that any of that mattered to those who stood and applauded on this day as Bill Clinton officially signed the anti-Castro, anti-Cuba Helms-Burton bill into American law. "I sign it with the certainty that it will send a powerful, unified message from the United States to Havana that the yearning of the Cuban people for freedom must not be denied," Clinton said. The

---

19. "Supporting the bill was good election-year politics in Florida," Clinton would later write in his autobiography, *My Life: The Presidential Years*, "but it undermined whatever chance I might have had if I won a second term to lift the embargo in return for positive changes within Cuba." Clinton also claimed he'd later learned, "indirectly, of course, that the shootdown was a mistake. Apparently [Castro] had issued earlier orders to fire on any aircraft that violated Cuban airspace and had failed to withdraw it when the Cubans knew the Brothers to the Rescue planes were coming."

signing was a solemn occasion, made more so by the presence of families of the dead Brothers to the Rescue airmen. Mario de la Pena's mother and Armando Alejandre's 18-year-old daughter both wept as Clinton talked about the downed fliers.

But it was also not lost on anyone that this was "Super Tuesday" in the American presidential election race and that Bill Clinton was gearing up for his re-election run.

"What a coincidence!" declared Republican Representative Ileana Ros-Lehtinen, who understood the legislation would be just as politically beneficial for Florida Republicans like herself. She crowed that the law would send "a chilling message to people who would go to that island with their millions of dollars and prop up that brutal dictator."

Not that anyone expected the dictator could hold out much longer. As the invited guests lined up to shake Clinton's hand — the special among them receiving one of the pens Clinton had used for the historic autograph-ing session — Miami *Herald* reporter Juan Tamayo asked Jorge Mas Canosa what he intended to do with his pen. As the law's behind-the-scenes chief orchestrator and lobbyist, the Cuban American National Foundation chair had certainly earned his pen. Mas Canosa didn't miss a beat. "Put it in my office in Havana," he replied.

"When?" Tamayo asked.

"Soon," he said.

Stinging the Wasp
May 22, 1996 – December 26, 1996

Miami, May 22, 1996

Running an intelligence network didn't just involve surveillance and counter-surveillance, assignments and reports, clandestine meetings and secret codes. Sometimes you had to immerse yourself in the personal lives of your agents — René's desire to be reunited with his wife, Tony's concerns about his relationship with Maggie — to make sure they performed as efficiently and effectively as possible. But for Gerardo Hernández, there was more to it than that. He prided himself on his personal relationships with the agents under his control.

Though it wasn't the stated reason for today's meeting with Joseph Santos and his wife, Amarylis Silverio, Hernández eventually steered this conversation again to the impending arrival of Joseph's mother from Cuba. They'd lived with her once before, Amarylis had told Hernández, and the woman "stuck her nose in everything."

But Amarylis also acknowledged, Hernández reported back to the CP after the meeting, that her mother-in-law was now "completely alone, old and it's her only son and only grand-daughter."

Hernández suggested various options, including finding a nearby efficiency apartment for the mother-in-law after a transitional period living with them. By the end of the meeting, Santos and his wife "came to an agreement," Hernández wrote, adding "the sentiments and reasons expressed by each one seemed sincere to me." Would that all problems could be so easily resolved.

Miami, June 1996

While the Brothers' shootdown and its fallout continued to be a primary topic of agitated conversation in the cafés and domino parks of Little Havana, it registered barely a blip on the radar of Cuban State Security as the CP issued new marching orders to Gerardo Hernández and his Avispa agents in mid-1996. Though the more than 40 single-spaced pages of background, commentary, analysis, praise, prodding and direction from Avispa's Havana handler, Edgardo, was intended primarily for Hernández, he, as usual, shared it with everyone.

"Family," Hernández wrote in an accompanying note, "this is what we received in the last mailing regarding you all." As usual, of course, the report only used the agents' code names so one agent still wouldn't know the real identity of any of the others. Written in the bureaucratese favoured by memo writers everywhere — "According to new work projections that have been assigned to our department, which are based on new prioritized objectives that have appeared in the Miami area" — the document featured updates on the latest plans of half a dozen counter-revolutionary groups and an equal number of individuals.[1] It concluded pessimistically, "the violent actions against Cuba should increase in the short term as a result of the extreme euphoria prevailing in Miami" following the shootdown.

There was praise for individual agents. Amarylis Silverio was "outdoing herself in matters concerning the Internet." But there were also gentle nudges too. "We have noticed that on occasion [René González] has mentioned people's names, which we do not have registered [and] essentially we do not know in detail who it is about. Hence, one of [his] main assignments… is to make a list of all his relations [and] his activities… so we can guide him towards better objectives." Tony Guerrero needed "to increase his work with friends who bear information [and] be more aggressive with them, and look for new relations in the objectives that would be of interest." The CP was still worried about Tony's "restlessness," which was code for his relationship with Maggie and the "operational difficulties it could bring us."

The report noted that Gerardo had recently been recognized for the "outstanding results achieved on the job during the provocations by the Government of the United States" following the Brothers' shootdown. On June 6, the anniversary of the founding of Cuba's Ministry of the Interior, both he and René González had been promoted to captain. It was less an earned honour than official acknowledgement that they'd completed their requisite four years of service as lieutenants. Because Nilo Hernández and Tony Guerrero were members of the reserves and Linda Hernández the militia, the report added with appropriate bureaucratic regret, none was considered a MININT combatant. "Therefore, in spite of the number of years that they have worked for us, we were only able to ascend them to sub-lieutenant."

Edgardo also offered detailed assessments of each agent's perfor-

---

1. They included the usual suspects: CANF, PUND, Alpha 66, Orlando Bosch and Luis Posada, along with their various offshoots and interconnections. Havana, for example, worried that Hector Viamonte, the PUND boss who two years before had founded the CLF, might be in cahoots with his friend Jorge Mas Canosa. The CP also worried that a group called Cuba Independencia Democracia (CID) was acquiring weapons in Central America, which was where Luis Posada also appeared to be planning to attack Cuban targets.

mance, current situation and future assignments. Joseph Santos and his wife Amarylis's "main assignment" involved "penetration" of the Southern Command headquarters under construction in Miami. "Stay apprised and immediately inform regarding everything that appears on said Command, via public information, secret,[2] visual, as well as everything referring to employment opportunities," Edgardo instructed. Joseph was to look for work around the base "in the computer field." The CP also had more mundane chores for their newest agents: they were to detail the steps they had taken to acquire a beeper and driver's licence so future agents could get up to speed on navigating American officialdom.

Nilo and Linda Hernández, the other husband-and-wife agents, were assigned letter-writing chores for the CP's "Active Measures" department: sending a letter, for example, from a "supposed Cuban exile" to the Mexican ambassador to Washington saying a Cuban-born Mexican mercenary — a real one by the name of Manuel Camargo — had been in Miami recently meeting with "terrorist elements"; and a more mischievous one to Congressman Alan Simpson threatening him on behalf of an exile group for his opposition to the Cuban Adjustment Act.

Agent Alejandro Alonso, the boat captain known by his code name Franklyn, should line up a volunteer job as a captain on one of the Democracy Movement's boats. But the CP definitely didn't want Alonso to give up his day job with the American Fish Company because he "needs money" now that his family had arrived from Cuba, and quitting would make him stand out from the crowd. More importantly, he shouldn't take the job he was considering taking with a shipping company because it would mean he'd be away from Miami often and "we wouldn't be able to count on him… in case something were to happen."

Tony's recent visit to Cuba had been "very positive for both parties," but there were concerns. Visits to "the native land," the report noted disapprovingly, had become all too rare for Tony, and this one had been especially brief — just 10 days and in the company of his girlfriend Maggie Becker. "As we well know, [visits home are] of vital importance to our operational base," Edgardo wrote. Although the CP had decided Tony should spend the "greatest portion" of his time with his family, and especially his son, Tony himself needed to spend more time in Cuba in order to see "everything we have built… the firmness of our people in their political ideology." There was

---

2. Gerardo Hernández told me "'secret' for the CP is not *secret*" in the way the official U.S. classification is understood. "Cubans are not so stupid as to pretend to get secret information from Southcom or from a military base through people with handyman jobs who barely speak English… For the CP, secret had to do with how the agent gathered the information. If it's from a newspaper it's public. But if Antonio says he was told an officer's wife was cheating on him, it would be secret because… it's not common knowledge."

also the hint in Edgardo's report that Tony needed to become more productive and deliver more reports "since it's been some time [since] we received things of interest from him." He should also try to land "better [jobs] with the aim of achieving greater penetration and gathering of information at the base."

The CP had been thinking too about René González's role as an FBI informant. They were concerned that by working too closely with the FBI, he "may get burned" and be forced to testify in a drug case. Informants, Edgardo noted, are "marked for the rest of their lives and… never have access to any kind of information" again, which, after all, was what González was in Florida to get. Still, he added as if arguing with himself, an agent "shouldn't always avoid" playing such a role either because it could lead to information about a possible "terrorist operation and we are removing ourselves from it."

Edgardo also reported the latest twists in the plan to bring González's wife and child to Florida. Because of Roque's defection and the fallout from the shootdown, Cuba had decided "it was necessary to wait until emotions subsided." Even after that, Edgardo added, everyone would need to be careful to make sure the process seemed routine, more so because Olga's cousin was an immigration official. The new plan called for Olga to write a letter to Cuba's Ministry of the Interior complaining that, while it had given her 12-year-old daughter the okay to go to the U.S., it was arbitrarily denying permission to her. She was then to take her concerns to the United States Interest Section in Havana to ask for its assistance.

Eventually, Edgardo explained, Olga's complaint would work its way back from the minister's office to the Intelligence Department, where, after a suitable delay, the department would resignedly report back that, "in order to avoid any type of international campaign regarding violation of human rights or another reason… there is no objection to [Olga] being given an exit visa and therefore we get rid of this problem." The key, Edgardo suggested, was for González not to make too much "noise."

Meanwhile, Edgardo had plenty of urgent agent work to keep González busy. "On March 16, Andres Alvariño, who works in the prisons and is a member of the National Guard in Miami, told [an M-19 agent] about having a project with CANF" to assemble a rigorously vetted group of 40 mercenaries with professional military experience — or even soldiers on active duty — "for the execution of paramilitary missions against Cuba." Operating in tightly controlled four-man cells, "they would be paid commission and they would have life insurance policies of $100,000 U.S. for their families."

The key figures behind this latest plot, which Edgardo said was being supported "indirectly" by the CIA, were two prominent CANF members: Roberto Martin Perez, who would be in charge of the force, and Enrique Bassas,[3] one of its "financial backers." Martin Perez, the son of one of former

---

3. In the message, as translated by U.S. authorities, Bassas's name is spelled as Casas.

Cuban president Fulgencio Batista's senior military officers, claimed the distinction of having been the longest serving political prisoner in Cuba; he'd spent 27 years in jail for his part in an early conspiracy against Fidel Castro.[4] Released in 1987, he'd moved to the U.S. and married Ninoska Perez Castellón, an incendiary anti-Castro host on Radio Mambi. Both were now on the board of CANF, and Ninoska often served as its media spokesperson. Enrique Bassas had been a co-founder of the infamous CORU and, two years earlier, had provided some of the bomb-making material Percy Alvarado was supposed to use at the Tropicana.

"This information," the CP told Hernández, "merits watching." The Cubans, of course, had other agents inside CANF, but you could never have too much information. Edgardo assigned González to the task with "the goal of obtaining new facts on it or expanding upon the data already at hand." Even if nothing materialized as a result, Edgardo added, "it serves [González] as a background to get to know the plans and the way the different counter revolutionary groups act and their ties to the special services."

Edgardo also wanted González to find out everything he could about another plot, this one to launch bomber planes against Cuba. Although the plan was "initially conceived with the purpose of launching two planes loaded with explosives, remote-controlled from a helicopter, directed against a public gathering in the Plaza de la Revolucion during a speech by the commander in chief," it had since been modified to include other possible targets: Castro's house in Jaimanitas, or some strategic target like an oil refinery or thermo-electric plant. The plotters had already tested the idea in a remote section of Texas, where one of the participants had accidentally been injured, as well as in the Bahamas and Puerto Rico. The plan had been postponed "due to the incident on February 24," but it hadn't been abandoned — and the CP wanted González to find out more.

Finally, there were those UFOs. In March 1995, the Cuban military first reported seeing unidentified flying objects on their radar. Birds? Drones? Balloons? At first, officials concluded they were probably American drones that had since been dispatched to Bosnia. But recently the objects had begun appearing again. They were detected in the skies north of Havana on the day of the shootdown and then, more recently off Santiago de Cuba at the other end of the island. "The subject continues to be of great importance to comrades" in the Cuban Air Force, Edgardo wrote. René González should check it out. Yes, René González would have plenty to keep him occupied while he waited for Olga and Irma.

---

4. In fact, another Cuban political prisoner, Mario Chanes de Armas, served 30 years.

STINGING THE WASP

Key West, July 1996

Tony Guerrero had a new proposal. During his brief meetings at the Centro Principal in April, Edgardo had raised concerns about his intelligence reporting routines. The intelligence rationale for basing Guerrero in Key West, of course, was so he could keep an eye on whatever was going on at the Boca Chica Naval Air Station and alert Cuba to any signs the U.S. might be planning an invasion. Senior military officials in Havana considered such an invasion likely. And who could blame them? In just over a dozen years, American forces had invaded Grenada (1983), Panama (1989) and Haiti (1994). Given the United States' longstanding hostility to the Castro regime and the ever-growing influence on America's Cuba policies of groups like the Cuban American National Foundation, it would have been foolhardy to have ignored the possibility.

Based in part on what Guerrero had reported in the lead-up to the Haiti invasion, the CP had compiled a checklist of what it considered the "main indications" that an attack was imminent. They included unexpected visits by military brass, increased landings of executive jets, a sudden influx of air combat and reconnaissance aircraft, an increase in the numbers of Coast Guard and naval vessels offshore and, of course, any sudden increase in security around the base. Observing those indicators wasn't the problem. You didn't need a security clearance — or even Guerrero's low-level civilian job at the base — to see them. You could see everything, Gerardo Hernández would say, from Highway 1.

The problem was reporting it all back to the CP in a timely fashion. In order to get Guerrero's written reports to Havana, Gerardo Hernández had to drive three and a half hours from Miami to Key West, implement complex, time-consuming counter-surveillance measures to make sure their clandestine, disk-handover meetings weren't observed and then drive all the way back to Miami so he could dispatch the coded material to Havana using high frequency radio transmissions. Given all Hernández's other responsibilities, carving out a day for such adventures was never easy.

If the message was urgent, of course, there were faster ways to communicate. Guerrero could use his beeper to alert Hernández. But what constituted urgent? Havana, of course, wanted to know everything, and immediately. The CP complained it had already received some vital information long after its best-before date.

So Guerrero had come up with a complex new series of 10-digit beeper codes[5] in which the first three digits represented various types of aircraft and ships or other military presence. Other numbers would flesh out details,

---

5. "If I enter 930-4032-400 and 289-8919-620," Guerrero wrote by way of example, "that means I am reporting the deployment of 18 F-14 airplane of the aircraft carrier wing and 6 FA-18 airplanes of the aircraft carrier wing."

such as numbers of planes or ships. If the first three numbers were 5-5-0, that meant Guerrero had spotted one of the "main indications" — increased high-level activities, sudden landings of fighter aircraft — and the numbers that followed would incorporate coded specifics detailing what was happening. But Guerrero also made it clear he only intended to use the beeper system to report unusual activities. "When I do not call during the week," he explained, "it means that the situation at the base is normal." They'd have to trust his judgment. "I await your opinion regarding the code," he wrote hopefully, ending with his sign off: "An embrace from your vegetarian brother."

Miami, Late Summer 1996

René González didn't say anything directly, but Gerardo Hernández could see it in his eyes and in the smile that played at the corners of his mouth. González knew. González had become trusted enough within Ramón Saúl Sánchez's Democracy Movement that he'd been invited to join a Democracy-linked affiliate known as the Cuban National Commission. That was a coup, especially considering the paranoia that had followed Roque's re-defection.

In order to join the CNC, you first had to be recommended by a member. Marcelino García, one of Sánchez's most trusted lieutenants, had put González's name forward. Then you had to fill out a detailed questionnaire about your background and be interviewed by members of the group before you could finally be accepted.

During their most recent debriefing session, González told Hernández he'd been interviewed along with several others, including a former Cuban merchant marine officer with a background very similar to his own. The man had been born in the United States, returned to Cuba with his family as a child and then come back to America as an adult without his family, although González said he'd heard the man's family had recently arrived in the U.S.

"The guy's a little strange," González confided to Hernández.

"Why did he seem strange?" Hernández wanted to know.

"I don't know. He just caught my attention, that's all."

"Be very careful with this person," Hernández replied evenly. "You can't lose sight of the fact that Democracy must be penetrated by everyone — DEA, FBI, us and maybe even Interpol — so you should be very careful with this person, study him and keep us informed."

Their conversation had moved on to other topics, but Hernández couldn't help but wonder about it later. If González had been Roque, he thought, "he would have come in saying that he uncovered a guy that he bet his life had to be one of ours." But González was "a very reserved person. Although he expressed his observation very tactfully," Hernández told Edgardo, their boss back at the Centro Principal, "the matter will require special handling by us."

That's because the American-born, Cuba-raised former merchant marine officer González referred to was Alejandro Alonso, another Cuban agent Hernández supervised. Alonso's task had been to use his boat pilot's background to insinuate himself inside the flotilla's operations so he could provide navigational details as well as information about Coast Guard activity. Alonso wasn't the easiest agent to manage. Though he invariably signed off his reports with a stirring "Fatherland or Death," Alonso sometimes "forgot" to return pager calls. Hernández had had to remind him he needed to maintain "full combat readiness status." Worse, his personal life could attract unwanted attention: he kept running up huge credit card debts and his brother was a drug dealer.

Was that why González had singled him out as strange, as a veiled warning? While Hernández told Edgardo he would "work with the marine, without his knowledge, to keep him from drawing attention to himself in that environment," Hernández's more immediate concern was to find ways to keep the two men separate "to guarantee the required compartmentalization." The less one agent knew about the activities of another, the safer everyone was.

Miami, September 11, 1996

Vicente Rosado knew Gerardo Hernández, but not his real name. He knew his cover name was Manuel Viramóntez, but he understood that wasn't his real name. In FBI parlance, he was an "Unsub," an Unknown Subject. The agents in his squad had already given him a code name: Royal Sovereign.

During the summer, Rosado, an FBI special agent with the Computer Analysis Response Team within the FBI's Miami-based F-1 (Foreign Intelligence-Cuba) Squad, had rented an apartment across the street from Hernández's place at 18100 Atlantic Boulevard in North Miami Beach in order to keep watch on his comings and goings.

Tonight, while Hernández was out, Rosado and his agents surreptitiously entered Apartment 305 for the first time.[6] Their job was to itemize everything inside. While the other agents went about their tasks, Rosado created an exact duplicate of every 3.5-inch computer disk in the apartment. The goal was to complete their work without leaving behind the slightest sniff they'd ever been there.

The apartment was small: a single bedroom with a closet, kitchen, din-

---

6. Over the course of the next two years, FBI agents made three more surreptitious entries into Hernández's apartment, copying an additional 300 disks. How did they initially identify Hernández as a Cuban agent? That isn't clear and was deliberately fudged during his trial. Prosecutors weren't required to disclose that information for national security reasons. But it appears as if they were already following at least one other intelligence officer, Ricardo Villarreal, who led them to Hernández, who probably then led them to other members of the network. Villarreal apparently returned to Cuba before the FBI arrested the others in September 1998.

ing room, living room, bathroom and two more closets. The furnishings were spare too, except for electronic equipment, of which there seemed an abundance. There were two laptop computers, an Epson and a Tandy 1100, an external Smart One Traveler modem and two Sony shortwave receiving radios. The agents made note of each item, but left them exactly where they'd found them.

Meanwhile Rosado laboriously duplicated each computer disk — over 200 in all, most of which were in the open on a dining room table — using a special machine. As he inserted one of Hernández's disks, he would carefully take one from his own stack of blanks, "mark it chronologically by numbering it" and then pop it into the second drive. As soon as the freshly cloned disk popped out of the machine, Rosado would flick the write-protect tab to make sure it couldn't be copied over. He'd learned that lesson the hard way.

The first time he'd used his new FBI copying machine during a surreptitious entry a month earlier at a Miami Beach apartment occupied by a man using the name Ricardo Villarreal, Rosado had accidentally copied one of the subject's disks onto another disc, also belonging to the subject. And then another, and another... 12 in all. They'd had to leave the overwritten disks behind so Villarreal wouldn't realize they'd been tampered with; they could only hope he didn't try to use them again. Whatever interesting, important information had been on those original disks, of course, had been lost.

It took Rosado several hours to finish copying all the disks. The agents left as stealthily as they'd entered. The next step was for Rosado's team to discover what was on those disks and figure out what it meant.

Miami, September 1996

Gerardo Hernández's JC Penney card had arrived, and he'd already used it to buy some clothing. On the one hand, having a credit card made him seem more ordinary, more American and therefore less likely to attract unwanted attention. On the other hand, creating a credit card paper trail risked attracting unwanted attention from U.S. tax authorities, who might reasonably ask why a man who'd been in the country for two years working as a freelance photographer hadn't filed an income tax return.

At a practical level, Hernández didn't need the card. "As you know," he explained in a report, "we don't buy many clothes here and what we do buy, I, at least... look around for specials at the cheapest shops." But, at the CP's urging, he had finally applied for the card — and, as instructed, documented the process so his bosses could pass the information to legend-preparing future illegal officers.

Speaking of legends, Hernández was still thinking about his. The original plan — to pass himself off as a photographer — had turned out to be "an expensive cover... with all our limited resources." He'd then toyed with the idea of changing his back story and calling himself a writer or scriptwriter but he had no scripts to show. He then considered tapping into his natural artistic talents to pass himself off as an artist but discovered it, like photography, was prohibitively expensive. "It's incredible what good construction paper costs, let alone canvas and paint," he wrote. He'd even imagined assuming his "best cover" as a caricaturist, a skill he'd developed a reputation for in university. In fact, he'd published his first cartoon while still in high school. But he worried that colleagues from Cuba who were now working in the United States "would certainly recognize my style, no matter how much I change it." Which was why he'd finally settled, for now, for calling himself a freelance commercial designer.

That's how he'd described himself to fellow students at the school where he was taking a course in English to improve his language skills. Though he sometimes missed classes because of "my operational duties," he reported that he'd learned a lot. Better, he noted, "you can now call me a 'social person,' with people who call me and people I call, with people I sometimes go out with and people I occasionally visit."

Now that he had his JC Penney card — with its $200 line of credit — he planned to apply for a gas card and a Costco membership. Welcome to America.

Miami, October 17, 1996

René González cut the man off, politely but firmly. "I'm not a Juan Pablo," he said, "or some delinquent who cooperates in order to get a pardon after he's been caught doing something wrong. I'm an honest citizen who got approached to be part of a drug deal, and whose principles led him to go to the authorities. But this… What you're asking me to do is different." They were sitting in the man's car in the parking lot of a shopping plaza. The man was an FBI agent named Albert Alonso. Alonso had been calling González all week, leaving messages, trying to set up this meeting.

It had begun with a call from Alex Barbeito, the FBI agent González had told last winter about that planned drug deal. Since the deal had fallen through, Barbeito told him the FBI was closing that file and transferring him to Alonso, an agent who handled anti-Castro groups. Alonso, Barbeito said, wanted to meet him.

González had put off returning Alonso's persistent pages, in part so he could discuss with Gerardo Hernández how to handle this latest development. Hernández thought Alonso might be fishing. So did González. "We can't forget how it stung them to have to endure the slap from Roque," Hernández said, "so they aren't going to stop seeking revenge." And he reminded González: "You have the same profile as Roque."

But they both knew helping the FBI sometimes also helped Cuban

Security. The trick, Hernández suggested, would be for González to respond to Alonso's come-on in a way that would be "different from the way they expect a Castro agent to act." González agreed. "It isn't logical to lend support to a group with which one supposedly has similar ideas and objectives, and from one day to the next offer to spy on that group," he told Hernández. "To me that seems to be so vile that even these people [the FBI] would be crazy to trust me after I did that."

So when Alonso finally broached the subject of feeding the FBI information about what happened inside PUND and the Democracy Movement, González responded like the exile he was supposed to be. "Look, I'm anti-Castro," he told Alonso. "That's why I joined these organizations, not to snitch on my brothers who carry on a legitimate struggle. You know, if somebody gave me an airplane and said, 'Here's a bomb. Go drop it on Fidel's head,' I wouldn't be too sure I would tell the U.S. government about it."

Alonso tried a different tack. "I understand that," he said, "but you know that Cuban moles are everywhere, even inside groups like Brothers to the Rescue and Democracy, and they're always planning plots. By telling us about those plots in time for us to stop them, you could help save those organizations from harm." González allowed that he understood, and that he would certainly be opposed to any criminal or terrorist activity. "If someday my conscience tells me to report something," he assured Alonso, "I will do it with great pleasure."

As González reported later: " I think I was very convincing in my sincerity and impressed him." But the truth was it was too late to convince Alonso. By following Gerardo Hernández and observing who he met with and then following them, the FBI had already identified González. To Special Agent Albert Alonso, René González was not really a potential informant but the subject of an ongoing national security investigation.

Miami, November 1996

"Edgardo, I've decided to mention a subject again, which I mentioned during my last trip to CP," Gerardo Hernández began the personal message he'd been pondering for some time. "It's related to the possibility of my wife being processed with the goal of joining me to fulfill this mission." That Hernández was thinking about Adriana was no surprise. He thought about her often. And wrote to her whenever he could. In July, they'd marked their eighth wedding anniversary with the unhappy acknowledgment they'd only been together for three of them. Adriana was ready to start a family. So was he.

To bring those personal issues into even sharper focus, Hernández had recently had to deal with the romantic relationships of two of his agents. Earlier this month, he and Tony Guerrero had met to consider "the state" of Tony's relationship with Maggie Becker. He and Tony had discussed — again

— the strategic pros of moving in together. Living with Maggie would, in the words of one of Tony's lists, "improve our entry into the American way of life and deepen our study of the language" as well as "eliminate the question of why I maintain a separate rent even though I live with her." There was also the more practical and not inconsiderable benefit of cutting his own monthly rent in half.

But then, of course, there was also a "most difficult" con. Since Maggie met her massage therapy clients in her home, she was there most of the time. Moving in with her would severely limit Tony's ability to receive radio messages "according to our established plan." But did that really matter? In Hernández's own lengthy analysis of their discussion for the CP, he noted that, "in the two years that we have been working with the comrade, there have been very few occasions that we have had to send him a radio message and, in most cases, he has found out the content of said messages through me first rather than through the transmission."

In fact, he and Guerrero had always found ways around whatever complications they'd encountered. Two months ago, they'd planned a face-to-face meeting in Miami to exchange reports and "monetary assistance," but then Maggie decided to tag along. They eventually arranged to meet at the health food store where Tony and Maggie often bought supplies. When Guerrero excused himself to visit the washroom, Hernández followed. They made that exchange "without speaking a word. [Tony and Maggie] left a few minutes later and I stayed a while longer to do some shopping," Hernández reported.

If the CP decided Tony should break up with Maggie for operational reasons, what would happen then, Hernández wondered? Tony would still need some form of companionship. What if, "instead of dealing with an American woman... decent... who is not 'into anything' except for yoga and her metaphysical deal and shit, the new one could be a Cuban militant, or spy maniac, or any other materialistic Latin woman, a bandit or a marijuana smoker..."

Hernández also made the point that, after working with Guerrero for two years, he believed his agent was ready to take on all "three fundamental steps being discussed: 1) moving into Maggie's house, 2) get married, 3) have a child." Maggie's desire to marry and have a child was "logical," he wrote, since they'd essentially been living together for three years and "her clock is ticking." But moving in together, he added, wasn't just a tactical way to preserve the relationship for appearance's sake or "out of consideration to Maggie," but it was also "closely related to [Tony's] well being."

Though he was writing about Guerrero, Hernández could have been describing his own frustrations with being alone in such a strange and different world. Living without a lover or even a companion to share the rent and the chores is "very strange in this environment, especially in a young man," he explained to his bosses in Havana, adding "it is not easy in this environment to find a woman with the minimum moral and social requirements necessary for having a relationship… The 'good ones' aspire to something a little better than the 'status' of [Tony] while the easiest ones to snap up are the ones with a 'turbulent' past… If the comrade feels good in this relationship," Hernández wrote, "I don't think… we should crush him" by forcing him to break it off. "In summary, and for all reasons explained, I think that we should allow the comrade to move in with the woman."

At the same time, of course, Hernández continued to be involved in the ongoing operation to bring René González's wife and daughter to Miami. One of the reasons the CP had approved that plan was because it hoped having his family with him would make González an even more effective agent. If that made sense for René, why not for Gerardo? Hernández knew from his last visit to the CP that Havana was considering allowing illegal officers to bring their spouses with them on assignment. Although he realized the subsequent silence from his superiors meant no decision had been taken, Hernández had decided to make his own case again "more in the spirit of reiterating and explaining my points than to try to prompt an answer."

Because, as he himself acknowledged, he was a "serious, meticulous and calculating" person, Hernández had filled up more than 10 single-spaced pages with an on-the-one-hand-this, on-the-other-hand-that assessment of "Operational Reasons," "Reasons Related to My Legend," "Reasons Related to Operational Work," "Possible Negative Factors" and "Conclusions" as to why his wife should join him. Many of his reasons, he acknowledged, were personal, but the personal and operational, he noted, were "linked and closely related."

There were operational complications to living alone, the most serious being it made him seem odd to his neighbours, "and it is not to my advantage to seem odd… in a country where people live so afraid and fearful of the possibilities of drug traffickers, serial killers or, even worse, spies (of which there is a case heard every so often, [the spy] usually [being] described as 'reserved and solitary')." Establishing a cover relationship to blend in might make sense, he allowed, except that even one night clubbing could cost "$50 easily, without eating," and there was no line item in his budget for such extravagance.

Besides, what would happen if he did find a woman to have even a casual relationship with? "With a radio [communication] plan every morning and at night, and with [agents] who beep me at seven o'clock in the morning or 11 o'clock at night — and I have to leave [the apartment] to call when I have a telephone in the house? It is too complicated for me to maintain a relation-ship for more than a month without running some type of risk to the security of my operational work."

Besides "permit[ting] me to find 'at home' everything that I have to go out to find," having a trained Adriana with him would mean she could share some of the operational workload, from carrying out counter-surveillance measures for his clandestine meetings to receiving radio messages, which would make him more efficient and effective as an illegal officer. And there were, of course, other advantages to having a woman as illegal officer that "I prefer not to elaborate much on... since you can deduce" them.

On the flip side, being an illegal officer meant "risking it 24 hours a day, constantly vulnerable to arrest and even death... When my wife becomes incorporated into the mission, she automatically assumes all the risks that I do, which means two could get screwed, with everything that this implies for the person as well as the mission."

But Hernández, who clearly wanted Adriana with him, managed to twist even that negative into a positive. Knowing that any mis-step could compromise his wife as well as himself, he said, would create "a very strong additional motivation to aspire to perfection in all aspects of the operational work." Although their conversations on the subject had been discreet, Adriana already knew enough about her husband's other life to have told him she was willing to "sacrifice" her profession[7] to join him in Miami.

At a personal level, he noted, he and Adriana complemented one another. "Among my defects as a person is that I am no good at domestic chores, besides being a little disorganized in my personal affairs and, at times, overly spontaneous at the hour of doing something or solving a problem." Adriana was everything he wasn't, and "we have faced the majority of our problems and situations in life over the years as a 'team.'"

Hernández already knew what some of the personal objections might be — and he had answers for each of them.

What if their marriage fell apart? "If, after 10 years together with heavy responsibilities and obstacles in the way, we have never had a problem that put our marriage in danger, it is even less likely to happen with such a great additional motivation," he answered.

What about having kids, which would be "in direct contradiction to our operational work?" In his letter, Hernández, perhaps disingenuously, downplayed the issue — "not actually a priority for us as a couple" — suggesting being together might be more than enough in the short term.

If they were together, he suggested, they could wait to have children "as long as biologically possible." If, on the other hand, they weren't allowed to be together, he added, "it is my intention to move up the matter of procreation so that at least the satisfaction of one aspiration will compensate for the lack of satisfaction in the other."

---

7. According to Hernández, Adriana "felt very fulfilled" in her profession but not in her job. "I know from her letters that her motivation in her work has suffered because of the incompetence and influence of people around her, and that has prompted me to repeat my request" to have her join him in Miami.

And living so many months away from his family in those circumstances, of course, could bring its own operational consequences...

Although Hernández insisted he'd only made his pitch "after much analysis and with as much objectivity as possible, including all positive and negative aspects," there was no doubt which way he believed the balance scales tilted. The question was, could he convince the CP he was right? In the end, he never got a direct response to his request.

Miami, November 20, 1996

The Democracy Movement was imploding. Its most recent attempt to re-create the success of its first flotilla was foundering on the rocky shoals of public indifference. Last night's meeting of its Cuban National Commission offshoot, for example, had attracted just 20 people and quickly degenerated into a four-hour "pandemonium" over the procedures used to elect the commission's executive board three months earlier. It was, René González reported to Gerardo Hernández, "the most sterile assembly I have ever seen in my life." Rodolfo González, the commission member who'd triggered the debate and dragged it out, "did a great job for us," González joked. At one point, Saúl Sánchez even threatened to resign. "He said it hurt to see how in a moment of crisis the movement was self-destructing," González reported. With so many things needing attention, he argued, time was being wasted on matters of no importance.

There definitely were important matters. The woman who'd sold the vessel *Democracia* to the group was threatening legal action the next day if she didn't get this month's $1,200 payment. The dry dock where another of the Movement's boats was supposedly being repaired had demanded the vessel be removed because Democracy couldn't come up with funds to pay for the contracted work. To complicate everything, Sánchez reported that his own health was "delicate, that on the previous Friday he had nearly suffered a heart attack" as a result of all this stress.

"After this touching moment," René González himself had suggested a way out of the meeting's procedural impasse, which was quickly and en-thusiastically endorsed by the exhausted, dispirited assembly. Given that the group — which had "no goals, [was] without definite objectives and no concrete plans — is wounded and can die if urgent measures are not taken," there was an irony in González's rescue effort. In the end, he concluded, it was worth it. "Although it means helping Democracy get out of the mess... I think this is a good moment to stand out." It was never easy for a secret agent to strike the right balance between enhancing his reputation within the "enemy" group he's attempting to infiltrate and not helping the group succeed in its broader objectives.

The day after the Cuban National Commission meeting, González had smacked up against the same dilemma during a second meeting with FBI agent Albert Alonso. Alonso continued to press him to become an informant on groups like Democracy and the Cuban National Commission. González resisted but didn't rule out cooperating under any circumstances. "Alonso listened patiently and said he respected me," González reported.

After making his pitch, Alonso had suddenly changed topics and asked him about Juan Pablo Roque. The FBI was still trying to reconstruct Roque's last days, Alonso said, to determine whether Roque had been sent from Cuba as a secret agent or was recruited after he'd arrived. What did González think? González said he thought Roque had been an agent from the beginning. How else to explain the fact he hadn't obtained his American pilot's licence or launched his own career? "Those seem to me to be signs he wasn't planning to spend a long time here," González said, "but that's just a guess, based on what I remember." It was also, of course, an attempt to draw a "subtle distinction" between Roque and González, who'd not only earned his flight instructor's licence and was trying to start his own flight school and who was also actively working to bring his family from Cuba to Florida.

René González still didn't realize the FBI had already linked him to Roque — and to Cuban intelligence.

Miami, December 1996

Vicente Rosado slipped the disk labelled RSA-105[8] into his computer's disk drive. The directory showed 17 files, mostly operating system files and a few DOS files. There were no text files on the disk but one — MS.EXE was an executable Micro Star file. Micro Star was an old and rarely used computer word processing program. The FBI agent opened the program, pressed the F10 function key to access the program's menus and selected the "Open File" command. He typed "a-f-i-n-a-c-i-ó-n," a Spanish word meaning refining. Instead of opening a file with that name, the computer asked him to "Insert a disk and press Enter to continue." Rosado followed the instructions, inserting another copy of one of the disks he'd duplicated. Like most of the disks he'd taken during the FBI's surreptitious entry into Gerardo Hernández's apartment in September, this one appeared to be blank: there were no files listed in its Directory index, and none of its 730 kilobytes of available space appeared to have been used.

But when he inserted the disk now, text appeared on the screen, and there was screen after screen of text in Spanish. The text appeared to be several reports dealing with Brothers to the Rescue and the Democracy Movement, all dated around the middle of October 1995, and all from someone named

---

8. "RS" stands for Hernández's FBI code name Royal Sovereign, the "A" signifies that it was a disk taken during the first entry, and the number is from the sequence of disk Rosado copied.

Iselin to someone else named Giro. Rosado didn't have a clue who either of those people might be, but he figured one of them was probably the man the agents called Royal Sovereign.

It had taken the FBI lab several months, but specialists there had finally discovered the password[9] that unlocked the contents of the disk. They'd done it, ironically, with an over-the-counter program called Norton Utilities Disk Editor. It allowed them to probe beyond the standard directory to examine the individual sectors of each floppy. Scrolling through a hexidecimal view of the disk contents, a researcher eventually discovered in cylinder 50, side 1, sector 8, a word — afinación — that Rosado would later explain "doesn't really fit into what I would expect to find on a disk that has a program." That hunch had proven correct. The FBI now had the key to unlock and decrypt the contents of the files hidden inside all those seemingly blank disks. They could finally begin to understand who Royal Sovereign was and what he was doing in Miami.

Miami, December 26, 1996

It had all taken much longer than René González expected. Even today, waiting at the Miami International Airport, Olga and Irma had had to jump more immigration hurdles than other arriving passengers because they were claiming permanent residency status. But, finally, they emerged from immigration's clutches and González had the opportunity to embrace his wife and daughter. Together. At last.

González hadn't come to the airport alone. He was accompanied by his mother's Aunt Gladys — who had prepared a "great welcome meal," which was waiting for everyone at her house — a few old friends and both Saúl Sánchez, the founder of the Democracy Movement, and Marcelino García, the head of the movement's aerial wing, and their wives, who'd invited themselves along.

Gerardo Hernández, of course, wasn't there. They'd had their usual clandestine meeting three days before, during which they talked of little else but the family's impending arrival and René's plans for the future. González, Hernández reported back to Havana, was "very happy and a little anxious." Part of that anxiety had to do with providing for his suddenly enlarged family. González had a job at the International Flight Center at Tamiami Airport, but the hours were brutal and the pay wasn't great. "The comrade," Hernández noted, often showed up for their meetings "with dark circles under his eyes [and] told me he was working a lot of hours."

González had been looking for a better paying position. Through his contacts with the Cuban Pilots' Association, he'd submitted his résumé to Fine Air, a charter company, and was considering taking a course for flight

---

9. He would later discover other passwords — "Mambi," Cientifico" and "Fuerte" — that also decrypted specific disks and files.

engineers in January. The problem was that the course would cost $6,500, meaning he'd have to take out a loan. But if he was lucky, he told Hernández, the course might lead directly to a better paying job after graduation and allow him to quickly repay the loan.

For now, Hernández, who noted that González had been reluctant to accept financial help because of "his character," did his best to ease his agent's money concerns. He handed him $2,838 in accumulated monthly "economic help." González had been entitled to $400 a month from the CP but had asked Hernández to hold most of this year's entitlement until his family arrived. This would help them get settled in their new lives together. Tonight, after dinner with Aunt Gladys, González would take his Olguita and Irmita back to the apartment he'd been readying for them and get on with that new life. It had been six long years since they'd all been together.

"Something Serious"
January 1997 – August 25, 1997

Miami, January 1997

He had a new problem, Tony Guerrero informed his Miami controller, Gerardo Hernández. His uncle, Roberto, the colonel, had divorced again — his third wife this time. That wasn't the problem. "I greatly admire, love and respect my Uncle Roberto," Tony wrote. "He has always been an example of sacrifice and commitment to our cause and an irreproachable member of our armed forces." The problem was that when Tony and Maggie visited Tony's family in Havana back in April, his uncle and one of his previous ex-wives had stopped by for a visit. This previous ex had since left Cuba illegally and was now living in Miami with Uncle Roberto's two daughters. That might not have been a problem either, except that Roberto had slyly let slip, in a recent conversation with Tony's mother, that he knew what Tony was doing in Florida. Tony's mother had passed on that information to Tony in a phone call earlier this month.

"My worry," Tony explained, was that Roberto might have also told the ex-wife, who might tell God-knew-who-else. "Everything is possible… It would be good, I'm thinking, of sitting down with the colonel and having a very detailed conversation with him," Tony explained.

Venezuela, February 21, 1997

Luis Posada was phoning from somewhere in Central America. "Nelly," he told his one-time secretary and friend, "I have to travel to see you around March 10 to discuss something serious that's going to take several months to prepare… that could change the fate of our country." Posada didn't explain what he meant. He didn't have to. Nelly Rojas and her husband, Pedro Morales, had been friends and anti-Castro allies for decades, and had worked together since Posada's earliest days in Venezuela.

Today, Posada was letting them know something big was coming and also introducing them, over the telephone, to "a great friend, a brother in the struggle." His name, Posada said, was Arnaldo Monzón, a New Jersey clothing chain owner and CANF board member. Posada called him "our angel in the northern zone." The introductions out of the way, Posada asked Pedro if he was "still traveling to Margarita?" Margarita?

The Cuban State Security agents who were listening in on the conversation, knew Margarita Island, off the coast of Venezuela, was the site for a Latin American leaders' summit this fall. Fidel Castro was supposed to attend. Was that the "something serious" Posada referred to, or was it something else? Posada had also been heard bragging in an interview with a Spanish-language TV station in November about a plan to set off explosives in Cuba to scare off tourists. It would be up to Cuba's intelligence networks to figure out the truth — and to stop whatever their old enemy was planning this time.

Tavernier, Florida, February 25, 1997

Shortly after 1 p.m., FBI Special Agent William Murphy identified the subject's vehicle — an older model burgundy Pontiac Grand Am, licence number RJK35F — as it arrived at the McDonald's in Tavernier in the Florida Keys. It wasn't the first time he'd followed this car, or its driver, a man he knew as Royal Sovereign. Murphy was the team leader of one of a number of FBI surveillance squads assigned to assist FC-1, the Bureau's National Security Squad, track a group of Cuban spies.

Another four-man squad, headed by Agent Johnny Davis, had already followed the subject this morning from his apartment in North Miami to a neighbourhood gas station — where he filled up his tank and made a call from a pay phone — and then along I-95 South to U.S. Highway 1 for about an hour until he arrived at the McDonald's. It was time to change surveillance teams to make sure the subject didn't recognize any of the cars or agents following him. In Miami, Royal Sovereign had forced them to call off their surveillance more than once. He'd thwarted them by smartly employing counter-surveillance techniques: driving slowly, changing lanes erratically, making sudden turnoffs, or not making a turn when he was in a turning lane, which meant they'd have been forced to expose themselves if they tried to follow. Royal Sovereign was a pro. But so were they.

As the subject pulled out of the restaurant and back on to the highway heading south, Murphy's team took over tracking. Today, Royal Sovereign drove directly to Key West, arriving at 4:20 p.m. Once in the city, however, he began what seemed like random driving up and down streets for close to 20 minutes before he finally pulled into a Burger King parking lot. He got out, went inside the restaurant, then immediately came back out, returned to the car, opened the trunk, took out a blue plastic bag. From a discreet distance, an agent in a car snapped photos. Royal Sovereign was wearing a white hat, white shirt, white shorts. Other agents followed at an equally discreet distance while their subject went for an equally aimless walk around the neighbourhood.

Twenty minutes later, Royal Sovereign met up with a second man in the parking lot behind Old Town Trolleys. The agents knew the second man too; in fact, another squad had followed Tony Guerrero from his job at the Boca Chica Naval Air Station to this meeting. Like Royal Sovereign, Guerrero had employed similar counter-surveillance techniques to make sure he wasn't followed. But he was.

As the agents continued to snap photos, the two men went into a nearby Miami Subs restaurant. Royal Sovereign exited immediately, then went back in to join Guerrero. Fifteen minutes later, Guerrero came out, made a call from a pay phone and returned inside.

After another few minutes, the two men came out of the restaurant together and walked toward Guerrero's grey Toyota pickup truck. Now, Guerrero was carrying the blue plastic bag. He opened the cab door, put the package inside, took out a brown paper bag, handed it to Royal Sovereign. At that point, the two men split up, got in their cars and drove away. Followed, of course, by their surveillance teams.

It wouldn't be until after the next secret entry into Gerardo Hernández's apartment, and after Vicente Rosado had decrypted more disks — including the ones Hernández and Guerrero had almost certainly exchanged inside their respective bags — that FBI investigators were finally able to piece together what Hernández and Guerrero talked about that day in Miami Subs. They had, as usual, talked about Maggie. She'd recently lost her part-time gig at the local Hilton Hotel. They'd talked yet again about what to do about their relationship. Tony and Maggie were planning another trip to Cuba. "I'll try to keep everything regarding the trip a secret, especially from those who work with me," Tony wrote, "but this can get out of my hands since Maggie may make a comment."

Guerrero also discussed the Valentine's Day wedding ("a special day for romantics and those in love like me") he'd attended for a young co-worker named Brian. Brian was just 18, his bride 16. Since Brian began working at the shop a few months before, they'd become close. "It's easy to go deep and get conversation out of him," Guerrero wrote. The most important intelligence he'd discovered so far was that Brian's father was in the military, some sort of "senior chief" in charge of the passenger terminal at the U.S. base at Guantanamo, and that Brian had recently signed up to begin military service himself.

Partly because of the ongoing pressure from Havana to increase his circle of useful friends, Guerrero had already promised to "continue to develop" the relationship and "offer the information we glean."

Guerrero told Hernández he had been the only one of Brian's fellow workers at the wedding, and Brian had also asked him to take photos. "These photos will be a gift from me to Brian," Guerrero noted, adding, "the important thing is to create a relationship, which will surely give us important information in the future."

Guerrero, of course, also included in his report his usual mind-glazing listing of which planes had been where and when on the base. But he noted several times that it was becoming more difficult for him to do this because, having recently been promoted to a four-year contract as a sheet metal mechanical helper in the maintenance shop, he didn't get to travel around the base very often anymore. But the job came with insurance and a bumped-up starting salary of $9.74 an hour.

Luckily, one of his recent assignments involved renovations to Building A1125. The work was being carried out with "extreme security" though he hadn't been able to learn what was so secret, probably because such information was well above the pay and security grade of a sheet metal mechanical helper.

Guerrero also reported he had gathered several important new pieces of information. The military had recently taken over responsibility from private contractors for guarding the base entrance from 6 p.m. to 6 a.m. each day, and responsibility for Caribbean security was to be officially transferred to the new Southern Command headquarters on June 1, 1997. How had he uncovered such highly sensitive information? By reading the base newspaper, the *Southernmost Flyer*. He had enclosed the articles, Guerrero noted helpfully.

Without wishing diminish the importance of any information — Cuban State Security was certainly eager to vacuum it all — the reality is that virtually every piece of military information Avispa gathered could have been found just as easily by reading local newspapers or glancing out a car window near the base. It certainly didn't merit the effort that went into collecting it — or the massive investment of American surveillance resources in detecting it.

Cuba's agents, of course, did discover information that saved Cuban lives and prevented disasters — just not from the U.S. military.

Miami, Late March 1997

The agenda for today's meet at the Piccadilly Restaurant on West Flagler centred around — as Gerardo Hernández knew it must — how Olga and Irma were settling into the land of the free and the home of the brave. The short answer, for Olga at least, was not well.

It had been almost four months since René González's wife and daughter arrived in Miami. Little Irmita, González had explained to Hernández, was adapting to English but not to her new surroundings. She'd even created her own "Cuba Spot," complete with Cuban flags and photos, in her bedroom. One day, René and his wife came into the room to find her staring at her Cuba Spot and crying. She'd already told her father two or three times she wasn't happy living in Miami, and he worried she spent too much time at home watching Spanish soap operas on TV.

Why not rent her some good American children's movies, Hernández suggested? "There are some with positive messages," he said, "and, at the same time, it would be good for her to practise her English." But they didn't have a VCR. And René, Hernández knew, wouldn't consider buying one for himself, "keeping in mind his austerity, which has always characterized him." Which had given Hernández an idea…

As for Olga, she was suffering the same culture shock they had all experienced. "Everyone in America," she marvelled, "lives under such tremendous hypocrisy." Her own adjustment had been made more difficult by immediately having to socialize with René's friends, who were, of course, not his friends at all but members of the exile groups he'd infiltrated. Olga found it difficult to suffer in silence their incessant anti-Cuban remarks.

Gerardo had tried to begin the process of integrating Olga into her husband's intelligence-gathering work by encouraging her to befriend Juan Pablo Roque's ex, Ana Margarita, whom Hernández now described disparagingly as the "Merry Widow." It hadn't gone well. Ana Margarita, Olga reported back, was a "jerk." Still, it had not been a total intelligence loss. She and René had attended a recent party at the home of Ana's dance teacher, where they'd overheard some trivial — but perhaps useful, one never knew — conversation involving one of Juan Pablo's Miami-based brothers. He'd recently visited Juan Pablo in Cuba, he said, and described JP as "fine." He was now carrying a weapon, his brother said, and seemed to be always in the company of a "bunch of segurosos," security guards. Despite his re-defection back to Cuba, the brother told party guests that he harboured Juan Pablo no ill will. "Blood is blood," he said. Might be significant, might not. González would report it back to Cuba, and let others sort out meaning for themselves.

Olga's most pressing need at the moment was to find a job. Partly because she didn't speak English, her professional experiences in Cuba counted for nothing in Miami. She'd filled out plenty of applications, she reported, but still hadn't landed a job — though she did have a line on one where English was not a pre-requisite. It was a telemarketing position, peddling cemetery plots to Hispanics in the United States. It wouldn't be a "fun job per se," Hernández told the CP, "but she is happy that she'll at least get something."

If Olga found a job, Hernández didn't have to remind the CP, René could stop spending so much time helping her adjust and focus more on his own intelligence assignments. The official purpose for bringing Olga to America, of course, had been to make González more efficient as an agent. And despite the inevitable family adjustment distractions, Hernández believed he'd "already started to notice an improvement in [González's] reporting performance."

Speaking of which, González had unearthed some potentially very significant intelligence. At a Cuban National Commission meeting a few days earlier, Saúl Sánchez confided that Jorge Mas Canosa, the chair of the Cuban

American National Foundation, had terminal cancer. "They don't think he will make it to the end of the year," Sánchez had said. Then he asked everyone to keep the information secret, González explained, even as he reported that secret information to the CP.

González had also spoken with another well-connected exile who told him there was jockeying within the ranks of CANF as to who should replace Mas Canosa. One of the names being bandied about was Roberto Martin Perez, the man the CP had recently identified as the head of a CANF-sponsored mercenary force. But reports of Mas Canosa's impending death — despite "the goodness it would do to humanity if a guy like Mas Canosa were to die," González joked — might be an elaborate "theatrical play" in which he would miraculously recover through "God's hand and the power of prayer, etc., etc.," gaining sympathy from the exile community in the process.

Hernández wasn't quite so cynical. "One cannot [but] doubt anything coming from Mas Canosa," he allowed, "but I don't think he's going to get into a story of that kind. And I actually think that if there is smoke, it's because there is fire." Whatever its ultimate truth, Hernández reported back to Havana, he and René and Olga "united our 'faith' in a brief mental 'prayer' that the news about the cancer is true, and we hope it cuts him in four pieces as soon as possible. Amen."[1]

Miami, April 1, 1997

Gerardo Hernández was on his way to the checkout at his local North Miami Costco — he had finally gotten his membership card — with a new VCR in his cart when, unexpectedly, "one of the most despicable characters alive" crossed in front of him.

The man was Felix Rodrígruez, the Bay of Pigs veteran, ally of Posada and Bosch and, worst, ex-CIA agent — "or agent, I don't know" — responsible for the death of Ché Guevara. Gerardo Hernández recognized him immediately from TV and newspaper pictures, but he knew he couldn't let his disgust show. He continued to the checkout, paid for the VCR, bought an ice cream and took a seat in the food court opposite the cash registers.

"Thinking that he could have detected some sign of surprise on my face when we passed each other," Hernández reported later, "I visibly placed the shopping cart and the VCR because, supposedly, if someone is there to observe him, they would buy something else as justification, but not something as expensive."

A few minutes later, after Rodríguez left the store, Hernández followed

---

1. Hernández says he now regrets having written that message. "One matures with time," he wrote me, "and learns that we shouldn't wish death to anybody — despite all the damages [Mas Canosa's] actions did to the Cuban people. We have to be different than they are."

discreetly, stopping at a pay phone near the entrance where he could observe Rodríguez get into his car, a late model metallic grey Mercedes with tinted windows, licence number VJG-4512. After he put his purchases in the trunk, Rodríguez walked the cart to a corral a significant distance from his car "with no logical justification at all. He did it in such as a way that, on his way back, he had the entire panoramic view" of the shopping centre and anyone who might have been attempting follow him. The man knew his counter-surveillance! Hernández only hoped his casual presence at the phone booth, talking with his beeper in his hand, apparently responding to a page, would not attract attention.

It had been a disconcerting encounter. "You can imagine," he told the CP in his report, "what it feels like to have... such an S.O.B. and who owes us such a big debt... so close by." The good news was that he'd managed to get his licence number and a description of his vehicle for those back at HQ who kept track of such information.

He'd also managed to get a good VCR for just $189. The VCR was a gift — "from all the comrades" — to mark René and Olga's 14th wedding anniversary, their first together in seven years! And, of course, so Irmita could watch those children's programs Hernández had recommended.

Miami, April 1997

"Are you the publicity manager for the theatre?" asked the man carrying a copy of *Time* magazine outside the Jackie Gleason Theater in South Miami Beach.

"No," responded the man in the blue pullover sweater and dark glasses. "Nelson is the manager."

Blue Pullover Man was, in fact, Gerardo Hernández. *Time*-Magazine Man was a fellow illegal officer named Ramón Labañino, and their conversational dance was the sign-countersign greeting they'd been instructed to use to identify one another for their handover meeting today. Labañino, an athletic 34-year-old who was most easily identifiable by his thick moustache and longish hair, operated in the United States under the fake identity of Luis Medina and employed a variety of code names: Allan, Johnny, Oscar and Oso, which was Spanish for bear. He'd been working undercover in the United States since 1992, mostly in Tampa keeping an eye on the comings and goings at the MacDill Air Force Base.[2]

---

2. Like the other illegal officers, Labañino hadn't been allowed to tell his wife, Elisabeth Palmeiro, where he was going or what he was really doing. Initially, he claimed he had to go to Spain to work as an economist on a joint venture there. Palmeiro, who was pregnant at the time, suspected Labañino had "another woman" in Spain. She confronted him during one of his vacations back to Cuba, and Labañino had come up with another, closer-to-true version. He was in the United States, he told her, on an important mission for the country... trying to smuggle medicines into Cuba that

Now, with the impending opening of the Southern Command HQ in Miami, the CP had decided to reassign him to Miami where he was to take over the supervision of three of Hernández's agents: Tony Guerrero and the husband-and-wife team of Joseph Santos and Amarylis Silverio.

Hernández had met with Santos and Silverio to let them know what was about to happen. They were clearly disconcerted. Hernández tried to be understanding. They should be "proud of the importance of the work" they had been doing. It was just one of the "bad things about this job," he allowed, "that, after working with a person for so long and being more or less adapted to each other, suddenly a change becomes necessary and you have to stop seeing each other and cut off any kind of relationship." But the important point, he added, was such change "is always done for the benefit of the work."

Hernández also explained to Silverio that the CP had decided she would need to quit her current job with Nilo Hernández and his wife Linda, the other agent-couple Hernández supervised. She could quit "by way of an argument with [Linda]… or claim she found a better job somewhere at another place, or that she will tend to her family for a while and return to work later on," Havana had advised Hernández. "We leave this up to you who are the ones that handle the situation." Whatever the method, the goal was to keep Labañino from inadvertently discovering that Nilo and Linda were also agents. Labañino "has nothing to do with [their] work and, therefore, doesn't need to know," the CP message explained. It was — always — all about compartmentalization.

Hernández, of course, didn't mention Nilo and Linda Hernández at his meeting with Labañino today. Instead, they discussed the agents Labañino would now be responsible for. Hernández gave him copies of their most recent reports. The handoff had begun.

Havana, April 12, 1997

Roberto Hernández Caballero got the call shortly before 4 a.m. Saturday morning. There'd been an explosion inside the Aché, a discotheque on the 3rd Street side of the Melia Cohiba, one of Havana's recently built luxury hotels. Hernández Caballero, a 34-year-old lieutenant-colonel in the Ministry of the Interior with a fondness for Sherlock Holmes stories, had been investigating crime scenes since he was 21. His specialty was terrorist attacks, which this certainly seemed to be.

A powerful explosive device planted in the men's washroom had ripped through the room, completely destroying a counter with three wash basins. The force of the blast had blown out a wall, damaging the ceiling above the dance floor, shattering the mirrored columns and dislodging large chunks

---

had been held up by the U.S. blockade.

of concrete from the walls. Luckily, there'd been no casualties. The disco normally shut down between four and five in the morning, but business had been slow tonight so the manager closed up early. Still, there'd been the usual coterie hanging around after hours — bartenders, security people, a DJ who was now freaking out at how close he'd come to death.

Hernández Caballero would need to make sure his men interviewed everyone. Had they seen anyone suspicious? Had there been any incidents inside the club tonight? He would have to wait for the official report from the department's explosives experts to determine what caused the blast, of course, but for now it was enough to know it had been powerful and appeared to have been deliberately set. Was it a random act? An unhappy patron? Or something more sinister?

Miami, April 15, 1997

"My regards," Ramón Labañino began his message to two of his other new Miami agents, code-named José and Tania. "This is a brief encounter to relay important interesting information that I received from the CP." The CP wanted its Miami eyes and ears to find out anything they could about just who was behind the weekend bombing at the Aché. "Apparently there are Cubans involved," the CP had suggested in its day-after message to Labañino, noting a possible connection with the Cuban American Military Council (CAMCO), yet another militant Miami-based exile organization. Labañino gave José and Tania their marching orders: "To search for active information on this act or any attempt for future acts by CAMCO. Details on any activities they may be planning or organizing. Introduction of explosives. Identifying the participants. Identifying the people who are carrying it out."

Havana, April 30, 1997

At least Roberto Hernández Caballero wouldn't have to go far today. One of the hotel gardeners had discovered something suspicious inside a planter beside an elevator on the 15th floor of the Melia Cohiba. Could he take a look? After the explosion at the Aché two and a half weeks ago, Hernández Caballero had set up his investigative team's command centre inside the hotel. Now he simply took the elevator to the 15th floor. It was a bomb all right. The device — plastic explosives connected to some sort of calculator-clock detonator — had been placed inside a plastic bag and slipped into the hollow between the plant and the planter. The timer had been activated, and the clock was ticking.

Hernández Caballero immediately ordered the entire 426-room hotel evacuated and called in the bomb squad. From a cautious distance, he watched as a deactivation expert cut the wires and defused the device before it could wreak its intended havoc. It might very well have wreaked havoc. Tomorrow was May Day. Thousands of Cubans, marching through the streets to celebrate, would have paraded directly in front of the hotel.

There seemed little doubt the Aché bombing on April 12th and this latest attempted one were connected. But how? And who was behind the attacks? Orlando Bosch? Cuban intelligence agents, who'd been keeping an eye on his activities, reported recently that Bosch had been boasting to associates he'd "sent some explosive materials to Cuba but did not know if 'they' had used them." Luis Posada, of course, was also near the top of any suspect list. Could this be the "something serious" he'd been hinting about on the phone two months ago?

The fact that this bomb hadn't detonated meant there'd be no property damage or casualties this time, but it also meant Cuban crime lab technicians could closely examine the unexploded bomb for clues. They would find an important one — a human hair, along with a number of dog hairs — but it would take 13 years before they could definitively match the human one to the man who'd actually planted the device, a Salvadoran gangster named Francisco Chavez Abarca.[3]

The bomb in the hotel planter wasn't the only one discovered that day. A second device was found, not by police but by school children. They were among 40 students taking part in an international chess tournament at the Commodore Hotel in Miramar. While waiting for their matches to start, one boy found a plastic bag filled with something on the hotel grounds. He didn't bother to look inside; the bag was shaped like a soccer ball. He began to kick it around in the field beside the hotel. Others joined in. Eventually one of the adults came outside to announce it was time to start the tournament. That was when one of the boys looked inside the bag, saw a calculator, a marker and some wires, along with some malleable, putty-like material. He showed it to the supervisor.

"Leave it," he instructed. "Some tourist probably left it by accident."

"No, look," the boy said, "the calculator's broken. See the wires. Can I take it?"

"Oh, all right," the supervisor allowed, "but we need to go inside now. Everything is about to start. Let's go."

Another boy grabbed for the marker, quickly discovered it didn't write and threw it away." A few boys argued over who should get the "putty."

"Share it among yourselves," the supervisor urged. "We really have to get inside."

No one would think any more about the incident until two years later when — during the trial of a man accused to planting other bombs at other

---

3. Chavez Abarca was arrested in Venezuela in 2010 and extradited to Cuba, where he confessed to working for Posada, planting several bombs, and hiring other mercenaries to set off more.

hotels — Cuban television showed the accused bomber's paraphernalia. One of the boys immediately recognized it as the guts of their pre-tournament soccer ball. "I have a calculator just like the one on the TV," he told his teachers. At first no one believed him — or realized just how close he and the other children had come to being killed.[4]

Havana, July 12, 1997

The server at the National Assembly offices in Playa finished setting out the usual refreshments — juice, water, coffee — for President Ricardo Alarcón and his guest, then left the room so the two could talk in private. As director of the State Department's Cuba desk during the first Bush administration, Vicki Huddleston had helped negotiate the deal that ended Cuba's involvement in Angola. She'd since moved on to other assignments and was now the department's deputy assistant secretary for African affairs. But she still kept a watchful brief on Cuban-American developments. While she was in Havana this week, she decided to pay a courtesy call on Alarcón.

They'd barely begun the getting-reacquainted preliminaries, however, when Huddleston's cell phone rang. It was a newly arrived American functionary beginning her posting at the United States Interest Section in Havana. Like most newcomers, the woman had booked a few days at the elegant Hotel Nacional before she settled into more permanent accommodations. She'd been leaving the hotel for the few-block walk to the Interest Section, she reported breathlessly to Huddleston, when a powerful bomb rocked the main floor of the hotel. She hadn't been hurt but there'd been injuries — no Americans, but a British citizen, a couple from Chile, a man from Jamaica and a Cuban woman who'd suffered serious cuts to her face.

Huddleston relayed the news to Alarcón who barely had time to take it in before there was another call. Another bomb had exploded, this one at the Hotel Capri, a block away.

The Capri? For years, Alarcón had lived in an apartment across from the Capri. The bombs kept getting closer, the damages more serious, the need to find whoever was responsible more urgent.

---

4. After he was arrested in 2010, Chavez Abarca confessed to planting the bomb at the Commodore too, enabling investigators to finally connect the boy's find to the bombing campaign. According to Cuban State Security, the only reason the bomb didn't explode that day was that — like the device stashed in the planter at the Melia Cohiba — the transistor used in the device was of a lower capacity than required. When Chavez Abarca returned to El Salvador after unsuccessfully planting those bombs, Posada refused to pay him because, he said, the bombs hadn't exploded.

Guatemala City, August 25, 1997

Tony Alvarez carefully re-read the words on the page in front of him. And again. Tried to make sense of the cryptic, handwritten note he'd just retrieved from his company fax machine. The note was not addressed to him, but to two Cuban co-workers at WRB Enterprises, the Tampa firm whose Guatemala office he headed. Alvarez read it anyway.

"This afternoon you will receive via Western Union four transfers of $800 each," the note began, explaining that the money was coming from four men in Union City, New Jersey. The author went on to instruct the men to use the cash to "liquidate" a "hotel bill." Tony Alvarez knew the cash transfers weren't for a hotel bill.

A Cuban-American engineer, Alvarez had relocated to Guatemala City the year before to set up a utility company to bid for contracts to build electric power plants in rural areas of the Central American country. Alvarez had hired the Cubans to work for him, but quickly became suspicious. They seemed to spend more time making personal phone calls — to El Salvador, Venezuela, Honduras, Spain and the United States — than doing the jobs he'd hired them to do. And they spent way too much time in furtive meetings, often at the office, with a secretive, grey-haired man who slur-spoke his words as if he were trying to keep from spilling a mouthful of marbles. The man carried at least four different passports and went by even more different names. Was he Ramón Medina Rodríguez, the name on his Salvadoran passport? Or Juan José Rivas Lopez, which is what it said on the one issued by the Government of Guatemala? Mostly, he seemed to prefer to be known by one of his own many clever nicknames: Comisario Basilio… Bambi… Lupo… Solo. This fax was signed "Solo," the name of one of the spies in the famous American TV series, *The Man from Uncle.* By now, Alvarez knew the man's real identity — Luis Posada Carriles — along with his history and his reputation.

Posada had recently showed up at the office with thick wads of cash, which he'd given to Alvarez's co-workers. They, in turn, had gone on a shopping spree, returning from a local electronics store with bags full of pocket calculators and timers. Later, Alvarez discovered explosives in an office closet. He had finally connected all the dots of his own suspicions in April after hearing reports about a bombing at a discotheque in a popular tourist hotel in Havana. Alvarez couldn't help but notice the mood of self-congratulation among the men. Their celebratory spirits rose with each report of another explosion.[5]

After Alvarez overheard the men discussing plans to assassinate Fidel Castro, he'd reported what he knew to Guatemalan State Security, but no one there seemed interested in following up. Now, Alvarez looked again at the words of the fax. "As I explained to you," Solo had written, "if there is

---

5. There'd been another blast at the Melia Cohiba on August 4, 1997. It destroyed furniture in the lobby, but didn't injure anyone.

no publicity, the work is useless. The American newspapers don't publish anything that hasn't been confirmed... If there is no publicity, there will be no payment."

Perhaps Alvarez should send a copy of this fax to a friend in Venezuela's security service. Or perhaps he should contact the FBI. After all, the money for whatever it was these men were doing seemed to be coming from the United States.

"This Is Really Fierce"
September 4, 1997 – November 1997

Havana, September 4, 1997, 10:30 a.m.

"Bucanero." The olive-skinned young man could have been any tourist in Havana. Raúl Ernesto Cruz León, a 26-year-old Salvadoran, was casually dressed in yellow polo shirt, shorts, sandals and a tan baseball cap. He carried a small blue backpack slung over his shoulder. To the bartender in the lobby bar of the Copacabana Hotel in the city's Miramar district, Cruz León would certainly have seemed unremarkable. The waiter nodded, turned and went to the fridge to get the tourist his beer.

Cruz León's family and friends back in San Salvador also assumed he was vacationing. They'd been surprised in early July when he had unexpectedly announced his intention to travel to Havana the first time. They'd never heard him mention Cuba before. He told them a friend had won a Cuban vacation but couldn't go. The man had sold Cruz León his ticket at a bargain price. That first trip appeared to have had a profound effect. Cruz León was so taken with Cuba's beauty, he told his brother William, he planned to go back again as soon as he could afford it.

Even the bombs didn't deter him. His brother had seen TV news reports about bombs going off in Havana hotels and asked Raúl about them. Raúl admitted he'd witnessed one attack himself. He'd been frightened like the rest of the tourists, he told his brother, but not so badly he wouldn't go back. Cruz León didn't tell his brother everything he knew about the explosions, or explain why he wasn't afraid. Cruz León had planted the bombs at both the Hotel Nacional and the nearby Hotel Capri.

It had been remarkably easy to do. Just as his friend "Gordito" had told him it would be. Although he'd been strip-searched at Havana's José Martí airport, the security guards didn't check his shoes — even after Cruz Léon asked, "My shoes too?" So they hadn't discovered the C-4 concealed in them. [1] They hadn't twigged to the real purpose of some of the other items in his

---

1. After they'd served their purpose, Cruz Léon gave the shoes to a Cuban he'd met on the island. After police arrested Cruz Léon, they recovered the shoes and tested them. They discovered traces of C-4 in the heel.

luggage either. The clocks and pocket calculators he claimed were gifts for Cuban friends, for example.

On July 12, Cruz León had armed the first bomb inside a washroom at the Capri, placed it beside a couch in the hotel lobby. He then calmly walked two blocks down Calle 19 toward the Malecón and up the long, palm-lined entrance drive to the Hotel Nacional. Cruz León placed his second timed-to-explode bomb under a couch in the Nacional's lobby near the public telephones and was about to leave when he noticed a tourist sit down on the couch. "There's a call for you at the desk," he improvised. He didn't want to hurt anyone. He'd told Gordito that. Gordito didn't seem to care. Just make some noise, he said. Create some confusion.

It had worked. Cruz León retreated to a safe corner of the lobby to watch the bomb explode and savour the noise and confusion that followed. He'd even mingled with a group of hotel guests — one of them perhaps the U.S. Interest Section employee who'd telephoned Vicki Huddleston at Ricardo Alarcón's office — joining them in their horrified recollections of what they'd all just witnessed and then slipping off into the Havana sunshine after the police arrived. Gordito would have been proud.

Gordito's real name was Francisco Antonio Chávez Abarca. He and Cruz León had become friends through the San Salvador car rental agency where Cruz León sometimes worked. Chávez Abarca, one of the agency's big-spending customers, often rented four-wheel-drive luxury vehicles — and not just because he fancied them. Chávez Abarca's father, a notorious local gangster, would copy the documents from the cars his son rented and use them to turn stolen cars of the same make and model into apparently legal ones he could re-sell.

Gordito's father — or, more accurately, one of his father's friends — had been the person most responsible for the fact Cruz León was now sitting at the bar in the lobby of the Copacabana.

"Gracias," Cruz León said as the bartender placed the beer in front of him. He took a sip, put down the glass, walked through the lobby to the washroom.

Gordito's father's friend was Luis Posada. During the mid-eighties, when Posada was part of the supply train ferrying weapons to the Nicaraguan Contras, Gordito's father had been one of his local arms suppliers. Last year, after Posada concocted his scheme to hire Central American mercenaries to bomb Havana hotels, he discussed it with his friend, who, in turn, discussed it with his son.

Gordito himself carried the first bombs into Cuba. The bomb in the bathroom next to the Aché discotheque? That was his. So was the bomb police discovered — and disarmed — a few weeks later in a planter near an elevator at the Melia Cohiba hotel,[2] and the bomb/soccer ball the young chess

---

2. According to a report Cuban State Security handed over to the FBI in June 1998, Chavez

players had discovered.

Nothing to it, Gordito had reassured Cruz León when he recruited him for "a little job." When Gordito told him he'd be planting bombs in Cuban hotels, Cruz León figured Gordito must have had a beef with some hotel owner. Not that the reason mattered all that much. Cruz León needed the money. He was so deeply in debt his mother had had to mortgage her jewellery store to help him get out from under. In December 1996, he'd almost lost his car to the repo man and he was now three months behind on payments for his colour TV. But debt wasn't his only motivator. "I thought of that movie, *The Specialist,* with Sylvester Stallone and Sharon Stone," Cruz León would remember later. "That guy planted a bomb, and he ended up a hero."

Cruz León loved the "rush of adrenalin" that came with danger. He had grown up in the middle of a decade-long bloody civil war between El Salvador's U.S.-backed military rulers and leftist insurgents that left 75,000 El Salvadorans dead. But his own attempts at military adventure inevitably turned into misadventures. He enrolled in military school twice, and dropped out each time. He signed up for a civilian parachuting course, but that came to a crashing end — literally — when he broke his leg on his third jump.

After he recovered, Cruz León landed a less dangerous job providing security on the sets of television programs being filmed around San Salvador. "Mostly," his sister would recall, "he just kept girls from bothering the stars." His easygoing nature brought him to the attention of a local promoter, who hired him to chauffeur visiting performers around town. Although those gigs were fun — he'd amassed a collection of photos of himself with one-named Latin American singing sensations like Selena and Thalia — Cruz León was always looking for the bigger score.

Gordito offered that. When he recruited him for his first Cuba bombing run, Gordito said he would take care of all the details: buying the airline tickets, arranging visas, fronting travel expense money. All Cruz León had to do was learn to assemble the bombs; he turned out to be very good at that, assembling an explosive device from "a small wad of plastic explosive, a detonator, a thin Casio alarm clock and a nine-volt battery" — in just over a minute. For every bomb Cruz León detonated, Gordito promised, he would earn $2,000 (U.S.).

After Cruz León returned from his first mission to Cuba, Gordito had paid him $3,000 and promised he would get the rest after his next trip. Cruz León was eager to return, and not just for the money. "I thought that I had accomplished a heroic mission," he would say later. "I thought it was an action against the evil." On August 31, Gordito had driven Cruz León to the

---

Ararca may also have been responsible for the bombing of a Cuban travel agency in Mexico City on May 25, 1997. "Available information" shows he was in the city from May 22 to 25. After he was arrested in 2010, he confessed to setting that bomb too.

airport again and helped him carry a heavy box to the check-in counter. Cruz León told the agent it contained a television set he was bringing to a friend in Cuba. The box did contain a TV, but it wasn't for a friend, and the inside was lined with C-4.

Now, inside the washroom at the Copacabana, Cruz León reached into his backpack, removed one of four plastic bags, connected the pieces of a bomb, set the timer and returned to the lobby. He paused beside a standing metal cylinder ashtray and gently placed the bag inside, then he returned to the bar. He looked at his watch. He had more than enough time to finish his beer.

Havana, September 4, 1997, 11:00 a.m.

Fabio Di Celmo was apologetic. Another day perhaps, he suggested into the telephone. The person at the other end of the line was a representative of Biconsa, a division of Cuba's Ministry of Domestic Trade, with whom he hoped to make a deal. But not today. Their appointment was for noon, but Fabio had a more pressing commitment. Enrico and Francesca, his best "buddies" from his school days in Italy, had honeymooned in Cuba and were flying home this afternoon. Fabio, who'd suggested the honeymoon destination, had promised to treat them to one final lunch before they left. Perhaps, Fabio suggested into the phone, he could meet with the Biconsa representative next week. He really did want to do some business. "*Of course. Yes, yes, that would be fine.*"

Fabio hung up, explained the new arrangements to his father. Giustino nodded. While Fabio met with his friends in the lobby bar at the Copacabana, Giustino would return to his room on the fourth floor to rest. Perhaps he'd join them for a drink later.

Fabio was feeling good. About himself, about business, about life. At 32, he sensed he was finally emerging from his father's business shadow. Although Gisutino Di Celmo was 77 years old, he still cast a long shadow. Giustino had been — still was — a natural-born salesman, a larger-than-life figure who could peddle anything to anyone. After World War II, Giustino left war-ravaged Italy for a better life in the new world. He and his wife Ora settled in Argentina, where Giustino could weave his selling magic while Ora raised their two young children, Livio and Titania.

But Giustino's friendships with anti-government union leaders soon brought him into conflict with Argentinean strongman Juan Peron. After some friends were murdered, Giustino packed up the family and returned to Italy. Fabio — in Roman times, a name given to a "special person" — was born there in 1965. From his base in Genoa, Giustino developed a thriving export business, selling much-needed furniture for hotels in outposts of the Soviet empire. In the early 1970s, he began travelling to Canada, peddling stylish Italian jewelry in Montreal. In 1976 — the year of the Montreal Olympics —

the family became permanent Canadian residents, allowing them to spend part of the year in Montreal and part in Italy.

The collapse of the Soviet Union in the early 1990s threatened Giustino's business, but he quickly parlayed an old friendship with the Czech trade minister into an introduction to Cuba's minister of domestic trade.

The loss of its Soviet benefactor had forced Cuba to turn to tourism to generate desperately needed revenues. Attracting visitors to the island meant building world-class resorts. And that, of course, meant a need for beds, furnishings, carpets, cleaning supplies, everything. Di Celmo was more than ready to supply those needs. In 1992, Giustino and his youngest son Fabio flew to Havana to meet with Cuban Domestic Trade Minister Manuel Vila Sosa.[3] Fabio was impressed, he would tell his older brother Livio afterward, and not just by the fact the first thing Vila Sosa did was to pick up his cell phone and call Czechoslovakia to make sure the Di Celmos really were friends of the Czech minister, but also because the minister, a colonel in the Cuban army, wore jeans and a T-shirt. Fabio was going to like doing business in Havana.

Fabio had joined his father in business after high school. At first, he'd just been his father's assistant, listening and watching while Giustino spun his salesman's web. Over time, Fabio had assumed more and more responsibility for finding the products they sold and for maintaining quality control over them. Thanks to competitive prices, on-time deliveries and quality products, sales had been brisk. One of their first big jobs was a contract to supply Italian furniture and carpets at the Hotel Nacional. There always seemed to be more opportunities. Cuba, as Fabio liked to say, needed "everything."

Recently, Fabio had finalized the first two contracts he'd negotiated completely on his own. One was for sewing machine needles. For some reason, no one in Cuba had been able to find a supplier for the machines. Fabio had. The deal had been a personal breakthrough, Fabio explained to Livio two days before, because he'd accomplished it all by himself. Fabio tried to convince his brother — who was then living in Montreal and had just lost his own job with an airline — to abandon life as "an office rat" and come work with him in Cuba. "We'll have fun together," he'd said.

Fabio had clearly become enamoured with life in Cuba. While he hadn't been interested in politics in Italy or Canada, he developed such an obsession with the speeches of Fidel Castro his friends had begun to tease him about it. After watching Castro deliver one of his famously spellbinding three-hour orations, Fabio told friends he'd never heard anyone speak so passionately about anything. After that, he'd read every Fidel Castro speech he could find and had even begun to read Cuban history.

Fabio also had a Chinese-Cuban girlfriend, and there was talk he and his father might buy a condo in the Monte Carlo Palace, a proposed con-

---

3. Three years later, Vila Sosa was ousted from his job over corruption allegations.

dominium project for foreigners in Havana's Miramar district. Since it had been impossible for foreigners to buy real estate in Havana when they'd begun coming to the city, Giustino, like many other outside entrepreneurs, had turned a room in the Copacabana into his local headquarters. He'd chosen the Copacabana, a Brazilian-themed waterfront hotel that had been among the first to be renovated in 1992, because he liked its tropical ambience, its friendly staff and convenient location. Although it nuzzled up against the Atlantic coast — its natural saltwater pool filled directly from the ocean — the hotel was still an easy commute to almost anywhere.

By 1997, he and Fabio were spending close to four months a year in Havana. That, in part, was a reflection of their success, but also of the nature of doing business in Cuba. Cuba was not like other countries, Fabio had confided to his brother; in Havana everything took twice as long. Giustino and Fabio began their daily sales calls at 8 o'clock each morning and scheduled meetings, one after the other, until noon. There were few formal meetings after lunch. That was just the Cuban way of doing business, Fabio explained.

Today, with their last meeting of the morning on hold, Fabio was eager to hear how Enrico and Francesca had enjoyed their honeymoon in Cuba. He'd already been talking with Enrico, who was worried about his bride. She'd become obsessed with an irrational fear something "bad" was going to happen to them in Cuba. Fabio would be happy today to remind her that she'd been wrong. He turned the corner, saw Enrico and Francesca seated at the glassed-in lobby bar waiting for him. He made his way past the tan couches, the high-backed rattan chairs, the potted palms, a canister ashtray. It was time for a drink, a celebration.

Havana, September 4, 1997, 11:40 a.m.

"Señor! Señor!" the boy shouted after the man in the yellow polo shirt, shorts, sandals and a tan baseball cap. "You left something." The boy, who was just eight years old, was visiting from Spain with his parents. They were staying at the Triton, another Havana beachfront hotel a kilometre from the Copacabana. This morning, the boy had been playing in the lobby with his babysitter when he noticed a man get up from a seat in the lobby, shrug his blue backpack over his shoulder and walk out of the hotel, leaving a small black notebook behind. "Señor, señor," he called again, but the man didn't look back.

Havana, September 4, 1997, 12:00 p.m.

Roberto Hernández Caballero and his team of State Security investigators were already on their way to the scene of the blast at the Copacabana when they received a second urgent call. There'd been another explosion just up the street at the Hotel Miramar. Two bombs close together. Just like at the Capri and the Nacional. What did that mean? About the person — or persons — planting the bombs?

Hernández Caballero knew enough to know that the Cuban American National Foundation's recent statement to the Miami press suggesting that the bombs were signs of some sort of internal rebellion was self-serving claptrap. It was far more likely that CANF itself was behind the whole thing.

But Hernández Caballero knew investigations started at the bottom. In order to find out who was behind the bombs, he would first have to figure out who was planting them. In the four months since the Aché explosion, four more had gone off and another had been discovered and defused. Two weeks ago, the most recent explosion occurred at the Sol Palmeras, a hotel in the resort area of Varadero. It was the first blast outside Havana, but it was still clearly targeted at the tourist industry. Was that bombing connected to the others?

In June, immigration officials arrested a Florida woman who claimed she'd come to Cuba to visit her brother. Authorities found traces of C-4 in her handbag, but hadn't been able to connect it to any of the bombings. Then in late July, police had responded to a report of an explosion in the highway tunnel leading into downtown Havana. It turned out to be a false alarm — just a stupid German tourist setting off a firecracker — but even that had ratcheted up tensions in a city wracked by rumour.

Cuban authorities weren't saying much publicly about the bombings. At first they denied they'd even happened. When the blasts at the Capri and Nacional forced them to acknowledge the obvious, officials did their best to minimize their significance. And no wonder. Would tourists come to Cuba if they thought there was a chance they'd be blown to bits? So far, luckily, none had. But...

Another urgent call. Another explosion. This one a little further up the street from the first two. At the Triton. Hernández decided he would go to the Triton while the rest of his team fanned out to the Copacabana and the Chateau Miramar. It was going to be a long day.

Havana September 4, 1997 , 12:30 p.m.

Fabio dead? How could that be? Giustino had been resting in his hotel room when he'd heard a deafening noise from somewhere below. A few minutes later, the receptionist telephoned him urgently from the hotel lobby. There'd been an explosion. His son had been wounded. He was being whisked by ambulance to the Clínica Central Cira García, the closest hospital.

Giustino rushed downstairs, past the shattered remains of the lobby bar, past the overturned furniture, past the spot where the still wet puddle of his son's bright-red blood stained the dark green carpet. The journey to the hospital was a blur, the news there as unexpected as it was incomprehensible.

Fabio was dead, the doctor explained. He had died almost instantly, killed by a sharp piece of shrapnel from the blast. The projectile had ripped into his throat, slicing a major artery.

Havana, September 4, 1997, 5:30 p.m.

It had been a good day. Four bombs. At $2,000 a bomb, that was $8,000. Not to forget the thousand Gordito owed him from the last trip. Cruz León would be able to pay off his debts and have plenty left over for other, better things.

He should call his girlfriend, Yohana, in San Salvador. Tell her... not the truth, of course. She didn't need to know what he was really doing in Havana. Just that he was happy, having a good vacation. Perhaps next time she could come with him... He had called her three nights ago to let her know he'd arrived safely. "Tell mama I'm fine," he'd said, "and I'll call back Wednesday or Thursday." It was already Thursday. He'd better call. He'd been dating Yohana Flores for 10 years. Maybe it was time to ...

It had been so easy. After planting the first bomb in the ashtray at the Copacabana, Cruz León had walked 300 metres up First Avenue to the Miramar, another oceanfront hotel, placed the second plastic bag behind some furniture in the lobby and then did the same a few minutes later in Hotel Triton, 500 metres along. After his initial experience in July, Cruz León decided he liked seeing and hearing the results of his handiwork so much he would plant these explosives in close-to-each-other hotels too, and he timed the detonations so he could still be in the neighbourhood when they went off.

By the time he made his way back to the Copacabana, the first bomb had already exploded. The scene was pandemonium. Some journalists, foreign he guessed, had tried to quiz him about what he'd seen. "No español, no español," he'd answered. But they persisted, asking him again in French and English. He kept shrugging his shoulders as he walked quickly away. The first police officers had already arrived with their sniffer dogs; no need to stick around for that. Not that there was any way anyone could connect the bombs to him. He was just another nameless tourist.

Like other nameless tourists, Cruz León enjoyed a late lunch that afternoon at a rooftop table at La Bodeguita del Medio, the famous, funky bar and restaurant in old Havana where Ernest Hemingway had once imbibed more than his share of mojitos. Cruz León saw Hemingway's signed, framed declaration — "My mojito in La Bodeguita; my daiquiri in El Floridita" — on the wall behind the bar, admired the photos, signatures and initials that the famous (Gabriel García Márquez, Pablo Neruda, Salvador Allende) and the unknown had scrawled on or carved into the restaurant's walls as mementoes of their visits.

Cruz León didn't write his name anywhere, but he did leave something behind so people would know he'd been there. After he finished his meal, he reached into his backpack, took out his last plastic bag containing yet another bomb, stealthily armed its timer for later that night and slipped it between a wall and a restaurant freezer. Then he left the restaurant and hired a bicycle taxi for the six-block trek back to the Hotel Plaza. The bici-taxi driver couldn't help but notice when his passenger tossed a calculator into the street as he drove.

Like the Ambos Mundos, where Cruz León had stayed in July, the Plaza was an upscale historic hotel in the tourist heart of old Havana. The hotel was conveniently close to all of old Havana's attractions: the Museo de Bellas Artes, the Museo de la Revolución, the stunning El Capitolio Nacional, which had been designed to look like the Capitol Building in Washington back in the days when Havana still aped American style. None of that especially interested Cruz León. But it was a sweltering September day. Perhaps he would take a stroll down the Prado, the equally famous, tree-shaded, marble-balustraded, terrazzo-floored central boulevard linking Parque Central to the Malecon and enjoy a little cooling breeze from the Bahia de la Habana.

But first he needed to call Yohana. He picked up the phone. Began to dial. As he did, the door to his room burst open. Police filled the hotel room. Raúl Ernesto Cruz León was no longer just another nameless tourist.

Montreal, September 4, 1997, 7:30 p.m.

Livio Di Celmo knew he shouldn't have said it, knew almost before the words had escaped his lips. But he couldn't help himself. His brother had just been murdered. The reporter from Montreal's *Le Devoir* had reached him while he was still packing for the flight to Havana. Who do you think is responsible for your brother's death, the reporter asked?

Livio didn't know. Not for sure. But he had his suspicions. He couldn't help but remember that day, less than a year ago, when he and his younger brother had driven from Montreal to Vermont for what was supposed to be a pleasure trip. Instead, guards at the border stopped them, ripped apart their car and questioned them for six hours. Why? For no better reason than that Fabio's passport carried a commercial visa stamp from Cuba. After that, Fabio vowed he would never set foot in the U.S. again. Livio also knew some Cuban-Americans "hated their country," that they would do anything to defeat its government. Who did he think was his responsible for his brother's death?

"The dogs of the CIA," he told the reporter. And instantly regretted it. What did he really know? It would turn out that he knew far more than he knew.

Havana, September 4, 1997, 11 p.m.

As soon as he heard the description from a fellow employee, Nicolás Rodríguez Valdés, a bartender at La Bodeguita, realized the hotel bomber the police were searching for must be the same strange, nervous young man he'd served just a few hours earlier. Rodríguez was a popular veteran bartender. "I make the best mojitos at La Bodeguita," he would boast, then laugh loudly. "But don't ask anyone else who works here, because they'd say the same thing."

That afternoon, he'd been working the restaurant's upper level. There were two dining rooms in the upper level, one large, the other small. Rodríguez remembered the man had specifically asked to sit in the smaller, empty room rather than in the larger area, which was crowded with tourists at the time. He'd been a "weird one," Rodríguez remembered. Even before his food arrived, he had taken out a calculator and seemed to be adding up the bill. After he served him, Rodríguez noted, he barely touched his food. Rodríguez assumed the young man must not be feeling well. "I offered him a liqueur to maybe settle his stomach," Rodríguez would explain later. "Afterwards, he went to the bathroom and I could hear him throwing up. I attended to him, took care of him and did my best to try and make him feel better."

Back in the restaurant, the grateful young man took out his camera and asked if he could take a picture of the two of them together. He set the camera's controls to automatic, snapped his photo and then left. Rodríguez wouldn't have thought any more of it except that, a few hours later, police circulated a description of the man allegedly responsible for the bombs at the Copacabana and other hotels earlier that day. Rodríguez immediately informed his manager, who also remembered the man. After learning investigators had taken someone into custody, the manager and another co-worker hurried to police headquarters to see if they could identify him.

Rodríguez remained behind. He closed the restaurant's upper level, urging diners to move downstairs into the main bar area to continue drinking. That accomplished, he headed back upstairs to shutter the drinks' area and complete his day's paperwork "when suddenly — boom!! — I heard the explosion." Cruz Léon's bomb ripped through La Bodeguita's upstairs, blowing holes in the freezer and the wall where the device had been planted, destroying a nearby showcase filled with souvenirs, shattering the bar's second-floor windows and ripping a gaping hole in the floor big enough that the table where Cruz Léon had been sitting fell through on to a group of four Mexicans dining below.

Rodríguez, who'd been just a few metres from the freezer when the device detonated, couldn't see anything for the smoke and dust, couldn't hear a sound. His ears had been blown out by the concussion.[4] "I had no idea what was go-

---

4. Rodríguez suffered permanent loss of hearing in his right ear, and remained off work for a month. "But more than the physical damage, something like this creates emo-

ing on and I was afraid that there might be another bomb. So I jumped over the bar and made my way down the stairs… It was mass confusion… People were screaming and crying and trying to get out as fast as they could. This is a small bar, and the door is narrow, so people were pushing and shoving to get out. It was total panic."

Luckily — thanks to the fact that Rodríguez had closed the upstairs section, thanks also to the fact also Cruz León had not chosen to place his bomb in the main bar area — no one was seriously hurt. But the reality, as everyone would quickly realize, was that Raúl Ernesto Cruz León had kept that last deadly ticking time bomb a secret while he confessed to everything else.

Havana, September 4, 1997, 11:30 p.m.

It hadn't taken the police any time at all to get Raúl Cruz León to start talking. About Gordito, about how much Gordito was paying him, about how easy it had been to plant the bombs… But he'd kept news about La Bodeguita to himself.

The connections that led them to Room 314 at the Plaza had begun with the black notebook Cruz León left behind on the lobby table at the Triton. The boy's babysitter gave investigators a detailed description of the man she'd seen walking away from her charge: a man in his mid-twenties wearing shorts, a polo shirt, baseball cap and sneakers and carrying a blue baseball cap. Her description matched those given by eye-witnesses to the earlier incidents at the Nacional and the Capri. Within the hour, police had distributed sketches of their suspect all over Havana. More witnesses began coming forward, including employees from the Bodeguita, as well as the bici-taxi driver, who remembered picking up a strangely behaving young man near the Bodeguita and delivering him to the Plaza. From there, it was a simple matter of connecting Cruz León to his room.

In the room, police discovered electrical cables and tools as well as a schematic design of a bomb, along with a list of 12 hotels and restaurants that could serve as future targets. They also found traces of C-4 in Cruz León's backpack, on his night table, in the room safe, on his clothing and under his fingernails. (Later, when they checked out the hotel room where he'd stayed during his first trip in July, they found traces of C-4 in its room safe too.)

They were still questioning Cruz León at 11 p.m. when the bomb he'd planted at the Bodeguita del Medio finally went off. Cruz León explained he didn't say anything about it in advance because he hoped they would assume someone else was responsible since he was already under arrest. He was wrong about that.

---

tional damage," he later told author Keith Bolender. "Every time I see someone with a package, I react to it. And every day, tourists bring in packages. Many times tourists come in and leave packages. They forget them. Every time that happens, I feel it again, in the pit of my stomach, that same fear. All the time."

WHAT LIES ACROSS THE WATER

Venezuela, September 5, 1997

"Paco," the caller demanded, "are you up to date on all this?" Paco was Francisco Pimentel, a Cuban-born Venezuelan businessman with close connections to Venezuela's secret police. During the early seventies, he'd become friends with Luis Posada. The two men had remained close. Posada was calling today to update him on his latest success.

"You have no idea," Posada gloated. "Three in a row in three hotels in Miramar, all synchronized and with no chance of them detecting the envoy." Posada hadn't yet heard the news of Cruz León's arrest. "And this is just starting. I promise you that several more envoys are on their way to Cuba to carry out new actions… This is really fierce," Posada gloated.

Miami, September 6, 1997

On Saturday, September 6 — just two days after Fabio Di Celmo's death — Liz Balmaseda began her twice-weekly column in the Miami *Herald* this way: "Fabio Di Celmo could have been a poster boy for the ugly foreigner in Havana." Cuban-born, Miami-raised Balmaseda represented what passed for liberal opinion in Miami. Although she did occasionally challenge the *exilio* status quo — in one 1992 column, for example, she described a report by the international human rights group America's Watch that described Miami as a dangerous place for dissenters as "this brutal truth" — she mostly shared, and gave voice to, the views of so many in Miami who regarded anyone who did business with Cuba as treacherous and despicable an enemy as the bearded one himself. In this morning's column, in fact, she'd approvingly quoted local anti-Castro radio talk show host Ninoska Pérez — Roberto Martin Perez's wife — describing the bombing campaign as a legitimate "last resort" for those who had tried everything else to bring democracy to their homeland.

"Until his death," Balmaseda added, Fabio Di Celmo was just one among "the morally vacant capitalists rushing to Cuba to make a buck." But now, she fretted, he had become "a symbol for something else… Castro authorities could point to Di Celmo as an innocent victim. They could point northward and blame their enemies. And the victim's family could blame the CIA, or whoever else they wanted to blame… The tilt of international opinion could favor the Cuban state."

Or not. The fact of where he was born and where he'd lived made Fabio Di Celmo's murder front-page news in both Canada and Italy — Cuba's two largest sources of tourists each year — while the fact that another bomb had gone off the same day at a popular tourist restaurant once favoured by Ernest Hemingway magnified the reverberations from the explosion in media around the world. The Miami *Herald* reported would be-visitors were already calling Italian tour operators to ask whether Cuba was "safe, and a Spanish travel agent said he had received two cancellations of Cuba packages from people who mentioned the bombs."[5] Luis Posada had gotten his wish.

Havana, September 9, 1997

"And why don't you come, Fatty, to get me out of here? You know how the hell to do that!" Raúl Cruz León sounded angry. And frustrated. He had been trying to reach Gordito for three days. He had called Gordito's father, his brother, even his wife. Tell Gordito I need money *now,* he told them. He didn't tell them he was under arrest, didn't tell him the Cubans were recording his conversations.

Finally, Gordito himself had called back. "Don't fuck around," Cruz León continued his tirade. "You're the one who put me in here and I don't know what the hell to do."

Gordito did his best to placate his clearly off-the-rails bomber. "No, I know, I know," he said soothingly. "I won't leave you by the wayside." He would make the necessary arrangements, get some cash together, get it to him as soon as possible. "Stay put," Gordito said, not knowing that Cruz León had no choice in the matter. "I'll talk to you tomorrow. Cuban State Security investigators listened in on the conversation with quiet satisfaction. Another dot had been connected. It was time to tell the world.

Miami, September 10, 1997

Cuban State Security wasn't the only one connecting dots. In the Miami *Herald* newsroom, reporter Juan Tamayo carefully re-read the official statement Cuba's Ministry of the Interior had issued earlier in the day announcing the arrest of one Raúl Ernesto Cruz León. *Salvadoran passport... mercenary agent... El Salvador...* Tamayo considered. Dot... to dot... to dot... to Luis Posada Carriles!

Posada's name was not mentioned anywhere in the official release. At least not directly. Instead, State Security had pinned the blame on one of its other favourite targets. "The investigation revealed, without any doubt, that the operations were carefully planned and executed from Miami by a subversive organization controlled by the Cuban American National Foundation headed by counter-revolutionary leader Jorge Mas Canosa."

Tamayo didn't buy that. The Foundation's political connections ran all the way to the White House. While Mas may once have been involved in violent attacks against the Castro regime, setting off bombs in Havana hotels no longer seemed to be his — or his organization's — *modus operandi.* Still,

---

5. The Cuban government would eventually claim the bombing campaign cost the island's tourism industry $181 million, not to mention close to $80 million in extra security measures.

Tamayo knew he would have to call a CANF official to get their official denial for tomorrow's story.

Tamayo was more intrigued by the possibility of a Posada connection. Posada, he knew, was now based in El Salvador. And last year the aging Cuban militant had talked about launching new actions against Castro. If the Cuban authorities were telling the truth — a proposition Tamayo never took for granted — and this Cruz León fellow's "sole motivation" for planting bombs had been money, then it stood to reason Luis Posada could be supplying the money.

How to begin? Juan Tamayo was the *Herald's* Spanish-Caribbean reporter, which, in practice, meant covering all things Cuban. There were more than half a million Cuban-Americans in Miami, and, for all sorts of diverse reasons — politics, nostalgia, family — every one of them seemed desperately eager for news of their homeland.

Tamayo was also Cuban-American. Born in Santiago, Cuba, to a pharmaceutical salesman and his wife, he was just 13 when the family abandoned their homeland for the United States in 1961. But he hadn't grown up in the volatile sub-tropical stew of *el exilio* Miami. His family had settled farther north, in Bridgeport, Connecticut, where Juan's father landed a job in a factory. Because Bridgeport at the time was a booming industrial area, it had attracted other like-minded, opportunity-seeking refugees from Castro's Cuba. They created their own small but vital community, including even a local Cuban club where Juan attended Saturday night parties and social events. Though his parents left Cuba "because they did not like Castro," Tamayo says they were never "political in an activist kind of way. They just wanted to make a new life for themselves in a new country."

Juan Tamayo's own new life involved becoming a journalist — with a special interest in Latin America. By 1979, he was a UPI correspondent in Mexico City, where one of his first assignments was to cover the twentieth anniversary of the triumph of Castro's 1959 revolution. Like most of those who'd left after the revolution, Tamayo hadn't been allowed to return to Cuba, even to visit, up to that point. Though he was returning now as a journalist, he brought his non-Cuban wife along to meet relatives he hadn't seen for 18 years. His overwhelming impression, he says, was of a place "trapped in time. It was as if nothing had changed. There were no new buildings, there was nothing to buy..." Even visiting his relatives produced a sense of déjà vu. "When we left Cuba, we couldn't take anything but a suitcase. My parents had to give away a lot of their stuff. I saw those things, all the same knickknacks, in the apartments of my relatives."

In 1982, Tamayo left the wire service to join the Miami *Herald* as a general assignment reporter on the foreign desk. Partly because of geography and partly because of the city's large Hispanic communities, the *Herald* covered

Latin America "like no other newspaper. The foreign desk was really the Latin American desk."

Although Tamayo did broaden his journalistic horizons — in 1986, he accepted a *Herald* posting to the always volatile, always newsworthy Middle East, and then, after a year's sabbatical as a Nieman fellow at Harvard in 1989–90, served for three more years as the *Herald*'s European bureau chief in Berlin, where he covered the fall of communism and the first Gulf War — Miami and the lure of Latin America eventually reeled him back.

In 1993, he returned to Miami as the *Herald*'s foreign editor. He was in charge of a staff that included reporters in Rio de Janeiro, Bogota, Managua, Jerusalem and Washington as well as what the paper described as "three correspondents who cover Cuba, the Caribbean and other regions of Latin America from Miami." Tamayo laughs. His new job, he says, "didn't work out in a spectacular way." He discovered he was not cut out to be an editor or manager. "I'm a reporter," he explains simply. Two unhappy years later, he returned to the reporting he did best, and to the Spanish Caribbean beat he loved most.

Covering Cuba — the primary focus of the beat — was never easy. For starters, the *Herald* was a lightning rod. Tamayo took heat from all sides for the paper's editorial positions, whatever they were. Tamayo tried to distance himself from those distractions, and from even his own views on his home-land. He would acknowledge, if pressed, that he'd drunk at least a little of the exile Kool-Aid, but he was, in the end, more interested in following the story, wherever it led, than in scoring exile points.

To complicate matters, Tamayo wasn't based in Cuba. Not that that was necessarily a handicap. The foreign correspondents who were based in Havana, Tamayo would explain, "didn't report what the Cubans didn't want them to because they knew they couldn't — at least not if they wanted to con-tinue to live and work in Cuba." To compensate for not living there, Tamayo undertook "almost monthly" visits to research stories and develop contacts. That, in fact, is how he first learned about the hotel bombings.

Getting the story confirmed, however, had been another matter. Cuban officials wouldn't talk. It wasn't so much they were denying bombs had gone off, he explains today with a laugh, but "I'm not sure if there were any active verbs used in their responses." Officials at the Melia hotel chain's headquarters in Spain were even less helpful. They claimed the explosion that had rocked their Havana hotel's discothèque in April had been caused by a "burst pipe."

So Tamayo began making cold calls. Somehow, he'd managed to get his hands on a copy of a 20-page collection of Cuban telephone exchange codes that listed the local routing numbers for every Cuban town and village, even down to specific neighbourhoods and city blocks in larger urban areas. Using this precise exchange information, Tamayo could call up ordinary people living near where events occurred.

By the end of May — two-and-a-half months after the first bombs — Tamayo had finally gathered enough information to be able to file a report. It began: "At least one bomb exploded and two others were deactivated in tourist hotels in Havana and Varadero in the first such incidents reported in Cuba since the early 1960s." Within hours, all of the Havana-based reporters had filed their own matching stories confirming the *Herald* scoop. "They all knew," Tamayo says. "It was all over the Havana cocktail party circuit. But they couldn't report it themselves until someone else had. I wasn't such a terrific reporter, but I could write what they couldn't."

The unanswered question, however, was who was responsible. Tamayo had put that question to a number of unnamed experts he identified in his story only as "longtime Cuba-watchers outside the island." They essentially offered four theories, the least interesting and least likely being that the perpetrator was "a lone bomber, either deranged or bent on a quixotic campaign against the Castro government." While it was possible — there were plenty of anti-Castro crazies in Cuba as well as in Miami — Tamayo thought the bombings were too sophisticated to be the work of a single obsessive.

He also thought the plot was beyond the capabilities of a second group of suggested authors: "Cuban exiles in the United States who want to create panic in the Cuban capital to drive tourists away and shake up the Castro government." None of the many and various Miami exile plotters Tamayo knew about — and he knew about plenty — "had managed anything like this in 30 years of trying. And, of course, everyone knew Cuba had a huge and very effective security service."

The third theory, which was being promoted by dissident sources on the island and which Tamayo thought could be true, was that the bombings were an "inside job," that elements in the Cuban administration were "unhappy with the direction of the government. These would have been people in the military or in the Ministry of Interior," Tamayo says. "Remember, we're still in the aftermath of the Special Period and also in the aftermath of Ochoa,[6] and there were questions about the loyalties of various officials. So there was a certain logic to that."

Tamayo also thought there could be some merit in a fourth theory, one more worthy of Machiavelli — or exile Kool-Aid: "The bombings," he wrote, paraphrasing his sources, "could be part of a campaign by Cuban authorities to stage incidents, blame exiles or U.S. agents and then impose tough security measures." As evidence, Tamayo's sources noted that Cuban authorities had arrested four dissidents in the weeks after the Aché blast and questioned

---

6. In 1989, General Arnaldo Ochoa Sánchez, one of Cuba's most respected military men — Castro himself had awarded him the title "Hero of the Republic" in 1984 — was arrested, convicted and executed for a variety of crimes ranging from drug trafficking and corruption to treason."

them about the bombings. Castro himself had recently launched a new "anti-American campaign… accusing Washington of stepping up efforts to topple the regime…"

"The timing of these bombs," suggested one of Tamayo's sources, described as a U.S. official, "is awfully convenient for them."

All of that, of course, had been the speculation *before* today's announcement by Cuban State Security. Could the real Machiavelli, Tamayo now wondered, be none other than that most Machiavellian of exiles, Luis Posada? It was at least a possibility. Tamayo picked up the phone, called Lafitte Fernandez, the editor of *El Diario de Hoy,* a San Salvador daily. Tamayo had met him when he was covering El Salvador's civil war. They'd become friends. Perhaps Fernandez might be interested in a joint investigative project to learn who this Cruz León really was and — if he really was responsible — who had financed him.

Miami, September 10, 1997

Tamayo was right. The Cuban American National Foundation quickly and categorically dismissed Havana's claim that it — or some "subversive organization controlled" by it — was responsible for the hotel bombings. "The Foundation had absolutely nothing to do with those events," CANF President Francisco 'Pepe' Hernández declared. Such a spurious allegation, he added, was "not worthy of a serious response." During its 17-year existence, "the Foundation has always used legal methods to get rid of Fidel Castro." The devil — along with the more complex, more nuanced and less categorical truth — could only be discovered in details that would never appear in any official CANF statement.

Havana, October 5, 1997

The man from MINREX — officially the Ministerio de Relaciones Exteriores de Cuba, Cuba's foreign affairs ministry — slid the formal note he had just finished reading aloud across the conference room table toward Michael Kozak. Kozak[7] was the chief of the USINT, similar diplomatic shorthand for the United States Interest Section in Havana. USINT was what the Americans called what would have been their embassy in Cuba if they had one, which they hadn't since the Americans and the Cubans broke off diplomatic relations in 1961. During the Jimmy Carter presidency, the two countries agreed to establish "interest sections" in their respective capitals — under the sheltering

---

7. Kozak, a career diplomat, was no stranger to Latin America, or to Cuba. By the time Clinton appointed him chief of the U.S. Interest Section in Havana in 1996, Kozak had already served as a U.S. negotiator during the Mariel boatlift and as the go-to guy on Cuban-American relations for both of Clinton's immediate predecessors, Ronald Reagan and George H. W. Bush.

umbrella of real embassies of other countries — "to perform diplomatic and consular activities, for which both governments reasserted their compromise to comply with the international agreements on consular and diplomatic relations." Whatever that meant.

"Regarding the information about a possible bomb attack on a tourist facility in Havana on October 1 or 2," this morning's Cuban note began, "we would like to say that although there was no explosion, it has been confirmed that this information was strictly accurate and the attack's characteristics were similar to earlier plans." The note's awkward, bland bureaucratese masked something quite extraordinary, at least to a casual observer of the traditional, almost invariably hostile public posturing between Washington and Havana. The Americans had quietly given the Cubans information about a planned attack and the Cubans were thanking them for it.

It had all begun four days earlier with an 11 p.m. phone call from Kozak to an official in MINREX. The United States, he said, had received information from sources in a third country that someone was planning another bomb attack on a Cuban tourist facility. He could provide no names or other details. The U.S. hadn't been able to confirm the information either, he added, but he wanted the Cubans to be aware of it. The next day, Kozak was summoned to MINREX, in part to quiz him about what the Americans really knew — not much — but also, and perhaps more important, to officially convey the Cuban government's heartfelt thanks for the information.

Now today — three days later — the Cubans had summoned Kozak back to the MINREX conference room on a Sunday, this time to report on the outcome of their own investigation. "Insomuch as this might be of interest and of use to U.S. authorities," the official note continued, "we wish to let them know that the source which provided them with this information has been shown to be truthful. We have acted with utmost discretion, as we were asked to do. We are very appreciative."

The Cubans didn't tell Kozak they'd found one unexploded bomb in a small shoulder bag at José Martí Airport and another in a minibus that shuttled tourists between the airport and Havana hotels. Neither did they explain that, on their own, they'd connected those explosives to yet another of Posada's Central American mercenaries, who had already escaped. It was enough for now that the two antagonists were, however tentatively and delicately, working together to prevent more bombings.

Kozak, for his part, thanked the Cubans for their information. Washington hadn't been sure how much credence to give its source or his "rumour," he said, but now his colleagues would be able to place more credence in future tips from this individual. Although Kozak told the Cubans he had no new developments to report regarding any possible American connections to the hotel bombings, he added Washington was now pursuing other leads in

Central America, especially after Wednesday's story in the Miami *Herald*.

On October 1 — the same day Kozak initially contacted MINREX with his tip — the *Herald* had published the first, still-unripened fruits of Juan Tamayo's investigation into the life and times of Raúl Ernesto Cruz León. "Extensive inquiries in El Salvador, Guatemala and Honduras have so far uncovered no hard evidence linking Cruz to the blasts or to any Cuban exiles in El Salvador or Miami," Tamayo wrote, but then added that the investigation so far "points to a puzzling attempt to shroud [Cruz León's] trips to Cuba in secrecy."

According to the travel agent who booked his flights, two different men — neither of them Cruz León — purchased the flight-and-hotel packages with cash. A third man — also not Cruz León — picked up the ticket and vouchers for the first visit. "There were a lot of different people paying for the tickets, picking them up and telephoning me," the travel agent told the newspaper. "Whatever [Cruz León] was doing, he was not alone."

On July 14, the day Cruz León was scheduled to return from Havana the first time, a man claiming to be Cruz León's brother telephoned the travel agent to say he had come to the airport to meet him but couldn't find him. Had he changed his flight? The newspaper then tracked down Cruz León's brother, who insisted he wasn't at the airport that day and he didn't even know the name of the travel agent his brother had used.

Two of Cruz León's co-workers told the paper Cruz León had once pointed out "a chubby man" and claimed he was the person who'd won his first Cuba vacation in a raffle. Since his arrest, Cruz León's friends had been trying to figure out the identity of the mystery man, Tamayo added, "but no one seems to know anything about him."

Back at MINREX, Kozak didn't say exactly how the Americans might be following up on the information they'd gleaned from the newspaper. Like his Cuban counterparts, Kozak still kept much to himself. But he did end his visit today with a request that "any information that Cuba has and that it can provide to the United States will be very useful." The Cubans asked for the same.

Off Puerto Rico, October 27, 1997

Drugs… What else would four men with dodgy answers to routine questions be doing floating listlessly in a fancy but battered cabin cruiser off Puerto Rico? Officers aboard the U.S. Coast Guard cutter *Baranof* had first spotted the tan, 46-foot *La Esperanza* during a routine patrol 11 miles off Puerto Rico's southwest coast at 3 p.m. Two of its hull portholes were broken and the vessel appeared to be taking on water. The officers initially assumed that the damage resulted from a storm in the area the day before and that the men aboard might need assistance.

One of the officers radioed the captain and asked where they'd come from and what they were doing. They'd sailed from Miami to do some fishing, the captain explained, which made sense, but then he claimed the vessel had made the 900-mile journey from Miami to Puerto Rico in a single day, which didn't make any geographical or nautical sense at all.

Despite protests from the Spanish-speaking men aboard *La Esperanza* that they were fine, thanks very much, the curious officers decided to take a closer look. When they boarded, there was no sign of any fishing gear. One of the officers asked about that. Another man claimed they were actually on their way to St. Lucia to sell the boat. Which was interesting too, thought one of the agents. The vessel had recently been outfitted with 2,000 gallons of extra fuel tanks as if in preparation for a long voyage. "Why would I invest more money in a boat that I am going to sell?" the agent asked himself. Equally intriguing, the navigational coordinates programmed into the vessel's computer were pre-set, not for St. Lucia but for Margarita Island off the coast of Venezuela.

When the officers asked to see the vessel's documents, the best the captain could provide were photocopies. Aristides Jiménez, a U.S. Maritime Enforcement Agent working for the U.S. Customs Service, asked the men if the boat was carrying drugs or weapons. It was a routine question in the circumstances. The men claimed it wasn't, an equally routine answer in the circumstances.

More than curious now, the officers decided to escort *La Esperanza* to the Puerto Rico police department dock in Aguadilla for a closer look. They expected to find drugs. They didn't.

At 9 p.m., half an hour after beginning their search, a Coast Guard engineer noticed a loose piece of rug on the stairs leading down from the deck. He pulled back the rug and discovered a wooden plank, also loose. When he lifted that, he saw a secret compartment. Inside was an assassin's treasure trove: two $7,000 semi-automatic, .50-calibre, armour-piercing Barrett assault rifles, each equipped with night scopes. Such a rifle could take out a target, including even an aircraft, from up to a mile away. Fishing?

There was more. Seven 10-round boxes of ammunition,[8] six ammunition clips and two tripods. Rummaging around in other parts of the vessel, the inspectors found three military fatigue outfits, field rations, rifle-range ear protectors, six portable radios, a satellite telephone and night vision goggles.

A federal agent had barely begun reading the men their Miranda rights

---

8. While inspectors didn't find the .357 handgun that went with 12 rounds of ammunition discovered aboard, the likelihood is that one of the men tossed the gun overboard, standard practice whenever the exiles were stopped at sea with illicit cargo. José Toñin Llama would later tell a reporter about another incident in 1996 when a Bahamian patrol vessel approached one of their yachts, which was carrying explosives. Those aboard quickly dumped the cargo into the ocean. "Soon after, we went there to recover it," Llama explained, "but didn't find it."

when one of them, 57-year-old Angel Alfonso Aleman, whose day job was as the administrator of a New Jersey textile factory cut him off. "He burst out and started yelling that the weapons were his," one of the customs investigators would recall later. "The others know nothing about them," Alfonso shouted. "I placed them there myself. They are weapons for the purpose of assassinating Fidel Castro."

The agents tried to stop him now because he was making incriminating statements, but Alfonso refused to keep quiet. "Look at all the entries in my passport going to Venezuela," he told them. "Do you think I went there on vacation? I have a contact on St. Lucia. I have a contact on Margarita." His only mission in life, he added proudly, was to assassinate Fidel Castro.[9]

It didn't take the Coast Guard long to call in the FBI. The man in charge of the FBI office in Puerto Rico at the time was Hector Pesquera, who... well, let's not get ahead of ourselves. FBI investigators quickly discovered a number of interesting facts: One of the two assault rifles found aboard *La Esperanza* turned out to be registered to Pepe Hernández, the president of the Cuban American National Foundation, the man who'd once promised Percy Alvarado he'd live "like a king" for the rest of his life if he would help assassinate Fidel Castro. The vessel itself — licence FL1390EM — was registered to a Florida company called Nautical Sports, whose director, president, secretary and treasurer were all listed as one José Antonio Llama, a member of CANF's executive board.

The vessel had set sail in mid-October from a private dock behind a home in the "tony section" of Gables-by-the-Sea. The home was owned by Marco Antonio Sainz, a Cuban exile businessman whose daughter was married to a son of CANF's treasurer. Sainz was also friends with Llama and had business connections with another CANF member. Sainz claimed he'd kept the vessel at his dock as a "favour" for his friend but that, one morning at dawn a few weeks earlier, he'd seen some people he didn't know sail off in it.[10]

When the FBI contacted Llama, he claimed the men were on their way to sell *La Esperanza*... but in Venezuela. Margarita, Venezuela, the pre-set destination listed on the boat's computer, just happened to be where Latin American leaders, including Fidel Castro, were scheduled to meet in less than two weeks. A spokesperson for the Cuban American National Foundation said she knew "absolutely nothing" about any boat. And CANF was certainly not involved in any assassination plot. Of course not.

---

9. During later court hearings, Alfonso denied making those statements.
10. One of Cuban State Security's ubiquitous "reliable sources" reported that a Cuban-American businessman named Carlos Martinez, one of Sainz's neighbours, also noticed "a small remote control guided plane covered with a sail cloth" near where *La Esperanza* was docked.

WHAT LIES ACROSS THE WATER

Miami, November 15, 1997

Special Report: The Plot Behind Cuba Bombings… The headline on the front page of Saturday morning's Miami *Herald* was stunning: "Cuban hotels were bombed by Miami-paid Salvadorans," it declared flatly. Juan Tamayo's 2,500-word report — based on a "two-month *Herald* investigation" — picked up where the headline left off. "A spate of bombings in Cuba this summer was the work of a ring of Salvadoran car thieves and armed robbers directed and financed by Cuban exiles in El Salvador and Miami," it began. "Luis Posada Carriles, a veteran of the Cuban exiles' secret war against President Fidel Castro… was the key link between El Salvador and the South Florida exiles who raised $15,000 for the operation."

With help from his friend Lafitte, the editor of *Diario de Hoy* — who'd assigned an energetic young Spanish journalism intern to handle much of the feet-on-the-ground legwork — Tamayo had slowly fit the scattered puzzle pieces together. The investigation, he would write, involved "dozens of interviews with security officials, friends of the bombers, Cuban exiles and others in El Salvador, Miami, Guatemala and Honduras."

It hadn't taken long to discover that Cruz León's "chubby" friend was Francisco Chávez Abarca, "a man described by several acquaintances as having a tough face and an even tougher attitude, a man who always packed a pistol and often had a bodyguard."

The reporters managed to obtain immigration and airline records showing that Chávez Abarca had purchased tickets to Havana for himself on two separate occasions during the previous year, including in April 1997. His return flight from Havana departed just hours after the explosion in the Aché. The reporters also tracked down half a dozen witnesses who identified Chávez Abarca as the man who'd arranged Cruz León's Cuban flights and drove him to the airport on both occasions.

Perhaps most significant, from Tamayo's point of view, the travel agent who handled the ticketing remembered that another man had called once to ask about the tickets. He knew it was not Chávez, the agent told the reporters, because the man who called had a distinctive "mumble." Luis Posada! But how were Posada and Chávez linked? Two Cuban exiles who'd fought alongside the Contras told the reporters about Chávez Abarca's father's arms deals with Posada.

In Miami, Tamayo also interviewed three "exiles who support armed attacks on Cuba" and who helped him connect Posada back to the project's mystery exile financiers. Tamayo's sources claimed Posada had "contacted Miami exiles in mid-1996 for the cash to pay the Salvadoran mercenaries. '[Posada] was the political, financial and thinking head on this [operation] because he's too old to be in the front lines,'" Tamayo quoted one of the exiles as saying. "But you can write that he commanded the operation," added another. "He doesn't mind even bad publicity, because it keeps up his image while protecting the safety of the operational commanders."

According to Tamayo's story, Posada himself "did not answer several *Herald* messages left for him with friends." Tamayo did manage to track Posada down in El Salvador and even talked with him on several occasions. But always off the record. "He was a very likeable guy," Tamayo would remember later. "He dressed like a teenager. Preppie. Tan pants, madras shirts, loafers or dock shoes. He was an engaging guy to talk to, but it was clear he was accustomed to dissembling. He'd say anything to back up his point of the day. But then, you'd see him the next day and he was making a different point, so he'd change his story again."

Not that Posada seemed worried that anything he might say would prompt authorities in El Salvador — or anywhere else outside Cuba — to arrest him. His confidence seemed well placed. Salvadoran officials admitted the case had not been investigated "vigorously," partly because no bombs exploded in El Salvador and partly because Salvadoran officials were skeptical of Cuba's allegations. "How could [Cruz León] smuggle explosives into Cuba, a tough police state," asked El Salvador's deputy public security minister, "when we're sure we can detect them at our airport? That is, how to say it, incredible.'"

Guatemala City, November 1997

Tony Alvarez found something else even more incredible. Alvarez had been trying for months to interest someone in authority in his information about Luis Posada. Well now, finally, he had a response. It was not what he expected. Alvarez had written a letter about Posada to a friend in Venezuela, enclosing a copy of the fax. That letter eventually made its way to the office of the Joint Terrorism Task Force in Miami, where it ended up on the desk of George Kiszynski, a veteran FBI agent.

Kiszynski didn't need to be told who Luis Posada was. Five years earlier, Kiszynski had interviewed Posada for six and half hours, the only formal police interview Posada ever agreed to. The United States Office of Independent Counsel, which was looking into the Iran-Contra scandal — including Posada's role in Oliver North's secret arms shipments to Nicaraguan contra rebels in the mid-1980s — had asked the FBI to interview Posada in Honduras, where he was living. On February 7, 1992, Kiszynski and another agent met with Posada in the U.S. embassy in Tegucigalpa. Kiszynski would remember him later as a "very engaging man, helpful, cooperative, not in any way abrasive." He had a speech impediment, Kiszynsi says, "but he wasn't hard to understand." They spoke in both English and Spanish. "He was a cooperative witness."

Posada, as he often did, had his own reasons for being helpful. Most of the agents' questions, of course, had focused on the Contra supply chain and what Posada knew of its various players. Posada told the agents that former Cuban exile and CIA operative Felix Rodríguez "arranged" for a private aircraft to bring him to El Salvador from Venezuela after he'd escaped from jail in 1985[11] and hired him for the Contras operation.

Posada said the Cuban American National Foundation's Jorge Mas Canosa knew about their resupply operation but wasn't directly involved. Though he described Mas as a friend, Posada noted their relationship had cooled after the Iran-Contra scandal broke. "Mas did not support Posada after the resupply operation in late 1986 [because] Mas is too busy in his lobbying activity," the agents noted.

Though Posada was "truthful for the most part," Kiszynski recalls, it was clear he was also — as always — playing the angles. "He was a senior citizen by then, an old warrior who was tired of living the life he'd lived and was ready to come home." In the second last paragraph of the 31-page interview report, the agents state, without preamble or explanation: "Posada was not responsible for the downing of the Cubana airliner as he was accused. Posada was involved in the armed struggle against Castro, but he was not responsible for blowing up the Cuban airliner in 1976."

Posada's reasons for denying any connection to the bombing soon became transparent. He told the agents that, before the interview, he'd gone to the Venezuelan embassy "and identified himself to them." Posada claimed officials there told him Venezuela "does not have a political problem" with him returning to the United States. Posada, the report summed up, "is tired and wants to move on with his life. He also misses his family in Miami." If he could be assured he wouldn't be arrested, Posada said he would even be willing to fly to Washington to talk with the Independent Counsel directly. That hadn't happened and, now, five years later, Posada was still in Central America, still seemingly mixed up in the "armed struggle against Castro."

When Kisynzski telephoned Tony Alvarez to follow up on his letter, he did not mention any of that. Nor did he indicate any intention to come to Guatemala to interview him. He simply told Alvarez he was dealing with dangerous people and that he should leave the country as soon as possible. Alvarez would later describe the FBI's attitude to the information he'd given them as "surprising indifference." Perhaps the *New York Times* would take him more seriously.

---

11. The official "record of interview" doesn't mention that Posada had escaped from a Venezuelan jail or that he was being held there in connection with the 1976 Cubana Airlines bombing that killed 76 people. Instead, it simply states that "Rodríguez and other Cuban friends of Posada helped Posada get out of Venezuela and relocate in El Salvador."

"A Duty to Prevent"
November 15, 1997 – December 1997

Key West, November 5, 1997

Like many of the other changes Tony Guerrero had made in his life — giving up smoking, taking up vegetarianism — attending this week's "silent retreat" on a Florida golf course had been Maggie's idea. Not that Tony had been hard to convince. Pritam Singh, a Florida developer who'd made millions "building pseudo small-town housing developments with front porches and picket fences," had recently decided his "long, hard drive for wealth was a self-destructive Yuppie delusion." He had determined to change his life. He'd given away his Mercedes-Benz, his art collection and his two-million-dollar Alaskan fishing lodge, and embraced Buddhism instead. Now he was ready to share the pleasures of enlightenment with his fellow Floridians.

This week, Singh was staging a silent retreat at his still-not-yet-given-away Key West Golf Club. Singh, along with a Vietnamese zen Bhuddist master and 600 followers and might-be followers "were practising monastic silence and performing slow-motion, deep concentration walking meditations that," suggested a Miami *Herald* report, "made them look like a flock of egrets hunting in the shallows."

No matter. Tony was as healthy — as happy — as he'd been in years. The CP had finally agreed to his expanding his relationship with Maggie. She'd bought a house, a fixer-upper in Big Pine Keys, and they were planning to move in together, to share everything. Well, almost everything.

Havana, November 14, 1997

He could see the look in their eyes. Disappointment? Mistrust? Hostility? What was *he* doing here? Percy Alvarado had hurried back from Miami to attend the funeral of his father. The other mourners appeared to wish he hadn't bothered. If he was not a traitor to his country — and some certainly believed he was — he was certainly a traitor to the ideas, and ideals, his father represented.

His father, Carlos Conrado de Jesús Alvarado Godoy Marin, had been a captain in the Guatemalan police force when CIA-backed mercenaries overthrew his country's democratically elected government in 1954. He escaped and later joined forces with a young revolutionary named Ché Guevara. They fought together on a number of fronts, including in the Cuban Revolution. By 1960, Godoy had moved his family to Cuba, where he joined the new government's new State Security Department.[1] He became a renowned and revered secret agent, operating for 37 years under the code name "Mercy." Much of what he had done was still secret. And now he had died, suddenly, unexpectedly.

Many of those attending his funeral today were former colleagues, including "Barbarroja," Manuel Piñeiro Losada, another of the pioneer revolutionaries who'd gone on to become the first head of Cuba's State Security. Alvarado tried to catch his eye. Piñeiro looked the other way.

Though Percy Alvarado Godoy did not seem to be cut from the same revolutionary cloth as his father, he was, of course, very much his father's son. When he was just 18, Alvarado would recall, he was walking down 60th Street with a girlfriend after a party when someone told him Ché Guevara had died. As a boy, Alvarado had met Ché with his father. "I started to cry, bawling. It was an indescribable pain and I said to myself that I was going to do everything I could, not to be like Ché, but to do, in everything, what he did."

Ten years later, he took his own State Security oath and "was told I had to begin to change my behavior... who I was." What he had been was a proud communist, a teacher at the Lenin school, general secretary of his trade union sector, president of his local Committee for the Defence of the Revolution, secretary of the International Committee of Solidarity with Cuba. "To start to change all that..."

He'd had to learn to be somebody he wasn't. He'd learned well. And his work was not yet done. Which was why he hadn't been able to tell his father and mother the truth and why, even now, he couldn't explain himself to the mourners at his father's funeral. Not even to Piñeiro, a man Alvarado greatly admired and a man who would have understood. "Today we leave Carlos here," Piñeiro had declared in his eulogy, "with the conviction that some day Cubans will have a better idea of this man's life... We are left with the duty to talk about him — when we can — and to tell who this man really was."

Later, standing at the edge of the crowd of mourners, Alvarado noticed a colleague — one of the few who knew the truth about him — approach Piñeiro and whisper something in his ear. They looked over at Alvarado. Soon after, Piñeiro himself approached to offer his condolences. Later, in a corner away from the others, Alvarado would recall, he "embraced me effusively."[2]

---

1. During the Bay of Pigs invasion, Alvarado says his "enraged" mother, Marta Alicia Godoy Muñoz, fired her .38 caliber weapon into the air at attacking war planes to defend Cuba's Liberty City.

2. According to the 2005 book *Tania: Undercover with Ché in Chile,* Alvarado's father's

"A DUTY TO PREVENT"

Miami, November 26, 1997

As a lone trumpeter played "Taps" and TV station helicopters hovered in the overcast sky above, Jorge Mas Santos Jr., emerged from the teary, black-clad clutch of family — his mother Irma, his two brothers, Juan Carlos and José Ramón, and their wives — and approached the coffin as it was slowly lowered into the ground. He sprinkled handfuls of dirt — precious soil from Cuba — into the hole and onto the remains of his father. "We shall return soon," he said softly.

Jorge Mas Canosa, the most successful Cuba-American businessman in the United States, the undisputed leader of Miami's anti-Castro exile community, the founder of the Cuban American National Foundation, the creator and shaper of American foreign policy, the *eminence grise* behind the ongoing war to win his homeland back from Fidel Castro, the man who believed he would replace Castro, the man who had promised his followers they would all one day return to a "free" Cuba would now not make that journey. He was dead at 58. He had died Sunday — three days earlier — at his gated home in Coral Gables. Dr. Alberto Hernández, a fellow exile-in-arms and his personal physician, said he'd died as the result of complications — renal failure, cardiac arrest — from the lung cancer that had been slowly eating away at his insides.

In May, the family announced he had Paget's disease, a usually manageable bone disorder, mostly to dampen gossip and speculation about the more deadly diagnosis that had been confirmed two months before. On September 28 — just two weeks after Cuban State Security publicly linked him to the hotel bombing campaign — Mas Canosa had been hospitalized for a lung infection. Despite fervent prayers for his health at exile churches all over America, his condition only got worse.

President Bill Clinton was quick to issue a statement to mark his passing: "Jorge was a born leader and organizer whose tenacity, strength of conviction and passion I greatly admired," Clinton said. "He galvanized his community, his adopted country and people around the world for the cause of freedom and democracy in Cuba."

As the body, surrounded by flowers in the shape of the Cuban flag, lay in state in Miami, thousands came to pay their respects. There were community leaders, unrepentant militants, ordinary exiles, politicians on the make. Jeb Bush, the son of the former president who was now seeking the Republican nomination for governor of Florida, showed up. The Florida congressional delegation organized a special memorial service in an ornate chamber in the Senate's Russell Office Building in Washington.

---

identity was as secret as his son's. "Until recently," notes author Ulises Estrada, "it was not possible to reveal 'Mercy's' real identity because his son, Percy Alvarado, worked as a Cuban agent who penetrated the ranks of counter-revolutionary and terrorist groups operating in Miami."

"For the [Cuban exile community], this has been a great loss," Orlando Bosch, who was among the Miami mourners, told reporters. "But for the cause of a free Cuba, this will be an even greater blow."

Luis Posada didn't make the ceremony. He was still in Central America, still planning and plotting to try to make Mas Canosa's dream reality.

There was no question that, on this day at least, thousands of Cuban-Americans shared Jorge Mas Canosa's dream. The day before, as his sons escorted their father's coffin from the hearse into St. Michael's Roman Catholic Church in Little Havana, a lone voice had begun to sing the words to the Cuban National anthem:

> "Hasten to battle, men of Bayamo,
> For the homeland looks proudly to you.
> You do not fear a glorious death,
> Because to die for the country is to live."

Others quickly joined in.

Today, thousands, some weeping, followed in the wake of the funeral cortege. Others stood on the sidewalk, tossing flowers or waving small Cuban flags as the procession made its mournful 11-block journey from the church to the cemetery. Along Calle Ocho, people hung Cuban and American flags from their windows. "Mas Canosa, we will never forget you," said one hastily written message on a bed sheet hung from a second-storey window.

At the Woodlawn Cemetery in the heart of Little Havana — the final resting place for two former Cuban presidents who'd fled into exile from Havana to Miami — Mas Canosa was buried. "We bury my father's body today," Mas Jr., declared, "but his soul will live in our hearts… Papi, we will finish what you started. We will do it. We will do it." As two military planes flew past, the crowd began to chant: "Adelante! Adelante! Adelante!" *Onward!* But to where? And behind what leaders?

Miami, December 1997

"We know you know people in Havana," the man began cryptically, "so we'd like you to take a message to your friends there. We want our counterparts in Cuba to invite us to meet with them." The "we" in this elliptical message was the FBI, the "our counterparts" Cuban State Security and the "you" Andrés Gómez. Gómez, a Cuban-American journalist, had been a lonely voice in the Miami exile wilderness for decades, one of the few who openly supported the Cuban revolution. He was the editor of *Areito*, a magazine of "progressive Cuban immigrants," as well as a leader of the Antonio Maceo Brigade, a pro-Cuba activist organization, and he travelled to Cuba on a regular basis. He certainly "knew people" who knew people who could arrange such a meeting. But would they?

Actually, that wasn't the first question Gómez asked himself. The first question was why were FBI agents so interested in setting up a meeting in the first place? Just as intriguing, why were they asking him to initiate the process? Why not just go through diplomatic channels? Unless…

Gómez understood that the FBI's Miami field office, like the Cuban exile community itself, wasn't a monolith. There were clearly at least some inside the Bureau who were interested in following up on Cuba's allegations of Miami connections to the Havana hotel bombings. And, if they were, Andrés Gómez would be happy to deliver their message.[3]

---

3. Gómez says he did deliver the messages to his contacts in Havana during a trip that winter, but the response at the time was non-committal.

The "Memphis Incident"
January 24, 1998 – April 14, 1998

Memphis, January 24, 1998

Gerardo Hernández placed his Manuel Viramóntez driver's licence and folded birth certificate on the customs counter.

"Passport?" demanded the agent.

"Don't have one," Hernández answered.

The customs agent examined his documents. "Name?"

"Manuel Viramóntez."

"Address?" Hernández repeated the North Miami address on his licence. The agent asked how long he'd lived at that address. Hernández answered.

"Why don't you have a passport?" the agent asked. Hernández knew he didn't need a passport to travel between the U.S. And Mexico. "I'm just coming from Mexico," he said.

The agent examined him again, put his documents aside. "Go to Office Number 3," he directed matter-of-factly, pointing with his finger down a hallway. Did the customs agent know? Had he somehow been unmasked? Was he about to be arrested?

Hernández had landed in Memphis from Cancun this evening on his — as usual — convoluted journey back to Miami after two intense, exhilarating, exhausting months in Havana. He and Adriana had spent their brief vacation time together "running against time," living each day as if it were "our last." Adriana booked off her job, Gerardo drove the car his father had left to him. They visited family, friends. They stayed in a hotel in Varadero, stopped in to see her grandparents in Villa Clara. They had her favourite foods — pizza and ice cream — every day. She joked that she'd gained 20 pounds. She hadn't, of course, but even if she had she would still have been as beautiful to him. They'd sat on the Malecón watching the water, revisited the sacred ground near Morro Castle where they'd shared their first kiss, danced 'til dawn at Havana discos. "Gerardo is a better dancer than me," Adriana would say, "but neither one of us is a great dancer. We're not even good dancers. We just enjoy dancing together."

On December 31, they'd had a party with friends to celebrate the New

Year, Adriana's birthday and their upcoming 10th wedding anniversary, which they knew they would not be together to celebrate in July. They'd kidded each other that they would have to stage a party like this every five years in order to celebrate their marriage. But they were just kidding. They had talked again — with more urgency — about finding some way, and soon, to be together all the time, to have that baby they talked about. And then, too soon, the visit was over.

"The taxi's here," Adriana said. She'd told him she'd rather not go with him to the airport. He hadn't told her he wasn't going to the airport — at least not yet. Gerardo said his goodbyes to the assembled friends and relatives and slowly made his way to the taxi. He put his bag in, got inside, got out again, came back to the house. He put his arms around Adriana. "I was missing you already, my queen," he said. They shared a last long embrace, and then he was gone.

After getting himself back up to work speed at a Havana work house, he had been dropped off at the Colina hotel, near the University of Havana, from where he would begin his journey back to Miami, back to Manuel. He'd sat at the bar, killing time, waiting to go to the airport. The bartender made small talk. About the Pope's upcoming visit to Havana, about the fact the streetwalkers had suddenly disappeared from the streets. The two events, he joked, were connected. He complained too about what he called "very, very low salaries" and the "terrible" food situation in Havana. Then, for seemingly no reason, he changed his tune. People were happy, pushing on, blah blah, blah. Hernández looked over, noticed a black man from the hotel watching them. Counter-intelligence, he thought.

In the taxi on the way to the airport, the driver complained about "Fidel Castro's government." Hernández prodded a bit — it wasn't hard — and the man began to "bad-mouth the country's situation and the Commander." Hernández quietly noted his name and taxi number. He'd pass the information to Edgardo later. He tried not to let himself think about the fact he was leaving his wife and risking his life in order to protect people like this taxi driver from attack. The rest of the trip — until Memphis — had been relatively uneventful, although Hernández would later document it all for the CP and for the benefit of future clandestine travellers.

Now he was inside Office Number 3. Had the sign on the door read "Immigration Inspection?" He should have been paying closer attention. He stood at a counter waiting for whatever came next. A few minutes later, the same customs officer entered the room and stood behind the counter. He was still holding Manuel Viramóntez's documents. He opened the birth certificate.

"Where were you born?"

"Cameron County, Texas," Hernández responded, adding an apology for his poor English, explaining he'd lived most of his life in Puerto Rico. *Father's name? Mother's name? Any other identification?* Hernández tried not to show his fear, tried to think how a "normal" person would respond in this situation — "screaming mad?" — and tried to react appropriately.

"I can't believe this is happening to me," he complained to the customs man, making the point he had to catch a connecting flight to Tampa in a less than an hour. He took out his wallet and offered a collection of cards — JC Penney, Costco — all bearing his fake name. "Look, you can call my home phone — my voice is on the answering machine — or my work, my friends. They can confirm I'm me." He opened his carry-on, took out a photo album showing photos of him in Florida. "See?"

The agent looked, handed the albums and the credit cards back. But he kept the original identification documents. "Taking these in one hand," Hernández would explain to his bosses later, "he hit his other hand with them, shaking his head 'no.' He left the office without saying anything."

What was going on? While he waited nervously for the man to return, Hernández re-rehearsed his legend to make sure nothing was amiss. He had sufficient luggage to justify how long he claimed he'd been in Mexico. And he'd bought souvenirs at the airport in Cancun to enhance his claim he was just an ordinary tourist visiting his girlfriend in Mexico. What if the customs agent took him up on his suggestion that he phone his friends to confirm his identity? Luckily, it was a Saturday night and no one was likely to be at any of the "numbers" he could supply. What if the agent asked him why his connecting flight was to Tampa instead of directly to Miami if that's where he lived? He was visiting a friend there, he would say. There was a phone number he could give if he wanted to call the "friend." She would know what to say… Which made him stop. He remembered suddenly that he'd bought his round-trip ticket in Florida. He wasn't another illegal trying to sneak into the country. That proved it! If that was what the issue was…

By now, another flight had de-planed and Room Number 3 had filled up with five other passengers who'd been dispatched here for further processing, including an old woman and her husband who'd lost his passport.

Finally, the agent returned with his papers. Hernández didn't wait for him to speak. "Look, here's my ticket," he told the agent. "I bought it in Florida. I only came through Memphis because there were no direct flights available. But my next flight leaves in a few minutes and if I don't get out of here soon…"

The agent didn't even bother to look at his ticket. Instead, he handed him back his licence and birth certificate — "You have to get a passport," he said pleasantly enough. "It helps" — and ushered him out the door, and on to his next flight.

What was it all about? "I don't think I gave off any signal," Hernández would explain in his report to the CP after he got back to Miami. "There is something I'm completely certain of and that is that the guy didn't like me and wanted to teach me a lesson. I don't know why... He knew I was a legal person; however, he took the documents for a while just to shake me up and his message was the last thing he said to me: 'You have to get a passport'... as if to say that I got into all those problems because I hadn't bothered getting one."

In the end, Hernández concluded, it had been a reassuring exercise. "I felt confident of the cards and the proofs I showed and the people to call. In conclusion, I did not panic and mess my pants." How might he have reacted if he'd known the FBI had been following him for months?

Miami, February 13, 1998

Tita! No, not Tita... Gerardo Hernández had been sitting alone in his apartment in North Miami, staring at the computer screen, deciphering one of those routine high frequency radio messages filled with all the usual information and instructions from Havana when he was brought up short by the brief note at the end of the transmission. His sister, María del Carmen, was dead.

Tita — he was the only one who called her that — was 10 years older than Gerardo. Growing up, he'd considered her his "hero," someone whose own successes had inspired him. A bright young woman and an avid reader, she'd graduated from the prestigious Military Technical Institute in Havana and had eventually returned to the school, a lieutenant colonel, a professor and the head of her department.

According to the message from the CP, she'd spent the day in one of Cuba's provinces, conducting admissions tests for potential students. Returning to Havana that night, her small plane had developed engine troubles and crashed. All four people aboard had been killed. María del Carmen was only 42 years old.

Gerardo was devastated. His big sister dead! What about María's two children? And Gerardo's mother? How was she dealing with this tragic news? He should be there with them. He was the man of the family.

He could ask Havana... But there was no way he could get back in time for her funeral. He was living illegally in a foreign country. He couldn't just hop on a plane. Besides, he'd only just returned from Cuba, and there were so many things he had to do here. Havana was pressing for more information about the bombings. And there were new projects in the works. He couldn't ...

What would María do in his place, he wondered? She wouldn't abandon her post — that much was certain. And she wouldn't want him to either. Hernández prepared a message to Havana. He would pay homage to his sister, he said, by doing his job. That would be the best tribute he could make.

WHAT LIES ACROSS THE WATER

Havana, March 9, 1998

The scene was becoming familiar. Officials from Cuba's Ministry of the Interior had once again invited Michael Kozak, the head of USINT, and one of his aides to a special meeting so they could read him an official response and thank you. "Concerning the information given verbally last Saturday March 7 about plans for terrorist attacks organized by Cuba exiles," the statement began.

Kozak had called a MININT contact on the weekend to speak with someone "urgently." The United States, he said, had received information from another "source of non-specified reliability" about another bomb that was likely to go off in Cuba in the next few days. He couldn't say when or where this attack might take place either, but the information he'd been given indicated the explosives were already in the country.

Now, two days later, the Cubans had invited Kozak to this official meeting, both to say thanks — "We sincerely appreciate the information provided" — and to explain the information had, once again, proved "absolutely reliable." In truth, the Cubans knew what Kozak told them was accurate when he'd first telephoned because — three days before his call — they'd arrested two Guatemalans sneaking through customs with bomb-making paraphernalia.

But, in a sense, confirming the source's reliability wasn't the real point of inviting Kozak for this face-to-face. "These criminal acts are extremely serious and affect not only Cuba and the United States but also other countries in the region," Cuba's statement continued. "We have a duty to prevent such acts being executed with impunity. This would not be difficult if Cuba and the United States coordinated, through the appropriate bodies, the fight against such actions." The Cubans were reaching out, looking to formalize and "coordinate" what had been, so far, ad hoc cooperation.

Kozak, for his part, seemed receptive. If the Cubans had any information or leads to nail down "who was supporting or controlling these activities, it would be very useful," he said. The U.S. government, he added, had already taken a firm decision "to pursue and enforce the law regardless of who may be responsible." But Kozak insisted that the Americans "still had no information about who was behind these acts, that there are several people with a record of such activities but that not all of them live, work or pass through Miami, or even through the United States, that some of them are in other countries, all of which made it more difficult to act against them."

One of Kozak's aides noted pointedly that he'd watched a recent Cuban television program in which a Colonel Rabeiro, the lead investigator in the Cruz León case, spoke about having recordings of telephone conversations between the Salvadoran and someone in Central America. Such information could be "very useful" in helping the Americans identify who was behind the bombings. Perhaps because the Cubans believed the Americans already knew all they needed to know in order to identify and apprehend those pulling the bombers' strings, their response to the aide's obvious fishing expedition was non committal. They didn't offer to let the Americans listen to the tapes. And they certainly didn't provide additional details about what they'd learned so far from the two Guatemalans they hadn't admitted they'd caught.

On March 4, Havana customs officials had arrested Nader Musalam Barackat, a 28-year-old Guatemalan, as he tried to slip past them with plastic explosives inside bottles of shampoo and deodorant. A few hours later, they arrested Musalam's associate, a 54-year-old former teacher and sometime fortune-teller named Maria Elena González Meza, who was waiting for Musalam at his hotel. In her luggage, they found two toothpaste tubes filled with explosives and two small alarm clocks.

Like Cruz León, Musalam and González were mercenaries, the terrorist equivalent of low-level drug mules. Musalam told investigators he needed the $1,300 per bomb he'd been promised to make a down payment on a taxi back in Guatemala City. He admitted he had reservations about planting bombs but confided he'd vacationed in Cuba years earlier and been eager to return. The girls, he explained cryptically.

González also needed money. Her daughter was seriously ill and required medications that cost $1,000 per prescription. "I thought this would be some quick money," she explained. Ironically, the man who'd asked her to carry the bomb to Cuba had made her charge her airline ticket to her own credit card and then offered her $500 less per bomb than he'd promised Musalam,[1] which of course, was also less than Cruz León had been promised. The man who'd made those promises? Francisco Chávez Abarca. Gordito.

In late 1997, González explained, someone hired Chávez Abarca to kill a woman González knew. The woman had somehow managed to run afoul of a prominent San Salvadoran. While stalking his prey, Gordito hung out at González's guest house in Guatemala City. One thing led to another and, soon, Chávez Abarca asked her and Musalam, another sometime guest at the house, if they'd like to make some quick, easy money.

González remembered snippets of information Chávez Abarca had mentioned during her tarot readings. He'd told her he was waiting for money from three different men, including "a man from New Jersey," a man named Ramón Medina — Luis Posada — and another whose name was Arnaldo Monzón. Monzón, of course, was the CANF member Luis Posada had described as "our angel in the northern zone." Thanks to the serial number on

---

1. González's husband, Jazid Iván Fernandez Mendoza, 28, an "undistinguished" Guatemalan government bureaucrat who devoted most of his free time "not to politics... but to whatever happened to be on television," was arrested three weeks later when he flew to Havana looking for his wife. Authorities would find traces of explosives on his hands from helping to pack the suitcase for his wife.

the cell phone CANF had given Percy Alvarado — not to forget an eagle-eyed Mexican customs officer — Cuban authorities had already fingered Monzón as the man who had "organized, supplied and financed" a March 1995 attack on a hotel in Varadero.

Still, the Cubans did not mention Monzón to Kozak or the other Americans that day. They assumed U.S. authorities were already aware of Monzón and his connections to the bombings. If they weren't, it was only because they didn't really want to know. The Cubans told Kozak they wanted to coordinate "through the appropriate bodies, the fight against such actions," but they didn't trust the Americans enough to share anything important with them. Just as the Americans did not trust the Cubans. And so it continued.

Miami, March 13, 1998

Gerardo Hernández watched them — not *them* per se, but for those who might be watching them. "Them" were René González and his wife Olga. Today's rendezvous was to take place at the Canton Chinese restaurant on sw 24th Street at five o'clock. González and his wife arrived early — as they were supposed to — and conducted their own counter-surveillance. They wandered through a few of the shops in the plaza near the restaurant, stopping at a counter for coffee. Gerardo Hernández observed the ordinary couple on their ordinary shopping expedition. He maintained a discreet distance, did not acknowledge them. Was anyone following them? Paying them too much attention? He didn't see any signs.

Hernández was looking forward to sitting down with the comrades again, hearing the latest about Olga's pregnancy. She was due in a month and a half. Perhaps he and Adriana would be next. Would they have their baby in Miami too?

If Hernández was eager to hear the latest news about Olga's pregnancy, he was less keen to have to deliver today's message from the CP. Officials in Havana, he would have to explain, were concerned that, after a year and a half in Florida, Olga "has not begun to 'produce' anything yet." They were right, of course, but Hernández understood there were all sorts of good reasons for that. Unlike Nilo and Linda Hernández and Joseph Santos and Amarylis Silverio, who'd all arrived in the United States as couples as well as agents, Olga had trained in the intelligence arts only in order to be reunited with her agent-husband. When she'd arrived in the U.S., she'd not only had to adapt to life in a strange new country herself, she'd had to help her daughter adjust too, all the while finding a job for herself and being there for René, who was struggling with his flight engineer's course.

The past few months, González had confided to Hernández, had "been the most difficult and stressful phase since he had been in this country… It seems that his economic future depends on this course," Hernández reported back to the CP, "and it seems that it is harder than he expected, so he has had to take on quite a load."

Now — for both of them — there was also the pregnancy. Doctors' appointments, preparing the apartment for a baby, etc. While Olga told Hernández it had been a "good pregnancy so far," she had "hemorrhoids that are driving her crazy," he reported, "and she may have to have an operation." No wonder she hadn't had time to produce useful intelligence!

Everything, Hernández thought, must seem so much simpler when viewed from the Havana side of the Florida Straits. Hernández had had his own recent encounter with those back at headquarters who claimed to know better. A few of the professional second-guessers, in fact, had dissected his actions during his encounter with the customs officer on his return from Havana — which had become known as the "Memphis incident" — and decided he had "proceeded too defensively… gave information that the guy did not ask you and answered questions he did not ask." They'd also chided Hernández for not being prepared "for any contingency before crossing any border checkpoint." That, they said, was "the interpretation we give your report."

Hernández had taken issue with their "interpretation." Last week, he'd fired off a nine-page rebuttal. He'd tried to respond to the situation, he explained, in the way he thought a "true citizen" would: expressing surprise the official would be questioning his identity and being eager to offer additional information to clarify matters. And the authors of the Havana report had clearly misinterpreted his point that he'd reviewed his legend while waiting for the customs officer to return to the room. "In my modest opinion," he wrote with evident frustration, "that paragraph in [my] report, in the manner it is written, explains the ideas rather clearly." He would have been a fool, he argued, not to have spent the time waiting for the customs agent to rehearse his legend *again*.

"Logically," Hernández noted acidly, actions "can always be given as many interpretations as you want… but I think that the last [interpretation] should have been that I waited to prepare myself until I had this problem." While Hernández acknowledged he may have had a reputation from his training days as a "wise ass, and of not giving certain things their full attention," he certainly knew the real-life risks and would never be "suicidal" by not preparing carefully at every step of the process. "No one should doubt it," he had concluded. He'd be curious to read their response.

René and Olga finished their coffees and left the plaza. By the time they returned a few minutes later, Hernández had positioned himself near the entrance to the Canton so he could watch them arrive. "There was no indication of enemy activity detected around them," Hernández wrote in his report, "so I let the comrades see me and they headed towards the restaurant where we met." During the meeting, González quietly slipped Hernández a disk with his latest report to Havana, which Hernández would pass on to the CP, along with his own note that expenses for the meeting — food, drinks and tip — had totaled $38.

West Hempstead, New York, April 14, 1998

Right on time. Thirty minutes before the brush pass was to take place, Carlos Fernandez saw the man whose photograph he'd been sent, standing at a pay phone across the street from the Wendy's on the Hempstead Turnpike on Long Island. The man was holding a black bag, making calls, checking traffic, watching for signs. Doing his counter-surveillance. He didn't see Fernandez, who was in a command post on the second floor of a nearby building with a view of three sides of the Wendy's. Neither, apparently, did he see any of the 35 other FBI agents planted in and around the fast food restaurant.

Two weeks ago, Fernandez, who was on the FBI's New York-based National Security Squad — his job was to keep an eye on the Cuban Mission at the United Nations — had gotten a phone call from his counterparts in Miami. They'd asked him to arrange to film a planned meeting between one of the Cuban agents they were following — neither Miami nor Fernandez knew at the time the man's real name was Ramón Labañino — and Leónardo Esteban Rodríguez Iglesias, officially a third secretary at the Mission, unofficially a legal Cuban intelligence officer.

The FBI folks in Miami had seemed to know everything there was to know about the meeting. Not only the date (today), the time (4 p.m.), and the place (inside the Wendy's washroom), but also even the spot (a bus stop a block from the Wendy's) where the two men were to establish their initial visual contact. Thanks to that information, Fernandez had been able to set up a Hollywood-worthy production. He had six video cameras — two in the command centre, one fixed on the front door of the Wendy's, one roving, one inside a vehicle in the parking lot, another in a van opposite the bus stop and two more inside the washroom — plus still cameras to record every stage of the process.

Fernandez had disabled the hand dryer in the washroom in case the men tried to operate it as a way to mask their conversation inside the washroom. Unfortunately, he'd forgotten to do the same with the air conditioning, which kicked in in the middle of the pass. No matter. His cameras had recorded the video of the exchange of black bags, as well as Labañino changing from a grey to a tan shirt — perhaps to throw off anyone following him — inside the washroom.

Fernandez watched the two men leave the restaurant separately. He didn't try to stop them. He didn't need to. Miami, Fernandez knew, was already reading the Cuban's mail, listening to his conversations and copying his disks. That's how they'd been able to provide such specific information about today's meeting. They probably already knew what Labañino had given Iglesias. They'd know soon enough whatever Iglesias had given him. Why arrest either of them, or the other Cubans they were following in Miami? If they did, the FBI would then just have to search for their replacements?

Gabo's Secret Mission
April 18, 1998 – June 10, 1998

Havana, April 18, 1998

Gabriel García Márquez needed to call Bill Richardson. Immediately. He needed to let the American ambassador to the United Nations know that plans for his upcoming visit to Washington had taken a sudden, "unforeseen and significant turn." García Márquez, the Nobel Prize-winning author, had stopped in Havana for a few days on his way to the United States to clear up some literary loose ends. He was writing an article about Pope John Paul's recent visit to Cuba. When the Pope made his historic speech three months before to hundreds of thousands of Cubans — believers and non-believers alike — García Márquez had been a front-row guest of Cuban President Fidel Castro in Revolution Square. It had been a fascinating speech. The Pope had publicly called for the release of Cuba's political prisoners while chastising the United States for its ongoing blockade and attacking what he described as a "capitalist neo-liberalism [that] subdues human beings and nations' development to the blind forces of the market." García Márquez was looking forward to writing more about its larger meaning.

Given that García Márquez and Castro had been friends for decades, it was hardly surprising the author would visit the Cuban leader during this stopover in Havana. Or even that Castro would ask his well-connected friend to carry a message for him to another of the novelist's good friends, United States President Bill Clinton.[1]

What was surprising — shocking, even horrifying — was the content of the message Castro wanted him to deliver to the president of the United States. Cuba had just discovered what Castro would describe as a "sinister terrorist plot" against Cuba, and he wanted Bill Clinton to know about it so he could take appropriate action. But Castro didn't want to put this information

---

1. Márquez had carried messages between the two men in the past. In August 1994, in the midst of the Cuban rafters' crisis, García Márquez attended a dinner party on Martha's Vineyard for the vacationing Clintons. Márquez had steered Clinton aside to outline Castro's proposals to settle the issue and personally urge Clinton to "try and come to an understanding with Fidel, as he has a very good opinion of you."

in an official letter in order "to avoid putting Clinton in the predicament of giving an [official] answer."[2]

Instead, Castro had prepared a written summary of the plot and "other subjects of mutual interest," which Márquez could crib from when he spoke to Clinton. The note, entitled "Summary of Issues That Gabriel García Márquez May Confidentially Transmit To President Clinton," touched on seven different subjects, but it was "Point 1" that really mattered: "Plans for terrorist actions against Cuba continue to be hatched and paid by the Cuban American National Foundation using Central American mercenaries… Now, they are plotting and taking steps to set up bombs in planes from Cuba or any other country's airline carrying tourists to, or from, Cuba to Latin American countries."

Thanks to Cuba's many and various intelligence agents inside the many and various plots, Castro was able to describe the plan in detail. The bombers intended to "hide a small device at a certain place inside the plane — a powerful explosive with a fuse controlled by a digital clock that can be programmed 99 hours in advance."

While the immediate threat was against Cuba, Castro predicted that the simple, "really devilish procedures" involved and the use of components "whose detection is practically impossible" made such attacks so easy "they might become an epidemic as the hijacking of planes once became.

"The American investigation and intelligence agencies are in possession of enough reliable information on the main people responsible," Castro's note concluded, throwing down the gauntlet. "If they really want to, they have the possibility of preventing… this new modality of terrorism. It will be impossible to stop it if the United States doesn't discharge its fundamental duty of fighting it. The responsibility to fight it can't be left to Cuba alone since any other country of the world might also be a victim of such actions."

Now, García Márquez picked up the telephone. He had promised to call Richardson a week before he was to arrive in the United States[3] to find out whether Richardson had been successful in lining up his meeting with Clinton. But now it was no longer "a simple personal visit." On the phone he explained to Richardson he was carrying an "urgent" message for the president.

---

2. The Cubans have continued to be relatively circumspect about who was involved in the plot and how they knew about it. When I asked State Security's Colonel Rafael Reyes, he mentioned "Posada and his friends, and the Cuban American National Foundation," but didn't elaborate. On August 9, 1998, however, the Miami *Herald* reported that Posada had told "Miami friends that he planned to blow up a jetliner on the ground in Cuba on April 25 [1998], but that Cuban police captured two of his agents as they tried to smuggle explosives to Havana aboard a TACA airline flight from Costa Rica."

3. García Márquez was in the United States to conduct literary workshops at Princeton University.

"Out of respect for the agreed secrecy I didn't mention on the phone who was sending it," García Márquez would write later, though he assumed Richardson would make the connection, "nor did I let it transpire that a delayed delivery could be the cause of major catastrophes and the death of innocent people." He also didn't mention the "two unwritten questions" Castro had suggested he could raise face-to-face with Clinton "if the circumstances were propitious."

Miami, May 1998

"Who are you voting for as chairman of the CANF?" the unsigned flier asked. The pamphlet wasn't written to support one of the many candidates vying to replace the late Jorge Mas Canosa as chair of the Cuban American National Foundation. In the words of its actual authors, the fine folks at M-9 — Cuban State Security's "active measures," or dirty tricks brigade — the document was "aimed at increasing the existing contradictions among the directors of this organization and discrediting it."

Such tactics were hardly unusual, even — or perhaps especially — in the United States, where political pranks have long been a regular feature of American campaigning. From the Cuban point of view, setting members of groups like CANF against one another or sowing discord within the larger exile community was an effective way to distract their enemies from actual schemes to attack Cuba. Given the jealousies and intrigues within *el exilio*, of course, pitting them against each other was remarkably easy to do.

"Flotin," for example, had been an M-9 scheme to spread a rumour that Brothers' José Basulto was discouraging other exile groups from participating in future flotillas organized by Raúl Saúl Sánchez's Democracy Movement. Playing on the reality that Sánchez's most recent flotillas had all turned out disastrously, the rumour mongers were to spread the word that Basulto was boasting to friends that "the only thing the Democracy Movement can show [for its flotilla efforts] is [Sánchez's] heart attack."[4]

With CANF's Congress to select Mas Canosa's successor set for late July, M-9's most pressing assignment was to make sure its anonymous flier — which was to be prepared by Gerardo Hernández's operatives and mailed to 40 key CANF members as well as the Miami *Herald* — attacked all the potential candidates with equal personal venom, therefore making each wonder who among the others might be saying such nasty things about them.

Mas Canosa's son, Jorge Mas Santos, "isn't interested in politics," the

---

4. Sánchez was a favourite target. M-9's letter writers also prepared letters claiming Sánchez had made disparaging remarks about another exile leader — "you are an envious person, an imbecile and jealous of his successes in the fight against Castro" — and suggesting Sánchez himself was a homosexual and that his new wife was in a lesbian relationship with a reporter.

flier declared. "His mother doesn't want him to assume leadership of the CANF. He doesn't have his father's charisma. He is not fluent in Spanish." As for Alberto Hernández, who'd been Mas Canosa's close confidante, "his extramarital relations don't allow him any extra time for politics. His most important distinction, he was Jorge Mas's doctor." Pepe Hernández, CANF's co-founder, "is a loser. He has no capital. He is under FBI surveillance because he is sloppy. He is not accepted by members of the CANF. He has no leadership charisma. He has prostate cancer…" And on and on.

The fliers, Edgardo wrote to Hernández, should be "deposited in several different mailboxes using different senders. [M-9] do not want any finger-prints left on the envelopes."

Washington, May 6, 1998

"After a warm embrace," Gabriel García Márquez would write in his report to Fidel Castro, "he sat in front of me with his hands on his knees and started speaking with a common phrase so properly said that it rang of truth: 'We are at your disposal.'" But the man sitting across from him in the White House this morning was not — as both he and Castro had hoped — U.S. President Bill Clinton. It was Clinton's oldest and closest friend, Thomas Mack McLarty, the president's advisor on Latin America.

Clinton was still in California and would be for another day. García Márquez had only discovered that after he'd arrived in Washington from Princeton six days before. A staffer from Bill Richardson's United Nations ambassador's office had suggested he meet with the president's National Security Advisor Sandy Berger instead. García Márquez had met Berger in September 1997 during an earlier face-to-face meeting with Clinton. Berger had seemed to be on the same wavelength as his boss on the issue of Cuba, but should he agree to meet with him instead of the man he'd been sent to meet?

García Márquez worried Richardson might be "interposing conditions" to prevent his message from getting directly to his intended recipient. If it was just a matter of timing in terms of meeting with the president himself, García Márquez told the staffer, he'd be glad to delay his own scheduled departure for Mexico by a day or two. We'll let the president know, the aide replied.

García Márquez passed that message on to Cuba's diplomatic representa-tive in Washington who used a "special envoy — confidential communications are so slow and hazardous from Washington" — to convey the latest develop-ments to Havana. "The response was a gentle request to wait in Washington for as long as necessary to fulfill my mission," García Márquez wrote. "At the same time I was humbly asked to be most careful to avoid offending Sam Berger for not accepting him as an interlocutor. The funny end of the message [from Havana]," he added, "left no doubt about the author, even without a signature: 'We wish you can write a lot,'" it read.

García Márquez, for his part, was "not in a hurry." During his literary workshop at Princeton, he had managed to produce "20 useful pages" on the memoir he was writing. And "the pace had not diminished in my impersonal room at the Washington hotel where I spent up to 10 hours a day." He would write, eat his meals and receive occasional visitors in the room.

One reason he rarely went out — even to enjoy the city's spring blossoms — was the sobering reality that he had placed Fidel Castro's written message for Bill Clinton inside his hotel room safe, and "it had no combination lock but a key that seemed to have been bought at a convenience store around the corner. I always carried it in my pocket and, after every inevitable occasion in which I left my room, I checked that the paper was still in its place and in the sealed envelope… Just the idea that I could lose it sent shivers down my spine, not so much for the loss itself as for the fact that it would have been easy to identify its source and destination."

Two nights earlier, however, García Márquez had agreed to attend a private dinner at the home of former Colombian president Cesar Gaviria. Gaviria had invited McLarty and his wife because she was eager to talk to the famous author about "some points" in his books.

After dinner, Gaviria — who knew the outlines of the message García Márquez was carrying — arranged for him to have a private chat with McLarty. "He did not conceal his apprehension over the terrorist plan," Márquez noted, "even if unaware of the atrocious details." McLarty said he hadn't known about García Márquez's request to speak directly to Clinton but promised to pass on the message.

The next morning, García Márquez sent another message to Havana. If he couldn't get to see the president himself, he asked, should he deliver the message to McLarty or to Berger. Havana's response "seemed to be in favor of McLarty, but always [being] careful not to offend Berger." In the end, the Cubans were happy to let García Márquez follow his instincts. "We trust your talents," the message said. García Márquez would call that "the most engaging consent that I have ever been given in my life."

After lunch with McLarty's wife — they hadn't found the time to talk at dinner the night before — the White House called García Márquez to tell him a meeting had been arranged for him the next morning with McLarty and three senior officials from the National Security Council. There'd been no mention of Berger. Had García Márquez's phone been tapped, or the communications between Havana and Washington been intercepted? He could only guess.

The next morning at 11:15 a.m., García Márquez was ushered into McLarty's office at the White House, where he was introduced to the three NSC officials: "Richard Clarke, leading director of multilateral affairs and presidential advisor on all subjects of international policy, especially for the fight on terrorism and narcotics; James Dobbins, senior director at the NSC for Inter-American affairs with the position of ambassador and presidential advisor on Latin America and the Caribbean; and Jeff Delaurentis, director of Inter-American affairs at the NSC and special advisor on Cuba... The three officials were gentle and highly professional."

There was none of the *pro forma* sabre-rattling or posturing that often opened such gatherings, García Márquez noted with satisfaction. There was "no mention of democratic reforms, free elections or human rights, nor any of the political clichés with which Americans pretend to condition any project of cooperation with Cuba. On the contrary," García Márquez reported hopefully, "my clearest impression of this trip is the certainty that reconciliation is beginning to grow as something irreversible in the collective consciousness."

The preliminaries out of the way, McLarty joined them from another meeting, and Márquez proceeded to outline the circumstances that had brought him to the White House today. He then handed McLarty the envelope with Fidel's translated letter — six double-spaced pages covering seven topics.[5]

McLarty quickly read the note, saying nothing, "but his changing emotions showed on his face as light in the water," García Márquez would report back to Castro. "I had read it myself so many times that I could practically know which of his expressions corresponded to the different points in the document. The first point, about the terrorist plot, made him grumble and he said: 'It's terrible.' Later, he suppressed a mischievous smile and, without interrupting his reading he said: 'We have common enemies.' I think he said it referring to the fourth point, where a description is made of a group of senators plotting to boycott the passage of the Torres-Rangel's and Dodd's bills and appreciation is expressed about Clinton's efforts to save them."

Once all had absorbed Castro's message, the rest of the meeting focused, understandably, on the threat to blow up the planes, "which made an impression on everyone." García Márquez understood why. He'd had to overcome his own "terror over a bomb explosion as I was flying to Mexico after having learned of it in Havana."

García Márquez knew the circumstances were "propitious" to raise the two unwritten questions Castro had asked him to raise and that García Márquez had carefully written in his organizer as "the only thing I was afraid to forget." The first question: "Wouldn't it be possible for the FBI to contact their Cuban counterparts for a joint struggle on terrorism?" Though it wasn't

---

5. The others included: "relative complacency over the measures announced on March 20 to resume flights from the United States to Cuba; Richardson's trip to Havana on January 1998; Cuba's arguments on refusing humanitarian aid; recognition for the Pentagon's favourable report on Cuba's military situation [which said that Cuba posed no danger to the security of the United States]; approval of the solution of the Iraqi crisis; and appreciation over the comments made by Clinton in the presence of Mandela and Kofi Anan with regards to Cuba."

part of the unwritten question, García Márquez added "a line of my own making: 'I'm sure that you'd find a prompt and positive reaction on the part of the Cuban authorities.'"

García Márquez was amazed at the "quick and strong reaction" of the NSC officials. Richard Clarke, for one, thought it would be a very good idea. But he cautioned that the FBI wouldn't be keen if information about such cooperation leaked out during an investigation. Would the Cubans be willing to keep the information a secret?

García Márquez couldn't help but smile. "There is nothing that the Cubans like better than keeping secrets," he replied.

His second question wasn't so much a question as a suggestion, a diplomatic opening: "Cooperation in matters of security," Castro had suggested, "could open the way to a propitious climate leading to the resumption of American travels to Cuba." García Márquez told his hosts he had personally met Americans from all strata of society who — knowing his friendship with Castro — asked for his help in making contacts for business or pleasure in Cuba. "I mentioned Donald Newhouse, editor of various journals and chairman of the Associated Press, who treated me to a lavish dinner at his countryside mansion in New Jersey at the end of my literary workshop in Princeton University," García Márquez reported. "His current dream is traveling to Cuba to discuss with Fidel personally the establishment of a permanent AP bureau in Havana, similar to CNN's."

By the end of their meeting, which had lasted just 50 minutes, Clarke had promised the NSC would take "immediate steps for a joint U.S.-Cuba plan on terrorism." Dobbins made a note in his pad that he would "communicate with their embassy in Cuba to implement the project." *Embassy?* García Márquez joked that Dobbins had promoted the United States Interest Section in Havana to a new level in America's foreign affairs hierarchy.

"What we have there is not an embassy," Dobbins replied with a laugh, "but it is much bigger than an embassy."

"They all laughed with mischievous complicity," García Márquez reported.

And then it was over. "I know that you have a very tight agenda before you get back to Mexico and we have also many things ahead," McLarty said. Then, looking him in the eye, he added: "Your mission was in fact of utmost importance, and you have discharged it very well."

García Márquez couldn't help but be pleased. "Neither my excessive honor nor my absence of modesty," he reported to Castro, "has allowed me to abandon that phrase to the ephemeral glory and the microphones hidden in flower vases." More importantly, "I left the White House with the firm impression that the effort and the uncertainties of the previous days had been worthy. The annoyance for not having delivered the message personally to the President had been compensated by a more informal and operative conclave whose good results would be forthcoming." Gabriel García Márquez had done his part.

Havana, May 9, 1998

Michael Kozak was bemused. And more than a little impressed. Three days after Gabriel García Márquez's visit to the White House, Kozak called on Cuban National Assembly President Ricardo Alarcón. "I don't know how you did it," Kozak told Alarcón, "but apparently Washington has gotten some message from your side concerning a terrorist plot — and we take it very seriously." Kozak wanted to discuss the logistics of getting an FBI delegation to come to Cuba to meet with Cuban State Security officials.

Miami, May 11, 1998

Miami's FBI office — one of the largest and most important in the country, with 400 agents trying to cope with all the usual manner of crime, from murder and bank robbery to public corruption and drug smuggling, as well as that most Miami of crimes, anti-Castro exile violence — had a new special agent in charge. His name was Hector Pesquera, and he was, perhaps surprisingly, the first Spanish-speaking FBI boss of the country's most Hispanic big city. He was not Cuban; he was Puerto Rican. He'd joined the FBI 22 years before and had worked his way up the ranks, hopscotching through postings in San Juan, Tampa, Uruguay and now Miami. His most recent appointment had been as special agent in charge in Puerto Rico and the U.S. Virgin Islands. During his three years there, he "oversaw cases that involved the indictment for fraud of three bank presidents, a former senator and several physicians charged with diverting AIDS funds, fraud in the Veterans Administration, and an increase in violent crime." He'd also been the agent in charge when the Coast Guard discovered those weapons aboard *La Esperanza*.

Pesquera told reporters he had no specific plans for the Miami bureau. "Whether it's Miami or elsewhere, I will always go after lawbreaking, regardless of where it takes me," he declared. As for Cuban exile violence? Pesquera told reporters he understood why Miami's Cuban exile community were eager to get rid of Fidel Castro by whatever means necessary, but "understanding doesn't mean I condone… The law has to be obeyed," he explained, insisting "we will not look the other way" if Miami-based exile groups violated U.S. Neutrality laws. Many would soon have reason to question Pesquera's sincerity on that score.

Havana, May 12, 1998

In the little less than a week since Gabriel García Márquez delivered Fidel Castro's message, there'd been a flurry of meetings and diplomatic conversations between American and Cuban officials. On May 9, the acting head of the U.S. Interest Section delivered a message from Washington that it had "no information on links between U.S. citizens and the terrorist attacks in the hotels." But the United States would be willing to "analyze any information or physical evidence" Cuba could provide to back up its claims. This was, the U.S. official emphasized, "a serious offer" and encouraged the Cuban government to "share" whatever it knew about "the risk of terrorist acts on flights" to or from Cuba.

Two days later, the head of Cuba's Special Interest Section in Washington was summoned to a meeting at the State Department, where one of the department's senior Latin American officials repeated the earlier offer. When the Cuban asked "if the offer included cooperation between the two countries in an eventual investigation," the American official said he "supposed so."

The next day — May 12 — there was yet another meeting between the head of the U.S. Interest Section and MINREX at Cuba's request to respond to the American invitation to cooperate. "The information we have is reliable," the Cuban statement said, "but it came through sensitive sources that cannot be revealed. We cannot work as you suggest. We are satisfied knowing that you are on the alert and paying attention to the problem." The ball, it seemed, was back in the American court.

Havana, June 3, 1998

The good news — despite all the cat-and-mouse, after-you-Alfonso, diplomatic back and forth — was that an FBI delegation was finally preparing to travel to Havana to talk with investigators from Cuban State Security about the evidence they'd uncovered. The bad news — which USINT head Michael Kozak personally delivered to Cuban National Assembly President Ricardo Alarcón — was contained in the draft of a warning Federal Aviation Administration officials planned to distribute to American airlines. "We have received unconfirmed information about a plot to place explosive devices on civil airliners which fly between Cuba and countries in Latin America," began the note, which Kozak handed to Alarcón. "The specific target, place and time frame have not been identified. We cannot dismiss the possibility that the threat may extend to international cargo flights from the United States. The U.S. government is still looking for additional information to clarify, verify or refute this threat."

This proposed warning, Alarcón understood immediately, was itself an explosive device, whose release could trigger exactly the fear and panic among tourists the Cubans had been desperately attempting to avoid by publicly downplaying the original hotel bombings and now confiding in the Americans the fact of the airplane plot. Could it be that, without even following through on the plot to blow up a plane, the terrorists had won?

Miami, June 7, 1998

If the FBI really wanted "information on links between U.S. citizens and the terrorist attacks" against Cuba — as the Americans claimed in their diplomatic exchanges — its agents could have done worse than read this morning's Miami *Herald* front-page story entitled "A Web of Conspiracy." Reporters Juan Tamayo and Gerardo Reyes had spent months turning over exile rocks in Miami, El Salvador, Guatemala, Honduras and Costa Rica, interviewed dozens of people and returned with "a trail of conspiracies" that all linked directly to Luis Posada Carriles and, from him, back to still secretive exile moneymen in Miami. Their 2,500-word story — which was a follow-up to Tamayo's November investigation linking Posada to Cruz León — showed that Posada's terrorism plans went well beyond the recent successful "bombing spree by Salvadoran mercenaries." According to the report, Posada's plots against Cuba — most of which had failed — had been intensifying ever since the 1990 assassination attempt against him.

In 1993, Posada, who was living in Honduras at the time, came up with a scheme to attack a Cuban freighter in a Honduran port. That attempt fizzled, explained an unidentified Miami exile who'd tried to raise money for the attack, because "we started getting so many people volunteering [to take part] we had to call it off."

The next year, Posada had hatched an even more audacious plan; he made a secret pact with the head of Honduras military intelligence to set up a camp in Honduras to train Cuban exile commando teams, who would then launch attacks on their homeland. Although the deal eventually fell through — apparently neither side trusted the other — there was a budget for the operation: $100,000 to bribe Honduran military officers and another $250,000 to pay for "weapons, explosives, fast attack boats and even small airplanes." According to the newspaper, a Honduran intelligence official had travelled to Miami to meet with four of the would-be exile financiers. Rolando Borges, the head of the Ex-Club, a militant Miami exile group with links to Posada, admitted he'd paid for the official's hotel room.

Also in 1994, Posada "led a team of six exiles" who tried to assassinate Castro during a summit of Latin American heads of state in Cartagena, Colombia. According to one of the would-be assassins the reporters interviewed, the security cordon around the Cuban leader made it impossible for the plotters to get close enough for a good shot. "I stood behind some journalists," one of them told the *Herald,* "and saw [Gabriel] García Márquez, but I only got to see Castro from a long distance." The plotters had spent more than $50,000 just to get that close.

Finally, in 1997, after Cruz León was arrested, the newspaper reported Posada switched Central American terrorism farm teams and recruited Guatemalan mercenaries to ferry explosives into Cuba. But those explosives either didn't detonate or the Guatemalans refused to go on the missions.[6]

During the course of their research, the reporters also obtained a copy of Tony Alvarez's letter outlining his suspicions about Posada and two of his employees, as well as a copy of the fax from "Solo" that Alvarez had lifted from the company fax machine. Rummaging through Alvarez's company phone records, the reporters discovered "several calls to offices Posada is known to use in El Salvador and Honduras." The reporters then talked to "a diplomat" who confirmed that Guatemalan state security officials had investigated some of Alvarez's allegations and found them "credible." They had also — the plot thickens — "alerted U.S. officials. The FBI, which is known to have a copy of the report," the reporters wrote, "declined to comment.

"Perhaps the biggest mystery surrounding Posada," they concluded, "is how he makes a living and manages to finance his conspiracies." They had their theories. Although he peddled his paintings of Cuban landscapes to supporters at "'patriotic prices' that are determined more by the political resoluteness of the author than the quality of the art," the bulk of his income came from other sources. Thanks to "powerful friends and protectors among Central American conservatives, especially in the security forces," Posada had not only avoided arrest but also got recommendations for jobs as a "security consultant" for kidnap-worthy Central American business owners. And Posada still occasionally earned healthy commissions by serving as an arms broker for Latin American governments.

In his 1994 autobiography, published in Honduras, Posada himself boasted about the financial help he'd received from senior officials of the Cuban American National Foundation, including the late Jorge Mas Canosa, Alberto Hernández and treasurer Feliciano Foyo. Posada claimed CANF officials paid his $22,000 hospital bill after the assassination attempt against him.

Had they individually — or the Foundation, or its still unacknowledged paramilitary wing — financed Posada's most recent plots? According to the *Herald,* "Posada prefers to rely on a single trusted friend in Miami to collect donations from exiles, then uses a courier to get the cash." The paper's sources "declined to identify the friend. 'That way the donors can deny any involvement in the operation, Posada can claim he doesn't know who gave

---

6. The reporters were not entirely right about the Guatemalan connection. While Posada did employ Guatemalan mercenaries, he also continued to use Salvadorans too. And while the Guatemalans didn't succeed, there were other reasons for that. The Cuban authorities had arrested three of them.

the money, and there's no paper trail on the cash,' said one person with first-hand knowledge of the system."

Although the reporters managed to find Posada in El Salvador, he declined their requests for an interview. But they did quote an acquaintance quoting him: "What choice do I have but to continue doing what I have been doing for so long?" Posada supposedly said, then added, enigmatically: "The airplane took off a long time ago, and now it's flown beyond the point of no return."

Havana, June 8, 1998

The Americans refused to budge. In the five days since Michael Kozak, the head of the USINT Section, blindsided Ricardo Alarcón with his heads-up about the proposed FAA warning, Cuban authorities — including Fidel Castro,[7] who personally drafted some of the key memos — tried desperately to convince the Americans not to issue it. Although their argument stemmed partly from self-interest — "The circulation of such a warning might create panic, thus causing considerable damage to the Cuban economy, which is exactly what the terrorists want" — the Cubans also believed that publicly releasing information about what their agents had uncovered could jeopardize the chances of arresting the culprits — and provide the terrorists with information that could help them identify the agents.

The Americans responded by saying they had no choice. Under U.S. laws and international agreements, they were "required to go ahead immediately with notification to the airlines, which have planes flying between the U.S. and Cuba directly or via third countries, and to notify the third-country governments." But not to worry, the officials declared. Each year, the FAA issued 15 to 20 such circulars. They were distributed only to those who needed to know. "In our experience," one American note reassured, "even when they become public, they do not normally have significant or lasting impact on air travel of passengers or cargo."

The Cubans were not reassured. Nor were they comforted by the American offer to delay issuing the warning if the Cubans would agree to advance the planned June 15 meeting of "experts" from the FBI and Cuban State Security by a week. If the Cubans agreed, the Americans said, "we would propose to make such notifications after we have had a chance to evaluate the

---

7. In his 2005 speech about the events leading to the arrest of the Five, Castro acknowledged that both sides had been doing their best to find a reasonable accommodation. "In my view, these exchanges they made in good faith, there was not a bad faith. We have tried to delve into this and we realize how much they insisted on certain legal procedures that forced them to do that… I have no doubts, really, that these exchanges they made in good faith. They were serious; we both were, and it's only fair to admit it."

information with the Cuban side." Cuban security officials were still vetting the documents and evidence they would share with the Americans; they couldn't be ready that quickly.

Which meant that, in the end, the American position — "We have no option in this respect as long as we believe the information to be credible" — prevailed. While that represented a welcome, if backhanded, acknowledgment that the U.S. side believed the Cuban information was credible, it also meant that, on June 8, 1998, the FAA went ahead and issued its information circular about the bomb threat.

Havana, June 10, 1998

"Open your bag please, sir." Otto Rodríguez knew he shouldn't have gotten off the plane. He'd hesitated when he spotted the uniformed men and their dogs — guard dogs? sniffer dogs? — on the tarmac outside his airplane, but then decided they couldn't have known. Could they? About the last time he'd been in Havana? About the bomb he'd set off inside the Melia Cohiba hotel last August? How could they?

Nervously, Rodríguez opened his suitcase for the customs agent at the José Marti Airport, tried to make diverting small talk. "I'm meeting a friend," he blurted. "His name is Juan. I have a picture of his granddaughter." He took the photo out of his wallet, showed it to the customs agent. The agent took it.

"Empty your suitcase, sir."

Rodríguez did as he was told. Shirts, pants, underwear, Nothing amiss here.

"Please take everything over to that room, sir," the agent said, pointing to a room across the hall. There, another official didn't waste time. He opened the false bottom of the suitcase the man had given him back in El Salvador. He knew! Inside, the agent found 519 grams of plastic explosives, two Casio PQ10 digital clocks —

"They're not mine," Rodríguez said. "I've never seen them before. I don't know how they got there."

"Take off your clothes." After he did so, the agent examined them, discovered C-4 inside his shoes but failed to find the detonators in his pants. If they found them later? It was too late now anyway. "Inside the small pocket in the jeans," Rodríguez said, pointing the customs agent to where he'd hidden them.

Otto Rene Rodríguez Llerena hadn't been caught by accident. Cuban officials hadn't known exactly who he would be, but they'd known he was coming. The photo of the little girl had simply confirmed he was their bomb-bearer. The Cubans knew because of Felix. Like Percy Alvarado, Felix was another Cuban secret agent burrowed inside a Miami exile organization.

Felix's real name was Juan Francisco Fernandez Gómez. During the 1960s, he'd been convicted of anti-Castro activities and served 10 years in prison with men who would later become key figures in the Miami exile community. During a trip to the U.S. to visit family in the mid-1990s, one of them — Rolando Borges Paz, a founder of the Ex-Club of Political Prisoners — recruited him to help carry out attacks inside Cuba.[8] Borges bragged to Fernandez Gómez that his plots were being underwritten by the Cuban American National Foundation. Borges eventually provided Fernandez with an invisible ink pen for composing messages and an ultra-violet light to read them. He also gave him one half an American dollar bill. If Borges sent an emissary to visit him, he explained, the emissary would be carrying the other half of the bill. As soon as Fernandez returned to Cuba, he reported Borges's offer to State Security and became Agent Felix.

Borges's plans — including one to attack a power station at Matanzas and another to place a bomb at the recently opened Ché Guevara mausoleum in Santa Clara — had been put on hold after Cruz León's arrest. But by the spring of 1998, when Fernandez paid another visit to Miami, Borges announced he was ready to resume the attacks. Borges's new plan was to use a Central American to carry explosives into Cuba. The courier would check into a Havana hotel and then call Fernandez — whom he would know as "Juan" — to arrange a face-to-face handover of the bomb-making material. Fernandez was to wear a black baseball cap Borges gave him — with the words "100% Cubano" emblazoned on the front — so the courier could identify him. How would Fernandez know the courier was who he claimed to be? Borges asked Fernandez for a personal photo — he gave him one of his granddaughter — and told him the courier would give it back to him when they met.

That courier, of course, turned out to be Otto Rodríguez, a 40-year-old ex-soldier who'd fought against the rebel FLMN guerillas during the Salvadoran civil war. Reminiscing about his military exploits fighting communists was how he'd come to meet the man who'd hired him to plant his first bomb in Cuba in the summer of 1997. At the time, Rodríguez was working as the security manager for a local Toyota dealership. He helped the man buy a car. The man claimed to be involved in real estate, said he was Cuban.

"I've always wanted to go to Cuba," Rodríguez told him.

"How would you like to see Cuba and help the struggle for Cuban democracy at the same time?" the man responded. The man had offered to pay for his trip and give him $1,000 if he'd set off a bomb in a tourist area in Havana. Though he didn't need the money, Rodríguez thought it sounded like a good "business deal." He agreed.

During his first visit to Havana, in early August 1997, Rodríguez had

---

8. Borges himself denied the allegations, made by Fernandez and a second former political prisoner, Oscar Madruga. "These are two poor viejos [old men] who were broken in prison," he told the Miami *Herald*. "Prison is hard and the government terrorizes you."

checked out both El Castillo del Morro and the Granma yacht near the Museum of the Revolution before finally deciding to plant his bomb at the Melia Cohiba — for no better reason than that he had met a couple of friends who were staying there. He didn't know at the time that the hotel had been the site of two previous explosions, or that Cuban police still had a command headquarters there. Luckily, he was able to plant his bomb in the hotel lobby, set the timer for 4 a.m. the next day and depart, undetected.

The day after he returned to El Salvador, the secretary at the car dealership handed him an envelope the man had left for him. It contained his payment for the mission. Six months later, the man approached him again to ask if he would plant another bomb. This time, Rodríguez said no. Figuring out where to plant the bomb and planting it had eaten up too much vacation time, and, besides, it was too dangerous. So the man made a second offer — another free trip to Cuba and $250 just to bring a "package" into the country for him. Foolishly, Rodríguez had said yes, and now, he knew, he was in very big trouble.

After questioning him — like Cruz León, Rodríguez quickly confessed — Cuban State Security arranged an "audio" line-up of voices to see if Rodríguez could pick out the voice of the man he said he had known as Ignacio Medina and who, he explained to his interrogators, spoke in a "a peculiar manner and appeared to swallow excess saliva quite often during conversations." He recognized the voice of Luis Posada Carriles as soon as he heard it on tape.

What made Otto Rodríguez's identification significant was not simply that he'd been hired by Posada himself — unlike Cruz León, who was recruited by Chavez Abarca and never met Posada — but also because Posada gave Rodríguez the photo to show at his meeting with "Juan." Posada would have had to have gotten that photo from Borges or someone else in Miami. Miami-Posada-bomb. Check and checkmate.

"I Sleep Like a Baby"
June 15, 1998 – August 13, 1998

Havana, June 15–18, 1998

The gathering, in a State Security protocol house on the outskirts of Havana, was unprecedented. For the first time in anyone's memory, a delegation of American law enforcement officials — from the Justice Department, the Federal Bureau of Investigation and the Transportation Security Administration — had travelled to Havana to meet their counterparts from Cuban State Security to discuss investigative details of violence against Cuba that allegedly originated in — or was financed from — the United States. Although these three days of secret meetings had been sanctioned at the very highest levels in Washington and Havana, each side was understandably wary of the other. The Cubans didn't want the Americans to know how they knew what they knew, partly because they were convinced the Americans already knew much of it, and partly because they didn't want to risk burning their sources by talking too candidly. (The Cubans didn't know then, of course, that at least some of those sources had already been scorched.) The Americans, for their part, fretted that Cuba's information might turn out to be disinformation, which would seem even worse if word leaked in Miami's exile leadership that they'd been consorting with the "enemy."

The U.S. delegation was led by Agustin Rodríguez, an FBI agent who'd been described to the Cubans as "representing the U.S. Justice Department," and Luis Rodríguez, a veteran Miami-Dade police officer and member of the Miami-based Joint Terrorism Task Force.[1] The Cuban delegation was headed up by Col. Adalberto Rabeiro, MININT's chief of investigations.

During their face-to-face sessions, the Cubans presented the Americans with a blizzard of material: photos, audio and video tapes, confessions, wiretap transcripts, bomb-making paraphernalia, even bomb fragments gathered during investigations into the hotel bombings so the Americans could test it

---

1. Through an intermediary, Luis Rodriguez turned down my request for an interview. According to Col Rafael Reyes of Cuban State Security, other Americans participating in the meetings included Daniel Hickey and Hector Vela of the Transportation Security Administration, as well as Thomas Monaghan.

in their own labs to determine if they could connect it to American sources. The spine of the Cuban case against Miami's exile groups, however, was laid out in three key documents.

Report on Terrorist Activities Against Cuba offered a 65-page panoramic overview of the landscape of exile violence from 1990 to the present, zeroing in on three dozen exile attacks and half a dozen assassination plots. Many of the descriptions of those incidents were accompanied by references to dated and numbered diplomatic protest notes the Cuban government had delivered to the American Interest Section in Havana at the time. The Cubans claimed that many of the attacks — even those ostensibly the work of other groups — had been financed by the Cuban American National Foundation.

The report also added some new details to what the Cubans described as the exiles' "last and gravest plot," the one to blow up an airplane. According to the Cubans, the plotters had targeted Cubana Airlines aircraft or other airlines flying to and from Cuba, "especially" those with stopovers in Central American airports "since the terrorist network has connections in these places and, thus, it is operatively easier to place the bombs." Unsurprisingly, the Cubans had names to connect to this particular plot. "We have learned from reliable sources that Luis Posada Carriles is the man responsible [for] this CANF-financed and macabre plan." Between March 15 and 21, the report said, Posada had met in Costa Rica and El Salvador with the Ex-Club's Miami-based Rolando Borges Paz to "coordinate actions for these and other plans."

The second document, *Elements Linked to Terrorism*, featured an alphabetically organized 61-page who's-who of 40 exiles the Cubans had identified as terrorists — from "Abreu Horta, Ernestino" to "Zuñiga Rey, Luis Manuel de la Caridad." Each dossier noted names, pseudonyms, physical descriptions, family histories, home and business addresses, phone numbers, beeper numbers, exile affiliations and involvement in alleged terrorist activities.

Operational Appendices, the third document, included 52 pages of not-so-random reports. There was a two-page accounting, for example, of thousands of dollars the Cubans claimed CANF had funnelled to ostensibly independent exile militants — including Andrés Nazario Sargen of Alpha 66 and Rodolfo Frómeta of Commandos F4 — to support their attacks against Cuba. That same document also noted — without explaining how the Cubans knew — that the FBI had summoned CANF President Pepe Hernández to its offices to question him about the purchase of several remote-control drone aircraft intended to be loaded with explosives and launched against Cuba.

There were transcripts of telephone calls the Cubans had surreptitiously recorded between some of the Central American mercenaries they'd captured and Francisco "Gordito" Chávez Abarca, the Salvadoran gangster who'd recruited them to plant the bombs. And summaries too of 14 wiretapped phone conversations between Luis Posada and various allies in Central America, during which he bragged about his role in the hotel bombings and referred in advance to the plan to assassinate Fidel Castro at the Margarita summit.

The Cubans helpfully included a detailed "movements and locations" listing for Posada — just in case the Americans ever wanted to track him down. There was the auto shop in El Salvador where he often met with Chávez Abarca, for example, and the art dealer's house in Costa Rica where he'd stayed in 1994 and again in '96, even the addresses of his mistresses in Tegucigalpa and San Salvador. Tantalizingly — and again without explaining how they knew — the Cubans noted that Posada had secretly visited Miami in August 1997 and April 1998.

The physical and documentary evidence the Cubans had accumulated seemed overwhelming — from "five Santeria necklaces [and] one used roll of toilet paper" seized from an Orlando Bosch-linked group to a listing of the phone numbers on Raúl Cruz León's beeper. The various reports were filled with tantalizing tidbits about other plots and operations too. During the First Ibero-American Summit in Guadalajara, Mexico, for example, the Cubans claimed that "CANF offered money to two individuals to travel to Mexico with the objective of eliminating the Commander in Chief. These plans were not completed," it added, "because the two individuals considered the pay too low, and there were no guarantees in place to deliver them from the country [after the assassination]." The Cubans didn't explain where they got that information. Nor did they say how they knew that CANF's Roberto Martin Perez had also travelled to Argentina at the time of the 1995 summit to look for opportunities to kill Castro. Nor, more importantly, did they offer the Americans details about what they described as a currently unfolding plan by two Cuban-born, Miami-based brothers, Jésus and Manuel Guerra Delgado, to assassinate Castro during the eighth Ibero-American summit in Portugal in October. "Today," the report simply explained, "both subjects are in the middle of preparations to acquire the documentation for their entry into Portugal."

The report also noted, almost in passing, that two Miami exiles the Cubans had arrested trying to bring weapons into Cuba in 1996 had also confessed to an unsolved murder in Miami. Fulgencio Chavez, a member of one of the exile paramilitaries, had been shot and killed in 1994. The men told the Cubans that Chávez had been killed because he was suspected of "collaborating with the FBI" — and that they'd been involved in the killing. Then there was the surprising footnote to the tale of two unexploded bombs the Cubans uncovered in Havana in October 1997, thanks to a tip from the U.S. Interest Section. Cuban investigators had already reported back that the bombers were two Guatemalan men who'd escaped before investigators figured out who they were. It turned out the men had travelled to Cuba using false identifies belonging to two other Guatemalan men. Their bodies, the

Cubans now said, were discovered two months later, shot in the head and deposited in a garbage dump.

As intriguing as all of that must have been for the Americans, the Cubans offered frustratingly little in the way of human source corroboration for most of their allegations, including the key charge that the politically powerful and well-connected Cuban American National Foundation was behind much of the violence directed at Cuba. The Cubans did identify some of their sources. For example, they singled out the two Cuban CANF agents — Agents 18 and 22 — they'd caught, outlined the sabotage missions they'd allegedly been instructed to undertake and even linked them to CANF officials Zuñiga and Otero. Intriguingly — given what happened less than two months later — the Cuban report made no mention of Percy Alvarado and his work inside CANF. Alvarado was the agent who could have drawn the most direct and damning lines from CANF to Posada and then to the bombs in Havana. But the Cubans weren't willing to lose Alvarado as a penetration agent — not yet — and they believed they'd given the Americans more than enough to make the connections for themselves.

The Cubans were also careful not to offer the Americans information that might lead them to Gerardo Hernández's Avispa network in Miami[2] — not realizing, of course, that the Americans were already following them. The documents clearly indicated that Cuba had agents inside many exile groups, including CANF. No surprise there. It was equally clear the Cubans weren't about to provide the Americans with their corroborators. No surprise there either. The FBI would need to develop its own sources and do its own investigations. But the Cuban material did point them in potentially productive directions.

The Americans seemed grateful. "They were very professional," one of the Cubans at the meetings would recall later, "very interested in what we had to show them."

Back home in the United States after the meetings, the Americans discussed what they'd read, heard and seen in Havana, and what it might mean. They were particularly intrigued by a surveillance video the Cubans had taken of Luis Posada and two accomplices outside the Camino Real Hotel in Guatemala City. The video, though the Americans didn't know it at the time, was taken during Posada's "secret" rendezvous with Percy Alvarado to provide him with the bomb-making materials he was supposed to set off at the Tropicana in Havana. "It occurred to [the FBI agents]," the American writer Ann Bardach reported later, "that the Cubans could easily have rid themselves of Posada forever; instead, they had opted to film him." One FBI

---

2. Hernández told me he knew nothing of the meetings in Havana at the time — even though some of the information the Cubans provided had been unearthed by his agents.

agent suggested to her that a live Luis Posada was "better propaganda" for the Cubans than he would have been as a dead exile martyr. "He's as good as it gets." But there was also, of course, the possibility the Cubans simply wanted the Americans themselves to finally take responsibility for Posada, whom their CIA had trained and unleashed on the world. It wouldn't happen.

Miami, July 4, 1998

Fernando González was back. The balding, mustachioed 35-year-old illegal officer — whose legend identified him as Ruben Campa and who used the code names Oscar or Vicky for his reports back to the CP — was usually based in Fayetteville, North Carolina, but he was no stranger to Miami. Last winter, he'd replaced Gerardo Hernández during his vacation. Now he had returned, sitting in for Ramón Labañino while he enjoyed some Cuban R&R with his family. Given handovers, overlaps and operations, González was scheduled to remain in Florida for four or five months, which is why he'd moved into Labañino's apartment in Hollywood. They'd continue to share the small space for a few months after Labañino returned in August.

González's marching orders were to take over a number of Labañino's operations: Aeropuerto, the ongoing search for signs of a possible attack against Cuba from Boca Chica; Surco, the attempt to find out whatever they could about what was happening inside the new Southern Command headquarters in Miami; Giron, the effort to penetrate the Cuban American National Foundation to ferret out more details about the organization's role in the bombing campaign; and Neblina, an offshoot of Giron that involved following CANF's Martin Perez, who was supposedly organizing a mercenary force to invade Cuba. González was also assigned to help out with Operation Paradiso, a project that involved sending René González and Alejandro Alonso to the Bahamas to determine if it was being used as a weapons-stashing and attack-staging base for Miami-based exiles. But Fernando González's priority, Havana said, should be Giron. Havana needed to know everything there was to know about what its nemesis, CANF, was planning.

New York, July 12, 1998

The story was as explosive as any well-placed bomb. It began: "A Cuban exile who has waged a campaign of bombings and assassination attempts aimed at toppling Fidel Castro says that his efforts were supported financially for more than a decade by the Cuban-American leaders of one of America's most influential lobbying groups." The story was incendiary for a couple of reasons. For starters, it appeared, not in some easily dismissed Cuban state media outlet like *Granma* or even an often-ignored regional American newspaper like the Miami *Herald*, but on the front page of the prestigious and influential *New York Times*. And the person making the allegations of collusion was not some self-serving Cuban government mouthpiece but Luis Posada Carriles himself, the man now claiming — and proclaiming — responsibility for the bombing spree.

The two-day series appeared under the joint byline of Larry Rohter, the *Times* Caribbean bureau chief, and Ann Louise Bardach, a contract reporter and veteran freelancer whose previous Cuba-related journalistic "gets" included interviews with both Fidel Castro and his sister Juanita, a Miami exile who had denounced her brothers and their revolution. Bardach and Rohter had already collaborated on a number of stories about exile militants, including stories linking the men arrested aboard *La Esperanza* off Puerto Rico to the Cuban American National Foundation.

In early June, thanks to a colleague at *Vanity Fair*, Bardach had met a Caracas-based businessman-friend of Posada's who'd promised to pass on Bardach's message: she wanted to talk. Two weeks later, she received a phone message from a "Ramón Medina." Medina — a.k.a. Posada — agreed to meet with her, but imposed a number of conditions: the reporters couldn't report where he was living or the alias he was now using, and they weren't allowed to photograph him because "not having pictures of my pretty face has kept me alive a long time."

On June 18, 1998 — the same day the FBI and Cuban State Security wrapped up their secret meetings in Havana — Rohter and Bardach arrived in Aruba, the site of their not-to-be-named rendezvous with Posada. Posada, dressed casually in Bermuda shorts and sandals, met them at the airport. He gallantly carried Bardach's suitcase to a waiting van, which ferried them to his "safe house, the home of a supporter, hidden from view by a high stucco-gated wall." Rohter, meanwhile, checked in to a local hotel to work other angles on the story.

Over the course of the next several days, Bardach spent 13 hours with Posada. She asked and Posada answered, mostly forthrightly, though sometimes elliptically. She managed to get six hours of it on tape, but sometimes Posada turned off her recorder so "he could tell me things that would not be recorded." Back at the hotel, Rohter would listen to the tapes and begin to draft the stories.

There were intriguing, almost eerie similarities to the interview Posada had given seven years earlier to Christopher Marquis of the Miami *Herald*. "'Let me have your hand," he told Bardach at one point. He guided her hand along the right side of his jaw to demonstrate — as he had done with Marquis — what the assassin's bullet had wrought. "My chin used to be an inch longer, very nice," he told Bardach. "I was very handsome once." And he lifted his shirt to show her "a torso ribboned with scars." Despite what seemed like the success of his hotel bombing campaign, Posada also seemed — again, as he had with Marquis — melancholic, summing up a life's worth of trying and failing to achieve his ultimate goal. "Right now is a bad time," he told Bardach. "Too many years. Everybody is very old."

Putting his own spin on the historical record may have been one reason Posada agreed to be interviewed by the world's newspaper of record. In her piece, Bardach noted that Posada had recently confided to a friend that he was "afraid he would not live long enough to tell his side of the story." But the more pressing reason, as Posada himself described it to Bardach, was that he wanted to generate "publicity" about the bombing campaign in order to achieve its real goal, which was to wreak havoc on Cuba's still fragile tourism economy.

When Bardach showed Posada her copy of the Solo fax — which made essentially the same point — Posada "seemed troubled by it and fretted it could cause him problems with the FBI." Not that he was *that* worried. At another point, Posada boasted of his "longstanding relationship with American law enforcement and intelligence agencies." "As you can see," he told her, "the FBI and the CIA don't bother me," noting his "close friendship" with two current FBI officials, including "an important official in the Washington office." Posada described George Kiszynski — the Miami-based FBI agent who'd telephoned Tony Alvarez to suggest he leave Guatemala — as "a very good friend... He's going to retire this year."[3]

Posada later asked Bardach not to include his comments about his closeness to Washington FBI officials in her story because "it had been years since he had had these close dealings." Whatever the larger truth, the fact — as Posada himself pointedly noted — was that he had not been questioned in connection with the bombings by anyone in American law enforcement.

Posada not only "proudly admitted authorship" of the bombings but also described Cruz León as only one of "maybe a dozen" mercenaries working for him in an "ongoing" campaign. "Very soon," he suggested "there will be exciting news."

He acknowledged that Cuban State Security had recently arrested three more of his operatives, but he seemed less worried about that — or their fates — than that their arrests hadn't yet generated any publicity. "Castro is keeping this a secret," Posada complained. "I don't understand why." The bombs, he said, were "acts of war" and Fabio Di Celmo and others were collateral damage in the greater cause. "We didn't want to hurt anybody," Posada insisted. "We just wanted to make a big scandal so that the tourists don't come anymore... It is sad that someone is dead, but we can't stop. That Italian was sitting in the wrong place at the wrong time... I sleep like a baby."

As startling — and disturbing — as those confessions were, it was

---

3. When I interviewed him in Miami in June 2010, Kiszynski said he'd only personally met Posada twice, including when he interviewed him as part of the Iran-Contra investigation.

Posada's claim that he had the financial backing of key members of the Cuban American National Foundation — a "tax-exempt foundation [that] has declared that it seeks to bring down Cuba's Communist Government solely through peaceful means" — that set off alarm bells in exile Miami and official Washington. Posada claimed he'd received more than $200,000 — all in cash — from the late Jorge Mas Canosa, CANF's chair.[4] Mas "never said, 'This is from the Foundation,'" Posada told Bardach. Instead, Posada explained "with a chuckle, the money arrived with the message: 'This is for the church.'"

What did Mas know about his terrorist plans? "You ask for money from him, and he said, 'I don't want to know anything,'" Posada explained. Discussion about actual plots was "not specific because [Mas] was intelligent enough to know who knows how to do the things and who doesn't know." Luis Posada knew. And Jorge Mas Canosa provided funds.

For all of his bragging and bravado, however, Posada seemed to sense his time was passing. Mas was dead. He worried again he too might die before he could kill Fidel Castro or before age claimed his enemy. When Bardach reminded Posada that Fidel's aunt had recently celebrated her 105th birthday, "Mr. Posada groaned. 'Oh my God,' he said. But then, shaking his head and wagging his finger, he quoted a popular proverb, as if to reassure himself. It is derived from the Cuban tradition of slaughtering a hog for a holiday meal: 'A cada lechon se le llega su nochebuena,' or 'Every pig gets its Christmas Eve.'" Perhaps. Would Luis Posada ever get his? Or his Christmas day?

Guatemala City, July 12, 1998

On July 12 — the day the first *New York Times* story appeared — Luis Posada was in Guatemala City wrapping up three days of meetings with three Miami-based exile militants: Enrique Bassas, Ramón Font and Luis Orlando Rodríguez. Bassas, you may recall, was the man alleged to have been tracking down one of the bomb components Posada gave Percy Alvarado for the attack on the Tropicana in 1994. A wealthy Miami businessman who operated a string of retirement homes, Bassas was now also, according to Cuban intelligence, the money man behind Martin Perez's new mercenary army. Like Posada, Ramón Font was a CIA-trained explosives expert. He'd been a member of Comando L, yet another of Miami's alphabetized paramilitary groups. Luis Rodríguez cut the most mysterious figure: he was described in

---

4. Jorge Mas Canosa's brother Ricardo — a former comptroller in the family business who had a falling out with his brother and eventually sued him — testified that, in 1985, his brother had instructed him to go to Panama, deposit a check for $50,000 in one of the company's Panamanian accounts, withdraw the cash and bring it back to Miami. According to Ricardo's testimony, Jorge said "it would be used to get Luis Posada Carriles out of jail [in Venezuela], that Carriles wanted out, that he might start talking... They had to get him out of jail."

a later news account as a fiftysomething Vietnam veteran from Miami who'd footed the bill for the other two at the local Holiday Inn.

They'd allegedly come to Guatemala City to talk about how to sneak guns and explosives into the Dominican Republic. The weapons were to be used to assassinate Fidel Castro at a summit of Caribbean leaders in Santo Domingo in August. Finding yourself on the front page of the *New York Times*, of course, was clearly not the best way to avoid publicity.

Washington, July 17, 1998

"The *New York Times* slandered," huffed Jorge Mas Santos, the son of the late founder of the Cuban American National Foundation, "and the *New York Times* lied." Mas Santos, now a member of CANF's board of directors, was front and centre at a Washington news conference to announce that CANF planned to sue the *Times* for having had the effrontery to connect the Foundation to the bombing attacks.[5]

CANF's attorney released a letter criticizing Bardach and Rohter as biased and demanded that the *Times* retract all references connecting CANF to the bombings, which, of course, CANF had publicly applauded in a full-page Miami *Herald* ad the year before. CANF also did its best to distance itself from Posada, formerly Mas Canosa's good friend and long-time ally. CANF's lawyer dismissed Posada as an "entirely questionable source," while Mas Santos, who clearly hadn't read his father's and Luis Posada's CIA files, insisted: "My father did not sustain any relationship with Luis Posada, had no contact with Luis Posada and did not support any of his activities."

When they weren't dissing Posada, CANF officials were, ironically, eagerly trotting him out to support their argument. During a CANF press conference in Miami, they'd even played a videotaped interview Posada had given an Hispanic Miami journalist. Posada, disguised by a bad fake beard and mustache, insisted he'd "never received any money from Mas Canosa or any other Foundation leader." He also claimed Bardach and Rohter were "very bad" and that they'd "magnified" his comments. When reporters asked if the Foundation had helped arrange the videotaped interview, Ninoska Perez Castellon, the Foundation spokeswoman, refused to answer. "Why is that an issue?" she demanded. "Why not ask how Ann Louise Bardach got to interview Posada?'"

---

5. On August 16, the *Times* published a carefully worded "Editor's Note" that was not an apology or retraction, but acknowledged an editing error had made it appear the Foundation "supported" the bombings. "The wording was not intended to mean that Mr. Posada said the Foundation leaders had paid specifically for the hotel bombings," the *Times* explained. But it noted again that CANF had provided Posada with funds and "asked not to be told how he used their funds." CANF never followed through on its threat to sue.

During that same Miami news conference, the *Herald* reported, CANF officials "heckled" and then tossed *Times* reporter Rohter from the room. Bardach, the paper noted, had "told friends that she is 'in hiding,' fearful of retaliation." Despite that, CANF did its best to present itself as the aggrieved party. Perez Castellon lamented the *Times* articles were "part of a pattern. We have seen a marked trend, specifically involving the *New York Times* and some other media, to try to discredit opponents of the Fidel Castro regime but not Fidel Castro, who is the real terrorist. "These latest malicious allegations," she said in a statement, "are simply part of the longstanding and systematic smear campaign against the Cuban American National Foundation designed to try and discredit Cuba's democratic opposition in exile."

Miami, July 23, 1998

One of Gerardo Hernández's many duties as an illegal officer in Miami involved monitoring the local media for news and gossip on exile groups, as well as for details on what American law enforcement agencies might — or might not — be doing to deter them. It was discouraging, often demoralizing work. Consider the opening paragraph on this July 23, 1998, article by Juan Tamayo in the Miami *Herald* under the title "Anti-Castro Plots Seldom Lead to Jail in U.S."

"Anti-Castro militant Tony Bryant still chuckles when he recalls the FBI agents who interviewed him after a 14-foot boat, loaded with high explosives and registered in his name, turned up near Havana. They said, 'You could hurt someone. Don't do it again,' said Bryant, former member of the Miami-based Comando L paramilitary group. 'I promised not to do it again, and they went away.'"

Tamayo went on to quote unnamed current and former prosecutors who told him there was an "unspoken policy... to gather intelligence and demobilize these people, to disrupt rather than arrest." That "yellow light" approach to law enforcement, they said, had "given comfort to people who should otherwise feel insecure about engaging in illegal activities."

The last major prosecution any of them could remember was Rodolfo Frómeta's conviction for trying to buy that Stinger missile... and he was now back out on the streets. "Judges or juries have set free some 17 Cubans accused of armed hijackings, shipping a 20mm cannon to Nicaraguan guerrillas or shooting a Cuban naval officer during a boat hijacking," Tamayo reported. "Some 90 Miami-area bombings remain unsolved from as far back as the mid-1960s, according to American Civil Liberties Union reports." Bryant himself told Tamayo authorities had only intercepted two of his 14 "missions against Cuba." In the story, prosecutors, the FBI, Alcohol Tobacco and Firearms agents and local cops all blamed someone else for the inaction. One prosecutor made the point that even if the police filed charges and prosecutors took them to trial, "it's very tough to get a jury in South Florida to convict people who are portrayed as freedom fighters."

Perhaps that was about to change now that the FBI had met with Cuban State Security and was finally on the case. Perhaps...

Miami, July 28, 1998

The story, which appeared on the front of the Miami *Herald*'s local news section five days later, was headlined "Anti Terrorism Raid Comes Up Empty." It told the story of an operation a few nights before. Members of Miami's Joint Terrorism Task Force had raided a marina along the Miami River. They were following up on an anonymous tip that they'd find explosives and guns aboard vessels headed for what an FBI spokesperson delicately described as a "third country." But the raid was a bust. "Our search didn't yield anything," the spokesperson said.

That wasn't quite true. Though searchers didn't find weapons aboard the two yachts or a Cuban-style shrimp fishing boat, they did discover that the bright-green 30-foot fishing boat, which had recently been retrofitted with a high-performance $25,000 engine and equipped with extra fuel tanks, had "documentation problems." The problem was it had no documentation. The agents seized it.

On one level, that may have seemed like yet another installment in the endless catch-and-release game endlessly played between police and Cuban exile gangs. And it was. But it was more too. As with most such Miami stories, this one had a back story. And the back story had a back story. And so on, and so on.

Let's pick up this particular ongoing, never-ending tale on July 18, the day Gerardo Hernández received an order from the CP. "It is urgent that you locate and verify info about boat bomb believed to be a fast white yacht, 17–19 feet, with windshield wipers on the lower deck, Registration number FL 1904 EY," the directive began. "Another boat called *Scala*, Registration number FL 8242 HJ, is currently having repairs done to its fuel tanks. The third boat, of Cuban construction, no registration number, blue/green color.

"Study feasibility of preparing measures to burn or damage. Have [agent Alejandro Alonso, Avispa's boat captain] study vulnerabilities by sailing along the river during the day or night." And it ended with a warning. "Take all security measures. Keep an eye out for any protective systems."

Hernández mobilized fellow illegal officer Fernando González — Labañino's vacation fill-in — and agents Nilo and Linda Hernández as well as Alejandro Alonso to scope out the most likely locations for the vessels along the Miami River.

By the next morning, they'd found what Hernández thought Havana was looking for at La Coloma Marina, which was located diagonally across the river from Joe's Seafood Restaurant. That should have been a good observation post. Unfortunately, Hernández reported, "because city commissioners were holding some kind of event at the restaurant... and the street was closed off," they hadn't been able to get close enough to verify the registration numbers of the boats, including one called *Flavia*, which Hernández believed might be the boat bomb. "I believe the *Scala* is probably the big white one with the blue stripe [nearby]," he added. "It hasn't moved. Perhaps for repairs being done on the tanks. Blue/green [vessel] is unmistakable... I will try to get a view of the registration number tomorrow." The easiest way to get close to the vessels, of course, would have been by casually sailing past in Alonso's boat. But Alonso, Hernández reported, seemed distracted by his own latest legal and financial crises.

By July 22, Hernández was able to report that he and the other agents had managed to get close enough to videotape *Flavia* and identify a partial registration number — "4 EY" — which matched numbers of the boat bomb.

The next issue, of course, was how to stop this floating bomb from reaching Cuba or that mysterious "third country" the FBI would later allude to. Hernández and his agents brainstormed various ideas — blow it up, set it on fire, sink it — but all the options carried risks. How would they get close enough to the vessel — swim out to it? rent a boat? — to plant a bomb or set it on fire and then escape without getting caught? There was a police station just three blocks from the marina, and the marina itself was patrolled by a security guard accompanied by "a Doberman the size of a calf." If they tried to set *Flavia* ablaze or plantexplosives, they very well might be killed themselves and — depending on the explosives aboard — blow the entire neighbourhood and all its residents to kingdom come.

"Rather than allowing them to sail quietly away," Hernández argued in a message to the CP, "I would suggest making an anonymous call to the FBI... to report the presence of a boat with such and such characteristics at such and such a place, which is ready to be used to commit an act of terrorism using explosives."

Two days later, the FBI — acting on an anonymous tip from what its lead agent would later describe in court as a "very reliable" informant — raided the marina.[6] But, as the *Herald* reported, the search turned up no weapons or explosives. Had the Cubans been wrong? Or had the owners of the vessels been tipped off in advance? And, if so, by whom?

---

6. FBI agent George Kisynzski did not identify his informant during his testimony at the trial of the Five, but he did say the informant was "very reliable" and "gave us a description of the vessels, primarily the Cuban vessel, the wooden vessel as he described it... It was green in color... He said it was... across the river from Joe's Seafood and Restaurant... The source stated that the wooden vessel was being equipped with a brand new diesel engine and being outfitted for a military attack. He gave us a general description of the vessel, actually a very good description of the vessel."

The FBI agent in charge of the raid was George Kisynzski, the same agent Luis Posada had described just two weeks earlier as a "very good friend." But the story gets murkier. The man who owned the blue-green boat as well as part of the docking and cargo facilities at the marina was none other than Enrique Bassas — the exile plot-financier who'd just returned from meeting Luis Posada in Guatemala City, a meeting to discuss how to get explosives and weapons into the Dominican Republic. The "third country?" Although it wasn't mentioned in the original *Herald* report, Kisynzski did interview Bassas following the raid, but didn't arrest him.

After a *Herald* reporter later discovered the Bassas connection to the Dominican Republic plot, the newspaper offered its own explanation for the raid. "Law enforcement veterans saw the search as an FBI hint to Bassas to cancel any conspiracies," the newspaper reported. "That's a common practice in South Florida… known as 'admonishing' or 'demobilizing' an operation." Conspiracies? Operations?

On August 9, the *Herald's* Tamayo — who'd been following up his own June report on Posada's various plots — would write yet another front page story, "Plot to Kill Castro in Dominican Is Exposed." The story identified Posada, Bassas and the others who'd met the month before in Guatemala City. "The plan," one of the plotters told Tamayo, "was to kill him any way we could: explosives on the road, grenades in a meeting, shots on the street. We would have strangled him if we had to." The plot collapsed, Tamayo would report, because it had been "betrayed" to U.S. authorities. By whom? Perhaps one of the plotters "got cold feet" or wanted to make off with the funds raised for the operation, Tamayo suggested, or else Cuban intelligence agents, "presumed by most law enforcement and exile experts to have penetrated many exile organizations, tipped the FBI to protect Castro's life during the visit to the Dominican Republic." In Miami, who knew?

Miami, August 1998

"Gerardo?" Gerardo Hernández had to improvise — and quickly. Running into someone from your old 'hood was one of the hazards that came with being a Cuban agent in a city filled with former Cubans.

"Miguel!"

Miguel López had grown up on the same street in Havana's Arroyo Naranjo neighbourhood as Hernández. They weren't close friends exactly, but López had been in Hernández's family's house and vice versa. López had even met Adriana once or twice, though he probably wouldn't remember her name. Now López was suddenly standing in front of Hernández in the parking lot of the Waterways shopping centre in Aventura, a community near Hernández's North Miami neighbourhood, wanting to reminisce about old times, calling him Gerardo instead of Manuel. Hernández looked around, made sure no one who knew him as Manuel was within earshot.

They exchanged the usual pleasantries. López told him he'd come to the United States in 1995 and was working as a delivery driver for the Carnival Fruit Company. Hernández told him his Cuban cover story — that he was working at the Cuban embassy in Argentina. He'd come to Miami, he confided, with an Argentinean woman with whom he was having a relationship. Would that story ever get back to Adriana, he wondered? She'd know better. Hernández asked López not to say anything — even the embassy didn't know he was in Miami, he said. The woman had paid for his flight. She wasn't with him now, Hernández riffed, because she was at her family's place in Miami delivering a package. Making it up as he went along…

They should get together, López suggested, and offered Hernández his phone number. Sure, Hernández said, not offering his own phone number in return. "I have to go," he said. Later that evening, Hernández did call López to tell him he was packing to fly back to Argentina. Perhaps they could get together the next time he was in Miami.

Havana, August 13, 1998

It all ended suddenly, unexpectedly. One day, Percy Alvarado was wending his way back from his clandestine work as a spy in Miami to his only slightly less clandestine life as a ne'er-do-well in Havana. He'd enjoyed his usual stopover in Nassau. "I drank my Bacardi in the Bahamas, fraternized with some Cubans and Puerto Ricans." But when his plane landed at José Martí Airport in Havana on August 5, 1998, two State Security agents were waiting for him. "They told me I had to do an interview with an American journalist." Alvarado says he was instructed to "tell [the reporter] everything about my life as an agent, without holding back." That order had come from on high, likely from Fidel himself. Havana had decided to "burn" Agent Monk. Percy Alvarado's days as a spy inside the Cuban American National Foundation were over.

There were any number of good reasons why the Cubans may have decided to sacrifice Alvarado's future usefulness inside CANF for the immediate good of exposing the links between Luis Posada and key officers in the Foundation. For starters, Alvarado wasn't that useful any more. After he'd refused to set off the bombs at the Tropicana in 1994, his CANF handlers had marginalized him, calling on him less and less often for assignments, which meant he had fewer revelations to offer his bosses in Havana.

The timing seemed right too. Two months before, Cuban State Security had shared its own findings with the FBI delegation. The American agents who'd come to Havana had seemed genuinely interested in what the Cubans had to offer. And a number of important mainstream American journalists had also finally begun to explore the money trail between CANF and Posada. In June, Juan Tamayo had tentatively raised the Posada-CANF link in a story in the Miami *Herald*. A month later, Ann Louise Bardach had quoted Posada bragging about it in the pages of the *New York Times*. Now, of course, CANF was threatening to sue the *Times*.

Which was why — or at least so the Cubans believed — the newspaper had dispatched reporter Timothy Golden to Cuba to follow up on the initial series. Golden specialized in reporting on Latin America. In 1984, still barely out of university, he'd landed a posting in El Salvador as the Miami *Herald's* Central American bureau chief. In 1987, he'd shared a Pulitzer prize for the *Herald's* reporting on the Iran-Contra affair. In 1989, he'd joined the *Times*. By 1991, he was the paper's Mexico City bureau chief. Now — after a stint in San Francisco and a year as a Nieman fellow at Harvard — he'd become the *Times* New York-based investigative correspondent on the foreign desk.

The Cubans set up an interview for Golden with Adalberto Rabeiro, one of the most senior officials in Cuba's Directorate of Intelligence and the man ultimately responsible for the bombings investigation. They arranged for Golden to visit the Villa Marista prison to talk with the Central American mercenaries who'd planted the actual bombs. And they organized — a sign of just how important the story was to the Cubans — interviews for Golden with two of the country's most powerful political figures, Ricardo Alarcón and Fidel Castro. The Cubans saw Percy Alvarado as the icing on this intelligence cake, the final, incontrovertible proof that CANF was orchestrating and financing the attacks on Cuba.

Alvarado and Golden met for more than an hour at a State Security protocol house in Havana. Alvarado says he offered a first-hand, naming-names account. Alvarado even played recordings of conversations he'd secretly taped. The Cubans believed Golden had everything he needed to finally tell the true story of Luis Posada and CANF. Golden left Cuba. And the Cubans waited. And waited. And waited. There was no story.

Actually, that's not quite true. On January 15, 1999 — five months after his trip to Cuba — the *Times* did publish Golden's "Plot to Oust Castro Run on a Shoestring, Lands 5 Underpaid Amateurs in Jail." But that 2,300-word story focused on the jailed mercenaries Golden had interviewed. There was not a single word from Golden's interview with Alvarado. What had gone wrong? The Cubans would eventually conclude they'd been duped and have since denounced Golden and the *Times* publicly and repeatedly.

In 2003, Ricardo Alarcón even called a press conference to criticize another *New York Times* story Golden had written about the Cuban Five. The byline "surprised me," Alarcón said, "as Golden is someone who knows a lot on the subject." He went on to describe Golden's 1998 trip to Havana and the "copious information on terrorism against Cuba and the individuals involved" he'd been given. "Tim Golden was the only person on the planet who knew [about Percy Alvarado] in '98," he said. In 2005, Fidel Castro continued the attack, suggesting that Golden's stories might have been spiked because "strong pressures were brought to bear" on the paper after the Bardach stories "scandalized the very powerful Foundation mob."

The truth, however, is almost certainly more prosaic.[7] As was the case in the missed signals, miscommunications between Cuban and American authorities in the lead-up to the Brothers to the Rescue shootdown, the Cubans seemed to fundamentally misunderstand how the American media and legal system actually worked. They didn't appreciate the level of corroboration the *Times* would have required to publish Alvarado's claim that he'd been a spy inside the Foundation and that prominent members of the organization had directed him to commit sabotage against Cuba. That would have been especially true after CANF's threats to sue the paper for the Bardach stories. At any rate, the story never appeared in the pages of the *Times*.

It would be a year before Alvarado's story finally became public, when he testified about his time inside CANF during Raúl Cruz León's Havana trial, and seven more years before a lawsuit by a disaffected CANF board member would finally more clearly connect the dots from CANF to the ongoing attacks against Cuba.

---

7. I conducted a year-long email correspondence with Golden to get his side of this story. His initial response to my inquiries was that this was "an old story and one that I've already spent more time with than I care to, in part because of the insistent complaints or accusations of the Cuban government." Eventually, he did agree to answer my questions off the record, reserving the right to decide whether I could publish what he said based on his reading a copy of the section in which he would be quoted. "I have to agree explicitly on anything you want to quote in my name." A curious position for a *New York Times* journalist to take, but there it was. In the end, he did not agree to be quoted. Without breaking confidence or getting into the specifics of what he told me, it is fair to say he rejects the Cuban suggestion there was any conspiracy at the *Times* not to publish — a view I agree with — and insists he did his best to corroborate Alvarado's story before he and his editors eventually gave up on it and he moved on to other projects.

"The Very Heart of Our System"
September 4, 1998 – September 15, 1998

Miami, September 4, 1998

Ramón Labañino telephoned Fernando González from a hotel room in Oakland with some — possibly very — bad news. The CP had dispatched him to California on a short-term assignment. His news, which González immediately relayed to the CP, was that "in hotel room in Oakland — repeat Oakland — they forced the window and robbed suitcase with computer and all the disks." Were "they" robbers who'd just happened to steal a laptop and disks belonging to a Cuban illegal intelligence officer? Or was this robbery not a robbery at all? Labañino immediately booked a flight back to Florida.

Miami, September 5, 1998

Gerardo Hernández's latest assignment was to track down the location of an exile terrorist training camp. Another one. This one, known as Rumbo Sur, was "a secluded South Dade training camp belonging to Miami's best-known anti-Castro militia, Alpha 66." Although reporter Kirk Nielsen's[1] description of a recent training exercise at the camp published in the *Miami New Times* had seemed more comic than menacing — a few, mostly geriatric commandos and an 11-year-old girl conducting a mock raid on a stack of old tires standing in for MiG aircraft on a non-existent Cuban airfield — the weapons they carried, including M-1s and Buckmaster AR-15s, were real. Hernández also knew that some of the recent raids the commandos boasted to Nielsen about taking part in — including a May 20, 1995, night attack in which machine gun fire was sprayed at the Guitart Hotel in Cayo Coyo from a speedboat — actually did take place.

The *New Times* article, Hernández reported back to Havana, ended with the ominous suggestion that the group was planning another action soon.

---

1. During his research for the story, Nielsen told me, he accidentally "made people in Washington very nervous." He called the FBI to ask for information on Alpha 66 at about the same time the FBI was gearing up to arrest the Avispa network and they were afraid Nielsen might trip over their operation. "I heard that a couple of years later from Paul Miller, who was the FBI spokesperson at the time."

The group's field commander had refused to say what it was. "Something's going to happen, you watch," he told Nielsen with a "stone-faced" expression. Hernández would await orders from Havana on what to do with that information gem.

It seemed he was always following up on reports about paramilitary training camps. Recently, he'd gone on a frustrating day-long, wild-goose-chase road trip looking for a camp Rodolfo Frómeta's F-4 group had supposedly set up. The directions he'd received from Havana's counter-revolutionary department, M-19 — "follow Okeechobee to Highway 27 and keep going north until you reach a sign that said Montura Ray, then make a left and go 12 or 13 miles to an Amoco station" — didn't help. He'd followed the directions, but there was no Montura Ray. Hernández asked someone who'd lived in the area for 27 years — the man had never heard of the place. And Hernández hadn't been able to locate the Amoco gas station either, even in the Yellow Pages or by calling Directory Assistance. He'd ended up returning to Miami and reporting on what he hadn't been able to find.

Now M-19 was asking him to follow up on a Latin American news agency report that another exile group, Brigade 2506, had just set up a paramilitary camp "for the purpose of training exile youth to keep the belligerent spirit alive." The CP wanted Hernández to get one of his younger agents — codenamed José — to "affiliate himself to find out about the kind of training, frequency, the number of people involved, their exact addresses and, if possible, film it."

José was keen. "Don't worry," he messaged Hernández. "I am always on the alert to fish for any information I can get about the bombs. I am also looking for a casual way to associate myself with the 2506 Brigade training camp. I don't want to be too aggressive in carrying out this objective so as not to draw attention to myself and I am thinking about asking for help from G-2 [a code name for another Avispa target/source] in this regard, but I am afraid he won't like the idea too much and might just exclude me from his plans."

Key West, September 1998

Maggie Becker would remember him as a "football type." Tall, blond. When he made an appointment for a massage, he said his name was George. He was pleasant, easy to talk to. Perhaps because he was Cuban-American, they'd ended up talking about Tony. Maggie was still trying to help Tony land a better job. She gave the man her business card. Maybe he could pass it along to someone he knew who was hiring, she suggested. The next time she'd see George — just before dawn on September 12, 1998 — he was no longer George. He was FBI Agent Sal Hernández and he — along with a dozen other armed agents wearing bullet-proof vests — had just smashed down her front door.

"THE VERY HEART OF OUR SYSTEM"

Miami, September 11, 1998

As soon as she saw them — René on his back on the bed, baby Ivette asleep on his chest, face up, arms open — Olga knew she had to take a picture. "Don't move," she said. It was close to midnight and Olga had just returned from the 2–11 p.m. shift at her new job. She was still in telemarketing but now selling English courses to Hispanics. Despite a year and a half in the United States, Olga still spoke only Spanish. English, she joked, was "impossible." Luckily, it was possible to get by in Miami speaking only Spanish.

On her way to work each day, Olga dropped off baby Ivette — who was now four and a half months old — at daycare. René would pick her up at the end of the day and be there at night for her and Irma, who was now 14. Unless, of course, René had to attend an exile meeting. In which case he brought Ivette along.

González had spent this morning running errands. Tomorrow, he was to begin flying from Opa-locka for a small company owned by a friend. He'd done his best to arrange his flight schedule so he'd be home each night. He and Ivette had developed their own feeding routine. René would lay on his back on the bed with his knees raised to create a kind of seat-cradle for the baby, who would sit with her back against his thighs. As she drank her bottle, she would stare straight into her father's face with her intense, all knowing eyes.

Tonight, she'd fallen asleep immediately after her feeding and René had carefully laid her on his chest, which was how Olga found the two of them. Olga found her camera. But then she realized René was wearing only his underwear. That wouldn't do. She found a blanket, placed it strategically, then took the picture. Snap. One last Kodak moment before the unknown tomorrow.

Big Pine Keys, September 12, 1998, 6:00 a.m.

Maggie and Tony were asleep in the rear bedroom of their new house when the sound of shattering glass woke her. Her first thought was that someone was breaking in. She reached for the phone to call the police when she heard the screams. "FBI! FBI!"

It was 6 a.m. and the house had suddenly filled with weapon-toting men dressed in flak jackets with F-B-I on their backs. Maggie noticed "George," her customer from a few days before. What the hell?

They had a search warrant but Maggie didn't read it. She was freaking out. "I had no idea." Tony knew. He remained, she would recall later, zen-like, "Tony-like," while the agents stationed themselves in every room. The FBI would spend the next two days taking photographs, sketching out rooms, rummaging through every nook and cranny and shelf and box. There were boxes everywhere. She and Tony were still in the process of moving in. And renovating. And...

Tony quietly signed consent forms, allowing other agents to search their old one-bedroom efficiency apartment in Key West — the one they hadn't yet fully moved out of, the one where Maggie had given "George" his massage — as well as Tony's locker at Boca Chica.

Inside the locker, the FBI's Evidence Response Team found Polaroid photos that appeared to be of an aircraft hangar. At the apartment, they confiscated a Sony shortwave radio, headphones and antenna but ignored the small Buddha statue beside it. They also removed a Sharp laptop computer, and Tony's and Maggie's passports. Inside the Big Pine Keys house, they found another computer, disks, some music cassettes Maggie had recorded, Tony's old application for maintenance work at Boca Chicha, more ads for more jobs there, web addresses for federal jobs listings, Tony's certificates from advanced courses in airport ground installation construction from his time in Kiev and — in a still unpacked box in the garage — a copy of a 1995 newspaper article about the appointment of the first woman to command the Naval Air Station. For all the drama of the raid, it hardly seemed a spy-worthy haul.

Miami, September 12, 1998, 6 a.m.

René González was asleep, still in his underwear, when the pounding on the apartment door woke Olga. She woke up René. He went to the door, returned. "It's the police," he told her calmly. He put on a pair of white shorts, went back to open the door. When he did, Olga heard screaming. In English.

She didn't know who it was, or what they were saying so she went to the living room to investigate. A man pushed her roughly up against the wall. She saw René in the doorway. He was face down, his head outside the apartment, his body in. One of the men cuffed him, then two of them stood him up.

"They're big," Olga remembers thinking to herself. "Rene's six foot two, and they're all taller than him." She heard what sounded like a helicopter overhead. "Sit down," one of the men ordered her.

"Are you René González... from Brothers to the Rescue?" another agent asked her husband. González said yes. And then they took him away.

Miami, September 12, 1998, 6 a.m.

Similar door-pounding, glass-smashing raids happened simultaneously across Miami that morning: at Nilo and Linda Hernández's home in Miami-Dade, at Joseph Santos and Amarylis Silverio's modest apartment in Flagami, at Alejandro Alonso's place in South Dade. The FBI used a battering ram to smash in the door of the third-floor apartment in Hollywood that Ramón Labañino and Fernando González were sharing. But the officers — two teams of them, one assigned to arrest each man — didn't have to unholster their weapons. The two men, who were asleep on a mattress, offered no resistance. The agents allowed them to dress, cuffed them and led them to waiting cars for the drive to FBI headquarters in North Miami, where they'd be photographed, fingerprinted, read their rights and processed before being sent to the federal detention centre downtown. They were being charged, the FBI officers explained, with being unregistered agents of a foreign government. Labañino and Fernando González — whose true identities the police would not know for more than a year — remained in character during their initial interrogations.

"My name is Ruben Campa," Fernando González told the officers in Mexican-accented Spanish. "I was born in Weslaco, Texas, on September 14, 1965. My father died in a car accident. My mother moved us to Mexico City…" He said he'd met Luis Medina, his Puerto Rican roommate, at a disco and they'd agreed to move in together to save on expenses.

When the police riffled through González's wallet, they found only "Ruben Campa" identification papers but they also discovered one of Tony Guerrero's compilations of aircraft at Boca Chica: "18 F-18s, six F-14s and 10 F-5s, as well as four E-2 surveillance planes."[2]

While FBI officers interviewed them separately, other agents back at their now-secured apartment waited for a search warrant. Once it arrived, they followed procedure: making a sketch of the apartment layout, photographing everything in its place before beginning the process of taking it apart, piece by piece, and carting it all off to be catalogued and examined. Investigators found the usual array of shortwave radios, radio scanners, tape recorders, computers, disks, a bulk eraser for erasing the disks and audio tapes, fake passports and IDs, membership cards for Sam's Club, AAA, the local library and other organizations, $5,409 in cash, ledgers and copies of 30 California death certificates and newspaper obituaries, possibly for the creation of future legends for future agents. In a desk drawer they also found an airline ticket to Mexico for Luis Medina. In five days, Ramón Labañino was supposed to be on his way to Havana.

Miami, September 12, 1998, 10 a.m.

Who was the governor of Puerto Rico in 1985? What bus did you take to get to school? Where did you catch it?

The man firing the questions was Hector Pesquera, the agent in charge of the Miami FBI office. Pesquera was Puerto Rican. The man he was questioning, Manuel Viramóntez, claimed to be Puerto Rican. Pesquera knew he wasn't,

---

2. During the trial, prosecutors introduced a small box seized from the apartment of Labañino and González. The box, identified as "War Planes," contained "glossy cards with photos of military aircraft," including a World War I vintage Albatross similar to one flown by the German ace Red Baron — and a receipt for $6.88 for the collection. "They are kind of like baseball cards, for us old-timers," Labañino's lawyer explained. "But instead they have pictures of aircraft on them."

knew he was Cuban, knew he was a spy, knew he was the king of the spy ring. Royal Sovereign. So he kept asking more and more detailed questions only a Puerto Rican would be able to answer. Gerardo Hernández — Manuel Viramóntez — answered them all. Which made Pesquera angrier and angrier. "I know you're Cuban," he shouted finally. "And you're going to rot in prison because Cuba isn't going to do anything for you." And then he left.

It had been a surreal Saturday morning already. There'd been no time for escape plans, no time to become "Daniel Cabrera" or any other emergency legend. Hernández could barely remember hearing someone jimmying the lock on his apartment door. He was still half asleep when whoever was outside smashed down the door and a SWAT team made up of men wearing helmets and carrying machine guns burst into the room. Hernández's bed was in the front room near the door. He didn't even have time to sit up in the bed before he was grabbed, lifted up, handcuffed. One of the agents squeezed open his mouth and peered inside. "I guess they had seen a lot of James Bond movies and they thought I would have cyanide in my mouth," Hernández would joke later. He didn't.

"Why am I being arrested?" he demanded.

"You know why," one of the agents said. He did. Within minutes, he was whisked out of the apartment and into a car for the drive to FBI headquarters. There, like the others, he was placed in a separate room, handcuffed to the wall and intermittently questioned.

After Pesquera left, other agents came and went, asking for this and that, proffering deals. "You know how this business works," one of them would say. "You know that you're an illegal agent. And you know what it says in the books is that Cuba isn't going to admit they sent you here with a fake passport. Cuba won't do that, so you will rot in prison. The best thing you can do is cooperate with us and we'll offer you whatever you want. We'll change your identity, give you bank accounts."

When Hernández continued to insist he was Manuel Viramóntez, a Puerto Rican graphic designer, they'd offered him a phone. "Call the consulate," they taunted. Hernández just looked at them, called their bluff. Once they were able to prove — and they would — that everything in his Manuel legend was false, Hernández — according to his original instructions from Havana — was supposed to confess that he had arrived illegally from Cuba during the Mariel boat lift and had paid $2,500 for his false documents from a Miami man who dealt in fake IDs.

The problem, of course, was that the FBI already had a copy of Havana's instructions on what to do in the event of an arrest. They knew what he was going to say before he could say it. Which left him with one final instruction, which Havana had long ago addressed, in third person, to his code name: "Under no circumstances will Giraldo ever admit to being part of or linked to Cuban intelligence or any other Cuban government organization." Gerardo Hernández had no intention of admitting anything. *¡Patria o muerte!* Fatherland or death.

Bronx, New York, September 12, 1998, 4 p.m.

Carlos Fernandez had surreptitiously followed Leónardo Esteban Rodríguez Iglesias all day, waiting for the right moment. The FBI agent didn't want to frighten the third secretary to the Cuban Mission at the United Nations. He just wanted to deliver a message, to let him know he knew.

Now, inside the Botanical Gardens, Fernandez finally sidled up close to Iglesias. He took a photo out of his jacket, showed it to him. "Do you remember who this guy is?" This guy was Ramón Labañino, the photo one of those Fernandez's surveillance team had taken during the April brush-pass exchange between Labañino and Iglesias in the washroom at the Wendy's on the Hempstead Turnpike.

Iglesias looked at the photo, turned away. He appeared to be in some kind of shock, Fernandez would remember later. He said nothing, simply turned on his heel and walked away. Fifteen minutes later, in another section of the park, Fernandez tried again. "Do you know what's going on?" he asked. Iglesias shook his head. "Geneva Convention," he said, then repeated it over and over again. "Geneva Convention, Geneva Convention…"[3]

Three days later, the CP sent an urgent message to Miami. "There was an approach made by FBI on officer Esteban who had a pass with [Labañino] past April," the message began "Showed picture of a person. Looked like [Labañino]… Use extreme security measures. Suspend operational activity until advised. We alerted [Fernando González] with whom you should have no contact. I will give you new instructions via this route. Update escape plan just in case."

It was already too late for updated escape plans, too late for Labañino to make his scheduled flight to Havana. The Wasp Network had been stung. The question was why — and, more intriguingly, why *now*, when the FBI itself was supposedly investigating exactly the kind of terrorist activities it had learned about, indirectly, from the work of La Red Avispa?

---

3. In December, the United States expelled three Cuban diplomats at its United Nations mission in connection with the Cuban spy affair. None was identified as Leónardo Esteban Rodríguez Iglesias. However, U.S. officials did say that two other "unidentified members of the Cuban U.N. delegations would have been expelled but left the United States weeks ago."

WHAT LIES ACROSS THE WATER

Miami, September 15, 1998

Hector Pesquera was crowing. "I have never seen anything like this in all my years in law enforcement," he gloated during a full-house press conference at FBI headquarters to announce his agents had smashed the biggest Cuban spy ring to hit Miami in... well, as long as anyone could remember. "This is a significant blow to the Cuban government. Right now they are in total disarray."

"This spy network was sent by the Cuban government to strike at the very heart of our system of national security and our democratic process," thundered federal prosecutor Thomas Scott, as if saying it could make it so.

Perhaps not surprisingly, Pesquera and Scott did their best to ignore the role the Cuban "spies" had played in breaking up terrorist plots against their homeland and in assisting the FBI catch exile drug smugglers[4] and focused instead on the weakest but most emotionally resonating part of their 20-page criminal complaint against the 12 Cubans[5] — that they'd attempted to "infiltrate" U.S. military bases in South Florida, singling out not only the new U.S. Southern Command Headquarters in Miami and the Boca Chica Naval Station at Key West but also MacDill Air Force Base in Tampa, where Ramón Labañino had previously been based,[6] as prime targets of the spy ring.

But neither they nor the investigators at the press conference could answer what seemed like the central question if that was really the case — what did Cuba plan to do with such intelligence? Attack the U.S.? In fact, authorities had a hard job making a convincing case that they had captured what Pesquera insisted was a "very sophisticated group."

During their first court appearance earlier in the day, reported the Miami *Herald*, "the alleged agents — eight expressionless men and two women — did not seem to fit the role. Appearing in blue prison garb before U.S. Magistrate Barry Garber in a packed Miami courtroom, most were assigned defence attorneys at U.S. taxpayers' expense. A majority said they lacked the money to pay lawyers. None had more than $2,000 in the bank. They drove old cars, lived in cheap apartments."[7]

When reporters fanned out to their old neighbourhoods to discover who these dangerous spies really were, what they came back with made them

---

4. Pesquera insisted the information René González provided to the FBI about PUND's Hector Viamonte, who was eventually indicted for drug smuggling, was "bogus."
5. The indictment also identified two Cuban illegal officers, Ricardo Villareal and Remjo Luna, it claimed had already "left the United States for other operational assignments."
6. During the trial, prosecutors didn't introduce any evidence about alleged espionage at MacDill.
7. Just as the Americans were determined to paint the agents in larger-than-life colours, the Cuban government initially did its best to pretend they knew nothing of their existence. "We only know what has been said on the wires." a Cuban Foreign Ministry spokesperson said. "This is a matter in which the American authorities are involved, and we don't feel it is responsible of us to comment on a matter we don't know anything about."

seem even less threatening. The FBI had painted Gerardo Hernández (whom they still knew only as Manuel Viramóntez) as "the mastermind, pasting his pictures above the organizational flow chart for hundreds of reporters to record." But he turned out to be "the kind of neighbor people liked — quiet and polite... 'Very nice, very intelligent,'" his neighbour, Victor Fonseca, told the *Herald*.

Amarylis Silverio's neighbour, Gertrudis Lopez, told reporters that "until someone proves it for sure, I won't believe [she's guilty]. We're laundry-room friends... Every night I talk to her on the balcony when she has a cigarette after dinner. I invited [Amarylis and her husband Joseph] to my house, to my son's birthday party. They just seemed like decent, hard-working people."

Even Ramón Saúl Sánchez, whose Democracy Movement organization René González had infiltrated, seemed hard pressed to say anything negative about a man he described as a "quiet type." Sánchez told the *Herald* about an incident earlier in the year when González saved his life. "Several members of [Democracy Movement] were returning from a flight to the Bahamas when a wing on their aircraft broke," the newspaper reported. "González-Sehweret managed to land at Homestead Air Reserve Base. 'He was one of my chief pilots,' Sánchez remarked. 'I am shocked.'"

If the espionage charges against the Cubans seemed thin — and they did, even then — why had the FBI decided to make such a big deal of that part of their case? "We have done this publicly," Hector Pesquera explained in Spanish in a message that was broadcast frequently on Hispanic radio stations for the next several days, "to gather information from the public." Huh?

Intentional or not, news of the arrests and the allegations against the Cubans did serve to ratchet up hysteria levels in the always-teetering-on-the-edge Miami exile community. WQBA-1140 AM commentator — not to forget CANF spokesperson — Ninoska Perez Castellon announced the FBI switchboard's number on air and invited people to call the Bureau (and her program) to report "suspicious characters." It turned out there were plenty of them. One caller said he could "die in peace" if the police charged all those involved with businesses promoting travel to Cuba or anyone who called for better relations with Cuba. "Let them shake down every place," declared another caller, "because there are many, many spies here."

Exile groups like the Cuban American National Foundation jumped on news of the arrests, "which we now see has been threatening vital security interests of the United States," to lobby for even tougher measures against Cuba. The day after Pesquera's press conference, CANF's chair Alberto Hernández and vice chair Jorge Mas Santos would fire off a letter to Senator Bob Graham, a supportive member of the Senate's intelligence committee, to ask him to stage a public hearing *in Miami* about Cuban espionage.

Only in Miami? Only in Miami.

Aftermath

September 15, 1998 –

Marianna Federal Correctional Institution, Florida, April 14, 2011

René González isn't surprised. But he is resigned. After 13 long years in the belly of the beast that is the American justice system, he has become reconciled to what he sees as its foibles and follies, its injustices and inconsistencies. I've emailed González at the Federal Correctional Institution in Marianna, Florida — his home for much of the past decade — to ask what he thinks about the recent verdict in Texas. The week before, after a complex, rollercoaster-ride 13-week trial, a jury in El Paso deliberated for less than three hours — the jurors having managed to complete their contemplative burden in time for lunch — before agreeing that Luis Posada Carriles was "not guilty." Of anything. At all. Ever.

Posada had been charged with 11 counts of perjury, obstruction of justice and immigration fraud in connection with his application to become a naturalized United States citizen. That application had followed his surreptitious return to the United States in March 2005, which had followed his controversial pardon from prison in Panama in 2004, which had followed his conviction for weapons offences in connection with yet another attempt to kill Fidel Castro in 2000, which had followed... but we'll come back to that.

During the trial, prosecutors offered many examples of how Posada had lied, including in answer to an immigration officer's question of whether he'd ever flashed a phony passport. He had, many times and using many different passports. Prosecutors also claimed Posada had even lied about how he'd arrived back in the United States in 2005. Posada said he'd paid a Mexican smuggler $6,000 to sneak him across the border into Texas in the back of a blue pick-up truck. The government countered that he'd actually sailed into Miami aboard a converted shrimp boat after a voyage from Mexico organized, financed and crewed by Posada's influential Florida exile friends. In either case, of course, he had come into the country illegally, but that seemed somehow beside the point to the U.S. justice system.

Posada told what the U.S. government considered his most egregious —

and germane to our story — lie on August 30, 2005, in the middle of an immigration review hearing in El Paso. Homeland Security lawyer Gina Garrett Jackson was questioning Posada about his 1998 interview with Ann Louise Bardach, during which he'd confessed to masterminding the hotel bombings. Posada, as usual, danced around the facts. His interview with Bardach, he claimed, was "made in a language I do not understand." The recording had been "illegal." And the *New York Times* later "retracted those interviews." None of his answers was true. As to whether Posada had told Bardach he planned the bombings, Posada answered: "I do not recall having said that."

So Barrett Jackson finally cut to the chase: "Were you involved in soliciting other individuals to carry out the bombings in Cuba?" she demanded. "No."

In April 2009 — after four years of legal to-ing and fro-ing[1] — the new Obama administration finally filed what would become the only sort-of substantive charge against Luis Posada ever filed in a U.S. court. Prosecutors said he lied when he answered "No" to Barrett Jackson's question about the bombings. What that meant was that the United States government had finally acknowledged — without explicitly doing so, of course — that the Cubans were right. About Luis Posada. About his role in the 1997 bombing campaign. And, likely, about much else. It had been a long and strange journey to this truth.

After the FBI swooped in on September 12, 1998, and arrested their agents, the Cuban government, not surprisingly, stopped cooperating with the Americans. Each side blamed the other for what didn't happen after that. The Cuban authorities complained the FBI did nothing with the treasure trove of material State Security had already handed it. The Americans counter-claimed that the Cubans refused to allow their agents to return to Cuba to interview witnesses and conduct their own investigations.

During the trial of the Five, in fact, prosecutors heaped scorn on the significance of the material Cuban State Security had given the FBI, material the public, of course, had never seen. "Obviously," one official sniffed to the

---

1. On April 13, 2005, Posada's lawyers had announced he would seek asylum in the United States based on his "well-founded fear of persecution" in Cuba. A month later, they unceremoniously withdrew that application, probably realizing that — having been convicted of a serious criminal offence in another country, to wit, trying to kill Castro in Panama in 2000 — Posada wasn't eligible for American citizenship. Eventually, U.S. Immigration and Customs Enforcement officials charged him with sneaking into the country illegally. But a Texas judge ruled Posada couldn't be extradited to Cuba or to Venezuela, where he was still wanted in connection with the Cubana Airlines bombing, because he might face "torture" there. The judge in his immigration case, Kathleen Cardone, a Bush appointee, had eventually dismissed all charges against Posada, claiming prosecutors engaged in "fraud, deceit and trickery... mistranslated... and manipulated evidence." Although her decision was eventually overturned on appeal, Cardone would again end up as the judge again when the Obama administration decided to re-file the charges.

Miami *Herald,* the information the Cubans provided "wasn't anything too dramatic, or we would have done something quickly."

Hector Pesquera, the FBI's agent in charge, told reporters after the trial that he took "full exception to the word cooperation" in describing the meetings between the Bureau and Cuban State Security in Havana. "There was some information brought to our attention through diplomatic channels," he said. "We — discharging our duties — looked into it. But to say and classify that we were cooperating with the Cuban government," he harrumphed loudly enough for the exile leadership to hear, "would be a misstatement."

After the arrests of the Cuban agents, the FBI also appeared to lose whatever interest it might have once had in pursuing American links to the hotel bombings. In August 2003, Pesquera quietly okayed shredding five file boxes full of material on Posada, including a large brown envelope labelled "Important Evidence," which was stuffed with crucial documents, such as copies of the cables transferring cash from exile financiers in New Jersey to Posada. An FBI spokesperson told author Ann Louise Bardach[2] the file cleansing had been the result of "routine cleaning," ordered, in part, because the Bureau believed Posada had "disappeared from sight and was out of action, [so] keeping his case file open was no longer warranted."

At the time those files were disappeared, of course, Posada himself had hardly disappeared. He was in a Panama jail awaiting trial for trying to assassinate Castro and had even been visited by the American embassy's FBI liaison there. His supporters in Miami were openly raising money for his legal defence and publicly lobbying for his release.

Despite the FBI's apparent official disinterest, elements inside the Justice Department and the FBI refused to let the Posada case die. And, shortly after his return to the United States in the spring of 2005, the FBI opened a new Luis Posada file. On June 10, 2005, an agent filed a 10-page affidavit in Posada's immigration case. Though the declaration relied heavily on Bardach's reporting, it also indicated that, in October 1998 — four months after the Havana meetings and a year after they'd first learned of his existence — FBI agents did finally travel to Guatemala to interview Tony Alvarez (referred to in the document as Confidential Source One, or CS-1). He handed over another copy of the "Solo" fax. Agents also ferreted out records showing that $19,000 worth of wire transfers from addresses in the United States to Posada's "Ramón Medina" alias in El Salvador and Guatemala had been sent between October 30, 1996 and January 14, 1998. "Based on the totality of the aforementioned information," the affidavit declared in backward but

---

2. Bardach discovered the files had been destroyed when an FBI agent called her soon after Posada returned to the United States and asked for her copies of FBI and CIA files on him. "When I asked why," Bardach would write, "he said, 'Do us a favor. We can't find ours.'"

straightforward bureaucratese, "the FBI is unable to rule out the possibility that Posada Carriles poses a threat to the national security of the United States."

In addition to the immigration proceedings unfolding in El Paso, a grand jury in Newark, New Jersey, began to look into links among Union City exiles — including CANF financier Arnaldo Monzón — Luis Posada and the 1997 bombings. The grand jury subpoenaed five men[3] who'd been named in the wire transfers. Two invoked their first amendment right against self-incrimination; the others denied any connection with the bombings, claiming their names had been "misappropriated" on the cables. The grand jury also subpoenaed Bardach and her Posada recordings. She fought their demands — as she had an earlier subpoena from the FBI in Florida — on freedom-of-the-press grounds. In the end, it didn't matter. The New Jersey grand jury never returned an indictment.

The closest the U.S. Justice Department could come to holding Posada to account for the Havana hotel bombings — forget Cubana Airlines, et al. — was the almost-but-not-quite-beside-the-point immigration fraud allegation that he'd fibbed about his role in them during his immigration review hearing. It was a far cry from the "Book 'em, Danno, murder-one" approach American justice took with the Cuban Five.[4]

Miami, Fall 1998

The Five — illegal officers Gerardo Hernández, Ramón Labañino and Fernando González, and agents René González and Antonio Guerrero[5] — were initially charged with being unregistered agents of a foreign government. The three illegal officers were also charged with using false identities. But those were relatively picayune charges. The prosecutors' prickly public relations problem was that the Cubans couldn't be charged with espionage because they'd never obtained anything more national-security sensitive than photographs of military planes in plain sight and yellowed clippings from base newspapers.

So prosecutors upped the ante — and lowered the bar for conviction. Instead of accusing them of actually stealing secrets, they charged Hernández, Labañino and Guerrero — who'd been assigned to gather information on

---

3. Bardach noted that one of those supboenaed — Abel Hernández — owned a Union City restaurant that featured one of Posada's paintings as well as a photo of Hernández "arm in arm with Jorge Mas Canosa."

4. After the 2001 verdict in the Cuban Five trial, the *Miami New Times* asked the FBI's Hector Pesquera "whether he would pursue local leads regarding the 1997 Havana bombings with the same vigor" as the Cuban agents. Pesquera pointedly refused to answer.

5. The other five — Nilo and Linda Hernández, Joseph and Amarylis Santos and Alejandro Alonso — quickly agreed to plead guilty and provide evidence against the others in exchange for lighter sentences.

Southcom and Boca Chica — with "*conspiracy to* gather and transmit national defense information,"[6] a convenient catch-all charge that didn't require them to prove they'd actually ever done so.

But why charge them at all? At one level, American law enforcement authorities would seem to have had the Avispa agents right where they wanted them — going about their intelligence-gathering business, blissfully unaware they were being watched. Spying on the spies had provided American intelligence with an ongoing primer on how Cuban intelligence operated. FBI agents could monitor the Cubans to see who else they met, thus expanding their who's-who of intelligence operatives. They'd even been able to surreptitiously enter their apartments, copy their disks, decode their messages. The FBI knew everything Havana was tasking the agents to do and what the agents were reporting back to the CP.

Given that Avispa's prime targets were militant Miami exile groups, the FBI could even have made law enforcement use of any Neutrality-Act-violating schemes the Cubans uncovered — assuming, of course, the FBI really wanted to enforce those laws. Thanks to their surveillance, the FBI knew the Cubans — whatever their desires — hadn't come close to penetrating Southcom or the Boca Chica Naval Station. By continuing to quietly keep tabs on them, the FBI could have retained the option to swoop in and break up their network in the unlikely event it ever did come too close to state secrets.

By arresting them, the FBI lost all those advantages. And taking them to court meant the government itself might have to disclose some of its clandestine methods for spying on the spies. Breaking up the network also meant the FBI would have to start over, uncovering the identities of the new agents the Cubans would send to replace those arrested. The only certainty was that there would be new agents.

Another question: why did the FBI choose to arrest the Cubans when they did? One theory was that officials were worried the Cubans might bolt the country after Ramón Labañino's laptop was stolen from his California hotel room. That robbery occurred on September 4, just eight days before their arrests. But Cuba had invested hugely in the development of its Avispa network. Havana wasn't about to order its total, instant dismantling because of what might very well have been a garden-variety robbery.[7]

Another, more plausible theory was that the FBI was trying to placate the Cuban American National Foundation. CANF had been badly singed by the agency's *La Esperanza* investigation. The FBI had easily tied those arrested aboard the vessel to CANF, then traced the vessel's ownership to Antonio Llama, a CANF board member, and one of the seized assault rifles to Pepe Hernández, CANF's president. The month before the arrests of the Five, Llama

---

6. Italic added.
7. The FBI has never disclosed whether it had any involvement in the Oakland break-in.

had been indicted as part of the conspiracy to assassinate Fidel Castro and a Justice Department official confirmed that Hernández was also a "target."[8] Given all of that, it might have seemed like a good time for the FBI to make nice with Miami's *el exilio* leadership. And how better to do it than by arresting a bunch of Cuban spies.

The man best positioned to explain why the FBI acted when it did — Hector Pesquera — isn't talking. At least not to me. It is known that, soon after he arrived in Miami that spring, Pesquera began to chum around with some of the most militant members of the Cuban exile community, including at least a few — Domingo Otero and Roberto Martin Perez — that Cuban State Security identified as terrorist plotters. Ann Bardach's FBI sources told her Pesquera had "decided to make his name with the Wasp network, rounding up Cuban agents in Miami and throwing the book at them. 'It made him a hero to the exile honchos,'" one agent told the author.

In an interview with a Miami radio station soon after the verdicts, Pesquera claimed he was the one who'd switched his agents' focus from spying on the spies to filing charges against them. "I was updated on everything there was," he explained of his first days in his new job. "We then began to concentrate on this investigation. As far as intelligence[-gathering] is concerned, [I decided] it shouldn't be there anymore. It should change course and become a criminal investigation."

After the verdict in the Cuban Five trial, Pesquera was quick to claim credit for persuading officials in Washington to okay his plan. He told the Miami *Herald* the case "never would have made it to court" if he hadn't lobbied FBI Director Louis Freeh directly. "To this day there are people in my headquarters who are not completely sold."

At the same time, Pesquera apparently discouraged investigations into incidents of exile terrorism. After FBI agents interviewed an "entirely credible" Tony Alvarez in Guatemala City, one of the agents told Bardach, "we thought it would be a slam dunk: we'd charge and arrest Posada. But then we had a meeting one day and the chief said, 'Hey, wait a minute. Lots of folks around here think Posada is a freedom fighter.' We were in shock. And they closed down the whole Posada investigation."[9]

I'd wanted to ask Pesquera — among many other questions — why, in the face of opposition from his own agents, he'd pressed so hard for the arrests so soon after the FBI and Cuban State Security had opened what seemed like such a promising, and unprecedented, dialogue. When I first contacted him, Pesquera, who retired from the FBI in 2003 and was now working for the

---

8. He was never charged.
9. The agents also told Bardach they were turned down when they asked to wiretap Orlando Bosch, "who we knew was working on bombing runs."

Miami Port Authority, was polite but cautious.[10] "It has been my policy not to discuss matters that occurred while I was a Bureau employee without the express approval from FBI HQ," he wrote in an email. But "if you so desire," he helpfully added, he included contact information for the FBI official who could provide that approval. I emailed the official, who shuffled me off to another official and then another, who finally wrote back that "since… Pesquera is a retired agent, you will need to contact the Society for Retired Agents to get permission to interview him."

That seemed strange. But I followed up and, after a good deal of phone tag, reached the Society's executive director, Scott Erskine, who seemed puzzled, surprised and perhaps a bit bemused the Bureau had referred me to him. The Society, he explained, is largely a social organization that has no role in providing permission for retired agents to speak publicly. He said it was up to Pesquera to decide what he can and cannot say and whether he'd willing to be interviewed.

After that, Pesquera stopped responding to my emails. Which leaves me to speculate on his motives in the case. Pesquera may indeed have been attempting to court favour with his influential new exile friends. But it's equally possible he may have been trying to deflect attention from the FBI's lack of success in holding anyone accountable for shooting down the Brothers to the Rescue planes two years before. That was still a festering wound in Miami's Cuban community. After the Five had been tried and convicted, Pesquera would draw a direct line between the 1996 shootdown and the 1998 arrests. "There was in my mind — in the [FBI] director's mind, [Attorney General] Janet Reno's mind — a concerted plan to murder those pilots," he told the Miami *Herald*. "When you blatantly cross the line between espionage to criminal activity — to murder — you have to draw the line."

The problem with that neat post-conviction justification is that there was no mention of the Brothers to the Rescue shootdown at the time the initial charges were filed. That's not quite true. Without waiting to see if there was any evidence connecting the Cuban agents to the shootdown, Congressman Lincoln Díaz-Balart[11] called on the Clinton administration to charge them for it anyway. "I am sure that the U.S. law enforcement agencies wish to proceed against those criminals" — note that they were still only *alleged* criminals — "as well as for the murder of four members of Brothers to the Rescue on February 24, 1996."

Seven months later, prosecutors did issue a revised indictment. It charged Gerardo Hernández with "conspiracy" — that word again — to commit

---

10. In April 2012, Pesquera took a new job as chief of police back in his native Puerto Rico.

11. Intriguingly, Pesquera had briefed Cuban American Congressmen Diaz-Balart and Ileana Ros-Lehtinen on the arrests three days before they were publicly announced.

murder in the shooting down of the Brothers to the Rescue fliers. But had prosecutors found smoking-gun evidence to link Hernández to the decision to shoot down the planes?

My own answer — after having read the 20,000-plus-page trial transcript and sifted through mountains of documents presented during the proceedings — is no. From other evidence, the decision to shoot down the planes appears to have been made by Fidel Castro himself, who issued standing orders to his military commanders in late January 1996 to do whatever was necessary to prevent further incursions into Cuban airspace. The military then waited for Brothers planes to make their next entrance into Cuban territory — and blew them out of the sky. Assuming, of course, you accept the Cuban claim the planes weren't in international waters when they were shot down.

One can argue — the Cubans certainly do — that the shootdown was a legitimate response to the ongoing provocations, as well as to the very real possibility that anti-Castro exiles, emboldened by publicity about Brothers' successes in violating Cuban airspace, would decide to drop bombs instead of bumper stickers on Havana. One can argue too — again, the Cubans do — that Brothers had been warned, and warned again, and again, about what would happen if they did again what they had already done several times before.

But one could also argue — I would — that the decision to shoot down the planes was wrong, that it was an over-reaction and that there were other, equally effective and dramatic ways to send their mad-as-hell-and-we're-not-going-to-take-it-anymore message to the Americans. Forcing the planes to land, for example, and then charging Basulto for violating its airspace might have brought global attention to Cuba's complaints without the loss of life.

But those arguments, however interesting, are beside the point to the charges against Gerardo Hernández. Was Hernández involved in a conspiracy to commit murder? Did he know in advance Cuba had decided to shoot down the planes? Did he have any role in planning, or carrying out the attacks? Did he have any control, or influence over the final decision to proceed, or even the intermediate decisions along the way?

One of the things that is clear from evidence presented during the trial is that Cuban State Security was obsessed with secrecy, with compartmentalization, with need to know. The decision to shoot down the planes appears to have been, primarily, a military matter. While the Cuban military and intelligence branches would have shared information about the specifics of those plans at the highest levels, that knowledge wouldn't have been disseminated widely, and certainly wouldn't have filtered down to officers in the field like Hernández. Those officers might get specific marching orders related to the mission without even being aware of the actual mission itself.

The prosecutors' "smoking gun" in the conspiracy to murder charge seems to have been a January 29, 1996, message from the CP announcing that "Superior Headquarters" had approved Operation Scorpion "in order to perfect the confrontation of counter-revolutionary actions of Brothers to the Rescue." But what did those words actually mean? Were they planning to shoot down the planes? Force them to land? Have their MiGs buzz them? Document their transgressions and escalate matters by complaining directly to the United Nations?

The rest of the message made it clear something was afoot, but not what that something might be. The CP wanted to know when Basulto would be flying a mission, for example, and who else might be flying with him. Basulto, unsurprisingly, seemed to be Havana's target. Cuban State Security also clearly didn't want their own agents, Roque or González, flying the day they "perfected" the confrontation. But there could have been a number of reasons for that: it could have been that they planned to shoot down the aircraft and didn't want their agents killed, of course, but it could just as easily have been that they planned to force the Brothers' planes to land and charge the pilots in Cuban courts, in which case they wouldn't want to risk having to arrest their own agents — or blow their covers.

Interestingly, this so-called smoking gun message wasn't even addressed to Hernández but to Manny Ruiz, the MININT major who'd replaced Hernández in Miami during his Cuban vacation and had remained in place for the hand back to Hernández. Interestingly too, the message mistakenly assumed René González was still flying missions. José Basulto had dropped González from the Brothers' roster two years before. While Hernández, who'd been supervising González for those two years, would certainly have known that, Ruiz might not. Which could explain why Havana's original error was repeated in a follow up-message to González two weeks later — a message supposedly from both Ruiz and Hernández.

In June 2010, Hernández, who didn't testify in his own defence at trial, finally told his version of the story in an affidavit filed as part of a last-gasp appeal of his murder conviction. In it, he insisted he never saw the message to González, and that Ruiz, who outranked him, probably appended his name to it as a matter of course.

Intriguingly, at the conclusion of the trial, prosecutors filed a last-minute emergency petition to prevent the jurors from voting on the murder count. During her instructions to the jury, Judge Joan Lenard outlined the level of proof required to convict Hernández of conspiracy to murder. Prosecutors, she said, needed to have proved there was a plan in place to shoot down the planes before they took off that day and that the shootdown was intended to happen in international waters, where the U.S. claimed jurisdiction.

In a petition to the 11th Circuit Court of Appeal on May 25, 2001 — before the case went to the jury — the prosecutors threw up their hands in despair. "In light of the evidence presented in this trial," the petition declared, the judge's instruction "presents an insurmountable hurdle for the United States in this case, and will likely result in the failure of the prosecution." The Appeal Court rejected their petition, but the prosecutors needn't have worried. The jury convicted the Five on every single count anyway, including conspiracy to murder. We'll come back to the jury. But we're getting ahead of ourselves. Even during the long lead-up to the trial, the universe — including the Cuban-American, Havana-Miami universe — had continued to unfold.

Havana, March 11, 1999

In the spring of 1999, Raúl Ernesto Cruz León finally went on trial in Havana for his role as the "material author" of the 1997 hotel bombings that killed Fabio Di Celmo. Over the course of four days, prosecutors introduced two tables-full of evidence to connect Cruz León — who'd already confessed to his role — to specific bombings. Prosecutors also attempted to link the bombing campaign itself to its "intellectual authors," Luis Posada and the Cuban American National Foundation. Percy Alvarado testified in public for the first time, outlining his infiltration of CANF, naming names and tightening the conspiratorial circle.

"CANF played the protagonist and hegemonic role in financing and organizing these acts of terror," declared Col. Adalberto Rabeiro, the MININT man in charge of the bombing investigation. He concluded his own testimony by showing a video about the life of Luis Posada.

"The unusually detailed testimony presented at the trial appeared to form part of a government effort to portray itself as being under constant attacks from Miami exiles," wrote Juan Tamayo, who'd travelled to Havana to cover the trial for the *Herald*. Tamayo, however, concluded that the most likely reason Havana wanted to publicize the attacks was to "justify harsh controls on domestic dissent." In the end, the five-judge panel found Cruz León guilty and sentenced him to death by firing squad.

San Juan, Puerto Rico, December 8, 1999

Eight months later, in another courtroom, this one in Puerto Rico, Juan Tamayo covered yet another exile-related trial with a very different outcome. Five CANF-connected exiles from *La Esperanza* were all acquitted of plotting to kill Fidel Castro. "Prosecutors had hoped that holding the trial in Puerto Rico would give them a better shot at convictions than in Miami, where juries regularly acquit anti-Castro plotters," Tamayo wrote. Instead, post-verdict comments by the jurors "showed that dislike for Castro and his government played a significant role in the jury's vote... In a stunning finale to the 14-day trial, two jurors later said the verdict was a 'message' to the Cuban people, embraced the defendants and went off to celebrate with them at a popular Cuban restaurant... Instead of going to jail, [the defendants] walked out of the federal courthouse singing the Cuban national anthem and accompanied by about 30 leading members of the Cuban community in Puerto Rico." One of the accused, Miami businessman and CANF board member — and CANF paramilitary financier — Tony Llama "sobbed openly and vowed that the verdict would invigorate 'our efforts to continue to get freedom for our country... This is not the end. This is just the beginning again.'"

Panama City, Panama, November 17, 2000

Less than a year after that — and less than a month before the trial of the Five was to begin in Miami — Luis Posada and three accomplices[12] were arrested in Panama City. In a dramatic turn of events, Castro himself had revealed the existence of this particular plot against him — and conveniently informed authorities that the plotters were staying at the nearby Coral Suites Hotel. During a press conference with selected reporters on the eve of a summit of Ibero-American leaders, Castro identified Posada as his chief would-be assassin and claimed the Cuban American National Foundation was the plot's financial puppet master. Panamanian authorities, Castro said, now had "the duty to find the chief terrorist and his accomplices, to make sure they don't escape by air, land or sea, to arrest them and to submit them to the proper courts."

Stunned by those unexpected revelations, Panamanian officials did just that. They arrested the four at their hotel and later recovered a Florida Marlins' black-and-aqua bag stuffed with "enough plastic explosives to level a building and kill people up to 200 metres away."[13] How did the Cubans know about the plot? The same way they knew about so many others, of course. They had at least one agent inside — or close to — those planning the attack.

Miami, Fall and Winter 1999

Necessity... In the end, necessity would become the primary legal defence strategy for Cuba's accused agents in Miami. Since Cuba could not depend on the United States government to protect it from American-financed and directed attacks, the argument went, it had had no choice but to send its

---

12. The accomplices included Gaspar Jiménez (you may remember him as Posada's sidekick during Percy Alvarado's bomb-making boot camp) and Guillermo Novo Sampol (another of the co-founders of CORU and the man whose cell phone was found in the possession of terrorists the Cubans arrested in 1995).

13. Posada, as usual, had an interesting explanation for his presence in Panama, if not for his stash of explosives. He claimed he was there to meet with a "senior official of the Cuban government who wanted to defect." The official, according to Posada's version: none other than Eduardo Delgado, the head of Cuba's Directorate of Intelligence and the man in charge of the by-now-arrested intelligence agents who'd been tracking Posada et al. for years.

agents to Florida to uncover plots and prevent terrorism against it and its leaders. A month after the arrest of the Avispa spies, Castro himself made that argument in an interview with CNN. "Yes, we have sometimes dispatched Cuban citizens to the United States to infiltrate counter-revolutionary organizations, to inform us about activities that are of great interest to us," Castro acknowledged in the interview with Lucia Newman, adding, "I think we have the right to do this."

The *Miami New Times* dubbed that the "Fatherland Defense," and quoted a U.S. security law expert "racking my memory to see if anything of this nature has ever been asserted before as a defense. I can't think of a parallel case." The Fatherland Defense would not have been an easy sell in Miami at any time, of course. But the 17 months between the arrest of the Cuban agents and the selection of a jury to hear their case were far from the best of times for pro-Castro Cubans.

On Thanksgiving Day 1999, a six-year-old Cuban boy named Elián González was plucked from an inner tube in the Straits of Florida by two fishers. Elián's mother, her boyfriend and a dozen others had died trying to cross from Cuba to Florida in bad weather in a small boat. The fishers handed Elián over to the U.S. Coast Guard, which, in turn, put him in the temporary care of his family's Miami relatives. They — with the vociferous support of the city's excitable exile community — unilaterally decided the boy should stay with his relatives in the United States and refused Elián's father's demands that the boy be returned to him in Cuba.

That family feud became the flashpoint for a highly charged five-month standoff between the Cuban government and the Miami exiles that only finally ended after armed U.S. Border Patrol officers braved a mob to seize Elián from his relatives. After two more months of legal, political and diplomatic wrangling that went all the way to the U.S. Supreme Court, Elián was finally returned to his father in Cuba. The Miami relatives' Little Havana home was quickly turned into a shrine — and Elián became a continuing *cause célèbre* for Miami exiles.

While the Elián affair played out on the streets of Little Havana and on TV screens around the world, reporters in South Florida's Spanish-language press were busily whipping their readers — including, of course, potential jurors — into a frenzy of hostility and hysteria against the accused Cuban spies. The day after the initial charges were announced, *El Nuevo Herald* reporter Pablo Alfonso insinuated — without offering any concrete evidence — that the FBI arrests "*may* be an action aimed at preventing a possible collaboration between the Cuban government and countries involved in terrorist actions against the United States." A week later, he resurrected Cold War rhetoric to suggest that "the idea to send Cuban spies en masse to Miami was developed more than three decades ago in the Georgian city of Pitsunda in the old Soviet

Union" during a post-Cuban missile crisis tête-à-tête between Soviet leader Nikita Khrushchev and Fidel Castro.

Writing in *Diario Las Americas* on September 20, 1998, Ariel Remos parroted and amplified Alfonso's claims that the arrests "*could be*" connected to Cuba's terrorist plans, then upped the ante yet again, tying together "the issue of spies and drug traffickers," and claiming — again without offering evidence — that it was "obvious" Castro "has been significantly involved in drug trafficking."

Two and a half years later, on the day the un-sequestered jury was set to begin considering its verdict, *El Nuevo Herald* trumpeted the headline: "Cuba Used Hallucinogens to Train Its Spies." In the article, Wilfredo Cancio quoted yet more anonymous sources, these ones suggesting that Cuba fed its spies LSD and other hallucinogens to train them for their missions, thus implying — again without specifically saying so — that the Avispa agents must have been drugged too.

At one level, the incendiary anti-Cuban rhetoric in South Florida's Hispanic press was par for the Miami exile course, but, as would later be discovered, it was also being surreptitiously, simultaneously funded by the same American government that was prosecuting the Five. At least 10 well-known South Florida journalists, including Alfonso, Remos and Cancio, all supplemented their salaries with tens of thousands of undisclosed dollars from the U.S. government-funded Board of Broadcast Governors and the Office of Cuba Broadcasting while moonlighting for Radio and TV Marti.[14] After the secret payments to the journalists were finally exposed in 2006, the *Herald* fired Alfonso and Cancio for violating the "sacred trust" between journalists and the public. But, by then, the damage had been done.

Given the emotionally roiling aftermath of the Elián González affair and the cauldron-stirring rhetoric about the Five in the local press, not to forget — how could anyone forget? — Miami's 40-year history of hostility to all things Havana, the defence's pre-emptive motion for a change of venue seemed a prudent no-brainer.[15] The track record of Miami juries in

---

14. The OCB operated Radio and TV Marti, ostensibly to broadcast into Cuba. But since the Cuban government jammed the Marti signals, their primary propaganda audience had turned out to be in South Florida's Cuban-American community. By paying the journalists who were attacking Cuba in the press to regurgitate their views on the air, the networks not only created an echo chamber effect for anti-Castro messaging but also possibly violated the U.S. Smith-Mundt Act, which prohibits the agency from "seeking to propagandize the U.S. public." According to information obtained using the Freedom of Information Act by the National Committee to Free the Five and others, Alfonso received $58,600 from the government during the period between the arrest of the Five and the end of their trial, Cancio received $4,725 and Remos $11,750. In total, the U.S. government paid more than $170,000 to seven journalists.

15. During the proceedings, the defence would try five more times to convince the judge

Cuba-related cases was so notorious federal prosecutors in the *La Esperanza* case had actually opposed a defence motion to have that trial moved from Puerto Rico to Miami, the home base for many of the accused, on the logical grounds the defendants would more likely walk in Miami. Prosecutors won the motion, but lost the case.

Prosecutors responsible for trying the Five — apparently detecting a previously undetectable strain of fair-mindedness among potential Miami jurors — opposed the defence motion. Judge Joan Lenard sided with the prosecutors. The five Cuban agents would face American justice deep in the deepest visceral, vengeful heart of anti-Castro Miami.

Although the defence managed to prevent any Cuban-Americans from serving on the jury,[16] it probably didn't matter. Dr. Lisandro Pérez, a professor of sociology at Florida International University and director of the Cuban Research Institute, analyzed survey and other data about community attitudes as part of a defence appeal of the verdicts. Pérez, a Cuban-American himself, concluded that the atmosphere in South Florida was so poisoned that "the possibility of selecting 12 citizens of Miami-Dade County who can be impartial in a case involving acknowledged agents of the Cuban government is virtually zero... even if even the jury were composed entirely of non-Cubans." Perhaps tellingly, the man who would be chosen jury foreperson made a point of proudly describing himself during the selection process as an "anti-communist."

The five defence attorneys — Miami lawyers without experience or expertise in espionage cases[17] — found themselves up against the full might of the United States government.[18] They had to get security clearances to see just some of what their clients were alleged to have done. Even though they were then allowed to peek at documents the government had classified secret, they had to convince the judge — over the inevitable objections of the prosecutors — to allow them to present any of those documents to the jury. In the end, less than 10 percent of the 15,000–20,000 seized documents was actually entered into evidence. During the trial itself, a national security

---

to move the trial. All were unsuccessful.

16. The jury ultimately consisted of five non-Cuban Hispanics, three non-Hispanic whites, three African-Americans and an Asian-American. Interestingly, 16 of the 160 members of the original jury pool said they knew the dead Brothers fliers or proposed trial witnesses about the shootdown.

17. During the early stages of the case, the Cubans — sticking to their original stories that they were not agents — accepted court-appointed lawyers. Even after the Cuban government decided to acknowledge the agents and fight the charges on the basis of necessity, the defendants retained their original lawyers.

18. At one point in the middle of the trial, Judge Joan Lenard estimated that investigating and prosecuting the Five had cost American taxpayers — up to that point — five million dollars.

advisor was on hand at all times to prevent allegedly sensitive material from slipping through the courtroom cracks. But none of that sensitive material, prosecutors had to concede, involved any American secrets the Avispa agents had stolen.

During the 17 months between their arrests and their trial, the agents were kept in solitary confinement while prosecutors played their best divide-and-conquer hands. They convinced five[19] of the 10 to cop pleas and cooperate in return for lesser sentences. None apparently had anything dramatic to offer. Only Joseph Santos testified at trial and, most of his testimony focused on how Cuban agents were recruited, trained and deployed. The other five — the agents who would become known as the Cuban Five — remained steadfast, despite the inevitable sticks connected to the government's carrots.

On August 15, 2000 — two days after his 40th birthday — prosecutors offered René González yet another deal.[20] He could opt out of going to trial by pleading guilty to a single count of being an unregistered foreign agent. "The last paragraph of the plea agreement draft [included] a not-so-veiled invitation to consider that my wife's resident status is at stake," González would later recall. With Olga's support, he responded to the offer by drawing a middle finger where his signature was supposed to go. The next day, authorities arrested his wife. On November 22 — just a few weeks before her husband was to go on trial — Olga was bundled onto a U.S. government plane and deported back to Cuba. Officials refused to allow her to take her children on the plane with

19. Nilo and Linda Hernández and Alejandro Alonso were sentenced to seven years each, while Joseph Santos was sentenced to four years, and his wife, Amarylis, to three and a half years. In 2001, U.S. prosecutors also arrested George and Marisol Gari, who they claimed were the Avispa agents code-named Luis and Margot. After pleading guilty to acting as unregistered foreign agents, George Gari was sentenced to seven years in prison, his wife to three and a half. In 2010, exile Edgerton Ivor Levy told an anti-Castro Miami television station that he and his wife were agents Ariel and Laura. He claimed that after their arrival in the United States, they'd acted as double agents, passing on information to American authorities. They were never charged.

20. The co-accused he admired most, Gerardo Hernández wrote me on September 10, 2010, was René González. While he didn't agree with the decision of the others to cop pleas, he understood it. Spy couples Nilo and Linda Hernández and Joseph Santos and Amarylis Silverio had young children to think about, while Alejandro Alonso's personal financial woes and family legal problems made him vulnerable. But René also "had his wife and two daughters with him... and he knew they will suffer the consequences — as they did — and he resisted all the pressure... [The authorities] didn't have much against him and they knew it, so they wanted to get him (and Fernando [the illegal officer caught filling in for Labañino's vacation who was not charged with conspiracy to steal American defense secrets]) out of the way to focus on the others... Even their lawyers told them that going to trial together would be a 'suicide.' They basically responded: 'Either with you or with another lawyer, but I'm going to trial with the other four.' Everybody said that, but of course the biggest merit is for those who would have benefited from a separation, like René and Fernando."

her. Her relatives in the U.S. and Cuba had to arrange separate transportation for teenaged Irma and the American-born toddler Ivette.

As for Gerardo Hernández, he was even unluckier. Because he was the alleged "spymaster" and because he refused to plead guilty, authorities punished him the way that hurt him most. They not only refused to grant Adriana a visa to visit him before or during the trial but they have also continued to refuse to issue a visa for all of the years he has been in prison since.[21]

Miami, December 6, 2000

The case of the *United States of America v Gerardo Hernández, a.k.a. Manuel Viramóntez et al.,* Docket No. 98-721, Judge Joan A. Lenard presiding, finally began in earnest in a small courtroom on the seventh floor of the Miami Court Building on the morning of December 6, 2000. A reporter for the British newspaper, the *Guardian,* described the scene: "The five Cubans sit in two rows, wearing dark suits and headphones to hear the trial in Spanish. [Fernando González], a small man with sleepy eyes and a moustache, sits quietly in a corner to Judge Lenard's right. Hernández is near the centre of the chamber; he has the bald head, goatee and sheer intensity of a young Lenin. Relatives of the dead fliers [sit] in a reserved row of the spectators section... A brother of one defendant sits a row back."

After instructing the newly sworn jurors on their duties — "Do not form any opinion until all the evidence is in" — Judge Lenard declared: "The trial will now begin."

The outcome was never really in doubt. For starters, the defendants' lawyers immediately fessed up to the basic charges: yes, their clients were unregistered agents of a foreign government, and, yes, some of them had used stolen identities. But they all vigorously denied trying to undermine the national security of the United States or, in Gerardo Hernández's case, to "brutally extinguish" the lives of the four Brothers to the Rescue fliers.

From the outset, the elephant in the room was Fidel Castro's communist government, and it occupied most of the space and sucked most of the air throughout. Paul McKenna, Gerardo Hernández's court-appointed lawyer, felt compelled to begin his opening statement by explaining to the jurors: "I do not represent the Government of Cuba. I don't represent Fidel Castro,

---

21. Despite international humanitarian appeals, neither Olga Salanueva nor Adriana Perez has been granted a visa to visit her husband in a U.S. prison. The U.S. government claimed Salanueva, who'd trained briefly so she could join her husband in Florida, "was a member of the Wasp Network who was deported for engaging in activity related to intelligence." But it's worth pointing out she was never charged with any such activity. Perez, who was hoping to join her husband so they could start a family, "was a candidate for training as a... U.S.-based spy when U.S. authorities broke up the network," so she too would not be allowed into the country.

and I am definitely not a communist." Not an auspicious beginning in the case of five Cuban communists representing Fidel Castro and the communist Government of Cuba.

In the end, the jury had to make sense of three inter-related issues within the larger case against the Five. The first was the government's contention that the Five — or at least the three specifically charged with "conspiracy to gather and transmit national defence information" — were actually seeking to steal American military secrets. That they didn't obtain any was acknowledged by all concerned.

The defence claimed the agents were "Cuba's early warning system of insurrection from the north." They were simply keeping an eye on American military activities — planes on runways, unusual movements that might indicate a planned attack on Cuba — but doing so using public means. Watching a runway from the side of a highway, reading base and other newspapers… The defence called former senior American military officers to testify that the information the Cubans did obtain didn't endanger U.S. security and that, as Four-Star General Charles Elliot Wilhelm put it, "the Cuban Armed Forces posed no conventional threat to the United States."

The defence pointedly noted too that Tony Guerrero hadn't even gone looking for his initial job at the Boca Chica base. His lawyer called Dalila Borrego, Guerrero's old employment counsellor, who testified she'd encouraged the personable young Cuban to apply for a low-level janitor's job at Boca Chica and even provided him with the necessary forms.

The prosecution counter-argued that the Cubans wanted to steal secrets, and would have if they could have. Prosecutors highlighted Havana's pressure on Guerrero to apply for more responsible positions so he could move up the security information food chain at the base and also focused in on Guerrero's reports back to the CP, in which he touted his efforts to befriend military personnel.

Score one for the prosecution. The Cubans clearly would have welcomed whatever information their agents could lay their hands on and encouraged them to ferret out more, and non-public information, if possible. But score one for the Cubans too. They were clearly foraging with a focus. Having seen what had already happened in Panama, Haiti, et al., they understood that their survival as a nation could depend on the success of their "early warning system."

The second key issue of the trial, and even more central to the Cubans' fatherland/necessity strategy, was the defence's contention that their clients were doing what the U.S. government should have — but didn't. They were preventing violations of American neutrality and international laws by infiltrating, uncovering and stopping attacks against Cuba by Florida-based terrorist groups.

Ironically, some of those same exile terrorists continued to make the Cubans' argument for them. In April 2001 — in the middle of the trial — three more Miami exiles were arrested trying to sneak into Cuba aboard a vessel filled with weapons. Cuban television even broadcast a telephone call the Cubans had recorded between one of those arrested and Santiago Álvarez, a prominent Miami exile with close ties to Luis Posada. During the conversation, which Alvarez didn't know was being recorded, Alvarez had mused about going ahead with the ever popular exile-chestnut scheme to set off a bomb at the Tropicana.

The defence did its best to focus the jury's attention on the long history of terrorism against Cuba, honing in on the 1997 Havana hotel bombings.[22] They convinced the judge to allow prosecutors and defence lawyers to fly to Havana to videotape interviews with eight potential witnesses to the bombings, including police investigator Roberto Hernández Caballero and Cuban State Security agent Percy Alvarado.

But they failed to convince the judge to allow them to introduce the full reports Cuban State Security had given the FBI in June 1998. They tried and failed to get access to FBI records of illegal activity by 17 individuals and exile groups, including the Cuban American National Foundation, Alpha 66 and Omega 7. They did call wannabe-Stinger-missile buyer Rodolfo Frómeta of Commandos F-4 to testify. Although Frómeta claimed to have discovered pacifism during his time in jail, he pointedly refused to denounce violent attacks by F-4 groups inside Cuba on the grounds of soldierly solidarity, thus bolstering the defence case. The defence lawyers also called FBI agent George Kiszynski, among others, to reinforce their point that exile terrorists were rarely arrested, rarely prosecuted and rarely convicted.

The prosecution limply countered by trying to show that, on some occasions, exiles were arrested and even convicted. Score one for the defence.

The third key issue — and the one that overshadowed everything else in the trial — was the prosecution's contention that Gerardo Hernández had been responsible for the deaths of the four Brothers to the Rescue fliers. The family members of the dead men were in the courtroom every day, bearing silent witness to the anguish they felt. Prosecutors did their best to focus the jurors' attention on them, showing photos of each of the dead fliers to the jurors and then using Arnaldo Iglesias, a Brothers' witness for the prosecution, to outline the circumstances of their deaths. Iglesias, the *Herald* reported, "paused, choked back tears and slowly read aloud from four death certificates."

The defence countered by calling José Basulto.[23] Hernández's lawyer, Paul

---

22. The judge ruled early on that evidence in the case had to relate to incidents that occurred between 1994 and 1998, the period of the alleged offences. That meant the defence couldn't refer to earlier attacks on Cuba.
23. Prosecutors apparently decided to use Iglesias as their main witness in presenting the

McKenna, egged on the easy-to-egg-on Basulto, blaming him for triggering the shootdown, and introduced evidence to show he'd ignored repeated warnings about violating Cuban air space. McKenna forced Basulto to concede Brothers had been test-firing potential weapons that could have been used against Cuba and confronted him with the letter he'd received from a man peddling used Czech military jets. Basulto, who blamed both of those incidents on Juan Pablo Roque, countered by asking McKenna if he was working for Cuban intelligence.

Judge Lenard admonished Basulto for that. She also tried — unsuccessfully — to prevent Basulto from staging, in the middle of the trial in front of a jury that was not sequestered, a showy memorial flight to mark the anniversary of the shootdown. On the eve of his highly publicized flight back to the scene of the shootdown, Basulto also announced that Florida Governor Jeb Bush had agreed to deliver a letter from a relative of a downed pilot to the governor's brother, who just happened to be President George W. Bush, asking him to indict Fidel Castro in connection with the shootdown.[24] Score an inadvertent one for the prosecutors.

The defence seemed to get bogged down trying to prove Basulto was the real author of his fellow fliers' misfortune (an argument some of the dead men's relatives also believed) and, most importantly, that the planes had been shot down inside Cuban territory rather than in international waters, as the prosecutors — and the International Civil Aviation Organization report — declared. The distinction was important legally because the wording of the conspiracy to commit murder charge said the incident had taken place within the "special maritime or territorial jurisdiction" of the United States. In fact, it was the judge's reference to the location of the shootdown that sent prosecutors scrambling to try to prevent the jurors from voting on the charge.

But that legal debate had little to do with the only significant central question: did Gerardo Hernández himself have any role in, or advance knowledge of the shootdown? The best witness about that would have been Hernández himself, but he was never called. That was strategically understandable, but testifying would have allowed Hernández to lay out his own, very different version of the events leading up to the tragedy and poke logic-holes in the prosecution version. Hernández knew René González hadn't flown with

---

conspiracy to murder case because they worried Basulto would be a loose cannon. He was.

24. In 2006, 10 years after the shootdown, the U.S. Attorney's office told the Miami *Herald* the investigation was still "an active case." A source told the *Herald* the "best hope" for laying charges against Raúl Castro was to get Gerardo Hernández to agree to testify against him. Hernández himself scoffed at what he called "their 'wild dream,' the true reason behind their psychological torture [of me]." In a 2010 letter to me, he wrote "it explains why they haven't let me see my wife for 12 years like every other prisoner, why they haven't let me write an email to her like every other prisoner, etc., etc."

Brothers for two years, for example. Why would he have included that misinformation in a message to González himself? Hernández was busy organizing Juan Pablo Roque's return to Havana during the lead-up to the shootdown. Why would he have warned Roque not to fly on a Brothers mission if he knew Roque would have been on his way back to Cuba? Yes, Hernández got a promotion after the shootdown, but he got it for years of service as a lieutenant and as a routine next step in the intelligence department pecking order, not for anything connected with blowing the planes out of the sky.

In the end, however, even Hernández's testimony probably wouldn't have changed the outcome. For Hernández. Or for the others, whose own less dramatic cases became inextricably entangled in the public — and jurors' — mind with the murder charge. On June 8, 2001, after just five days of deliberation following a complex, contentious seven-month trial, the jury in the case of Gerardo Hernández, a.k.a. Manuel Viramóntez et al. returned its verdicts. Guilty on all counts, including the conspiracy to commit murder charge the prosecution itself had tried to take off the table.

Cuban-American exiles celebrated the verdict at a Miami party attended by prosecutors and the FBI's Miami agent in charge Hector Pesquera. The Cuban American National Foundation,[25] led by CANF's executive vice president Dennis Hays,[26] immediately began lobbying U.S. Attorney General John Ashcroft to indict Fidel Castro for the shootdown.

During the three years since the Five had been arrested, American politics had changed — and not for the better, certainly not in terms of Cuban-American relations. Bill Clinton was no longer president, but the Helms-Burton Act he had so ill-advisedly signed, was now the draconian law of the land. Florida's exile leaders, who had played such a critical getting-out-the-vote role to ensure George W. Bush's victory in the controversial, hanging-chad 2000 presidential election, were ready to claim their reward. The Cuban Five had been convicted, and the new administration in Washington seemed finally ready to do whatever was necessary to rid the world of Fidel Castro and his communist regime. But then, on September 11, 2001, the world changed. And didn't.

---

25. Four months after the verdict, key members of CANF — including spokesperson Ninoska Pérez Castellón, her husband Roberto Martin Pérez, Alberto Hernández and Luis Zuñiga — all resigned from the Foundation to protest what they saw as a softening in its opposition to the Cuban government. They formed the hard-line Cuban Liberty Council to lobby Washington. CANF continues to operate, but its credibility was shaken in 2006, when former director José Antonio Llama filed suit against the organization, claiming he'd helped finance the often-denied paramilitary wing.

26. Yes, Dennis Hays was the same State Department official U.S. Under Secretary of State Peter Tarnoff had kept out of the Cuba loop during the rafters' negotiations because he was thought to be in league with CANF.

Havana, February 2011

Before we consider what happened to the Cuban Five after 9/11, let's briefly jump forward to the trial of Luis Posada in 2011, to understand its similarities and differences with the case of the Five, and what — if anything — that says about juries, trials and American justice. In February 2011, in the middle of Posada's trial in El Paso, I was in Havana doing interviews for this book. One of those I interviewed was a Cuban criminal lawyer named Roberto González, who also happened to be the brother of defendant René González. During preparation for their 2000 trial, González had worked with the Five's Miami-based lawyers, helping them line up evidence and witnesses in Cuba. He then spent the entire seven months of the trial in the courtroom in Miami, observing American justice up close. What did he see as the main differences between the American and Cuban systems of justice, I asked him?

"The objective in each system is the same," González told me, "but the procedures are very different." In Cuba, he said, most of the real action happens outside the courtroom during the "preparation" phase. Lawyers for the accused and the prosecution spend their time discovering each other's witnesses, sorting out evidentiary truth from lies away from the glare of publicity — and then submit their reports and responses for the judge to consider. That's why the public phase of the process — actual trials — happen late in the day and don't usually last long in Cuba. While North Americans often question what we consider speedy "show trials" in countries like Cuba, González makes a compelling argument that our own system offers no greater guarantee of justice.

González says the trial of the Five was an eye-opener. "In the U.S.," he marvelled, "the 'discovery' happens during the trial, which makes trials go on for so long. And what is important in that sort of trial is not truth or facts, but theatre. The outcome has to do with the acting capacity of the lawyers, the personality of the witnesses — more sympathetic witnesses, less sympathetic witnesses, a very attractive woman witness, a less attractive woman witness…"

While we like to believe our jury system is a guarantee we will be fairly judged by our peers, González sees its actual workings differently. Juries aren't selected for their expertise or their wisdom, he points out, but often because they don't know anything about anything that matters in the case before them. "I call it 'trial by ignorance.'"

González, of course, was talking about the trial of the Cuban Five in Miami, but he could just as easily have been discussing the Posada case going on as we talked in El Paso. I'd been in El Paso for the opening days of the Posada trial. It was definitely theatrical. Posada's Miami lawyer, Arturo — "call me Art" — Hernández, had filled the courtroom with his strutting ego and his histrionics. During the trial's 13 weeks, he filed 13 separate motions for mistrials. He badgered witnesses, launching personal and often specious attacks. He insinuated — without ever having to prove — that Tony Alvarez, the Guatemala City businessman who had connected Posada directly to the bombings, had once been the lover of a Castro relative. And that meant...? He unfairly, and with impunity, sliced and diced the journalistic reputation of author Ann Louise Bardach before she testified. He even attacked the credibility and credentials of a Havana coroner who simply came to El Paso to testify that Fabio Di Celmo, the Italian-Canadian businessman killed in one of the hotel bombings, had died instantly of a shrapnel wound!

Given the number of witnesses, the conflicting testimony and the sheer volume of the evidence presented during more than three months of on-again, off-again courtroom dramatics, how was it possible for the jury in El Paso to have reached its unanimous conclusion before lunch on its first and only day of deliberation?

The Posada jury — as Roberto González noted in the case of the Cuban Five — was chosen more for what it didn't know about the accused and his history of exile terrorism than for what it did. So, while the jury in El Paso rendered a swift and decisive verdict — as had the jury in Miami in the case of the Cuban Five — that doesn't mean they rendered justice in either case.

Roberto González's brother René emailed me soon after the verdict in El Paso. "There are few things in the life experience of an average American that can make him an arbiter on justice, unless injustice is brought on himself. An unfair legal system," he concluded, "is no more than a reflection of a society built on unfairness."

Miami, Fall 2001

You might have imagined 9/11 would have made Americans more sympathetic to — or at least understanding of — Cuba's right to defend itself against terrorist attacks plotted and financed from the United States. After all, George W. Bush's ringing, post 9/11 line-in-the-terrorist-sand declaration — "A government that harbors a terrorist in its territory, that permits him to act, to live, to raise money, to organize himself, is as guilty as the terrorist" — could apply equally well to Florida in its role as a staging ground for terrorism against Cuba.

"Orlando Bosch," Cuban National Assembly President Ricardo Alarcón noted sardonically, "has been defined by the U.S. Department of Justice as a terrorist... Where does he live? In Afghanistan? Or does he live in Miami? Is he keeping quiet? No."

The 25th anniversary of the 1976 terrorist bombing of Cubana Airlines Flight 455, which killed 73 people, occurred just four weeks after 9/11. The Cubans marked the occasion with a march and a speech by Fidel Castro. Castro, who'd been among the first world leaders to offer his condolences to the American people after the September 11 attacks, noted that Cubans knew all too well the awful impact of air terrorism long before 9/11. "On a day like today," he said, "we have the right to ask, What will be done about Posada Carriles and Orlando Bosch, the perpetrators of that monstrous, terrorist act? And about those who planned and financed the bombs that were placed in the hotels?" The response from Washington was a deafening silence.

In Florida, where the Five were still awaiting their sentencing hearings, the response was anything but silence. In fact, *El Nuevo Herald* attempted to hike the hostility level, running a story on November 14 citing unidentified federal investigators connecting 9/11 terrorist Mohammed Atta with Cuba. The connection was more than just tenuous. There was no connection. According to the otherwise unattributed story, the investigators "suspect" that Atta had contact with "a top Defense Ministry officer with personal ties to Castro, who entered the United States under cover of assignment to a Cuban-government delegation escorting Elián's two grandmothers." The *Herald* took that unsourced, unconfirmed possibility and ran it under the headline, "They Affirm That Atta Met in Miami with a Cuban Agent." The next day, Congressman Diaz-Balart issued a press release stating it as gospel truth: "Al Qaeda terrorists have been linked to Cuban intelligence operatives." And so it went.

Miami, December 12, 2001

On December 12, 2001, three months and one day after 9/11, Gerardo Hernández stood in a Miami court room, the first of the Five to be sentenced. In his statement to the court, Hernández inked in what he saw as the obvious connection between what he had done for Cuba in Florida and what Americans were now doing in Afghanistan to respond to Osama bin Laden's "condemnable" terrorist attacks. "The sons and daughters" of America who were putting their lives at risk to stop future attacks against their homeland, he told Judge Lenard, were rightly considered "patriots… Their objective is not that of threatening the national security of any of the countries where these [terrorists] are being sheltered."

The real issue with terrorism and the United States' response to it, he pointed out, was American hypocrisy. "As long as the acts of some of these criminals are condemned while others are sheltered and allowed to act with impunity against the security and sovereignty of other countries, and considered 'freedom fighters,' this scourge will never be eradicated," he explained. "As long as this is the case, there will always be nations that need to send some of their own people to carry out dangerous missions for their defense, whether it be in Afghanistan or South Florida."

By the time of their sentencing, the Cuban Five had become national heroes in their homeland. On July 26, 2001, an annual national holiday to mark the beginning of what became the Cuban Revolution, Fidel Castro had

led 1.2 million chanting citizens — many wearing T-shirts and carrying plac-
ards with the images of the Five — in a march past the U.S. Interest Section
in Havana. Declaring that the five patriots had "risked their lives daily to
discover and inform on the terrorist plans hatched against our people by the
Cuban-American Mafiosi," Castro promised they would return to a proper
heroes' welcome. Later, the Cuban Parliament unanimously agreed to bestow
on them the country's highest honour, Heroes of the Republic of Cuba, and
Castro declared 2002 to be the Year of the Heroes: Prisoners of the Empire.

It was the beginning of an ongoing war of words — fought with legal
briefs and speeches, protest marches and newspaper ads, websites and offers
of prisoner exchanges — whose goal is not only to win freedom for the Five
but also to validate and vindicate their mission. The families of the Five —
particularly Gerardo's wife Adriana and René's wife Olga and daughter Irma,
along with Tony's mother and sister, and Ramon's and Fernando's wives —
have put a human face on their case, speaking out in interviews and attending
events around the world.

Beginning with the National Committee to Free the Five, a San Francisco-
based group that was set up in the aftermath of their convictions, there are
now more than 400 committees in over 100 countries working for the freedom
of the five Cuban agents. They conduct research (the National Committee
uncovered details of U.S. government payments to Miami journalists who
inflamed passions in the lead-up to the trial), organize demonstrations (the
International Committee for the Freedom of the Five staged "Five Days for the
Five" in Washington in April 2012) and even conduct mock trials (solidarity
groups in Canada organized a "People's Tribunal & Assembly" in Toronto in
September 2012 to create a public forum and "break the silence of the mainstream media"). The movement has found more converts — and greater legal
and diplomatic success — in the international community, where the story of
the Five is actually better known and understood than in the United States.

On May 27, 2005, the United Nations Human Rights Commission's
Working Group on Arbitrary Detentions concluded that the U.S. treatment
of the Five had contravened Article 14 of the International Covenant on
Civil and Political Rights. Citing the long periods the men spent in solitary
confinement, the fact their lawyers got only limited access to the case against
them (shades of third-world dictatorships), the irredeemably hostile climate
in Miami and the "severe sentences" handed them, the group "requested
the U.S. government to adopt the necessary steps to remedy the situation."
Nothing happened.

On October 13, 2010, Amnesty International released its own report on
the case. While acknowledging that the charges against the Five were serious,
the international rights watchdog raised "doubts about the fairness and im-
partiality of the trial... the strength of the evidence to support the conspiracy

to murder conviction in the case of Gerardo Hernández, and whether the circumstances of the pre-trial detention of the five men, in which they had limited access to their attorneys and to documents, may have undermined their right to defense." Again, nothing happened.

The Five have virtually exhausted their legal appeals. On August 9, 2005, they won their only American legal victory when a three-judge panel of the U.S. 11th Circuit Court of Appeals unanimously agreed to reverse all of their convictions and ordered a new trial — not in Miami.

Describing a "perfect storm" of "improper [prosecutorial] assertions, insinuations or suggestions" that had the potential to "inflame the jury's prejudices" in a community already hostile to anyone connected to the Government of Cuba, the judges declared the original trial had violated "one of our most sacred freedoms… the right to be tried fairly in a non-coercive atmosphere." But that judicial triumph was short lived. A year later, the full appeals court reversed its panel's decision.

In 2008, the courts affirmed the sentences initially handed out to Hernández and René González but determined that Judge Lenard had made serious errors and ordered that the others be re-sentenced and their periods of incarceration reduced. Fernando González, originally sentenced to 19 years for general conspiracy, conspiracy to act as a non-registered foreign agent and false identity, had his sentence reduced to 17 years and nine months. Tony Guerrero's life term plus 10 years for general conspiracy, conspiracy to commit espionage and conspiracy to act as a non-registered foreign agent was reduced to 21 years and 10 months. Ramón Labañino, sentenced to life plus 18 years for general conspiracy, conspiracy to commit espionage, false identity and conspiracy to act as a non-registered foreign agent, had his sentence reduced to 30 years.

The case of the Five never made it to the United States Supreme Court. On January 20, 2009, the Five's defence team, now led by famed American civil rights lawyer Leonard Weinglass, petitioned the court to order a new trial. "The pervasive and violent anti-Castro struggle of the Miami community," he argued, couldn't have helped but "infect the jury with hostility [and] cause jurors to fear for their (and their families') safety, livelihoods, and community standing if they acquitted." Ten Nobel Prize winners, as well as lawyers, parliamentarians and public figures from more than a dozen countries filed friends-of-the-court briefs urging the Supreme Court to hear the appeal. But the new U.S. administration, led by Barack Obama, petitioned the court not to take up the case. The trial, it claimed, had been fair and there was therefore no need to review the case. On June 15, 2009, the U.S. Supreme Court, without explanation, denied the petition. There would be no new trial, no legal victory. The Five would have to look elsewhere for justice.

AFTERMATH

Havana, December 3, 2009

The man Cuban authorities arrested was no low-level Central American mercenary. Neither was he your run-of-the-mill Miami-based Cuban-exile true believer. Instead, he was a gregarious, grey-haired, 60-year-old social-worker-turned-telecommunications-specialist from Bethesda, Maryland. Alan Gross — all six-feet, 250-pounds of him — had arrived in Cuba 11 days earlier on a tourist visa. But he was no ordinary tourist. Despite U.S. restrictions that still limited most legal American travel to the island to Cuban-Americans and organized groups, Gross — a Jewish American — was in the process of wrapping up what would have been his fifth visit to Cuba in 2009 alone.

In 2001, Gross founded a company called Joint Business Development Center, which specialized in "Internet connectivity in locations where there [is] little or no access." Essentially, that meant Gross worked as a freelance contractor for U.S.-government-funded organizations setting up satellite communications equipment in remote corners of troubled countries, like Iraq and Afghanistan, in order to "circumvent state-controlled channels."

Gross had first travelled to Cuba in June 2004 at the behest of a man named Marc Wachtenheim. Wachtenheim ran the Pan American Development Organization, which was partly funded by the United States Agency for International Development. USAID — set up in 1961 as a "humanitarian" extension of U.S. foreign policy — is supposed to "extend assistance to countries recovering from disaster, trying to escape poverty and engaging in democratic reforms." In the U.S., of course, the phrase "engaging in democratic reforms" inevitably translated into American-sponsored schemes to promote "regime change" in Cuba, especially after passage of the 1996 Helms-Burton Act. During the Bush administration, USAID spending on Cuba-related projects jumped from $3.5 million a year to more than $45 million. Much of that spending went on in secret with very little oversight or accountability. "The Cuba programs," noted Fulton Armstrong, a former senior advisor to the Senate Foreign Relations Committee, in a December 2011 column in the Miami *Herald*, "have an especially problematic heritage, including embezzlement, mismanagement, and systemic politicization… The secrecy surrounding them, the clandestine tradecraft… and the deliberate concealment of the U.S. hand, had all the markings of an intelligence covert operation."

But what Wachtenheim actually asked Gross to do back in 2004 seemed innocuous enough. He was simply supposed to deliver a video camera to a man named José Manuel Collera Vento, a pediatric cardiologist and the grand master of Cuba's Masonic Lodge. Wachtenheim offered to pay Gross $400 for his troubles. What neither Gross nor his handlers back in Washington realized at the time was that Collera — also known as Agent Duarte — was a Cuban State Security agent who reported back to Cuban intelligence on his meeting with Gross. Alan Gross had popped up on the Cuban intelligence radar.

Gross returned in 2007 — again posing as a tourist, again under the auspices of Wachtenheim and PADF — to distribute more communications equipment. The equipment this time was more sophisticated and included several BGANS, or Broadband Global Network Systems. Gross, who brought one into the country in his backpack, described it to a Cuban customs official as a "modem." Not quite. A BGANS not only functions as a satellite phone bypassing the local phone system but it can also provide Internet signals and be used to establish its own WiFi hotspot. That allows it to operate undetected by government servers. Which, of course, was the purpose. But also illegal in Cuba.

Later that year, Gross submitted his own proposal to PADF to bring communications equipment into Cuba using "multiple conduits such as tourism, humanitarian missions and diplomatic pouches." Although PADF turned down his pitch, Gross was more successful the next year when he submitted almost the same proposal to yet another USAID-connected firm, Development Associates International, which was looking for ways to spend its "Cuba Democracy Program" budget. On October 30, 2008, Gross signed a one-year deal with DAI. He was to bring the necessary equipment onto the island, set up three WiFi hotpots — one each in Havana, Camaguey and Santiago — and train Cubans to use them. For his troubles, DAI agreed to pay him $258,264.

Although Gross applied for U.S. Treasury and Commerce Department licences to travel to Cuba and to export equipment there, he never informed Cuba of his mission, and invariably flew into the country on a tourist visa. To smuggle his various pieces of equipment into the country without arousing suspicion, Gross contacted a New York Jewish group involved in organizing religious and humanitarian missions to Cuba. He managed to convince at least two participants — Suzanne Andisman, the senior vice president of the Jewish Federation of Broward County in Florida, and Richard Klein, an executive at the Jewish Federations of North America — to act as unsuspecting mules, ferrying sophisticated equipment into the country in their luggage and carry-ons. Gross would later rendezvous with them at Havana hotels to retrieve his equipment.

Gross sometimes travelled with the religious groups, both to make his own Cuban visits seem more innocent and also to be there in case anything went wrong. Once, one of his mules was stopped by a customs officer who wanted to know more about a WiFi range extender in the person's carry-on. Gross quickly stepped in to explain it was for personal use and even managed to negotiate a reduction in the hundred percent customs fee the officer initially wanted to impose. In a report back to DAI on that adventure, Gross allowed that it had been "better to be lucky than smart."

On March 30, 2009, Gross made his own first trip to Cuba as a USAID subcontractor. After passing through customs "without being detected," Gross visited the Gran Patronato, Havana's main synagogue, where he explained to its leaders he had brought with him a gift from American Jews "to improve communication between Jewish communities." After installing his communications gear, Gross showed two members of the synagogue how to use it and instructed them in how to set up email addresses for themselves. But he warned them not to use their real names, in order — as he put it in his report — to "make their identification even more problematic for Cuban authorities." Gross also used the network himself to communicate with officials at DAI in Washington.

On his next 10-day visit — at the end of April — Gross travelled to Santiago de Cuba, where he set up yet another WiFi location at that city's synagogue. He did the same again in June, this time renting a car in Havana for the seven-hour drive to Camaguey rather than risk a further encounter with Cuban airport authorities. He returned in July for another week to repair part of the system he'd installed in Camaguey and to distribute a collection of new electronic goodies — 12 iPods, 11 Blackberry Curves, three MacBooks, six 500-gigabyte hard drives, three more BGANS, three routers, three controllers, 18 wireless access points, 13 memory sticks, three Internet phones and an assortment of networking switches.

In his report back to DAI, Gross proudly declared that he'd succeeded in creating the three wireless networks, which now had 325 users, and noted that "communications to and from the U.S. have improved and [are] used on a regular basis." But, he added, it was all a "very risky business." He didn't know the half of it.

Gross arrived for his fifth visit of the year on November 24, 2009, travelling to Santiago de Cuba and Camaguey to train his BGANS users in their "operation and upkeep." Gross's final assignment in Cuba this trip was to deliver a replacement BGANS device to Raúl Capote Fernández, a Havana university professor. Capote, who'd been using the U.S.-supplied device to send information on "the Cuban situation" to his handlers in the United States, was yet another ubiquitous agent of Cuban State Security. Although Capote's damaged BGANS wasn't one Gross had distributed — it had been originally delivered in 2008 — Gross agreed to visit the Cuban to replace it. He never showed. Instead, a few days later, Marc Wachtenheim's assistant called Capote to warn him that "the person designated to carry out the replacement had been arrested in Havana because he had been careless."

More than careless. When Cuban authorities arrested Gross, they not only seized his Rosetta Stone Spanish-language CDs but also his laptop, several flash drives and a very special SIM card. While SIMS — subscriber identity module cards — are standard equipment in cell phones, this one was a much more sophisticated device, capable of preventing its satellite phone transmissions from being detected within 400 kilometres. You can't buy SIM cards like that off the shelf. In the United States, they're most frequently used by the CIA and the Defense Department.

Ferreting through the records on his computer and flash drives, Cuban investigators uncovered a treasure trove of Gross's reports back to his bosses in Washington in which Gross acknowledged the dangerous nature of the work he was doing. "This is very risky business in no uncertain terms," he wrote at one point, adding that "detection of satellite signals would be catastrophic." One local Cuban community leader he'd talked to, he wrote, "made it abundantly clear that we are all 'playing with fire.'" Alan Gross had been burned.

After news of his arrest became public, the U.S. State Department issued a statement declaring him a humanitarian do-gooder and demanding his immediate release. A spokesperson suggested vaguely and blandly that Gross had been working on "a program designed to play a positive constructive role in Cuban society and governance by helping Cuban citizens to gain access they seek to information readily available to citizens elsewhere in the world." Gross's wife, Judith, who also insisted her husband had "done nothing wrong," claimed he was "helping the Jewish community improve communications and Internet access." There were problems, of course, with that benign, benevolent explanation.

While recognized U.S. Jewish groups had been permitted to travel to Cuba for more than 20 years — delivering everything from kosher goods and medicines to, in fact, communications equipment — the Jewish Telegraphic Agency, a global Jewish news service, noted that "the main Jewish groups in Cuba denied having any contracts with Alan Gross or any knowledge of his project." "The saddest part," said Adela Dworin, president of Havana's Beth Shalom Temple, the central headquarters for Cuba's Jewish community, "is that [Gross and the U.S. government] tried to involve the Jewish community in Cuba, which has nothing to do with this."

In truth, Cuba's 1,500-member Jewish community not only had generally good relations with the island's government — in 2010, Raúl Castro himself would attend Shalom Temple to take part in Hanukkah services and praise "the Hebrew community in Cuba and the fabulous history of the Hebrew people" — but they already had their own Internet connections that allowed them to communicate with other Jews around the world.

Did Cuba's Jewish community really need James-Bond-style SIM cards, satellite phones and secret, undetectable WiFi hotspots? Or did all that high tech equipment have a more sinister purpose? The Cuban government certainly thought so. On February 4, 2011, it charged Alan Gross under Article 91 of the Cuban Penal Code with "acts against the independence and territorial integrity of the state." When he went on trial a year later, the Cubans used Gross's own reports to DAI to show, in the words of his sentencing document, the "lucrative, conspiratorial and covert" nature of what he had been doing in Cuba.

Prosecutors asked for a sentence of 20 years. Gross's defence lawyer urged the judges to simply fine him, credit him with time served and send him on his way. The judges weighed the competing arguments. On the one hand, Gross had been cooperative after his arrest, but he'd also been "evasive… and tried to distort certain points of fact that were already established." While his age was a mitigating factor, the fact he'd been motivated by financial gain worked against him. In the end, the court sentenced him to 15 years in prison — meaning he would be 77 before he was finally allowed to return to his wife and family. Gross's lawyers appealed, but Cuba's Supreme Court ultimately upheld the sentence. Like the members of the Cuban Five, Alan Gross would have to look beyond the justice system of the country in which he'd been arrested for mercy.

Marianna Federal Correctional Institution, Marianna, Florida, October 7, 2011

The guards woke him at four in the morning. René González had spent his last night in prison in "the hole." But this time, it was not a punishment. It was to facilitate the publicity-free, pre-dawn prison departure both sides wanted. González dressed now in the same unfamiliar civilian clothes — light green golf shirt, dark slacks — he'd tried on the week before as part of his pre-release routine. Paperwork, signatures, fittings, more paperwork, more signatures.

Still, it was nothing compared with… The situation was "almost surreal," he thought to himself as he dressed, marvelling at "how easy it is to get out after they have made everything [so difficult] to have you in for so long." Best not to think about that now. González had promised himself he would live in the moment. Still…

Just after 4:30 a.m., the guards escorted González to the prison door, opened it. His lawyer, Philip Horowitz, was waiting to greet him on the other side. Horowitz then drove him to a pre-arranged "place nearby" to reunite with his family. His daughters[27] Irma, now 28, and Ivette, 14 — had she really been only four months old the morning the FBI dragged him away in September 1998? — were there, as was his brother Roberto and his father Cándido. But not Olga. The U.S. Government continued to refuse to grant her a visa. She was in Havana at the other end of the cell phone. Waiting for a call from her husband.

The original plan had been for them all to jump into a waiting van and drive to a secret hideaway to enjoy their reunion in peace. But it turned out there were no hovering reporters — they wouldn't begin gathering for a couple of hours, anticipating González would be released later in the day like other

---

27. By this point, Irma had a job teaching psychology at the University of Havana while Ivette was a Grade 8 student with "outstanding grades," explained her proud father.

prisoners — so Roberto took out his video camera and began recording the moment: the smiles, the laughter, the hugs, the tears.

"The first word that comes to my mind is elation and lots of happiness," René would write later, "but it is more complicated than that... At times I realized how long I had been away from my family — looking at how my daughters had grown — and it made me sad. Hugging them and my father and brother made me happy. At times, I thought on my other comrades and it also made me sad. Then I would talk to Olguita and happiness would come back, and so on."

There was also, of course, the even more emotion-conflicting "expectations as to the new life." After 13 years and 25 days as Prisoner #58738-004, René González was finally free. Sort of.

After the Five were convicted and sentenced in 2001, they had been scattered to separate prisons across the country. While they waited out all their various and sundry legal appeals, each coped with incarceration in his own way. Tony Guerrero immersed himself in his poetry, taught himself to paint and eventually began to tutor other prisoners, not only in art but also — perhaps surprisingly, given his earlier difficulties with the language — in English, preparing other inmates for their high school equivalency tests. Gerardo returned to his early love of cartooning and became actively involved as the most public face of the Five.

"From day one," René González says, "[I decided] I would get out of prison better fitted, be it emotionally, physically or intellectually." He developed a daily routine of morning exercises — he eventually ended up completing half-marathons — followed by afternoons reading and studying, especially economics, and responding to the huge volume of letters and cards that arrived each day from supporters. His fellow prisoners "were amazed at the amount of letters, the magazines with our pictures in them, the stamps made after us and some of those things," he recalls. His celebrity helped in his relationship with other prisoners — as did the fact he had opted to go to trial rather than cooperate with the authorities in exchange for a lesser sentence. "It gives you the trust of the other inmates because they know you won't turn against them." Though he didn't push his own political views, other inmates, knowing what he'd been convicted of, were naturally curious. "For most of them, I would be the first 'commie' that talked to them about Marxism, and it was interesting to see their reactions after so much manipulation."

González also spoke by phone each day with his wife Olga, "provided I managed to count the minutes so as not to exhaust the allocation of 300 minutes a month." He and Olga didn't exchange regular letters — sending mail to Cuba through the U.S. Interest Section in Washington was slow and cumbersome — but they added email to their daily correspondence after René was allowed to use a prisoners' email system in the latter stages of his incarceration. They also managed one, supposedly secret personal visit. After 10 years of denying Olga a visa to visit her husband in prison, American authorities tendered a surprise offer in late 2010. Without officially granting them visas, they agreed to allow both Olga and Gerardo's wife, Adriana, to visit their husbands in prison. The deal was almost certainly an American tit for tat after Cuba had agreed to allow Judith Gross to visit her husband in jail in Havana — and perhaps a dangled carrot for a hoped-for larger deal to free Gross himself, though that never materialized. The only caveat was that the Cubans had to agree to keep the visits secret — probably to avoid raising the red flag of humanity to the bull of Miami's exile leadership. The Cubans kept their part of the bargain, but someone on the American side leaked the story. Republican Congresswoman Ileana Ros-Lehtinen predictably "raised hell" with the State Department.

Still, René González did finally get to spend time with his wife, if only three days. Olga was kept under "virtual arrest" at a nearby hotel, René recalls, and then driven each day to the prison, where "a guy from the [Federal Department of Corrections] and a lady from the State Department would watch on us" in the prison visiting room. Despite the awkward circumstances, "they were very professional and allowed us a normal interaction."

As the prisoner with the shortest sentence — at 15 years, the shortest only relatively speaking — González was also the first to be released. Under federal law, prisoners must serve at least 85 percent of their sentence inside the penitentiary, then — if their record inside has been exemplary, which González's had — live their remaining time outside the prison walls under what is known as supervised release.[28]

About 10 months before González's scheduled October 2011 release date, his lawyer began talks with U.S. authorities over where he would serve the final years of his sentence. González, not surprisingly, wanted to return to his family in Cuba. He also — not unreasonably — feared for his safety if he was forced to remain in the U.S. Although there was no particular legal purpose to forcing him to remain in America — he was not about to be "reintegrated" into American society, and the U.S. government would almost certainly deport him to Cuba as soon as his sentence expired — the prosecutors insisted González renounce his American citizenship before they would even consider an application to complete his sentence in Cuba. González initially resisted — he didn't trust the prosecutors — then relented. But the judge — the same Joan Lenard who'd sentenced the Five to their long sentences in 2001 — turned down his plea to return to Cuba. "Of course, I wasn't at all surprised," González says today. "I was ready for it." But he wasn't quite ready for what came next.

"If they need someone to send to Mars for three years," René González

---

28. González's supervised release is scheduled to end on October 7, 2014.

joked with his wife on the phone in the spring of 2012, "I'm ready for it. I can spend some time on a spacecraft [prison] followed by time on another planet [supervised release]. I've been trained for it."

González lives somewhere, but he can't tell you where. He doesn't have a driver's licence, a bank account or any card or any document that lists his current address. "I can't leave a record that would allow the terrorists from Miami to locate me." He can't get a job because that too might make him vulnerable. He can't even talk to his neighbours across the fence — if there is one — or engage in any of the ordinary social interactions with anyone except his lawyer, occasional visiting family members and — by phone — his wife. So he does what he did in prison: exercise, read, study. "The only difference," he says with a laugh, "is that the recreation yard is bigger and the food is better — save for the cook, of course."

There have been only a few breaks from this monastic existence. In early November 2011 — three weeks after his release from Marianna prison — González showed up, unannounced, at a party in Miami to celebrate the end of a U.S. tour by the famed Cuban children's theatre group, La Colmenita. Founded in 1990 by Cuban director Carlos Alberto Cremata,[29] the troupe's repertoire includes everything from lively children's fairy tales and musicals to *Abracadabra,* a show written by the children themselves to celebrate the story of Cuba's "five heroes."

The 22 children, ranging in age from five to 15, had performed that show — among others — for appreciative audiences in Washington, New York and San Francisco, and were on their way home when they made one final stop in Miami. After a day visiting with some of their exile family members in Miami — many of whom the children had rarely, if ever, met — and just a few hours before boarding their flight back to Havana, the young actors were bussed to a house in the city where, they were told, a surprise was waiting for them. After they'd gathered in a circle in the backyard in anxious anticipation, René González, real-life hero and one of the subjects of their play, suddenly entered their circle. "Abracadabra!" The children surged forward as one, surrounding him, hugging him, kissing him, squealing, shouting, some crying with excitement.

"Here you have another 'Colmenita,'" González boasted, showing off his own La Colmenita T-shirt. "What's new, pal?" he added, scooping up Federico León Burgos, La Colmenita's youngest performer, in his arms. Inside the house, he asked the children what they'd liked best about their tour of the United States. "New York," answered one. "This meeting," said another.

González's second respite from his virtual house arrest was less joyful. In late March 2012, he applied for court approval to fly to Cuba for two weeks to visit his brother Roberto, who was in the final stages of terminal cancer. This

29. Cremata's father was one of the pilots killed in the 1976 Cubana Airlines bombing.

time, Judge Lenard, over the objections of the government, gave her blessing. While the visit was private — the Cubans only announced his return to Cuba as a final item on its daily newscast the day of his arrival and scheduled no public events during his time there — and González himself returned as promised following his two weeks, the decision to allow him to visit his dying brother instantly became part of a wider debate over the fate of Alan Gross.[30]

Judith Gross — who'd already asked Pope Benedict to intercede with Cuban authorities on her husband's behalf during his March 2012 papal visit to the island — now appealed directly to Cuban President Raúl Castro. She asked him to allow her husband to visit his own 89-year-old mother, who was dying of inoperable lung cancer in Texas. "She longs to see her son," Judith Gross wrote in an opinion column in the *Washington Post*, adding that, "so far, the Cuban government has not decided to reciprocate the humanitarian gesture extended to González. Are Cuba's leaders really that cold and uncaring? Why will they not allow Alan the same humanitarian privilege granted to González?"

The two situations weren't quite so tit-for-tat comparable as Judith Gross had understandably attempted to paint them. For starters, the U.S. government had objected to González's application. It was the judge who ultimately gave him permission to travel. And, while such judicial dispensations are relatively routine in America for well-behaved prisoners at the supervised release end of their prison terms, Gross was barely three years into his own 15-year sentence. A more apt comparison: the U.S. offered no similar "humanitarian gesture" to Gerardo Hernández when his mother was dying during his incarceration.

That said, finding common ground is the best hope for Alan Gross — and for the release of the Cuban Five.

There are similarities between the cases. Both failed to register as foreign agents. Both violated the laws of the countries in which they worked. Both were sentenced to unconscionably long prison terms for the actual crimes they committed. And both are now hostage to larger political and diplomatic interests, which neither side — for its own reasons — wants to acknowledge.

But there are important differences in their cases too. The Five were all trained intelligence agents who understood the risks they were taking. Gross

---

30 On May 3, 2013, in the middle of a second court-sanctioned González visit to Cuba — this time for a memorial service for his father who had died the month before — Judge Lenard issued a surprise ruling on his lawyer's latest "renewed motion to modify conditions of release." Declared the judge: "If Defendant voluntarily renounces his United States citizenship … and if he is issued a certificate of loss of nationality by the U.S. Department of State, then Defendant shall serve the remainder of his supervised-release term in Cuba on a non-reporting basis, and he shall not return to the United States." For René González, the long legal fight had finally, belatedly come to an end.

was a bumbling amateur who may — or may not — have been misled. At the same time, the goal of the Cuban agents was to protect their homeland from terrorist attack, while the ultimate purpose of Gross's mission was to undermine a sovereign government and promote "regime change." Whatever the similarities and differences between them, however, it was probably inevitable the two cases would become entwined, both in the public mind and in the political calculations between the two countries.

The Cubans have expressed a willingness to find what they call a "humanitarian solution" to the case of Alan Gross — by which they mean they would be willing to send Gross home in exchange for the release of the Cuban Five. Such prisoner swaps are not uncommon, not even in the recent political history of the United States. In June 2010 — six months after Alan Gross was arrested in Havana — the United States rounded up 10 Russian spies it claimed were on a "deep cover" quest for America's "nuclear and diplomatic secrets," then promptly swapped them, without trial, for four prisoners the Russians previously claimed had been caught spying for Washington. And — as Gross himself pointed out in a conversation with his rabbi — the idea of trading him for five Cubans is hardly a stretch when you realize that, in the fall of 2011, Israel freed 1,100 Palestinian prisoners to get one of its soldiers back.

Unfortunately, we're talking here about relations between the United States and Cuba where *realpolitik* — not to mention reality — intrudes even more rarely than it does in the Middle East. In May 2012, U.S. State Department spokesperson Victoria Nuland — responding to the Cuban offer to negotiate a deal — persisted in the fiction that "there's no equivalency in these situations, and the Cuban government knows that. On the one hand, you have convicted spies in the United States, and on the other hand, you have an assistance worker who should never have been locked up in the first place." If the Americans really do want Alan Gross back, however, it is almost certain they will eventually have to bargain with the Cubans over the fate of the Five. And — perhaps — finally come to terms with their own hypocrisy about Cuba. As Alex Trelles put it to me so succinctly — and wisely — back on that spring day in 2009 on the terrace of the Hotel Nacional in Havana, "nothing will change between Cuba and the United States until they resolve the issue of the Five."

Whatever Happened to...

Percy Alvarado Godoy: Lives in Havana, where the Cuban government supplies him with a car and driver, as well as a secretary. The author of the memoir *Confessions of Fraile* and other books, he is now a writer and journalist. Alvarado came under fire in 2012 when in one of his columns he wrongly accused some Cuban intellectuals of being in the pay of the Americans. He quickly apologized, but many in the intellectual community were not placated.

José Basulto: Collaborated with a Miami writer on a 2010 memoir, *Seagull One: The Amazing True Story of Brothers to the Rescue*. He continues to run the Brothers group.

Orlando Bosch Avila: Died in April 2011, shortly after his memoir *Los Años Que He Vivido (The Years That I Have Lived)* was published. In it, Bosch insisted he "categorically had no responsibility" for the Cubana Airlines bombing, though he'd previously said the truth about the plane crash would only be revealed through tapes and documents after his death.

Francisco Antonio "Gordito" Chávez Abarca: Venezuelan authorities arrested him in 2010 and extradited him to Cuba to face charges in connection with the Havana hotel bombings. He confessed, testifying that he had operated under the direction of Luis Posada. Sentenced to 30 years in prison.

Raúl Ernesto Cruz León: Initially sentenced to death for his role in the bombing campaign, in 2010 Cuba's Supreme Court commuted his sentence — along with that of *Otto Rene Rodríguez Llerena* — to 30 years in jail.

Rodolfo Frómeta: In 2006, he unveiled a videotape of himself leading a bunch of fatigues-clad, semi-automatic-weapons-carrying commandos storming a shack in South Florida, where they "captured" two men dressed up to look like the Castro brothers. "In the last scene of the 15-minute video," the Miami *Herald* reported, "Frómeta yells at the Fidel Castro look-alike, calling him "dog" and asking him why he killed Frómeta's son and brother. As Frómeta played the video for a *Herald* reporter, he smiled in triumph as Castro's character kneels in defeat before him."

Fernando González: Serving 17 years and nine months. Expected release date: February 2014.

René González: Sentenced to 15 years for general conspiracy and conspiracy to act as a non-registered foreign agent. Released on parole, October 7, 2011.

Antonio Guerrero: Serving 21 years and 10 months. Expected release date:

September 2017. He and his American girlfriend, *Maggie Becker,* are still in contact though no longer in a relationship. She is a massage therapist in Key West.

Francisco "Pepe" Hernández: Continues as president of the Cuban American National Foundation. In 2009, CANF, which now has offices in Washington, Miami and New Jersey, published an article calling for lifting U.S. restrictions on aid and travel to Cuba that would "chart a new direction for U.S.-Cuba policy." "For 50 years we have been trying to change the Cuban government, the Cuban regime," Hernández explained to the Miami *Herald* at the time. "What we have to do is change the emphasis to the Cuban people — because they are going to be the ones who change things in Cuba." Perhaps not surprisingly, the Cuban government doesn't believe this latest change of heart is genuine either.

Gerardo Hernández: Sentenced to two life terms plus 15 years for general conspiracy, conspiracy to commit espionage, conspiracy to commit murder, false identity and conspiracy to act as a non-registered foreign agent. Expected release date: Never.

Ramón Labañino: Serving 30-year sentence. Expected release date: October 2024.

Luis Posada Carriles: Lives in Miami, where he continues to call for the overthrow of the Cuban government.

Juan Pablo Roque: Cubans affiliated with Commandos F4 allegedly wounded Roque in a December 2002 assassination attempt that killed a police officer and one of the commandos. The Cuban government denied Roque had been wounded, though they refused to confirm or deny the attempt. Roque himself later told an American reporter, "I'm fine. Can't you see?" In August 1999, his American wife, *Ana Margarita*, charged Roque — and the Cuban government — with rape because he'd married her under false pretences. She ultimately won a $27-million judgment — the Cuban government refused to appear to contest her claim — but hasn't managed to collect much of it. In 2005, U.S. President George W. Bush ordered she be paid $200,000 out of frozen Cuban assets. In 2010, she sued eight Miami-based charter companies trying to garnish the fees they were paying to the Cuban government to operate Florida-Cuba flights, but a judge threw out her claim. She has written a book about her experiences and has — so far unsuccessfully — tried to turn her story into a movie.

Ramón Saúl Sánchez: Acquitted in 2002 of illegally entering Cuban waters. The jury, according to the Miami *Herald*, were "persuaded by arguments [Sánchez] believes he should be able to enter the waters of his homeland." Sánchez, who also went on a hunger strike in 2006 to protest the U.S. government's Cuban immigration policy, continues to head the Democracy Movement.

Acknowledgments

What a long, strange, complex, fascinating journey I've been on ever since that spring day in 2009 when Alex Trelles introduced me to the longer, stranger, more complex and even more fascinating story of the Cuban Five. I want to thank him for that, and for his encouragement to "look it up."

As a novice in the ever "other galaxy" of Cuban-American relations, I desperately needed a guide. Enter John Kirk, a friend, a professor of Latin American Studies at neighbouring Dalhousie University in Halifax, the author or editor of 13 books on Cuba and a man who has visited the island more than 80 times, researching everything from the history of José Martí to Cuba's contemporary medical internationalism. It was John who counselled "patience, persistence and passion" as I negotiated the labyrinth of the Cuban bureaucracy, desperately seeking someone — anyone — who could give me permission to interview the people I needed to talk to for the book I wanted to write. And it was John, as well, who eventually introduced me to the always cheerful, ever efficient Silvia Garcia in Cuban National Assembly President Ricardo Alarcón's office. It was Silvia who made things happen!

I could not have managed most of my interviews in Cuba without the aid of my translator, Jesús Magán Mena, who made the sometimes stuttering complexities of simultaneous translations into a seamless conversation. I thank him for that, and for introducing me to his wonderful family and the joys of Havana taxi rides.

As I began my research, I wrote letters to each of the Five, asking page after page of detailed, often personal questions about everything from their childhoods to their clandestine lives in Florida. They took the time to answer — and then to answer my follow-up questions, and the follow-ups to the follow-ups. They never sought anything in return.

Later, I asked Gerardo Hernández and René González to read and comment on sections of the manuscript. They turned out to be excellent copy editors and careful proofreaders. When they disagreed with something I'd written, they were always careful to preface their remarks with, "It's your book and you must write it the way you want, but…" Would that all the journalists I met along the way had been as understanding of the concept of editorial independence!

That said, I want to single out Juan Tamayo, the veteran Miami *Herald* journalist. Although a Cuban-American who cheerfully admits he has drunk of the exile Kool-Aid, Juan remains, first, last and always, a curious, determined reporter who can't help but follow a story wherever it takes him. Which is why his stories are required — if not always welcome — reading in Havana, Miami and Washington. Juan was invariably generous with information, background and advice, not to mention an excellent dinner companion when we ended up in El Paso together in the winter of 2011 to cover the trial of Luis Posada.

Many others were equally generous with their time and expertise. While some of them do not wish to be acknowledged publicly, my thank-you list is still long: Ricardo Alarcón, Percy Alvarado Godoy, Jean Guy Allard, Jose Antonio Alvarez Fernández, Miguel Alvarez, Sue Ashdown, Ann Louise Bardach, Maggie Becker, Keith Bolender, Gilbert Brownstone, Livio Di Celmo, Giustiono Di Celmo, Carlos Alberto Cremata, Bernie Dwyer, Martin Garbus, Danny Glover, Timothy Golden, Thomas Goldstein, Andrés Gómez, Roberto González, Maruchi Guerrero, Bill Hackwell, Roberto Hernández Caballero, Manuel Hevia, Bethany Horne, Alicia Jrapko, George Kiszynski, Richard Klugh, Peter Kornbluh, Saul Landau, Gladys Larrona, Max Lesnik, Arturo Lopez-Levy, Jose Luis Méndez Méndez, Kirk Nielsen, Adriana Pérez, José Pertierra, Gloria La Riva, Rafael Reyes Rivero, Mirta Rodríguez, Ana Ruiz, Olga Salanueva, Wayne Smith, Daniel J. Steinbock, Teresita Vicente Sotolongo, Leonard Weinglass and Vivien Lesnik Weisman.

I would be remiss if I also didn't thank my agent, Anne McDermid and her colleagues, Chris Bucci and Monica Pacheo, at Anne McDermid & Associates. I think it's fair to say they were surprised — as was I — by just how hard a sell this book turned out to be for mainstream North American publishers. We heard all sorts of explanations, of course, but the key one seemed to be the belief that there wasn't an audience in America for a book that might present a sympathetic portrait of a bunch of "Cuban spies."

I hope this book proves them wrong. For that, I thank Errol Sharpe, Bev Rach and their team at Fernwood Publishing. I have known Errol and Bev as friends for many years, and it is a pleasure to finally have the chance to work with them — and with my editor, Brenda Conroy — on a book project.

Generous and timely financial support from the Canada Council, as well as from University of King's College's Committee on Research & Travel Funding made it possible for me to continue to research the book while we sought a home for my Cuban orphan project. My colleagues at King's, particularly in the School of Journalism, have always been supportive of my writing life, and I thank them for that.

Finally, my thanks — as always, as ever — to my wife Jeanie and my children, Matthew, Emily and Michael and my son-in-law Greg, who make all things possible. And worthwhile.

Endnotes

"What a word is truth. Slippery, tricky unreliable." — Lillian Hellman

The truth is — everybody lies. It is the nature of the clandestine world, and you should never take it on faith that anyone is telling the whole truth. The Cubans lied in September 1998 when they claimed to know nothing more than what they'd read on the newswires about 10 Cubans who'd been arrested by the FBI in Miami. But the Americans lied when they claimed Cuban State Security had given them nothing more than a few meaningless newspaper clippings at a meeting in Havana in June 1998. The FBI lied — and continues to lie — about whether they have any documents of their own relating to those meetings. Luis Posada lies. Always.

So how is anyone supposed to figure out who is telling the truth, or which truth, or how much of the truth? The issue matters in a book like this: a narrative *nonfiction* account. So how did I decide whose versions to believe?

Take, for example, the stories that René González and Gerardo Hernández, two members of the Cuban Five, tell. They were trained to lie, to live as people they were not in order to do the jobs they'd been given. How can their accounts be trusted?

In my correspondence with them, they each acknowledged there might be questions I would ask that they would not — could not — answer. There turned out to be few of those. But they also promised not to lie or mislead me. I don't believe they did. In some instances, their answers to my questions did not conform to the official Cuban version. It was René, in fact, who, early on in my research, steered me away from the conventional wisdom that the FBI had used information the Cubans had given them during those Havana meetings to identify and arrest the Five. In most cases, there were also other materials — court documents, testimony, news accounts, interviews — against which to check their accounts. In all but one case, that other evidence corroborated their versions.

The exception — perhaps — concerned a small story about Olga Salanuevo. I'd written that Gerardo had met her in late 1995 or early 1996 at a workhouse in Havana where she was being trained in intelligence matters so she'd be ready to join her husband in Miami. Gerardo said he didn't remember meeting her then, though a Cuban intelligence document suggested they'd been in the workhouse at the same time. Given that American officials have refused to grant Olga a visa to visit her husband based on claims she'd trained as an agent, Gerardo's failure to "remember" may be understandable — if it is not, in fact, simply an honest failure to remember. Or even a mistake in the official documentation. Who knows, for certain?

The conventional American wisdom is that you shouldn't trust anything the Cubans say. That was likely one reason the *New York Times* didn't publish Percy Alvarado's explosive allegation in 1998 that he'd infiltrated the Cuban American National Foundation. But, in this, as in many other disputes about what really happened, I found the Cuban version rang truest to the known facts. Consider Cuba's allegation that the Cuban American National Foundation was involved in financing the 1997 Havana hotel bombing campaign. Shortly after Cuban State Security arrested Raúl Cruz Léon in September 1997, the government issued a statement accusing senior officials in the Foundation of being the "intellectual authors" of the bombings. CANF officials indignantly denied it. The news media dutifully reported those denials as gospel.

In 1999, during Cruz Léon's trial, the Cubans introduced evidence — including testimony by Percy Alvarado — revealing new details about that secret CANF paramilitary, including at which meeting it was established, who was there, even the details of who was to run it. Once again, CANF dismissed this as more Castro propaganda. And once again, the media reported the denials as if they were true. But then, in 2006, CANF board member Antonio Llama — himself a militant anti-Castro Cuban exile-in-good-standing — sued his compatriots in CANF for not paying him back the money he'd fronted to finance their secret paramilitary organization. Uh, right... The very same paramilitary the Cubans said existed and CANF denied. Much of the detail Llama offered could have come straight from the earlier statements by Cuban State Security.

Despite that, few mainstream media outlets connected CANF's dots of deception. Or, perhaps more importantly, ever questioned CANF's other blanket denials, including their insistence that Percy Alvarado had not penetrated their secret, inner organization. Alvarado's allegation that CANF had recruited him to plant bombs at the Tropicana and that Posada himself had trained him to assemble the bomb components were impossible to verify but I did examine Alvarado's passport, which indicates he was in Guatemala City when he claims the incident occurred, and Cuban surveillance video shows Posada and his partner-in-crime, Gaspar Jiménez — Pumarejo — at the hotel. My money's on Alvarado.

Not that the Cubans always tell the truth. They insist their agents were only in Florida to monitor the activities of exile terrorists groups. But at least one of them, Antonio Guerrero, had an almost exclusively military — if entirely defensive, and defensible — mission.

In the end, I tried to examine the evidence as fairly as I could and come to my own conclusions. Wherever possible, I've incorporated differing versions, quibbles and outright denials — as well as source material — mostly in footnotes and endnotes. But the final judgements — and the responsibility for them — are mine.

ENDNOTES

Building the Nest

Only in Miami! ... The Miami *Herald* provided in-depth coverage of Bosch's release from prison and subsequent press conference. Bosch's personal history is drawn from a variety of sources, including a number of feature stories in the *Herald,* in particular, Heather Dewar's June 29, 1989 profile: "Passion for a Free Cuba Drove Bosch to Extreme." Much of the information about Bosch's terrorist activities, including once classified CIA documents, can be found on the website of George Washington University's National Security Archive. Ann Louise Bardach's *Atlantic* magazine article, "Twilight of the Assassins," and Dick Russell's "Little Havana's Reign of Terror" in the *Miami New Times* both offered additional detail, as did "Keeping Things in Perspective: Cuba and the Question of International Terrorism," a 2001 report for the Center for International Policy by Anya K. Landau and Wayne S. Smith. Bernard Benes' treatment is examined in Robert E. Levine's *Secret Missions to Cuba.*

U.S. Navy air controllers picked up... The account of René González's defection is based on my correspondence with González as well as accounts of his defection in the Miami *Herald* on December 10 and 14, 1990, and after his arrest, on September 20, 1998.

"She'd known it as soon as she came round the corner..." Based on an interview with Olga Salanueva in Havana on February 15, 2011.

José Basulto was — he would insist to anyone who asked... Basulto recounts his version of his life story in *Seagull One,* an authorized 2010 biography-collaboration with Miami-based writer Lily Prellezo. You can find a more nuanced account in "Bird of Paradox," Kirk Nielsen's 2001 profile of Basulto for *Miami New Times.* The quote from the Miami *Herald* is from a January 20, 1996, profile. And the Cuban intelligence information comes from interviews with and documents from Cuban State Security agents.

Christopher Marquis pressed the telephone receiver closer against his ear... Marquis wrote a number of stories about the assassination attempt on Posada, including one on May 13, 1990. His profile of Posada, on which this section is based, appeared in the November 10, 1991, issue of *Tropic* magazine. Marquis later served as chief foreign affairs writer for Knight-Ridder Newspapers and as a Cuba and Latin American specialist at the *New York Times,* where his editor described his coverage of Cuba as "legendary." He died in 2005 at the age of 43 of complications from AIDS.

It ended with faux smiles and a handshake... The *Herald,* which covered Mas's campaign against it in some detail, is the primary source of information about that. Jorge Mas Canosa's official and unofficial biography was stitched together from a variety of sources, including the Cuban American National Foundation website, the Jorge Mas Canosa Freedom Foundation website, a 1993 *Esquire* profile by Gaeton Fonzi and a 1999 *Monthly Review* obituary by Saul Landau.

By 1992, the Miami exiles' ever hopeful... The Cubans were the first to accuse CANF of setting up a secret paramilitary when it linked the Foundation to the Havana hotel bombing campaign in 1997. CANF officials denied it, but details later emerged as part of a lawsuit a disgruntled Llama filed against his former CANF associates in 2006. CANF's plans for Cuba were detailed in an October 11, 1992, report in the Miami *Herald:* "Jorge Mas Canosa: The Road to Havana."

Though most of the participants were quick to characterize ... Mas Canosa's pivotal role in the presidential campaign was documented in a number of articles that year — including April 26 and October 28 and 29, 1992 — by Miami *Herald* political editor Tom Fiedler.

Maggie Becker wasn't sure what to call it... Based on a June 12, 2010, interview with Maggie Becker, supplemented with additional biographical details from interviews with Guerrero's mother and sister in Havana on February 10, 2011. The information about Guerrero's assignments in Panama comes from a document introduced into evidence at the trial of the Cuban Five.

The Cuban diplomatic note began... This was one of a number of Cuban diplomatic notes defence lawyers read into the record during the 2001 trial of the Cuban Five.

Dalila Borrego had another job Antonio could apply for... Guerrero's May 1993 application for the job at the base was among the items seized from his house at the time of his arrest. Borrego testified as a defence witness at his trial, essentially to demonstrate that it had been her idea — not Guerrero's — to apply for jobs at the Boca Chica base.

At first glance, it might have seemed like... From several stories in the Miami *Herald,* including one published October 16, 1993.

Abel Viera was excited for his old friend... Alvarado chronicled his exploits in a book entitled *Confessions of Fraile: A Real Story of Terrorism.* Because the English version of the book, which was originally published in Spanish, read like a bad Google translation, I took some minor liberties with the text's awkward dialogue. But I have been true to the meaning, both from the context and from my own extensive interviews with Alvarado in Havana on February 3 and September 9, 2011. His tale as what he calls a "penetration agent" inside the Cuban American National Foundation was the most difficult to document. Because he wasn't arrested or tried like the Cuban Five, there are very few documents on the public record to corroborate what he says. The Cuban American National Foundation has denied all of it. But I have examined his passports from that time and they do show the pattern of travels he's claimed. And much of what he disclosed about the inner workings of the Cuban American National Foundation during his testimony at the trials of the Havana hotel bombers in 1999, including the roles of various CANF officials, was inadvertently substantiated in a 2006 lawsuit filed against CANF by a disgruntled former member of its board. Details about Alvarado's day-to-day routine while in Miami were published in a March 10, 1999, article in the Miami *Herald.* The details of Zuñiga's terrorist history can be found in a book called *Welcome Home: Torturers, Assassins and Terrorists in Refuge in the U.S.*

Perhaps it was because they'd both fled Fidel Castro's Cuba..." Both

Basulto in *Seagull One* and Roque in *Desertor* write about that day's mission by the former Cuban pilots.

The 55-word story was so seemingly routine... In addition to the Miami *Herald* brief, this section is based on a variety of news reports about these incidents as well as the testimony of Frómeta, U.S. Customs Agent Raymond Crump and Alcohol Tobacco and Firearms Special Agent Julie Torres during the 2001 trial of Cuban Five.

He took the unfamiliar coins from his pockets... Gerardo Hernández's anecdote about the grape soda was mentioned in his correspondence with me. The information about how he and Adriana met, as well as the development of their relationship, emerged from my correspondence with him as well as my February 15, 2011, interview with Adriana. The trial transcript provided the source material for my description of Gerardo's various identifies, while retired FBI expert Stewart Hoyt, who advised the agency on Cuban counter-intelligence, testified in detail about how Cuba's intelligence structure works.

Rescuing the Brothers

Pepe Hernández was apologetic... From *Confessions of Fraile*. After Alvarado testified at the 1999 trial of Raúl Cruz Léon, Foundation officials were quick to deny his allegations, insisting they'd had nothing to do with him. "We don't know who this person is," spokeswoman Ninoska Perez told the Miami *Herald*. "We've never heard of him... If he had infiltrated [the Foundation], you think he would go unnoticed?... We have repeatedly said this is not the type of activity we would get involved with." But again, much of what Alvarado claimed — including the role CANF's paramilitary wing played in launching attacks against Cuba — was inadvertently confirmed in Tony Llama's 2006 lawsuit against CANF.

"Remember I want to be with you at the beach in September..." René González's lawyer introduced this letter to his wife as a defence exhibit during his trial. Prosecutors objected, insisting the judge instruct jurors that the letter was not being introduced for its truthfulness but simply to reflect González's state of mind at the time. Olga Salanueva told me about her experiences during the Special Period in our interview.

The Sergeant unfurled the heavy poncho... FBI Special Agent Raymond Lopez testified about the sting operation against Frómeta during the trial of the Cuban Five. Frómeta himself also testified as a — reluctant — defence witness.

Pepe Hernández carefully checked the GPS coordinates... As described in *Confessions of Fraile* and my interviews with Alvarado.

It was 'there,' José Basulto would explain later... This incident is described in full in Basulto's biography, *Seagull One*. Portions of the video footage from Basulto's April 17, 1994, incursion into Cuban airspace were played for the jury during the trial of the Cuban Five. Basulto was also questioned about both incidents when he testified as a hostile defence witness during the trial.

The fact that nine Miami police officers had been assigned... The information in this section comes from the November 1994 report of Human Rights

Watch as well as coverage of its 1992 and 1994 reports in the Miami *Herald*.

Percy Alvarado heard the knock on his hotel room door... From *Confessions of Fraile* and my interviews with Alvarado, as well as a May 10, 2005, article Alvarado wrote about the incident for *Juventud Rebelde*. I also examined Alvarado's passport, which shows he was in Guatemala at the time of this meeting.

Given the almost festive mood among the spectators..." From a December 21, 1994, report in the Miami *Herald*.

"Dear Mr. Basulto," the letter began... The existence of this letter was disclosed during Basulto's testimony at the trial of the Cuban Five. Basulto claimed he hadn't requested the information. Instead, he said, "this document was requested by Mr. Roque and sent to my address, apparently."

Alfredo Otero had finally calmed down... As described in *Confessions of Fraile* and my interviews with Alvarado.

Arrested! Maggie Becker still couldn't believe what had happened... Based on my interview with Becker, supplemented by interviews with Antonio's mother and sister.

Percy Alvarado's handlers at the Cuban American National Foundation... As described in *Confessions of Fraile* and my interviews with Alvarado.

This time it wasn't Cuban State Security that had stymied... Manuel Hevia, the Director of Historical Research at Cuban State Security, who has written extensively about Miami exile terrorism, and Rafael Reyes Rivero, a colonel in State Security, told me this story during a February 14, 2011, interview in Havana. The incident is also documented in *Welcome Home: Torturers, Assassins and Terrorists in Refuge in the U.S.*

It was a marriage made in *el exilio* heaven... I gathered information from a variety of sources, including an account of the wedding in *Seagull One*, as well as news accounts from the Miami *Herald* (March 3, 1996), *New York Times* (August 14, 1999) and *Miami New Times* (April 1, 2010). The story of the incident involving Rene González comes from my correspondence with González as well as an account in the Basulto book.

The automatic garage door opened... Interview with Ricardo Alarcón, February 10, 2011.

Another day, another plot... From the transcript of the trial of the Cuban Five.

José Basulto had to do something... The narrative in this section comes from a variety of news accounts — including a July 14 Knight-Ridder account of the ramming written by a reporter aboard *Democracia* — as well as later testimony by Basulto and fellow Brothers pilot Arnaldo Iglesias. Information on Miami-Dade police intelligence reports come from a website called the Cuban Information archives. <http://cuban-exile.com/doc_301-325/doc0314.htm>

José Basulto wasn't the only one... Ramón Saúl Sánchez's personal history comes from a number of newspaper accounts, particularly a gushing July 6, 1996, profile of him by Miami *Herald* publisher David Lawrence. Information on Miami-Dade police intelligence reports come from the Cuban Information

Archives website.

"The United States of America Interest Section…" Introduced as a prosecution exhibit during the trial of the Five.

Saúl Sánchez had a plan… From evidence at the trial of the Five as well as news accounts in the Miami *Herald* from October 1995.

Juan Pablo Roque was exactly where he preferred to be… Roque's book launch party is described in *Seagull One* while the excerpts from *Desertor* come from translated excerpts published in the Miami *Herald* after Roque's defection.

Juan Pablo Roque was losing it… From evidence presented at the trial of the Cuban Five.

Manny Ruiz wasn't the only illegal officer… From the transcript of the trial of the Cuban Five.

Shootdown

Even a spy needs a break… In addition to other evidence presented at the trial, this section is based on a secret Cuban State Security document dated December 5, 1995, and entitled: "Agent German's Return and Proposal for Public Declaration (Denunciation) of BTTR."

While the CP prepared Gerardo Hernández… From evidence presented at the trial of the Cuban Five.

José Basulto was clearly enjoying himself… From a Miami *Herald* report about the overflight as well as a transcript of Basulto's Radio Martí interview, which was introduced during the trial of the Five.

The two men were both old baseball players… The story of the Richardson-Castro meetings is told in "Backfire," Carl Nagin's January 26, 1998, article about the shootdown in the *New Yorker.*

The early morning email from Cecilia Capestany… From documents presented during Capestany's testimony at the trial of the Cuban Five.

Juan Pablo Roque still wasn't keen… From the transcript of the trial of the Cuban Five.

It seemed the FBI — like Cuban intelligence… From the transcript of the trial of the Cuban Five.

Venecia wasn't the only Cuban operation… From the transcript of the trial of the Cuban Five.

While they tackled all their various assignments… Santos, who pleaded guilty to his role in the Wasp Network, testified during the trial of the Five. Information about Southcom's planned relocation comes from a Defence Department press release as well as a June 2, 1997, feature on the opening in the Miami *Herald.*

Eugene Carroll understood immediately… Carroll testified about this warning — and what he did with it — during the trial of the Cuban Five.

Yet another meeting at the Swiss embassy… Read into evidence at the trial of the Cuban Five.

Now that the final decision had been made… From the transcript of the trial of the Cuban Five, as well as Gerardo Hernández's March 16, 2011, affidavit filed in support of his application to vacate his conspiracy to murder conviction.

Cuban State Security wasn't alone... Plans for the Concilio meeting, Brothers' financial contribution to it and the Cuban response were all covered in the Miami *Herald* at the time. The information about the U.S. government's concerns come from Nuccio's testimony at the trial of the Five.

René González had asked for tonight's meeting... From René González's report to Hernández, admitted into evidence during the trial of the Cuban Five.

The squeak of his shoes on the tile floor in their bedroom... Ana Margarita described this scene in an interview with the *Miami New Times* published April 1, 2010.

Cecilia Capestany hit the Send button... From testimony at the trial of the Cuban Five.

The sky was cloudless as the three Cessnas... The story of the shootdown of the Brothers aircraft comes from a variety of sources, including transcripts of testimony by Basulto and others during the trial of the Cuban Five, the International Civil Aviation report into the incident and news stories in the Miami *Herald*.

After more than seven months of formal and informal complaints... The question of exactly where the planes were when they were shot down became a key issue during the trial of the Five. This section is drawn from testimony as well as the report of the ICAO and Cuba's later requests for satellite data from the day of the shootdown.

René González was reaching into the refrigerator... From correspondence with González.

Like René González, Gerardo Hernández found out ... From correspondence with Hernández.

José Basulto speculated that Cuban authorities... From reports in the Miami *Herald* as well as the transcript of Roque's CNN interview.

The coded shortwave message was brief... From testimony at the trial of the Cuban Five.

"Why the hell didn't you call?"... Agent Barbeito testified about this meeting during the trial of the Cuban Five.

"As I sign this bill into law..." The signing ceremony was reported in the Miami *Herald*. There are many sources concerning the backdrop leading up to the signing, including Bill Clinton's own memoir.

Stinging the Wasp

Running an intelligence network didn't just involve... This incident is described in a report to the CP written by Gerardo Hernández and introduced as evidence at the trial of the Five.

While the Brothers' shootdown and its fallout... From the memo Edgardo wrote to Hernando, which was introduced as evidence in the trial of the Five.

Tony Guerrero had a new proposal... From a message sent by Guerrero to the CP through Hernández and introduced during the trial.

ENDNOTES

René González didn't say anything... From a message Hernández sent to the CP following a meeting with Hernández and introduced during the trial.

Vicente Rosado knew Gerardo Hernández... From Rosado's testimony during the trial.

Gerardo Hernández's JC Penney card had arrived... From Hernández's report to the CP.

René González cut the man off... From González's report to Hernández and Hernández's response, introduced during the trial.

"Edgardo, I've decided to mention again... From Hernández's letter to Delgado, introduced during the trial.

The Democracy Movement was imploding... From González's report to Hernández, introduced during the trial.

Vicente Rosado slipped the disk labelled RSA-105... From Rosado's testimony during the trial.

It had all taken much longer than he'd expected... From evidence presented at the trial, as well as correspondence with González.

"Something Serious"

He had a new problem... From Guerrero's report to Hernández, introduced as evidence at the trial of the Five.

Luis Posada was phoning from somewhere in Central America... The telephone conversation was surreptitiously recorded by Cuban State Security and included in documents Cuba provided to the FBI in June 1998.

Shortly after 1 p.m., FBI Special Agent William Murphy identified... From Murphy's testimony at trial. The account of what actually happened at the meeting between Hernández and Guerrero is based on the reports Hernández and Guerrero sent to Havana, which were decrypted by the FBI and submitted as evidence in the trial.

The agenda for today's meet at the Piccadilly Restaurant... From Hernández's report to the CP, entered as evidence during the trial.

Gerardo Hernández was on his way to the checkout... From Hernández's report to the CP, entered as evidence during the trial.

"Are you the publicity manager for the theatre?"... From documents introduced during the trial.

Roberto Hernández Caballero got the call shortly before 4 a.m. ... From his testimony during the trial.

"My regards," Ramón Labañino began his message... From Labañino's report to Havana, introduced during the trial.

At least Roberto Caballero Hernández wouldn't have to go far today... From testimony during the trial. State Security historian Manuel Hevia told me the story of the discovery of the chess tournament bomb during an interview in Havana on February 14, 2011.

The server at the National Assembly offices in Playa... From my interview with Ricardo Alarcón.

Tony Alvarez carefully re-read the words... FBI Special Agent Thomas H. Rice recounted the story in a 10-page affidavit sworn on June 10, 2005, and obtained by the Miami *Herald*. Versions of the story have also appeared in Ann Louise Bardach's *Cuba Confidential* as well as in several articles in the *Herald*.

"This Is Really Fierce"

"Bucanero"... Cruz León's personal biography is drawn from a number of sources, the most comprehensive being three separate Miami *Herald* articles published on September 17, October 1 and November 16, 1997. Cruz León himself was interviewed on Cuban television following his arrest, and Cuban State Security filmed him re-enacting how he had placed the bombs at each location. He was also interviewed by the United Nations Special Rapporteur, who travelled to Cuba to investigate that country's complaints about the 1997 bombing campaign. His report was published December 31, 1999. The description of Cruz León's initial belief about his "heroic" role and the "adrenalin" rush he felt from planting the bombs come from several interviews he gave, including an August 6, 2005, interview from prison as well as a 1999 interview with Timothy Golden of the *New York Times*.

Fabio Di Celmo was apologetic... Much of the information in this section comes from an interview with Fabio Di Celmo's brother, Livio, in Montreal on June 3, 2010.

"Señor! Señor!"... As reported by the Miami *Herald* September 18, 1997.

Roberto Hernández Caballero and his team... From his testimony during the trial. The story of the firecracker in the tunnel and the woman arrested with traces of C-4 in her handbag comes from a July 25, 1997, report in the Miami *Herald*.

Fabio dead? How could that be?... Interview with Livio Di Celmo.

It had been a good day... Cruz León re-enacted his bomb-planting path and process that day in a video prepared by Cuban State Security. His recollections of the events come from his confession, his interview with the United Nations Special Rapporteur and from accounts in the Miami *Herald*. The story of the bicycle taxi driver is from an interview with Colonel Rafael Reyes of Cuba's Ministry of the Interior in Havana, February 14, 2011.

Livio Di Celmo knew he shouldn't have said it... Interview with Livio Di Celmo.

As soon as he heard the description from a fellow employee... Nicolás Rodríguez's account of the bomb blast is based largely on Canadian author Keith Bolender's interview with him as described in *Voices from the Other Side: An Oral History of Terrorism Against Cuba* (Pluto, 2010).

It hadn't taken the police... This section is based on a variety of news stories from the time, as well as the report of a United Nations Special Rapporteur.

"Paco"... Cuban State Security provided transcripts of the conversation to the FBI in June 1998.

On Saturday, September 6... "Cuba Bombings: Terrorist vs. Terrorist" in the Miami *Herald*, September 6, 1997.

"And why don't you come, Fatty"... From a transcript released by Cuban authorities. Other details are drawn from a 1999 report by the United Nations Special Rapporteur, as well as from reports published in the Miami *Herald*.

Cuban State Security wasn't the only one... From an interview with Juan Tamayo in Miami in June 2010.

Tamayo was right... From a Miami *Herald* report.

The man from MINREX... This comes from Fidel Castro's May 25, 2005, speech about the bombing campaign. According to Castro, Kozak referenced Tamayo's October 1 Miami *Herald* story during the meeting.

Drugs... What else would four middle-aged men... From various press reports as well as testimony during their 1999 trial.

Special Report: The Plot... Based on an interview with Juan Tamayo and his November 15, 1997, article in the Miami *Herald*.

Tony Alvarez found something else... The story of the FBI's failure to seriously investigate the Alvarez letter comes from a number of different sources but is best told by Ann Louise Bardach in *Cuba Confidential*. The account of Kiszynski's 1992 interview with Posada is based on the declassified report of the interview from the Office of Independent Counsel. I also interviewed Kiszynski in Miami in June 2010.

"A Duty to Prevent"

Like many of the changes Tony Guerrero had made... From an interview with Maggie Becker in Key West in June 2010, plus a November 8, 1997, report in the Miami *Herald* about the retreat.

He could see the look in their eyes... This section is based on Alvarado's account of his father's funeral published in cubadebate.cu on September 27, 2007.

As a lone trumpeter played "Taps"... Mas Canosa's death was widely covered in the Miami press.

We know you know people in Havana... Based on an interview with Andrés Gómez in Miami in June 2010.

The "Memphis Incident"

Gerardo Hernández placed his Manuel... From a document entered into evidence during the trial as well as correspondence with Hernández and an interview with Adriana Perez in Havana February 15, 2011.

Tita! No, not Tita... From my correspondence with Hernández and my interview in Havana with Adriana.

The scene was becoming familiar... From Fidel Castro's 2005 speech. The backgrounds on the would-be Guatemalan bombers come from 1999 prison interviews with the *New York Times* and the U.N. Special Rapporteur. Further information, including the connection to Arnaldo Monzón, is detailed in an October 1998 report released by Cuba's Ministry of the Interior.

Gerardo Hernández watched them — not *them* per se... From documents introduced during the trial of the Five, as well as from correspondence with Hernández and González, and my interview with Olga Salanueva in Havana.

Right on time… From Carlos Fernandez's testimony during the trial of the Five.

Gabo's Secret Mission

Gabriel García Márquez had to call Bill Richardson… This account is based on Márquez's May 13, 1998, report to Fidel Castro on his secret mission to Washington, as recounted in the Castro speech.

"Who are you voting for as chairman of the CANF?"… From a document entered into evidence during the trial.

"After a warm embrace"… From Márquez's May 13, 1998 report to Fidel Castro.

"There was nothing more beautiful"… From a document entered into evidence during the trial.

Michael Kozak was bemused… From my interview with Ricardo Alarcón.

The Miami FBI office… Based on several news reports published at the time of Pesquera's appointment.

In the little less than a week since… From Fidel Castro's May 25, 2005 speech.

The good news… From Fidel Castro's May 25, 2005 speech.

If the FBI had really wanted to uncover… Miami *Herald*, June 7, 1998.

The Americans had refused to budge… From Fidel Castro's May 25, 2005 speech.

"Open your bag please, sir"… There are a number of sources for this account, including Rodríguez own 2006 deposition in the immigration fraud trial of Luis Posada, the report of U.N. Special Rapporteur, my interview with Manuel Heviz and Rafael Reyes and "Chronology of an Aborted Plot," a May 11, 2007 report on the website <juventudrebelde.cu>.

"I Sleep Like a Baby"

The gathering, in a State Security Protocol House… Cuban State Security provided me with copies of the materials they turned over to the FBI. And I was able to interview Col. Rafael Reyes Rivero and Manuel Hevia to flesh out the words on the page. I also filed freedom of information requests in the United States to attempt to get access to FBI memos and reports written before and after those meetings, but they were not forthcoming.

Fernando González was back… From evidence presented during the trial of the Five.

The story was as explosive as any well-placed bomb… This section is based on the *New York Times* series, which appeared on July 12–13, 1998, as well as Bardach's November 15, 2007, statement to the U.S. House Committee on Foreign Affairs, Subcommittee on International Organizations, Human Rights and Oversight and her testimony at the 2011 trial of Luis Posada in El Paso, Texas.

ENDNOTES

On July 12 — the same day the first *New York Times* story appeared… The Miami *Herald* published details about the plot August 9, 1998.

"The *New York Times* slandered"… Based on stories published in the Miami *Herald* on July 15 and 17, 1998.

One of Gerardo Hernández's many duties… Based on Juan Tamayo's July 23, 1998, account in the Miami *Herald*.

The newspaper story, which appeared… Based on testimony at the trial of the Five, correspondence with Gerardo Hernández and the Miami *Herald's* July 28, 1998 report of the raid as well as its August 9 story detailing the assassination plot.

"Gerardo?"… From Miguel López's testimony at the trial of the Five.

It had ended suddenly, unexpectedly… Based on Percy Alvarado's own account of the encounter, as well as on 2011 email correspondence with Timothy Golden. The Cuban website <http://www.antiterrororistas.cu> carried an account of Ricardo Alarcón's press conference, while Castro's comments about the story come from an April 17, 2005, speech at <http://www.cuba.cu/gobierno/discursos/2005/ing/f170405i.html>.

The Very Heart of Our System

Ramón Labañino telephoned Fernando González… From documents presented during the trial of the Five.

Another day, another exile terrorist training camp to track down… From testimony at the trial as well as my interview with Kirk Nielsen and his article, "Alpha Males," which appeared in the *Miami New Times* on August 27, 1998.

Maggie Becker would remember him as a "football type"… From an interview with Maggie Becker and the trial transcript.

As soon as she saw them… From an interview with Olga Salaneuva and correspondence with René González.

Maggie and Tony were asleep… Based on my interview with Maggie Becker, as well as testimony at the trial of the Five.

René González was asleep… From an interview with Olga Salaneuva and correspondence with René González.

Similar door-pounding, glass smashing raids… From testimony at the trial of the Five.

Who was the governor of Puerto Rico… From an interview by Saul Landau, my correspondence with Hernández and testimony at the trial of the Five.

Carlos Fernandez had been surreptitiously following… From Fernandez testimony at the trial of the Five.

Hector Pesquera was crowing… From reports in the Miami *Herald*.

Aftermath

René González isn't surprised… From my correspondence with González. I covered the first week of the 2011 trial of Luis Posada in El Paso and continued to follow the case through reports in the Miami *Herald*, the Associated Press, the *New York Times* and in the brilliantly detailed and evocative daily blog posts of

José Pertierra, a Cuban-born American lawyer who observed the trial on behalf of the Venezuelan government. I also quote from documents presented during the trial, including the 2005 FBI affidavit. The details from the trial of the Cuban Five are from news accounts at the time. The story about the FBI's shredding of Luis Posada's file is described in author Ann Louis Bardach's November 17, 2007, statement to the American House Committee on Foreign Affairs, Subcommittee on International Organizations, Human Rights and Oversight. The detail that an FBI liaison officer met with Posada while he was in jail in Panama was mentioned in court during Posada's 2011 trial. Accounts of the New Jersey grand jury investigation are drawn from various news reports of the time

The Five — illegal officers... From news accounts and the transcript of the trial of the Five.

In the spring of 1999... Primarily from Juan Tamayo's reporting on the trial for the Miami *Herald*.

Eight months later, in another courtroom... From Tamayo's report in the Miami *Herald,* December 9, 1999.

Less than a year after that... From various news accounts at the time.

Necessity. In the end... The "Fatherland Defense" is described in Kirk Nielsen's story "What Spies Beneath" in *Miami New Times* March 15, 2001. The Elián González affair was widely covered in the U.S. and international media. The details about government payments to Miami journalists who wrote about the Five were uncovered through freedom of information petitions filed by National Committee to Free the Cuban Five, the Partnership for Civil Justice Fund and Liberation newspaper. The legal arguments for a change of venue were reported in the press and detailed in various appeal proceedings. Both René González and his wife independently described the prosecutor's August 15, 2000, plea deal offer to me.

The case of the United States of America... From court transcripts and news accounts. The story of the 2001 foiled terrorist plot appeared in the Miami *Herald*.

Before we consider what happened to the Cuban Five... From my interview with Roberto González in Havana in February 2011, my observations of the Posada trial in El Paso and my correspondence with René González.

On December 12, 2001... From the transcript of Hernández's sentencing report, the reports of the United Nations Human Rights Commission's Working Group on Arbitrary Detentions and Amnesty International, and the rulings in the various appeals and sentencing hearings.

The man Cuban authorities had just arrested in Havana... The story of what Alan Gross actually did in Cuba is contained in a statement-of-facts sentencing document that was eventually leaked to a Miami blog, Café Fuerte, and covered in detail by other news outlets, including the Miami *Herald* and Reuters. Philip Peters translated and summarized the document in another blog, Cuban Triangle. An investigative report by the Associated Press connected the dots back to the DAI and USAID.

The guards woke him at four in the morning... The details of René

ENDNOTES

Gonzalez's prison experience, release and his life on supervised release primarily come from my correspondence with him, although there is a YouTube video of his reunion with his family: http://www.youtube.com/watch?v=Ojh-ocSutnw. His meeting with the children of La Colmenita is documented in *Esencias*, a documentary about their American tour by director Roberto Chile.

Selected Bibliography

Allard, Jean-Guy. 2006. *Miami-FBI Terrorist Connection*. Bogota: MasAlla Publishing.

Alvarado, Francisco. 2010. "Cuban Spy Juan Pablo Roque's Jilted Ex-wife Won $27-Million for Deception." *Miami New Times*. April 1.

Alvarado Godoy, Percy. 2004. *Confessions of Fraile*. Havana: Editorial Capitán San Luis.

Arboyleya, Jesús. 1996. *Havana Miami: The US-Cuba Migration Conflict*. Melbourne, Australia: Ocean Press.

Bardach, Ann Louise. 2002. *Cuba Confidential*. New York: Random House.

___. 2006. "Twilight of the Assassins." *The Atlantic*. November.

___. 2009. *Without Fidel: A Death Foretold in Miami, Havana and Washington*. New York: Scribner.

Bramson, Seth H. 2007. *Miami: The Magic City*. Charleston: Arcadia.

Bran, Zoë. 2002. *Enduring Cuba*. London: Lonely Planet Publications.

Brenner, Philip, Marguerite Rose Jiménez, John M. Kirk and William M. LeoGrande, eds. 2008. *A Contemporary Cuba Reader: Reinventing the Revolution*. Lanham, MD: Rowman & Littlefield.

Calvo, Hernando, and Katlijn Declercq. 2000. *The Cuban Exile Movement*. Melbourne, Australia: Ocean Press.

Castro, Fidel. 2005. "A Different Behavior: Special Address by Dr. Fidel Castro Ruz, President of the Republic of Cuba, at the Anti-imperialist Square." May 20.

Clinton, Bill. 2001. *My Life*. New York: Knopf.

Corbett, Ben. 2004. *This Is Cuba: An Outlaw Culture Survives*. Cambridge: Westview Press.

Cordescu, Andrei. 1999. *Ay, Cuba!* New York: St. Martin's Press.

Dávalos Fernández, Rudolfo. 2006. *United States vs The Cuban Five: A Judicial Cover-up*. Havana: Editorial Capitán San Luis.

Eire, Carlos. 2003. *Waiting for Snow in Havana*. New York: Free Press.

Erikson, Daniel P. 2008. *The Cuba Wars*. New York: Bloomsbury Press.

Esteban, Angel, and Stéphanie Panichelli. 2009. *Fidel & Gabo*. New York: Pegasus.

Estrada, Alfredo José. 2007. *Havana: Autobiography of a City*. New York: Macmillan Palgrave.

Fonzi, Gaeton. 1993. "Jorge Who?" *Esquire*. January.

Franklin, Jane. 2002. *Cuba and the United States: A Chronological History*. Melbourne, Australia: Ocean Press.

García, María Cristina. 1996. *Havana USA: Cuban Exiles and Cuban Americans in South Florida, 1959–1994*. Berkeley: University of California Press.

George, Paul S. 2006. *Little Havana*. Charleston: Arcadia.

González-Pando, Miguel. 1997. "Developmental Stages of the 'Cuban Exile Country.'" *Cuba in Transition* 7: 50–65.

Gott, Richard. 2004. *Cuba: A New History*. New Haven: Yale University Press.

Guerrero, Antonio. 2001. *From My Altitude*. Havana: Editorial José Martí.

Guillermoprieto, Alma. 2002. *Looking for History: Dispatches from Latin America*. New York: Vintage.

____. 2005. *Dancing with Cuba*. New York: Vintage.

Hinckle, Warren, and Bill Turner. 1992. *Deadly Secrets: The CIA-Mafia War Against Castro and the Assassination of J.F.K*. New York: Thunder's Mouth Press.

James, Ian Michael. 2006. *Ninety Miles: Cuban Journeys in the Age of Castro*. Lanham, MD: Rowman & Littlefield.

Kornbluh, Peter, and Erin Maskell. 2011. "The CIA File on Luis Posada Carriles." The National Security Archive (NSA), George Washington University. <http://www.gwu.edu/~nsarchiv/> posted January 11.

Lamrani, Salim, ed. 2005. *Superpower Principles: U.S. Terrorism Against Cuba*. Monroe, ME: Common Courage Press.

Landau, Anya K., and Wayne S. Smith. 2001. *Keeping Things in Perspective: Cuba and the Question of International Terrorism*. Washington: Center for International Policy. November 20.

Lawrence, Matt, and Thomas Van Hare. 2009. *Betrayal: Clinton, Castro & the Cuban Five*. New York: iUniverse.

Levine, Robert M. 2001. *Secret Missions to Cuba*. New York: Palgrave Macmillan.

Levine, Robert M., and Asís Moisés. 2000. *Cuban Miami*. New Brunswick, NJ: Rutgers University Press.

Marquis, Christopher. 1991. "The Shadow Warrior." *Tropic Magazine*. November 10.

Martin, Gerald. 2008. *Gabriel García Marques: A Life*. Toronto: Viking Canada.

Mendoze, Tony. 1999. *Cuba — Going Back*. Austin: University of Texas Press.

Miller, Tom. 1992. *Trading with the Enemy: A Yankee Travels Through Castro's Cuba*. New York: Atheneum.

____ (ed.). 2001. *Travellers' Tales: Cuba*. Berkeley: Publishers Group West.

Moses, Catherine. 2000. *Real Life in Castro's Cuba*. Lanham, MD: SR Books.

Murphy, Dervla. 2008. *The Island That Dared*. London: Eland.

Nagin, Carl. 1998. "Backfire." *New Yorker*. January 26.

Nielsen, Kirk. 1998. "Alpha Males." *Miami New Times*. August 27.

____. 2001. "Cuban Missive Crisis." *Miami New Times*. February 1.

____. 2001. "What Spies Beneath." *Miami New Times*. March 15.

____. 2001. "Inside the Wasp's Nest." *Miami New Times*. February 22.

____. 2001. "Bird of Paradox." *Miami New Times*. April 26.

____. 2001. "Spies in Miami, Commandoes in Cuba." *Miami New Times*. July 5.

____. 2001. "Fidel Made Them Do It." *Miami New Times*. August 9.

Nielsen, Kirk, and Tristram Korten. 2008. "The 'Coddled' Terrorists of South Florida." January 14. <theinvestigativefund.org>.

Nuñez, Iraida, ed. 2007. *Welcome Home*. Havana: Editorial Capitán San Luis.

Oppenheimer, Andres. 1992. *Castro's Final Hour*. New York: Touchstone.

Prellezo, Lilly, with José Basulto. 2010. *Seagull One*. Gainesville: University Press of Florida.

Quirk, Robert E. 1992. *Fidel Castro*. New York: W.W. Norton.

Rieff, David. 1992. *The Exile: Cuba in the Heart of Miami*. New York: Simon & Schuster.

Russell, Dick. 1976. "Little Havana's Reign of Terror." *Miami New Times*. October 29.

Saney, Isaac. 2004. *Cuba: A Revolution in Motion*. Black Point, NS: Fernwood.

Schoultz, Lars. 2009. *That Infernal Little Cuban Republic*. Chapel Hill: University of North Carolina Press.

Smith, Stephen. 1997. *The Land of Miracles*. London: Little, Brown and Company.

Smith, Wayne. 1987. *The Closest of Enemies*. New York: W.W. Norton.

Sweig, Julia E. 2009. *Cuba: What Everyone Needs to Know*. New York: Oxford University Press.

Tattlin, Isadora. 2002. *Cuba Diaries*. Chapel Hill: Algonquin Books.

Tucker, Lee. 1994. *Dangerous Dialogues Revisited: Threats to Freedom of Expression Continue in Miami's Cuban Exile Community*. Washington: Human Rights Watch. November.

Walker, Alice. 2005. "Introduction." *Letters of Love & Hope: The Story of the Cuban Five*. Melbourne, Australia: Ocean Press.

Index